The Gift of Speech

Papers in the Analysis of Speech and Voice

JOHN LAVER

Professor of Phonetics
University of Edinburgh

EDINBURGH UNIVERSITY PRESS

© John Laver, 1991

Edinburgh University Press
22 George Square, Edinburgh

Typeset in Linotron Times Roman
by Photoprint, Torquay and
printed in Great Britain by
Page Bros Ltd, Norwich

British Library Cataloguing
  in Publication Data
Laver, John
  The gift of speech: Papers in the analysis of
  speech and voice.
  I. Title
  414

ISBN 0 7486 0313 1

FOR

David and Mary Abercrombie
Peter and Jenny Ladefoged
Donald and Menucha Boomer

Contents

Acknowledgements

I have been fortunate in having advice and help from my colleagues R.E. Asher, Sandy Hutcheson and Mervyn Jack on making the selection of articles for reproduction in this volume.

Acknowledgements and thanks for permission to reproduce copyright material are due to my collaborating authors Janet Mackenzie Beck, Donald Boomer, Robert Hanson, Steven Hiller, Edmund Rooney, Peter Trudgill and Sheila Wirz, and to the following publishers and journals: Penguin Books, Harmondsworth for Chapter 1; the *British Journal of Disorders of Communication* for Chapters 2 and 9; Hoffmann und Campe, Hamburg for Chapter 4; Academic Press, New York for Chapters 5 and 8; Mouton, The Hague for Chapter 6; Lawrence Erlbaum Associates, Hillsdale and the European Commission for Chapter 7; the *Journal of the International Phonetic Association* for Chapter 11; Grune and Stratton, New York for Chapter 13; Cambridge University Press, Cambridge, and Editions de la Maison des Sciences de l'Homme, Paris for Chapter 14; the Voice Committee of the International Association of Logopedics and Phoniatrics and the *Journal of Voice* for Chapter 18; the *Journal of Phonetics* for Chapter 17; Edinburgh University Press, Edinburgh for Chapter 19; and *Historiographia Linguistica* for Chapter 20.

I also gratefully acknowledge the secretarial help of Alison Gardiner, Susan MacDonald and Maureen Anderson, and a grant in aid of the preparation costs from the Faculty of Arts of the University of Edinburgh.

Introduction

The task of preparing this collection of papers for publication in one volume has given me the occasion to reflect on the breadth of modern phonetics, and in particular on my own perspective on the subject. When I first came into contact with phonetics in 1958, as an undergraduate student at the University of Edinburgh attending a one-year introductory course which, in the vocabulary traditional to Scottish universities, was then called the 'Ordinary Course in Phonetics', the scope of the subject (in the Edinburgh view) was already wide.

The core of the subject was then (as it remains today) a general phonetic theory that chiefly addressed the obligation to provide a descriptive vocabulary to support linguistic interests in spoken language. Chomsky had just published *Syntactic Structures* (1957), the first of the books he was to write which changed the paradigm of linguistic theory. His contribution to phonetics and phonology with Morris Halle, *The Sound Pattern of English* (Chomsky and Halle, 1968) lay ten years in the future. Psycholinguistics had just appeared, and sociolinguistics lay on the distant horizon (at least, as names for subjects).

Experimental phonetics was already very well-established, with acoustic investigations dominated by spectrography, a technique which had been introduced to phonetics only in the previous decade by American researchers in speech communication, coming from military and industrial backgrounds. Another strand that was strongly evident in the interests of the phoneticians of that time at Edinburgh was speech therapy and pathology. Many members of the Department of Phonetics taught courses on phonetics to the students of the Edinburgh School of Speech Therapy, and common research interests and collaboration continue to the present day.

The scholar whose vision of wide professional horizons most influenced the scope and nature of phonetics as a subject at that time in Edinburgh was David Abercrombie, the Head of the Department of Phonetics. It was the custom then in Scottish universities that the most senior academic member of a department should teach the most elementary course in the subject – a practice which has much to commend it. The Ordinary Course in Phonetics, taught by Abercrombie with assistance from colleagues such as Peter Ladefoged, Elizabeth Uldall, Ken Albrow and Lindsay Criper, was a seminal experience for many phoneticians-to-be, as the products of the Department of Phonetics found posts in many other universities throughout the world. Equally, Abercrombie's influence extended to colleagues in related Departments, such as English Language, Applied Linguistics and General Linguistics. Contemporary colleagues in these other departments who were in their varying degrees influenced by Abercrombie during the earlier days of his tenure included John Lyons, Angus McIntosh, John Sinclair, Ian Catford, Peter Strevens, Michael Halliday, Jack Aitken, Pit Corder and Ron Asher.

It may be helpful to work towards a commentary on my own perspective on the subject by trying to give some flavour of Abercrombie's contribution which, though he retired in 1980, still endures. He had come to Edinburgh in 1948 from the London School of Economics, where he had been a lecturer from 1934, with intermissions in the Middle East during the Second World War (Asher and Henderson, 1981). In this early part of his career at London, he had interacted professionally with Bronislaw Malinowski, C.K. Ogden, J.R. Firth and Daniel Jones. But his intellectual ancestry as a phonetician sprang even more directly from a uniquely British tradition of phonetics stretching back to scholars of the previous four hundred years, such as Bullokar, Hart, Holder, Wallis, Bishop Wilkins, Cooper, Sheridan, Herries, Sweet, Ellis, Alexander Graham Bell (the elder) and Alexander Melville Bell – a tradition which insists on the inseparability of the physical and psychological aspects of language.

The hallmark of Abercrombie's approach to phonetics was the combination of a demanding attention to theoretical rigour, allied to the scrupulous development of practical skills of performance and perception. One of his chief concerns was the contribution of phonetics to the teaching of English as a foreign and second language, and he published a good deal on prosodic and rhythmic aspects of English. His work was grounded in an excellent appreciation of the historical roots of the subject, and while his theoretical framework was always strongly linguistic, it nevertheless encompassed a perspective that was wider than the formal symbolic functions of spoken language alone. The orientation that he brought to phonetics was based not least on a strong interest in semiotics, and the iconic and the indexical (or evidential) properties of the medium of speech were amongst his major concerns. He was as interested in the written medium of language as in the spoken medium, and was a specialist in the theory of transcription. He made some major contributions to the study of paralanguage and tone of voice, and to that of speaker-identifying voice characteristics. Nothing germane to the study of speech, in all its aspects, was alien to him as a phonetician, and it is perhaps this eclectic quality of his outlook that has most shaped the professional attitudes of his students.

His main impact on a wider international audience was achieved through one of the four books he wrote – his theoretical textbook *Elements of General Phonetics*, published after many years of preliminary versions used as teaching texts for students at Edinburgh (Abercrombie, 1967). This is still in print after nearly twenty-five years, and has been used in very many courses as a basic textbook. The continuing appeal of this book certainly lies in part in the elegant, lucid and humane style that so characterised Abercrombie's writing. The book is very easy to read, and undergraduates tend to read it quickly. To do so is quite to mistake the depth and quality of Abercrombie's thinking; there is not a phrase in the book, so ostensibly transparent at first reading, that on adequate contemplation is not revealed as the product of a deep theoretical understanding of the intricate structure of speech and language. A number of other books are perhaps better fitted to the role of an elementary pedagogical exposition of surface aspects of the architecture of speech, but not one published to date, to my mind, quite captures as well the essence of the underlying design.

I write on Abercrombie at some length partly because I think he has not been accorded his due as the *doyen* of phonetics of the British School. He published some seventy articles, chapters and reviews, but while these are internationally properly regarded, it is only those who have had the privilege of being taught by him, or of having had the benefit of direct interaction with him as colleagues, who perhaps can reach a full appreciation of his qualities.

Coming now to my own perspective on the study of speech, I would like to say first that the process of writing about speech has been in a number of senses its own reward. Analytic writing is both the most demanding and the most productive method of reaching precision about conceptual structures. Readers of this volume must be the judges of whether the view of speech offered in these chapters is adequately clear; but I have found the career-long process of trying to clarify my own thinking by writing both indispensable and enjoyable. The sensation of addressing readers who are both unknown and yet familiar, and who form a community whose solidarity is extended beyond one's immediate acquaintance in both space and time, becomes addictive.

Second, my own perception is that my approach to the description of speech owes most to three people. The first is David Abercrombie, about whose influence I have already said much, and whose imprint will be visible in many of the papers reproduced in this volume. To him I owe a semiotic orientation, a respect for the historical foundations of the subject, and an abiding concern with the architectural design of phonetic theory. The interest in the voice which is displayed in many papers in this volume grew from the stimulus of attending his lectures, both as an undergraduate and as a postgraduate. He acted as the supervisor for my PhD dissertation on voice quality, and many of the ideas on voice quality which are elaborated in my articles are foreshadowed in his own teaching, writing and guidance.

Another major influence has been Peter Ladefoged, from the time when he taught experimental phonetics to the students of the Ordinary Course in Phonetics at Edinburgh to today, where he has been the chief architect of the Phonetics Laboratory at the University of California at Los Angeles since 1962. A steady stream of PhD dissertations building linguistic phonetic theory from experimental phonetic data has flowed from this laboratory over the past twenty-nine years, each reflecting the profound influence of a scholar who is committed to the mutual illumination of meticulously observed data and stringently formulated theory.

Peter Ladefoged has been a prolific writer, and his influence has been very wide. Amongst his six books, the publication which has most influenced phonetic theory has probably been *Preliminaries to Linguistic Phonetics* (1971), and it is this book which perhaps most closely mirrors his habitual professional stance. Written partly as a response to Chomsky and Halle's *The Sound Pattern of English*, whose account of phonetic phenomena in spoken language he regarded as over-abstract, *Preliminaries* successfully took on the task of providing a more empirically substantiated theory of phonetic features systematically used in the sound-patterns of the languages of the world.

A formative part of my own career was spent with Peter Ladefoged in 1971 in the Phonetics Laboratory at UCLA, which might be claimed to have both inherited and amplified the traditions of an Edinburgh view of phonetics. My interests in the biological and cognitive foundations of speech, and a sense of the importance in speech research of the scientific method, were first stimulated by his writings. I think I probably appreciated the need for a general phonetic theory capable of responding to the astonishing breadth of phonetic phenomena in the detailed realities of diverse languages more from Ladefoged's writings than from any other source. But the most basic and personal lesson I learned jointly from him and his wife Jenny was the need in an academic career for stamina; not only the tenacity required to follow the evolution of a developing idea through to its full form, but also the resolve to adhere to a personal vision not just when one's life seems to be flowing with the current, but through times of adversity as well.

The third scholar to whom I feel very indebted is Donald Boomer, the experimental and clinical psychologist from the National Institutes of Mental Health in Bethesda, Maryland who came in 1966 to spend a sabbatical year in Edinburgh, and with whom I collaborated on research into slips of the tongue in spontaneous speech. The initial descriptive work which I did with him (reprinted here as Chapter 2) launched me into a continuing fascination with how the brain might control speech production. It was Donald Boomer who introduced me to the gladiatorial arena of modelling the control of speech production, where it is usually the researcher who is finally vanquished by the complexities of the data, rather than the brain which gives up its mysteries. I learned from him what he had understood from the neurophysiologist Hughlings Jackson, that the workings of an opaque system like the brain might at least be approached through an examination of its characteristic malfunctions, even though the understanding of the normally-functioning system reached by this avenue might never be comprehensive.

Donald Boomer had a formidable analytic talent that I never quite managed to emulate in full. He regarded experimental data as a prisoner captured in a hard-won battle, to be interrogated and kept under close scrutiny until it had yielded every last drop of significance and subtle implication. Collaboration with him was an indelible apprenticeship in the workings of the scientific imagination.

The neurophysiologist John Eccles once said of Charles Sherrington (in a Gifford Lecture in this university) that he regarded Sherrington as his 'great master'. I have dwelled at some length on the nature of the approach to speech of Abercrombie, Ladefoged and Boomer because it is these scholars that I regard as my own 'great masters'. To acknowledge my debt, I dedicate this book of collected papers to them. To their names in the dedication, I would also like to join the names of Mary Abercrombie, Jenny Ladefoged and Menucha Boomer: in all three cases, the achievements of their husbands have been enabled and underpinned by their support and by their generosity of spirit.

This book itself is of course a direct signal of my own attitudes to the domain and nature of phonetics. The book is organised in two parts. The seven articles of Part I deal with the production of speech and its control by the brain. Chapter 1, first published in 1970, surveys the state of the art in research on speech production at that time, and this might be read in association with Chapter 7, published nearly twenty years later, which tries to place a review of contemporary speech research in a unified cognitive framework.

Chapters 2 to 6 reproduce some of the work that began with my collaboration with Donald Boomer, on slips of the tongue as evidence for the way that the brain might control the otherwise hidden processes of generating and monitoring of the production of normal, everyday speech. Speech errors in these articles are treated not as psychopathological aberrations, as Freud would have us believe, but as part and parcel of the normal constructional process of preparing a neurolinguistic and neuro-muscular program for speaking. As such, they offer a window on cerebral phenomena which are normally largely inaccessible, and give us glimpses of an immensely skilled and creative process at work over which every speaker possesses the most remarkable mastery.

A special word of explanation about Chapter 3 may be helpful. This was a working paper distributed to colleagues in 1969, and never formally published by myself. It formed part of the background to 'The Production of Speech', published in 1970 and reproduced here as Chapter 1. The manuscript of 'The Detection and Correction of Slips of the Tongue' was then included in a collected book of articles on speech errors edited by Vicki Fromkin in 1973, however, and has been cited quite often since then in the literature on speech production. Because it was the original source of some of the material in Chapter 1, there was a certain dilemma of choice between the two articles. However, despite the repetition that necessarily results, it was decided to reproduce both, in the interests of making Chapter 3 available in the context of the other articles on speech errors reprinted here.

Part II collects together thirteen articles (four of them previously distributed only in informal 'Work in Progress' publications to colleagues) on the description and analysis of voice quality. Chapter 8, on language and non-verbal communication, sets an initial framework. It tries to place the function of vocal communication in the wider context of all the strands of communication in everyday face-to-face conversation – including non-vocal strands such as gesture, posture, facial expression, gaze direction, proximity and spatial orientation. The skill of speakers and listeners in managing to integrate their control of all these coded, convention-rich, time-sensitive dimensions of behaviour with all the subtleties of vocal communication comes close to defeating the imagination. The most appropriate term that comes to mind to describe such virtuosity of performance is 'orchestration'.

Chapter 9 considers the voice as a source of a wide range of information for the listener about the speaker, developing some of David Abercrombie's ideas about the evidential ('indexical') function of speech. It also develops Beatrice Honikman's notion of a 'setting' of the vocal apparatus, as a long-term bias on articulatory action. This treatment of settings as basic components into which voices can be analysed runs through all the remaining chapters in the book.

The next two chapters apply a number of semiotic concepts to the topic of voice quality. Chapter 10 offers some comments on the semiotic status of phonetic data, and tries to show that phonetic data is both highly abstract, and equivocal with respect to the communicative function it might fulfil. Spreading the lips, as a phonetic event, might be relevant merely to the performance of a single vowel segment, or to the vocal gesture of smiling, or might simply reflect the habitual speech posture of the speaker. Chapter 11 considers the problematic area of what both laymen and professionals might mean by their use of labels for the voice, and tries to bring some semiotic order to what remains a highly metaphorical field of discourse.

Chapter 12 attempts to come to grips with the componential analysis of voices as composites of settings. This article summarises two lectures, one given in Northern Ireland in 1978 and the other in Cambridge in 1979. The material was later modified and expanded for incorporation in my book *The Phonetic Description of Voice Quality* (Laver, 1980), but, since that book is now out of print, it may be helpful to make some of the source material publicly available here for the first time.

Chapter 13 was written with my friend of many years, Robert Hanson, a speech scientist trained at the University of California at Santa Barbara and the University of Texas at Austin, at that time working for Bell Laboratories. It was one outcome of a project supported by the Medical Research Council to devise a method for describing voices characteristic of genetic and other types of disorder. This paper explores a concept of the normal voice, to use as a baseline for the description of the more deviant voices of abnormality in a project described in detail in Chapter 15.

Chapter 14, on phonetic and linguistic markers (or 'indices') in speech that serve to reveal characteristics of the speaker to the listener, was written with Peter Trudgill, the noted sociolinguist, who was originally trained at Edinburgh. This chapter returns to a semiotic theme whose outline was sketched in Chapter 9, to classify the different types of marker according to what type of characteristic the listener is attributing to the speaker. It considers not only vocal evidence, but also patterns of language use such as vocabulary and grammatical patterns.

Chapter 15 is a previously unpublished paper from the Medical Research Council project mentioned in association with Chapter 13. My colleague Sheila Wirz, now with the National Hospitals College of Speech Sciences in London, was the co-director of this project to develop a perceptual scheme for describing profiles of both normal and pathological voice quality. The result was the 'Vocal Profile Analysis (VPA) Protocol' method, which has now been widely taught by Sheila Wirz and colleagues to speech therapists and pathologists in Britain, Holland and Australia, for use in clinical situations. The VPA scheme was based on the principles developed for the description of the normal voice, as described in Chapters 9, 12 and 13, and in Laver (1975: 1980). It extends this method to the often more extreme voices encountered in speech pathology, and one of its main objectives is therefore the unification of techniques for describing both normal and pathological aspects of voice quality.

The work on the VPA scheme described in Chapter 15 was consciously based on the perceptual ability of speech therapists and pathologists to hear voices as composites of contributory settings. The reliability of judges trained in the VPA system is reported in Chapter 15, and shows that the VPA method is learnable. It is desirable, however, to go beyond a solely perceptual scheme and to try to establish both the acoustic correlates of the setting categories and the underlying physiological phenomena. Chapter 16 gives an account of work which tries to establish the biological basis for one of these setting categories in the area of phonation, namely 'harshness'. The label 'harshness' captures some of the semantics of the phonatory quality to which reference is being made – the perceptual effect of harsh voices is of a certain 'roughness'. This roughness is due acoustically to small-scale dysperiodicities or 'microperturbations' in the fine detail of the mode of vibration of the vocal folds. In their turn, these microperturbations (in the case of pathological voices) are caused by asymmetric changes in the layered structure of the vocal fold tissue which disrupt the regularity of the vibratory pattern of the vocal folds.

The work described in Chapters 16 and 17 was the product of a second Medical Research Council-funded project, where my research colleagues were Janet Mackenzie Beck, Steven Hiller and Edmund Rooney. Janet Mackenzie Beck (who is a qualified speech therapist as well as a biological scientist by training) was the first author for Chapter 16, in which we consider the anatomical and physiological foundation to these dysperiodic microperturbations in the laryngeal waveform. We also try to relate the anatomical situation of different types of disorder to their possible acoustic consequences, with the motivation of beginning to move towards a diagnostic support function in such work. Our intention was to try to make some of the medical knowledge in this area available to phonetics and speech pathology, and to synthesise a typological approach to laryngeal pathology in the light of an understanding of the disruptions of the layered structure of the vocal folds that characterised the individual pathologies.

Chapter 17 is the acoustic counterpart to the preceding chapter. It comments on our attempt to develop an automatic computer-based system for detecting the microperturbations in harsh voices, with a view to developing acoustic methods for screening voices for possible laryngeal pathology, and for monitoring changes over time with chemotherapy, radiotherapy or speech therapy. The great advantage of automatic methods which could analyse possible voice pathology from acoustic evidence is that such techniques are non-invasive. The accuracy of the system we produced could in principle support screening or monitoring applications. The scientific basis of such systems is not yet at a level that would reliably support diagnostic use, however, and in any case the ultimate responsibility for such an important decision should rest always with qualified medical specialists.

Chapter 18 is a more general survey of the topic of microperturbations and voice pathology, written for the Voice Committee of the International Association of Logopedics and Phoniatrics. It integrates part of the information in Chapters 16 and 17 in more compact form, and indicates some of the outstanding research publications in this field. It also identifies some of the work remaining to be done in this medically promising area.

Our understanding of the voice and its communicative functions is now reasonably well-advanced. But we should not forget that such understanding is cumulative, and that every generation owes a debt of knowledge to scholars of earlier times. Chapters 19 and 20 are historical essays, describing writings on different aspects of the voice from the time of antiquity to the nineteenth century. Some of the most lucid commentators on the voice are in fact the earliest. Both Cicero and Quintilian had much to say on the voice, often in strikingly modern-sounding terms. There is also a wealth of good observations in the writings of the sixteenth to nineteenth centuries, some of which is explored in these two chapters.

I believe it will be obvious from the papers reprinted here that the study of speech is now necessarily a multidisciplinary enterprise. To be a modern phonetician, one has to become familiar to some degree with aspects of the life sciences, the information sciences and the physical sciences. Over and above this, because speech is one of the intrinsically human activities, mediating our social and psychological relationships with each other in the web of everyday interaction, phonetics must be anchored in the social sciences and the humanities.

Compared with the range of the subject as I have described it in the 1950s, which was already broad, the modern discipline has grown extensively. The articles reprinted here are mostly accounts of expeditions to the frontiers of the subject. I have never felt, however, that the lines of communication connecting these ventures to the heartland of the subject (a general phonetic theory for use in the study of spoken language) have become fragile or tenuous. Rather, that the principles of phonetic analysis originally developed for linguistic phonetics stand one in good stead when extended to areas like the description of voice quality. Similarly, the obsessive interest of phoneticians in the study of the articulation of speech extends very naturally upstream to the strategies of neuromuscular and neurolinguistic control of that articulation.

It will no doubt therefore be self evident from the chapters offered in this book that I do not regard the domain of phonetics as restricted to the study of spoken language alone. To take one final example of this broader philosophy, the duality of normal and pathological speech should be part of the professional territory of phoneticians, supporting and supported by professionals in speech pathology and therapy. If speech is a gift, then unfortunately the gift is sometimes taken away, and we should do all we can first to understand, and then to try to restore such a precious facility.

No aspect of speech should be foreign to a phonetician, in my view. Linguistic, paralinguistic and extralinguistic aspects of speech are all legitimate topics of study. The chief responsibility of the theoretical phonetician, to my mind, is the obligation to show how the objective description of these seemingly disparate areas can be unified. The pleasure of phonetics is the discovery of the unifying principles underlying the manifest complexity of the gift of speech.

I hope that the chapters of this book will be of interest not only to professional readers in phonetics and neighbouring subjects such as linguistics, cognitive and social psychology, psycholinguistics, sociolinguistics, laryngology and phoniatrics, speech therapy and pathology, speech science and speech technology, but also to other academic readers and educated readers in general.

The papers reprinted in this volume are as they originally appeared, apart from minor corrections. Inevitably, some degree of repetition remains, for which I ask the reader's indulgence.

John Laver
Centre for Speech Technology Research
University of Edinburgh
February 1991

References

Abercrombie, D. (1967) *Elements of General Phonetics*, Edinburgh University Press, Edinburgh.

Asher, R.E. and Henderson, E.J.A. (eds) (1981) *Towards a History of Phonetics*, Edinburgh University Press, Edinburgh.

Chomsky, N. (1957) *Syntactic Structures*, Mouton, The Hague.

Chomsky, N. and Halle, M. (1968) *The Sound Pattern of English*, Harper and Row, New York.

Fromkin, V. (ed.) (1973) *Speech Errors as Linguistic Evidence*, Mouton, The Hague.

Ladefoged, P. (1971) *Preliminaries to Linguistic Phonetics*, University of Chicago Press, Chicago.

Laver, J. (1980) *The Phonetic Description of Voice Quality*, Cambridge University Press, Cambridge.

Part I

Speech Production

1 The Production of Speech

Originally published as Laver, J. (1970) 'The Production of Speech', in Lyons, J. (ed.), *New Horizons in Linguistics*, Penguin Books, Harmondsworth (pp. 53–75)

In his Introduction to the source-volume of this chapter, John Lyons suggests that in the past fifty years linguistics has tended to be 'somewhat insistent on the need for autonomy' (p. 8). There is an important sense in which phonetics has not participated in any insistence on autonomy that may have characterised the rest of linguistics in this period. Phonetics, as the study of the medium of spoken language (Abercrombie, 1967: 2), has always accepted that, in order to build a theory of how the apparatus of speech works and is used, it must employ a variety of concepts from a wide range of disciplines such as anatomy, physiology, physics and psychology. The boundaries of phonetics as a subject have been set primarily by the object of its study, speech, rather than by considerations of methodology. Phonetics stands at the intersection of all disciplines concerned in any way with the study of speech, and takes parts of its conceptual stock, and parts of its methodology, from each one of them. An essential characteristic of phonetics is thus that it is above all else a synthesising subject.

That linguistics as a whole should now be less insistent on the principle of autonomy is not an isolated tendency; it is part of a marked trend in all the behavioural sciences, perhaps exemplifying a general process of maturation that these disciplines are undergoing. Where earlier research tended to be somewhat constrained by disciplinary territorial barriers, these barriers now seem to be rapidly weakening, and multidisciplinary approaches to particular problems are increasingly being undertaken (Hymes, 1964; Smith, 1966; Lenneberg, 1967). As a direct result of this trend towards multidisciplinary synthesis, there has been a growth of interest in the exploration of topics in the borderlands between the territories of the older disciplines. Examples of such explorations which have a point of departure in linguistics are the fields of psycholinguistics (Saporta, 1961; Lyons and Wales, 1966) and sociolinguistics (Bright, 1966; Fishman, 1968; Pride, 1970: 287–301). A similar example, and one which will be the major topic of comment in this chapter, is the field of neurolinguistics.

The movement towards bringing multidisciplinary viewpoints to bear on particular problem areas is very attractive to phonetics, given the inherent synthesising character of the subject. The next decade or so may well see a number of attempts by phoneticians to locate the theory of speech in broader social, psychological and biological frameworks than have hitherto been used.

This chapter is specifically concerned with the production of speech. The most important new development in the study of this area in recent years, and one with far-reaching implications, is the attempt to use data from direct observation of speech to infer functional properties of the neural control systems in the brain's organisation of speech production.

It is difficult to find a satisfactorily specific and adequate adjective to characterise such a functional model of the brain's control of speech production. The terms 'neurophysiological', 'neuropsychological' and 'neurolinguistic' each reflect some characteristic of the model. Because the current state of neurological research into language activities restricts us largely to a consideration of functions rather than of detailed mechanisms, perhaps the least satisfactory of the possible labels is 'neurophysiological'. 'Neuropsychological' would be somewhat more acceptable, and would be compatible with a suggestion recently expressed by Chomsky (1968: 1) that linguistics is itself a branch of cognitive psychology. However, until this area of research becomes mature enough to acquire a commonly agreed label, the most neutral term, 'neurolinguistic', is probably the most satisfactory.

If phoneticians and linguists are to succeed in constructing a neurolinguistic model of the brain's control of speech, thus contributing to the necessarily multidisciplinary study of cerebral functions, they will have to modify their theoretical equipment to accommodate concepts and methods not only from neurophysiology and neuropsychology, but also from other disciplines such as control-systems engineering, computer science and information retrieval.

This expansion of phonetic and linguistic interests into the neurolinguistic processes of speech production may seem a novel departure, but I would like to show that it can be partly explained as a logical development of a trend which has its roots in the history of phonetics in the changing philosophy of articulatory analysis in the early part of this century.

The inherently dynamic nature of the articulation of the speech organs has been recognised for a long time. One of the first writers to comment on this was Hermann Paul (1886), when he wrote that 'A word is not a united compound of a definite number of independent sounds, of which each can be expressed by an alphabetical sign; but it is essentially a continuous series of infinitely numerous sounds, and alphabetical symbols do no more than bring out certain characteristic points of this series in an imperfect way'. Nevertheless, for a long time after Paul wrote this, phonetics continued to find it expedient to describe the articulation of speech as if it consisted of momentarily static postures of the speech organs, linked by glides from one posture to the next (Abercrombie, 1965: 21). The phoneticians of the early part of this century acknowledged that these segmental concepts were merely fictions convenient for the purpose of description and categorisation; but however nominal their adherence to this postural view of articulation, it had the unavoidable and prejudicial effect of focusing their theoretical attention on the static description of the vocal organs in the particular postures which they thought characterised the material of language. This was especially limiting, for three reasons: it distracted attention from the time-varying, parametric aspects of articulation; it overemphasised the individual independence of a small number of vocal organs; and it tended to perpetuate the attitude towards an alphabetic segmentation of the speech continuum that Paul had criticised.

Dissatisfaction with the unnecessary and inhibiting restraints of the static, postural view grew during the 1920s and 1930s in the teaching, for example, of J.R. Firth and Stephen Jones in London, and of a number of experimental phoneticians in other countries such as Stetson (1928) in America and Menzerath, Lacerda and von Essen in Germany. Gradually, speech has been recognised more explicitly as 'a dynamic process involving many coordinated articulatory processes, rather than as a sequence of relatively static postures involving only one or two of the articulatory organs' (Henderson, 1965: 16). The dynamic concept of speech production is now one of the foundations of modern articulatory phonetics, though the old-fashioned postural view has not entirely disappeared: it continues to exert an insidiously seductive influence, especially through some of the implications underlying parts of the established descriptive terminology (Henderson, 1965). Descriptive articulatory theory is still therefore far from maximally efficient (Fant, 1968), and the attempt to improve the adequacy and universality of general phonetic descriptive categories has produced a number of recent publications (Peterson and Shoup, 1966; Ladefoged, 1965).

The chief effect of the more dynamic view of speech was that it concentrated analytic attention on the time-varying parameters of articulation. This was particularly encouraged by the invention in the early 1940s of the sound spectrograph (Koenig, Dunn and Lacy, 1946; Potter, Kopp and Green, 1947; Pulgram, 1959). The advent of this instrument was a milestone in the study of speech, as it allowed phoneticians to have, for the first time, easy and relatively cheap access to a wide range of objective, quantifiable information about the acoustics of speech production, and hence to the underlying parameters of articulation.

The sound spectrograph provides graphic records of the spectral and temporal distribution of acoustic energy in any given utterance. The analysis of spectrographic data enabled phoneticians to formulate hypotheses about the nature of the acoustic parameters essential for the minimal specification of intelligible speech. For these hypotheses to be tested, they had to be able to produce synthetic simulations of the minimal acoustic specifications of the sounds of speech, and to use them as experimental stimuli to be presented to human listeners for identification in linguistic terms. People have been trying to produce synthetic speech by means of machines for a very long time, going back at least to von Kempelen in 1769 (Flanagan, 1965: 166), and by the time the sound spectrograph appeared, a variety of mechanical and electrical speech synthesisers had been invented which were suitable for testing hypotheses about the intelligibility of synthesised material.

Efforts to synthesise acceptable speech from a minimum amount of acoustic information received an additional impetus during the early 1950s from the requirements of telecommunications. Before the arrival of orbital satellite telecommunication links, there was a growing pressure on the limited capacity of the existing telecommunication channels. Transmitting the totality of the acoustic characteristics of an utterance was becoming increasingly uneconomical, and one way of economising was to transmit only those acoustic features of a speech message essential for intelligibility. This meant that a way had to be found of breaking down an utterance into its minimal acoustic parameters, and then reconstituting the transmitted parametric information at the other end of the telecommunication link into acceptable speech. There were two distinct problems: the automatic analysis of speech into acoustic parameters, and effective synthesis of the parameters into intelligible speech. Automatic speech analysis proved rather difficult, but a number of very successful electronic speech synthesisers were built, partly with a view to solving the problem of telecommunication economics, during the 1950s (Flanagan, 1965; Fant, 1968). The best synthetic speech is now indistinguishable from normal human speech.

Much of the early testing of hypotheses about the minimal acoustic specification of speech was done by means of programs controlling a synthesiser which were derived directly from phoneticians' interpretations of spectrographic analyses of actual human utterances, in a synthesis-by-analysis procedure. Enough is now known about the acoustic characteristics of typical speech behaviour to allow synthesis-by-rule, where the program controlling the synthesiser is produced by a computer according to sets of rules drawn up by phoneticians and communications engineers (Holmes, Mattingly and Shearme, 1964). The provision of computer speech immediately opens up a wide range of possible technological applications.

The acoustic analysis and synthesis of speech attracted a great deal of research in the 1950s and early 1960s (Lehiste, 1967). However, in this explosive growth of research effort, the attention of many workers tended to be monopolised by the study of the acoustic parameters themselves, to the relative disadvantage of the underlying articulatory parameters. This period of acoustic research did achieve remarkably comprehensive and important results, well represented by Fant's (1960) *Acoustic Theory of Speech Production*, but it seems generally agreed that in the last three or four years, interest has swung away from the acoustics of speech, back towards the study of articulatory aspects (Lehiste, 1967: vi).

An increasing variety of instrumental analytic techniques are now being applied to the study of articulatory dynamics, and these techniques all provide a continuous record of sequential articulatory events in real time, as they happen. The foremost technique, and one which is arousing wide interest, is electromyography – the registration of the minute electrical voltages produced by muscles as they contract (Fromkin, 1966; Fromkin and Ladefoged, 1966). This technique has been made extremely fruitful by the addition of a computer to process the vast amount of electromyographic data produced in even short utterances in (Fromkin and Ladefoged, 1966: 233).

Another promising technique is electrokymography, which records the continuous changes in oral and nasal airflow during speech. This produces detailed information about the timing and type of movements which the vocal organs superimpose on the out-flowing airstream during articulation. Complementary information about where in the mouth contact is made between tongue and palate can be gained from electropalatography, which uses an artificial palate into which is inserted a number of electrodes for registering the contacts (Kydd and Belt, 1964; Kozhevnikov and Chistovich, 1965).

A fourth technique used for recording the dynamics of articulation is cineradiography (Subtelny and Subtelny, 1962). Modern developments of image-intensification, which allows a correspondingly lower dosage of X-ray, should encourage its increasingly wide use.

I suggested above that, throughout the post-war period of research into acoustic phonetics, interest was mainly focused on the parametric approach to the acoustic analysis and synthesis of speech. This emphasis on parameters has been carried over into current articulatory studies (Abercrombie, 1965: 120–4), reinforcing the dynamic view of articulation inherited from the 1930s. A significant area of research which is emerging as the product of this interest in articulatory parameters is the exploration of the possibility of constructing a physiological speech synthesiser (Ladefoged, 1964). A working model of the vocal organs would have exactly the same usefulness for articulatory phonetics as the acoustic synthesisers had for acoustic phonetics: namely, it would enable a phonetician to test the validity of a hypothesis about the articulatory dynamics of an utterance by providing a synthetic simulation whose linguistic intelligibility could be judged by listeners.

An improved knowledge of the acoustic and articulatory characteristics of speech production has also served to strengthen the attitude that the physiological system for speech is not a set of independent vocal organs, but a single, complex system in which the continuous, interacting activities of the various linked components are intricately coordinated in time. In a parametric approach, temporal considerations thus assume a major importance, and modern phonetics increasingly recognises the need to give an adequate account, in describing the dynamics of articulation, of such temporal features as seriality, duration and rhythm.

Temporal behaviour in articulation can be remarkably delicately controlled: for example, one perceptually important difference between the articulations of the English words *bin* and *pin* is that the onset of vibration of the vocal cords is simultaneous with the moment of opening of the lips for [b], while in the case of *pin*, the onset is delayed for an interval, which can be as short as four hundredths of a second, after the moment of opening of the lips. The phonetician is led straight into speculation about the nature of the neural systems that can achieve such precise control of the intricately complex musculature of the vocal organs.

Phoneticians are thus being persuaded, by their interest in giving adequate accounts of the dynamics of articulation, to give some thought to the functional properties of the neural section of the neuromuscular speech-chain. I deliberately emphasise the distinction between the two different sections of the neuromuscular speech-chain: namely, between the muscles themselves, as the peripheral terminal of the chain, and the more central neural systems that control the activities of these muscles. The study of speech production could be said to be correspondingly divided, into two areas: the study of articulation, concerned with the dynamics of movements of the vocal organs; and the study of the neural functions which construct the neurolinguistic program of motor commands to be carried out by the articulatory muscles. Until very recently, phonetics has largely limited its interest in speech production to the study of articulation; it is now in the process of expanding its theoretical apparatus to include the study of neurolinguistic programming.

It seems quite certain, however, that the development of a really comprehensive model of neurolinguistic programming is a very long way ahead. A major difficulty is the scarcity of persuasive evidence. To all intents and purposes, the healthy adult brain is not itself accessible to neurolinguistic experiment. There is thus no possibility of directly observing the neural mechanisms involved in constructing a neurolinguistic program. However, it is a widely accepted research strategy that one can infer the properties of an unobservable control system from an examination of the output of that system. Hughlings Jackson, the great neurophysiologist, is reported as once saying 'The study of the causes of things must be preceded by a study of the things caused' (Beveridge, 1961). If we want to know how the brain controls speech, we must first look at speech itself.

There are likely to be two major benefits from any success that phonetics may have in inferring the properties of the neurolinguistic control system. Firstly, it is obviously desirable that we should be able to give a more comprehensive account of language behaviour by adding a neurolinguistic component to linguistic theory. (It is also noteworthy that in neurolinguistics, the sub-disciplinary boundary between phonetics and linguistics, which has always been of doubtful validity, is largely disappearing.) Secondly, and this is of wider importance, discoveries about the neural control of speech will have general applications to the whole range of cerebral control of voluntary, serial behaviour. Lashley (1951), in a classic article on this topic, supported the view that the study of speech production is a uniquely valuable point of entry into such speculations. He quotes Fournié (1887): 'Speech is the only window through which the physiologist can view the cerebral life', and suggests that 'the problems raised by the organisation of language seem . . . to be characteristic of almost all other cerebral activity' (Lashley, 1951).

The strategy of inferring properties of control systems from their output can be applied not only to the efficient operation of these systems, but also to their output when malfunctions occur. The evidence from characteristic malfunctions is, if anything, more penetrating than that obtained when the system is operating efficiently. We can distinguish five different conditions of speech to which this strategy can be applied: error-free, continuous speech; speech containing errors such as slips of the tongue, and their corrections; speech containing discontinuities such as hesitation signals; speech during the language-acquisition period in young children; and speech 'in dissolution', in the gross malfunctions of the speech production process in speech pathology.

It seems very probable that studies of language acquisition and speech pathology will eventually make an important contribution to the development of an adequate neurolinguistic model of the normal, healthy, adult brain, but I shall largely restrict discussion in this chapter to error-free continuous speech, slips of the tongue and their correction, and hesitation signals, which have so far provided the principal evidence.

Before going further, I should emphasise that error-free, continuous speech should not be equated with 'normal speech'. Spontaneous, normal speech is normally far from completely free from errors, and often contains slips of the tongue (Boomer and Laver, 1968); it is also nearly always far from completely continuous, almost invariably containing a variety of hesitation signals, such as pauses, repetitions and vocalisations such as 'er', 'ah' and 'um' (Boomer, 1965; Goldman-Eisler, 1968).

Using evidence from the speech output, any adequate neurolinguistic model will have to account in detail for the different functions involved in the generation of any speech utterance. The outline which follows below of the neurolinguistic functions is necessarily very simplistic, because of the highly speculative nature of the conclusions which have so far been reached, and because of the severe complexity of the problem.

There seem to be five chief functions: the ideation process, which initiates the approximate semantic content of any verbal message the speaker wishes to communicate; the permanent storage of linguistic information; the planning process, which constructs an appropriate neurolinguistic program for the expression of the idea; the execution of the neurolinguistic program by the articulatory muscle systems; and the monitoring function, which allows the detection and correction of errors. I shall refer to these functions as *ideation, storage, program-planning, articulation* and *monitoring*, respectively.

The least penetrable of the five functions, as far as neurolinguistics is concerned, is that of ideation. The initiation of ideas, of whatever degree of cognitive complexity, constitutes perhaps the most difficult issue raised in considerations of cerebral functions. Neurolinguistics can make two contributions of interest to the cognitive psychology of this area: firstly, it can bring the resources of the linguistic theory of semantics to the description of the semantic structure of the idea expressed; and secondly, it can say something about the relation between the ideation process and the program-planning and monitoring processes, as we shall see below.

In discussing the permanent storage of linguistic information, it is useful to distinguish between *what* is stored, and *how* it is stored. In considering *what* is stored, it is important to recognise that the various neural units used in speech production do not necessarily have any one-to-one correlation with the linguistic elements and the rules governing their combination currently posited by any theory of descriptive linguistics (Peterson, 1968). A starting-point is to say simply that storage consists of the neural correlates of potential linguistic behaviour. By itself, this is a self-evident statement, but its interest lies in the search which it implies for the nature of the relationship between neural units and linguistic elements and rules; a firm hypothesis about the actual relationship is crucial for any adequate neurolinguistic model.

I shall return in a moment to the current search for the characteristics of neural organisation of speech, but, before I do so, I would like to offer some comments on how neurolinguistic information may be stored.

The search for the neural memory trace, or engram, has occupied many neurophysiologists for a long time, without their reaching definitive and compelling results (Lashley, 1950). Two general hypotheses are the possibilities of local storage and non-local storage. Some evidence for local storage in precisely defined areas of the brain comes from speech pathologies correlated with known localised brain damage. It seems unlikely, however, that any extreme theory of local storage is valid for speech. Lenneberg (1967: 60) comments that 'The narrow localisation theory, which holds that engrams for words or syntactic rules are stored in certain aggregates of cells, cannot be in accord with the clinical facts'.

An interesting theory of non-local storage has recently appeared in a model of the memory process based on holography. Holography was originally a concept in the field of optics. The holographic principle is used in photography, using laser-illumination of optical interference patterns themselves originally produced by a laser, to give an apparently three-dimensional optical image. The relevance of holography for memory is that, on the holographic optical record, information about the recorded object is not stored locally, as it would be on a normal photographic film, but uniformly, at every point of the record. Holography thus supplies a model of non-local storage of information which has had an immediate application to the neurophysiology of memory (Longuet-Higgins, 1968; Pribram, 1969).

A major problem in considering the relationship between the storage system and the program-planning function is how the latter can retrieve necessary information from the former. Information retrieval is of course a problem which is not restricted to the field of human memory: in a sense, it is a central problem of our whole technological society, and not surprisingly a new discipline has appeared, devoted to its study. Many of the concepts which it has developed (see Bott, 1970: 215–28) can be applied directly, if cautiously, to the question of how the brain might retrieve neurolinguistic data stored in its memory.

For any retrieval system to work economically, an addressing system is needed for the data in storage. Errors of retrieval can tell us something about the characteristics of such an addressing system. Broadbent (1966: 289) writes 'It is extremely plausible that, in picking out a particular address in storage, one will occasionally go to the wrong address. But the errors which are made will presumably not be random, but rather will be linked to the way in which different possible addresses are organised together'. A clue to one sort of addressing system for lexical storage lies in the tentative hypotheses we explore in trying to recall a forgotten name or word. In these circumstances, we usually seem fairly confident of the rhythmic pattern of the word, and of the number and approximate segmental structure of the syllables, though less confident of the identity of all but one or two of the particular segments within the syllables (Brown and McNeill, 1966). On this basis, we can generate a number of words with a similar rhythm and structure to the forgotten word, which can act as associative stimuli leading to its eventual recovery. That is to say, we generally know what area of the lexical store to search for a partially forgotten word, in terms of a phonological rhythm-and-structure addressing system.

It seems extremely likely that the system of storage can have a variety of associative addressing indices. One principal index is almost certainly the semantic index. For example, some slips of the tongue show that lexical addresses can be organised on an associative semantic basis, in such slips as *sleast*, where, in the attempt to retrieve *least, slightest* was also activated, and the brain failed to complete its choice between them before the program was articulated. Another associative addressing system is the one based on experiential association that many 'Freudian' slips of the tongue suggest (Freud, 1901).

Finally, on the subject of storage, obviously very long-term memory is involved, and the processes of acquisition, retention and use of the memory store in speech are subject to the same factors of learning, recall, confusion, and forgetting as any other sort of utilisation of memory (cf. Johnson-Laird, 1970: 261–70). The storage system can thus be investigated by using the techniques of experimental psychology. In this connection, attempts to explore the properties of the lexical storage system by means of word-association tests have resulted in a very large body of literature (cf. Clark, 1970: 271-86). A particularly interesting recent approach is that of Kiss (1967, 1969), who is developing a computer model of lexical selection in which the retrieval operation works as a stochastic process.

I have implied that the retrieval of selected linguistic information from the memory store, with its necessary sub-processes of search and recognition, constitutes part of the program-planning function. The characteristics of the program-planning function make up the central core of any neurolinguistic model of speech production, and we have seen that we can infer some properties of the process of retrieving linguistic information from the memory store. However, we have to acknowledge that in general we still know very little about how the brain goes about constructing a neurolinguistic program, at least at the lexical, morphological and syntactic levels. We shall see below that neurolinguistic research has had some small success in reaching conclusions about the neural reality of some phonological units, and about the principles of their neural organisation into longer programs, but it would be very premature, at this stage of research, to suggest that the brain actually makes use of neural elements or operations that correspond directly to any of the higher-level structural units or rules laid down in current theories of descriptive linguistics.

A temporising formulation that avoids such premature commitment would be simply that the planning function organises a program specifying the neural correlates of the linguistic characteristics of the idea which the speaker intends to communicate. This commits us only to the simplistic and convenient position that program-planning involves the selection and eventual temporal organisation of the neural correlates of lexical items and their morphological and syntactic arrangement, together with their associated phonology – the criterion for each lexical, morphological or syntactic choice being that it should be semantically relevant to the expression of the speaker's initial idea.

This formulation emphasises that the relation between the idea and the neurolinguistic program is a semantic one. This is a difficult area to conceptualise, precisely because it is only possible to discuss ideas in terms of their expository linguistic programs. Miller, Galanter and Pribram (1960) quote a passage by William James (1890) which I think captures the nature of this difficulty with great clarity:

> And has the reader never asked himself what kind of a mental fact is his intention of saying a thing before he has said it? It is an entirely definite intention, distinct from all other intentions, an absolutely distinct state of consciousness, therefore; and yet how much of it consists of definite sensorial images, either of words or of things? Hardly anything! Linger, and the words and things come into the mind; the anticipatory intention, the divination is there no more. But as the words that replace it arrive, it welcomes them successively and calls them right if they agree with it, it rejects them and calls them wrong if they do not. It has therefore a nature of its own of the most positive sort, and yet what can we say about it without using words that belong to the later mental facts that replace it?

This passage implies that the planning function, in retrieving items from the memory store, activates more items than it finally selects for inclusion in the neurolinguistic program to be articulated. This is well supported by those slips of the tongue, mentioned above, where the brain fails to complete its planning choice between competing possible alternatives before the speech-program reaches the articulation stage. A lexical example would be the slip mentioned above: *didn't bother me in the sleast* with competition between *slightest* and *least* (Boomer and Laver, 1968: 10). A syntactic example would be: *He behaved as like a fool* with competition between *like a fool* and either or both of *as if he were a fool* and *as though he were a fool*.

A number of conclusions can be drawn from the suggestion that more items are activated than are selected for inclusion in the final program. Firstly, because the competing alternatives, from amongst which one candidate is finally selected, are presumably all relatively appropriate semantically, the initial activation of a given part of the memory store must be directed on a semantic basis, making use of a semantic addressing system. Secondly, the planning function has to be able to scrutinise the competing candidates, assess their degree of semantic relevance to the expression of the initial idea, and choose the most appropriate item. The semantic structuring of the initial idea thus serves as a predisposition towards both activating particular areas of the memory store, and choosing the most relevant of the individual items that have been activated.

That such a choice between competing candidates seems often to be made is one theoretical justification, following William James, for treating ideation as a separate function from neurolinguistic program-planning.

To separate the ideation function from the planning function is not to imply that the latter may not influence the former. It seems intuitively reasonable to assume that the specific restrictions and associations characterising particular items that are activated by the planning function may allow the brain to reach a revised, and perhaps more precise, formulation of the original idea, which in turn may lead to a revision of parts of the neurolinguistic program.

In trying to infer the characteristics of the neural organisation of a speech program from a detailed examination of articulation, one particularly important conclusion has been reached about neural correlates of phonological units: the preparation and articulation of a speech program is not performed on a sound-by-sound, or even on a word-by-word basis. It is much more likely that neural elements corresponding to much longer stretches of speech are assembled in advance and then allowed to be articulated as a single continuous program.

The concept of a series of skilled movements being prepared as a sequence, in advance of execution, has been recognised for some time. Craik (1947: 61) suggested that complex patterns of muscular movements, as in typewriting, could be prepared and 'triggered off as a whole'. In the field of phonetics, the concept of anticipatory adjustments in articulation is of very long standing; Stetson (1928: 203) aptly called it the 'law of prevision'. More recently, Lashley (1951) wrote that 'There are indications that, prior to the internal or overt enunciation of a sentence, an aggregate of word units is partially activated or readied'.

The linguistic unit in English which seems to be the most promising candidate for the typical preassembled stretch is what has variously been called a 'tone-group' (Halliday, 1967), a 'phonemic clause' (Trager and Smith, 1951), or a 'syntagma' (Kozhevnikov and Chistovich, 1965). For convenience, I shall refer to this unit as the 'tone-group'. The tone-group is a stretch of speech which lasts, on average, for about seven or eight syllables, and which contains only one very prominent syllable, on which a major change of pitch occurs in intonation. This prominent syllable, which I shall refer to as the 'tonic syllable', is usually located at or near the end of the tone-group, as in *Ask them to come into the* gar*den*. The tone-group is also characterised by pauses, which are usually optional but sometimes mandatory, at its boundaries. Here the pauses are not perceived as hesitation signals, unless unduly prolonged; while internal pauses of even very short duration are heard by the listener as hesitations (Boomer and Dittman, 1962). The boundaries of the tone-group often, though not always, coincide with those of the syntactic clause. Lastly, the tone-group is the major unit for carrying intonation patterns, and has a simple correspondence with units of rhythm.

Evidence in error-free, continuous speech that the tone-group is the usual unit of neurolinguistic pre-preparation comes from the fact that intonational and (sometimes) syntactic choices in the early part of the tone-group can depend on choices made in the latter part, and logically therefore have to anticipate the later choices.

Evidence also comes from observation of slips of the tongue. Boomer and Laver (1968) suggest, after Lashley (1951), that tongue-slips are the result of transient malfunctions of the neural organisation of a speech program, and show that slips can be plausibly explained as the neural interaction of elements 'simultaneously represented in an interim assembly' (Boomer and Laver, 1968: 9). In an analysis of slips involving segments representing phonemes, they note that the span of interference between an intended segment and the interfering segment usually comes within a single tone-group, and only rarely across a tone-group boundary. They also note that slips nearly always involve the tonic syllable, or the word in which the tonic syllable occurs (the 'tonic word'), usually as the location of the interfering segment. They comment that 'the typical slip involves interference from the tonic word *before* it is uttered' (1968: 8), since the tonic word is usually very late in the tone-group. This is good evidence for believing that 'the tone-group is handled in the central nervous system as a unitary behavioural act, and the neural correlates of the separate elements are assembled . . . before the performance of the utterance begins' (1968: 9).

The conclusion that the tone-group is probably the usual unit of neural pre-preparation was first suggested by Boomer (1965) in a study of hesitation pauses. Using the 'phonemic clause' (tone-group) as his frame of reference, he studied the location of hesitation pauses in the stream of speech, and addressed himself to the question of whether the phonemic clause or the word was the more plausible candidate for the unit of neural encoding in speech. He argued that if it was the word, any pauses should occur before points of least certainty on the part of the speaker about his next choice, that is, before words of low probability of occurrence, which carry high information value. The tonic word, typically occurring late in the tone-group (phonemic clause), tends to have the lowest probability of occurrence of all the words in the tone-group: the word-unit model thus predicts that pauses, if they occur, would do so before the tonic word, usually late in the tone group. Boomer found, however, that hesitation pauses tend to occur towards the beginning of phonemic clauses (tone-groups), often after the first word. This evidence, he suggested, 'argues strongly for the phonemic clause rather than the word as the molar encoding unit of speech' (Boomer, 1965: 156).

The suggestion that the preparation of a neural program for the articulation of a tone-group involves the assembly of a number of neural elements, leads us to speculate about the size of the minimal neural unit used in such an assembly process. A small minimal unit seems essential. Ladefoged (1967: 169) points out that 'there must be some stored units: all conceivable utterances cannot be stored as indivisible units in the cortex so that they are available should there be an occasion for their use'. A number of researchers have tried to discover the size of the smallest invariant neural unit in the program of motor commands to the articulatory muscles, by looking closely at the dynamics of connected speech with the help of some of the instrumental techniques mentioned above: electromyography, electrokymography, electropalatography, cineradiography and spectrography. The two favoured candidates are the phoneme and the syllable. In search of the necessary neural invariances, researchers have tried either to demonstrate directly corresponding invariances of muscular activities in articulation, or to find an explanation capable of accounting for discrepancies between the posited neural invariances and observed articulatory variabilities.

Variations in articulation arise from the fact that, in connected speech, neighbouring articulations very often exercise an assimilatory influence on each other, with a tendency for the influence to be largely anticipatory rather than perseverative. The characteristics of an articulation representing a particular phonological element thus often vary according to the context in which the element occurs, especially when the articulation precedes another articulation using substantially the same groups of muscles.

Some researchers have reported findings of articulatory invariances that support the phoneme as the minimal neural unit. Workers at the Haskins Laboratories in New York, investigating adjacent phonemes whose articulations involve different muscle groups, report that they have found invariances in the electromyographic records of the articulations of each phoneme 'regardless of the context in which the phoneme occurs' (Liberman, Cooper, Harris, MacNeilage and Studdert-Kennedy, 1964). Even when adjacent phonemes involve a common muscle group, they report that 'there appears to a common core of (electromyographic) activity that remains constant' when a phoneme appears in different contexts (Liberman et al., 1964: 84). Similar evidence comes from MacNeilage (1963): in an electromyographic study, he found an invariance in his records for the production of /f/ which was independent of phonetic context.

Fromkin (1968) offers different evidence, which favours the syllable, and which is still based partly on articulatory invariances: in an electromyographic study of /b/ and /p/, she found that there were invariances in the data for each phoneme for its occurrence in either initial or final position in a syllable, but clear differences between the data for the two positions. In this case, the brain obviously transmits different neural commands for a phoneme occurring in initial as opposed to final syllable position, and one hypothesis which could explain this is that the syllable constitutes the basic neural unit. She quotes Fry (1964: 219) in support, who writes 'it is at least plausible . . . that syllabification is one feature of the brain's control of motor speech activity, and that the true function of the syllable . . . is to form the unit of neural organisation'.

An observation from the field of slips of the tongue also supports the syllable: Boomer and Laver (1968: 7) found that 'segmental slips obey a structural law with regard to syllable place', in that syllable-initial segments interfere only with other syllable-initial segments, final only with final, and nuclear only with nuclear. This argues that the syllable is more than just a linguistic construct, and has a plausible reality as the smallest unit of neural programming, with segmental phonemes having neural invariance only in terms of their organisation within the syllable.

Other work which largely favours the phoneme as the smallest neural unit, but which allows for variability in articulation depending on context, is that of Lindblom (1963), Öhman (1966; 1967) and Öhman, Persson and Leanderson (1967), all from Stockholm. This particularly promising work posits neural invariance of phoneme-sized units, and accounts for variations in articulation which depend on context in terms of different temporal relations between the neural commands for successive articulatory gestures.

One difficulty in trying to account for the variability of articulation is that we do not yet really know enough about the neuromuscular physiology of the vocal organs. We lack, for example, a thorough knowledge of the detailed physiology of the tongue, which is extremely complex. This may be remedied by the growing amount of electromyographic work that is currently being undertaken. Another particularly important area of neuro-muscular physiology about which more information is needed is that of the detailed mechanisms of the brain's auditory, tactile and kinesthetic sensory feedback system (Ladefoged, 1967: 163; Fromkin, 1968: 62). The brain clearly uses some sensory feedback information to keep a continuous plot of the movement and position of the vocal organs; it may also use sensory feedback to modify the characteristics of some in-process motor commands, but Lashley (1951) points out that the execution of rapid, accurate movements is often completed in a shorter time than the reaction time for tactile or kinesthetic reports to be made on what happened. Control of continuous articulation thus cannot depend entirely for its accuracy on a chain of sensory-motor reactions. An interesting additional possibility of feedback-control of motor commands is the use of a neural scanning system to report on the motor commands themselves (Fromkin, 1968: 62), thus avoiding the time delay involved in sensory feedback.

While sensory information may not be of prime importance in controlling articulation directly, this information is nevertheless available to the brain for use in the last of the neurolinguistic functions noted in the early part of this chapter – the function of monitoring speech utterances for errors.

Monitoring an utterance for errors such as slips of the tongue is an automatic process which normally operates outside awareness. Not many slips of the tongue remain uncorrected by the speaker, so it seems fair to assume that the monitor system maintains nearly constant surveillance, and is therefore an integral part of the speech-producing process. A speaker also often makes a slip and corrects it without either the speaker or the listener being aware that a slip has occurred. The conscious perception of speech in some sense regularises and idealises the actual data of speech (Boomer and Laver, 1968). Conscious awareness is thus not a necessary part of the monitoring process.

The fact that a speaker does correct his slips of the tongue is fundamental evidence of a monitoring function in the speech-producing process. A logical prerequisite of the correction of errors is their detection, and it is useful to distinguish between the system which facilitates detection, and the system which allows correction. In discussing detection, we must be sure about what it is that is being detected. We speak of 'slips of the tongue', which implies literally that the slip is an error of articulation; in fact this is a misconception. Articulation consists of muscular actions, and any and every muscular contraction is the result of a specific neural control program. When errors occur, they are to be attributed to incorrect programs; 'slip of the tongue' is a misnomer: 'slip of the brain', or perhaps 'slip of the mind' would be more accurate.

Monitoring thus serves to detect errors in the neurolinguistic program. It is interesting to consider by what criteria a program can be said to be 'incorrect', or to contain an 'error'. One convenient approach is to say that an incorrect program is one which in some detail distorts the communication of the speaker's idea. It is striking that this leads us straight back into considerations of the relation between an idea and the linguistic program constructed to communicate that idea.

In this formulation, errors which distort accurate communication of the speaker's idea include not only slips of the tongue, but also linguistically orthodox programs which are in some detail semantically inappropriate to the speaker's idea. This gives two general categories of error: those which result in a form not found in the language, such as *didn't bother me in the sleast* (Boomer and Laver, 1968); and those which give linguistically permissible but semantically inappropriate results, such as Lashley's (1951) example of a spoonerism *Our queer old dean* for *Our dear old Queen*, and also such examples of corrections of imprecision as *He was sitting writing at his desk – er – table*. In other words, the revision of a semantically inappropriate choice in a program after its initial utterance is evidence of an error which can be discussed in the same overall framework as other sorts of program errors.

In the category of errors which give linguistically permissible results, it is often only the fact of correction that allows us, as observers, to know that an error has occurred.

The detection system that the monitoring function applies to the two categories of errors has to achieve two results: it has to establish the neurolinguistic characteristics of the program that was articulated, from sensory and neural reports, and it has to evaluate the appropriateness of the performed program for the semantic expression of the speaker's idea. On the basis of the evaluation, and taking into consideration the degree of the accuracy demanded by the situation, the brain can then take any necessary action towards stopping the current program and reprogramming an appropriate correction of the error.

The basic purpose of the monitoring system is to allow the brain to revise inappropriate neurolinguistic programs: it seems reasonable to suggest that the program-planning function may be similarly involved, as part of its normal creative activity, in editorial revision of programs before they reach the articulation stage. If revision is a shared purpose of the planning function and the monitoring function, then the revisionary activities of the two functions can be equated. The successful revisionary activity of the planning function leads to error-free speech, because revisions are carried out before the program is articulated; and the revisionary activity of the monitoring function is reflected in the correction, after articulation, of overt errors. The difference between error-free speech and speech containing overt errors, in this view, would be a fairly trivial difference of the point in time at which the brain's revisionary resources were applied – before or after articulation of the program. This is substantially the same conclusion as that reached by Hockett, in his distinction between 'covert editing' and 'overt editing', where he writes 'Editing in the internal flow is *covert editing* . . . In certain formal circumstances covert editing is thorough, and overt speech is unusually smooth. Much more typically, what is actually said aloud includes various signs of *overt editing*' (Hockett, 1967: 936). I would equate covert editing with revision carried out by the planning function, and overt editing with revision initiated by the monitoring function.

This is really a restatement of the view which I put forward early in this chapter, that normal speech is not necessarily error-free speech and, by extension, that errors are part and parcel of the normal process of speech production, and therefore worthy of study.

I have offered some generalities about some aspects of a possible functional model of the brain's neurolinguistic control of speech production. In the present stage of neurolinguistic research, these generalities are necessarily more than a little speculative. To conclude, I should emphasise that while models of cerebral functions are usually constrained by criteria of logic, some of these criteria may not be obeyed in the real situation. Donald Boomer wrote to me recently with a very salutary comment on this topic. He wrote 'Man's brain is an evolutionary outcome, and there is no reason to believe that the evolutionary process is subject to the logical canons of parsimony and elegance. On the contrary in fact'.

References

Abercrombie, D. (1965) *Studies in Phonetics and Linguistics*, Oxford University Press, London.

Abercrombie, D. (1967) *Elements of General Phonetics*, Edinburgh University Press, Edinburgh.

Beveridge, W.I.B. (1961) *The Art of Scientific Investigation*, Mercury Books, London.

Boomer, D.S. (1965) 'Hesitation and grammatical encoding', *Language and Speech* 8: 148–58; reprinted in Oldfield, R.C. and Marshall, J.C. (eds) (1968) *Language: Selected Readings*, Penguin Books, London.

Boomer, D.S. and Dittman, A.T. (1962) 'Hesitation pauses and juncture pauses in speech', *Language and Speech* 5: 215–20.

Boomer, D.S. and Laver, J. (1968) 'Slips of the tongue', *British Journal of Disorders of Communication* 3: 2–12 (reprinted in this volume, Chapter 2).

Bott, M.F. (1970) 'Computational linguistics', pp. 215–28 in Lyons, J. (ed.) *New Horizons in Linguistics*, Penguin Books, Harmondsworth.

Bright, W. (ed.) (1966) *Sociolinguistics* (Proceedings of the UCLA Sociolinguistics Conference, 1964), Mouton, The Hague.

Broadbent, D.E. (1966) 'The well-ordered mind', *American Educational Research Journal* 3: 281–95.

Brown, R. and McNeill, D. (1966) 'The "tip of the tongue" phenomenon', *Journal of Verbal Learning and Verbal Behavior* 5: 325–37.

Chomsky, N. (1968) *Language and Mind*, Harcourt, Brace and World, New York.

Clark, H.H. (1970) 'Word associations and linguistic theory', pp. 271–86 in Lyons, J. (ed.) *New Horizons in Linguistics*, Penguin Books, Harmondsworth.

Collins, N.L. and Michie, D. (eds.) (1967) *Machine Intelligence*, Volume 1, Edinburgh University Press, Edinburgh.

Craik, K.J.W. (1947) 'Theory of the human operator in control systems. I. The operator as an engineering system', *British Journal of Psychology* 38: 56–61.

Fant, G. (1960) *Acoustic Theory of Speech Production*, Mouton, The Hague.

Fant, G. (1968) 'Analysis and synthesis of speech processes', pp. 173–277 in Malmberg, B. (ed.) *Manual of Phonetics*, North-Holland, Amsterdam.

Fishman, J.A. (ed.) (1968) *Readings in the Sociology of Language*, Mouton, The Hague.

Flanagan, J.L. (1965) *Speech Analysis. Synthesis and Perception*, Academic Press, New York.

Fournié, E. (1887) *Essai de Psychologie*, Paris.

Freud, S. (1901) *Zur Psychopathologie des Alltagsleben* (translated as *The Psychopathology of Everyday Life*, E. Benn, London, 1966).

Fromkin, V.A. (1966) 'Neuro-muscular specification of linguistic units', *Language and Speech* 9: 170–99.

Fromkin, V.A. (1968) 'Speculations on performance models', *Journal of Linguistics* 4: 47–68.

Fromkin, V.A. and Ladefoged, P. (1966) 'Electromyography in speech research', *Phonetica* 15: 219–42.

Fry, D.B. (1964) 'The functions of the syllable', *Zeitschrift für Phonetik* 17: 215–37.

Goldman-Eisler, F. (1968) *Psycholinguistics*, Academic Press, London.
Halliday, M.A.K. (1967) *Intonation and Grammar in British English*, Mouton, The Hague.
Henderson, E.J.A. (1965) 'The domain of phonetics', School of Oriental and African Studies, University of London.
Hockett, C.F. (1967) 'Where the tongue slips, there slip I', pp. 910–36 in *To Honor Roman Jakobson*, Volume 2, Mouton, The Hague.
Holmes, J.N., Mattingly, I.G. and Shearme, J.N. (1964) 'Speech synthesis by rule', *Language and Speech* 7: 127–43.
Hymes, D. (1964) *Language in Culture and Society: A Reader in Linguistics and Anthropology*, Harper and Row, New York.
James, W. (1890) *Principles of Psychology*, Volume 1, Holt, Rinehart and Winston, New York.
Jeffress, L.A. (ed.) *Cerebral Mechanisms in Behavior*, Wiley, New York.
Johnson-Laird, P. (1970) 'The perception and memory of sentences', pp. 261–70 in Lyons, J. (ed.) *New Horizons in Linguistics*, Penguin Books, Harmondsworth.
Kiss, G.R. (1967) 'Networks as models of word storage', pp. 155–67 in Collins, N.L. and Michie, D. (eds) *Machine Intelligence*, Volume 1, Oliver and Boyd, Edinburgh.
Kiss, G.R. (1969) 'Steps towards a model of word selection', in Michie, D. and Meltzer, B. (eds) *Machine Intelligence*, Volume 4, Edinburgh University Press, Edinburgh.
Koenig, W., Dunn, H.K. and Lacey, L.Y. (1946) 'The sound spectrograph', *Journal of the Acoustical Society of America* 17: 19–49.
Kozhevnikov, V.A. and Chistovich, L.A. (1965) *Speech: Articulation and Perception*, Nauka, Moscow (translated by the US Department of Commerce, Joint Publications Research Service, Washington DC).
Kydd, W.L. and Belt, D.A. (1964) 'Continuous palatography', *Journal of Speech and Hearing Research* 29: 489–92.
Ladefoged, P. (1964) 'Some possibilities in speech synthesis', Language and Speech 7: 205–14.
Ladefoged, P. (1965) 'The nature of general phonetic theories', *Monograph Series on Language and Linguistics*, Georgetown University, Washington, DC.
Ladefoged, P. (1967) *Three Areas of Experimental Phonetics*, Oxford University Press, London.
Lashley, K.S. (1950) 'In search of the engram', in *Physiological Mechanisms in Animal Behavior, Symposia of the Society for Experimental Biology* 4, Academic Press, New York.
Lashley, K.S. (1951) 'The problem of serial order in behavior', in Jeffress, L.A. (ed.) *Cerebral Mechanisms in Behavior*, Wiley, New York; reprinted in Saporta, S. (ed.) (1961) *Psycholinguistics: A Book of Readings*, pp. 180–98, Holt, Rinehart and Winston, New York.
Lehiste, I.L. (1967) *Readings in Acoustic Phonetics*, Massachusetts Institute of Technology Press, Cambridge MA.
Lenneberg, E.H. (1967) *Biological Foundations of Language*, Wiley, New York.
Liberman, A.M., Cooper, F.S., Harris, K.S., MacNeilage, P.F. and Studdert-Kennedy, M. (1964) 'Some observations on a model of speech perception', in Wathen-Dunn, W. (ed.) *Models for the Perception of Speech and Visual Form*, Massachusetts Institute of Technology Press, Cambridge MA.
Lindblom, B. (1963) 'Spectrographic study of vowel reduction', *Journal of the Acoustical Society of America* 35: 1773–81.

Longuet-Higgins, H.C. (1968) 'The non-local storage of temporal information', *Proceedings of the Royal Society, B*, 171: 327–34.

Lyons, J. (ed.) (1970) *New Horizons in Linguistics*, Penguin Books, Harmondsworth.

Lyons, J. and Wales, R.J. (1966) *Psycholinguistics Papers*, Edinburgh University Press, Edinburgh.

MacNeilage, P.F. (1963) 'Electromyographic and acoustic study of the production of certain final clusters', *Journal of the Acoustical Society of America* 35: 461–3.

Malmberg, B. (ed.) (1968) *Manual of Phonetics*, North-Holland, Amsterdam.

Miller, G.A., Galanter, E. and Pribram, K.H. (1960) *Plans and the Structure of Behavior*, Holt, Rinehart and Winston, New York.

Öhman, S.E.G. (1966) 'Numerical models of coarticulation', *Journal of the Acoustical Society of America* 41: 310–20.

Öhman, S.E.G., Persson, A. and Leanderson, R. (1967) 'Speech production at the neuromuscular level', *Proceedings of the Sixth International Congress of Phonetic Sciences, Prague*, Mouton, The Hague.

Oldfield, R.C. and Marshall, J.C. (eds) (1968) *Language: Selected Readings*, Penguin Books, London.

Paul, H. (1886) *Prinzipien der Sprachgeschichte*, 2nd Edition, Halle (translated by Strong, H.A. as *Principles of the History of Language*, London 1888).

Peterson, G.E. and Shoup, J.E. (1966) 'A physiological theory of phonetics', *Journal of Speech and Hearing Research* 9: 5–67.

Potter, R.K., Kopp, G.A. and Green, H.C. (1947) *Visible Speech*, Van Nostrand, New York.

Pribram, K.H. (1969) 'The neurophysiology of remembering', *Scientific American* 220: 1.73–86.

Pride, J.B. (1970) 'Sociolinguistics', pp. 287–301 in Lyons, J. (ed.) *New Horizons in Linguistics*, Penguin Books, Harmondsworth.

Pulgram, E. (1959) *Introduction to the Spectrography of Speech*, Mouton, The Hague.

Saporta, S. (ed.) (1961) *Psycholinguistics: a Book of Readings*, Holt, Rinehart and Winston, New York.

Smith, A.G. (ed.) (1966) *Communication and Culture*, Holt, Rinehart and Winston, New York.

Stetson, R.H. (1928) *Motor Phonetics*, North-Holland, Amsterdam (2nd edition, 1951).

Subtelny, J.D. and Subtelny, J.D. (1962) 'Roentgenographic techniques and phonetic research', *Proceedings of the Fourth International Congress of Phonetic Sciences*, pp. 129–46, Mouton, The Hague.

Trager, G.L. and Smith, H.L. (1951) 'An outline of English structure', *Studies in Linguistics*, Occasional Paper 3.

Wathen-Dunn, W. (ed.) (1964) *Models for the Perception of Speech and Visual Form*, Massachusetts Institute of Technology Press, Cambridge MA.

2 Slips of the Tongue

Originally published as Boomer, D.S. and Laver, J. (1968) 'Slips of
the tongue', *British Journal of Disorders of Communication* 3:2–11
(reprinted in Fromkin, V.A. (ed.) (1973) *Speech Errors as Linguistic Evidence*, Mouton, The Hague (pp. 120–31))

Summary

A general psycholinguistic interest in speech performance underlies the
study to be reported here. The specific focus is on the system of control of
sequencing of speech units, and even more narrowly on a class of speech
errors – tongue-slips – which result from transient malfunctions of this
system. The general strategy is that of inferring relevant properties of an
unobservable system on the basis of its output characteristics.

Introduction

Our usage of the term tongue-slip can be illustrated in a preliminary,
informal way by reference to a characteristic example. Consider the
following utterance, noted during a dinner-table conversation.

'But those frunds . . . funds have been frozen.'

'Frunds', here, is a tongue-slip, a form involuntarily produced by the
speaker instead of the intended 'funds'. Such fleeting misarticulations are
relatively common in ordinary spontaneous speech. They have been aptly
characterised by one of our colleagues as an aspect of 'the speech
pathology of everyday life'. This observation indirectly raises a theoretical
issue which is an essential part of the context of the study[1] to be reported
here.

Abercrombie (1965) has drawn an important distinction between 'conversation' and 'spoken prose', a distinction which is almost never explicitly
recognised in linguistics. The overwhelming bulk of daily use of spoken
language comes under the heading of conversation. Spoken prose includes
dramatic dialogue, monologues, prepared lectures, and – we would add –
linguistic citation sentences. These forms, Abercrombie points out, are
regularised, highly specialised abstractions from conversation and account
for only a very small part of spoken language. Despite this unrepresent-
ativeness, however, spoken prose continues unaccountably to be the
exclusive subject matter of linguistics.

In order to justify this delimitation of its area of interest, linguistics has established an explicit distinction between 'well-formed' and 'deviant' utterances. Implicit in this distinction, and nearly unnoticed, has been a corollary equation of well-formed with 'normal', and deviant with 'abnormal'. Deviations are thus dismissed as linguistically irrelevant, since they represent trivial departures from the hypothetical norms which linguistics seeks to describe.

It is important to recognise that in speech 'normal' does not mean 'perfect'. The norm for spontaneous speech is demonstrably imperfect. Conversation is characterised by frequent pauses, hesitation sounds, false starts, misarticulations and corrections. In choosing to define away these characteristic irregularities, linguistics discards a potentially powerful check on the veridicality of competing models of speech performance.

Capsule demonstrations of the operation of a given linguistic model on carefully selected citation utterances are not compelling, since any instance of spoken prose may be equally consonant with a number of internally consistent systems which have been expressly constructed to generate spoken prose. The study of natural, 'live' speech, however, with its characteristic irregularities preserved, can provide crucial theoretical leverage in that a careful analysis of the irregularities in context may reveal functional patterns which are consistent with one hypothetical model and contradictory to others. Neurophysiologists from Hughlings Jackson onwards have suggested that our understanding of complex mental processes may be facilitated by working into the system 'backwards' from its output rather than forwards from its input. This research strategy is one of the foundations of the study to be reported here.

This paper, then, is addressed to only one aspect of the speech process: the control of sequencing of speech units, and, even more narrowly, to the kinds of speech errors called tongue-slips which result from transient malfunctions of this system. To the degree that observed tongue-slips can be shown to be structured, and not simply the result of random malfunctioning of the speech-producing process, then their obedience to the constraints of a descriptive and explanatory theory may provide the basis for deriving some of the relevant properties or characteristics of the sequencing system, of interest to linguistics, psychology and neurophysiology.

Previous Work

Our search of the literature has turned up very few systematic studies of tongue-slips (Bawden, 1900; Cohen, 1966; Freud, 1901; Fromkin, 1966; Meringer, 1908; Meringer and Mayer, 1895; Oertel, 1901; Simonini, 1956; Sturtevant, 1917; 1947; Wells, 1951). In the light of the opening discussion this is perhaps not surprising. An additional explanation for this neglect may be afforded by the social-perceptual aspects of tongue-slips. In everyday circumstances we simply do not hear many of our own tongue-slips nor those made by others. They can be discerned in running speech only by adopting a specialised 'proofreader' mode of listening. In ordinary conversation it is as though we were bound by a shared, tacit, social agreement, both as listeners and as speakers, to keep the occurrence of tongue-slips out of conscious awareness, to look beyond them, as it were, to the regularised, idealised intended utterance. In this sense our everyday speech behaviour can be likened to the analytic behaviour of linguists, as discussed above. Thus it may be that the automatic perceptual screen which keeps tongue-slips out of social awareness has also operated to keep them out of scientific awareness, despite their frequent occurrence.

If this selective inattention toward tongue-slips which we posit helps to explain the limited amount of previous work, an additional explanation can be suggested for the general lack of penetration of the conclusions drawn from what work has been done. Most writers have been content with a superficial description of those tongue-slips they have observed, noting mainly a tendency for the contextual determination of the slip to be anticipatory in action, and borrowing chiefly from philology such descriptive categories as 'assimilation', 'dissimilation', 'analogy', etc. A possible reason for this superficiality is that tongue-slips have been assumed to constitute, for reasons outlined above, departures from 'normal' behaviour, and thus to lack the structure of normal behaviour. It is easy, though fallacious, to extend this assumption to support the belief that tongue-slips have practically no rigorous structure, and that a low-level description is adequately penetrating.

From the standpoint of psychology and of general phonetics such culturally conditioned labels as 'normal' and 'abnormal' are at odds with the fundamental scientific assumption that any aspect of human behaviour is potentially structured and thus subject to explanation.

Another possible influence here is the close and immediate psychoanalytic connotation of tongue-slip. Freud's careful observations and brilliant formulations concerning the unconscious motivations of tongue-slips have surrounded this term with an aura of psychopathology. It is our view, however, that the mechanics of slips can be studied linguistically without reference to their motivation. In the bulk of our examples a plausible origin for the intrusion can be found in the immediate environment of the slip. In many of Freud's examples no such immediate environmental origin is apparent. Freud recognised this distinction in *Psychopathology of Everyday Life*: 'The disturbance in speaking which is manifested in a slip of the tongue can . . . be caused by the influence of another component of the same speech . . . The disturbance could however be of a second kind . . .; it could result from influences outside this word, sentence or context, and arise out of elements which are not intended to be uttered and of whose excitation we only learn precisely through the actual disturbance' (Freud, 1901, trans. A. Tyson, 1966; 56).

Corpus

The speech material which was analysed for this study is a collection, made by the senior author over a period of several years, of more than a hundred tape-recorded brief excerpts of natural speech, each excerpt containing a slip and some context. These were taken from conference discussions, broadcasts, normal conversations, and from interviews with psychiatric patients whose speech was free from any pathological defects. Thirty-five different speakers are represented; all but one are native speakers of English. The accents of most of the speakers can be characterised as General American; those of the remainder represent one or another of the varieties of British English.

The conclusions reached on the basis of this corpus were validated against an additional corpus of over a hundred orthographically-recorded slips personally heard in normal conversation by the authors.

Definitions

Before any further discussion of tongue-slips, it will be necessary to distinguish clearly between these events and other non-fluencies in the sequencing of speech such as stuttering and restarts occasioned by in-process revisions of the speaker's linguistic intention.

A slip of the tongue (hereinafter *slip)* is *an involuntary deviation in performance from the speaker's current phonological, grammatical or lexical intention*. Slips involve units of varying size, from segments to sequences of segments, to whole syllables and words, on the phonological level; on the grammatical level units include morphemes and whole words, and, more rarely, higher-order constituent groups.

The deviation is almost always detected, not necessarily consciously, by the speaker, and corrected. In any given instance, the discrepancy between the aberrant utterance and the correction defies the slip. In a few instances in our corpus, where the deviation was uncorrected, we analysed the slip with reference to the inferred intention, or if the intention was unclear, we noted a number of alternative determinations and categorised the slip as not being unambiguously analysable by our procedure.

Classifications

There are three general modes of slip: *misordering* of units in the string, *omission* of a unit, or *replacement* of a unit. The units most often involved are segments, morphemes and words. Unit-mode categorisations allow descriptions of slips as *segmental replacement* (SR), *morphemic omission* (MO), *word misordering* (WM), etc., as summarised in the following table:

	Misordering	*Omission*	*Replacement*
Segment	SM	SO	SR
Morpheme	MM	MO	MR
Word	WM	WO	WR

Segmental slips are by far the most common, involving about sixty per cent of the examples. A detailed report including the higher-order classes of slips would take this article beyond its intended scope; hence this exposition of the analysis and results will be focused mainly on the segmental slips.

Within the class 'segmental slip', SR slips are the most common, and fall into three subcategories: (*simple*) *segmental replacement* (SR), where the slip has the same number of segments as the intended word; *segmental replacement with augmentation* (SR (A)), where the slip has more segments than the intended word; and *segmental replacement with reduction* (SR(R)), where the slip has fewer segments than the intended word.

Procedure

The exposition of the analytic procedure may be best understood by reference to Figure 2.1, a reproduction of the form which was employed in recording the analysis. The slip is the one which was quoted in the introduction.

---

1. Orthography: "But those frunds funds have been frozen"
                                    S   ↓ T
2. Utterance: /bət ðouz fr∧ndz f∧ndz hav   bın   frouzn/
3. Intention: /bət ðouz   f∧ndz hav   bın   frouzn/
4. Rhythm: W   S   S   W   W   Ś   W |
                                    ◄────────────────

---

5. Syllable structure

	I_1	I_2	I_3	N	F_4	F_3	F_2	F_1
Origin	f	r	—	ou	—	—	—	—
Target	f	—	—	∧	—	n	d	z
Slip	f	r	—	∧	—	n	d	z
Source of segments in slip	T,O	O	—	T	—	T	T	T

---

6. Notes   SR(A) slip
   (a) OI_2/r/ is substituted anticipatorily for TI_2 zero.
   (b) O is in tonic syllable, T is in immediately preceding salient syllable.
   (c) O and T share I_1 = /f/. O and T both in salient syllables.

Figure 2.1 Illustrative protocol for analysis of tongue-slips.

In Figure 2.1, Line 1 is a transcription of the utterance in ordinary orthography, including the slip, but excluding other non-fluencies and any parenthetic remarks the speaker may have made about the slip.

Line 2 is a phonemic transcription of the utterance listed in Line 1. The capital letters above the transcription, S, T, O, identify, respectively, the slip, the target, and the origin. The *target* word is the word at which the speaker was aiming when he made the slip. In the example cited, the word *frozen* has interfered with *funds* to produce *frunds*. *Frozen* is thus the origin, *funds* the target and *frunds* the slip. The short vertical arrow after *frunds* indicates the point at which the utterance was checked.

Line 3 is our reconstruction of the intended utterance, in phonemic transcription, omitting the slip and repetitions of any preceding function words which may accompany the correction.

Line 4 contains the rhythmical and intonational information about the intended utterance, as far as it could be established from the actual utterance and the corrected utterance. *S* and *W* signify *salient* (stressed) and *weak* syllables respectively in the unit of rhythm, the *foot*, a concept described by Abercrombie (1964). While this concept is applicable to the rhythm of both American and British English, one is less confident of the similarity of American and British intonation. We are only interested here, however, in two relatively uncontroversial aspects of intonation – the location of intonation unit boundaries, and the location of the most prominent syllable within units thus demarcated. We mark the former with vertical lines, the latter with an acute symbol (') over the syllable concerned. British readers can assume that the system uses Halliday's analysis of intonation (Halliday, 1963), marking *tone-group* boundaries and the location of the *tonic* syllable in each tone-group. This terminology will be adopted throughout. American readers may transpose these features into the system described by Trager and Smith (1951). For *tone-group*, read *phonemic clause*; for *tone-group boundary*, read *terminal juncture*; for *tonic syllable*, read *primary stress*. This equivalence obviously rests on our assumption that American and British forms of English do not differ importantly with regard to these particular features.

The sample utterance here, then, contains one tone-group or phonemic clause, with the boundary falling after *frozen*, and with the tonic or primary stress on the first syllable of *frózen*.

The horizontal arrow below Line 4 shows the span and direction of influence of the slip, from origin to target. A left-hand arrow, as is shown here, marks an *anticipatory* slip, in that the origin is in a word not yet uttered when the slip occurs. A right-hand arrow marks a *perseverative* slip, in which the origin is in a word already uttered.

Section 5 is an analysis of the segmental composition of the origin, target and slip syllables. The analytic framework is the canonical structure of the phonological syllable in English, in terms of which up to three initial consonant segments, (I), are possible, and up to four final consonant segments, (F), with the nuclear segment, (N), located medially. Any English syllable can be portrayed in this framework with dashes (——)

representing zeros in those positions not occupied by segments in that particular syllable.

The bottom line in Section 5 shows the provenance of each segment in the slip syllable. An entry T means that the segment also appears in the same position in the target syllable; an O that the segment also appears in the same position in the origin syllable; and T, O means that the slip segment appears in the same position in both the target and the origin syllables.

The tape-recorded examples were jointly analysed by the authors, using a tape-loop repeater. When we could not agree on a given feature, the opinion of one or more colleagues was solicited. It should be made clear that the present form of the analytic procedure grew out of the raw data rather than having been applied at the outset. Theoretical insights and procedural modifications growing out of the first analysis required a second and ultimately a third complete reanalysis of the entire corpus.

Results

Analysis of the segmental slips in the terms outlined above revealed a number of significant patterns. These are presented below as a set of tongue-slip laws, with 'law' to be understood in a statistical rather than in an absolute sense.

A. Slips involve the tonic word, either as origin or as target, with tonic origins predominating.

B. The target and the origin of a tongue-slip are both located in the same tone-group.

C. Exceptions to Law B form another structured class of their own: where target and origin are located in different (usually adjacent) tone-groups, each will be in the tonic word in its own tone-group.

D. The origin syllable and the target syllable of a slip are metrically similar, in that both are salient, or both arc weak, with salient-salient pairings predominating.

E. Segmental slips obey a structural law with regard to syllable-place; that is, initial segments in the origin syllable replace initial segments in the target syllable, nuclear replace nuclear, and final replace final.

F. Segmental slips obey phonologically orthodox sequence rules; that is, segmental slips do not result in sequences not permitted by normal phonology.[2]

A final generalisation will also be listed here although is not strictly a law, but rather a failure to find obedience to a law. 'Similarity' has been previously proposed as a determinant of tongue-slips in such terms as 'the coalescence of similars' (Bawden, 1900). In a matrix tabulation of origin and target segments we could discern no general tendency for interactions to occur between segments sharing one or more articulatory features.[3] We conclude, accordingly, that articulatory similarity is not an important determinant.

It should be noted that Laws A and B considered together account for the prevalence of anticipatory slips over perseverative slips. Since (1) origins are predominantly tonic words, and (2) the tonic usually falls on the last lexical item in the tone-group, and (3) the target is usually in the same tone-group as the origin, then most slips are necessarily anticipatory. Thus the 'law' of anticipation reduces to an artefact.

As emphasised above, these are probability laws, not exceptionless statements. Not every slip obeys every law. On the other hand, no slip in our corpus violates all the laws. An overall confidence estimate in statistical terms is not feasible since the complex probabilities of the underlying events cannot be satisfactorily combined into a single statement. As a rough indication of the power of this set of laws and the extent of their generalisability, however, their overall correctness as applied to the total corpus of segmental slips is over eighty per cent.

Interpretation

1. At a phenomenal level, the segmental tongue slip has been shown to be considerably more structured than has previously been believed. The origin of the interfering sound can now be identified more precisely. In any segmental replacement slip there is a high probability that its origin will be found (a) in the tonic word in the tone-group in which it occurs, (b) in the salient syllable of the tonic word, if the slip occurs in a salient syllable; in a weak syllable if the slip is in a weak syllable, (c) at the same syllable place, i.e. initial, nuclear or final.

It is necessary, in a discussion of segmental slips, to distinguish between different aspects of articulation. While suprasegmental aspects relevant to higher-order articulatory units such as the syllable, the foot, and the tone-group are centrally involved in determining slips, the segmental aspects of articulation of vowels and consonants as such seem to be much less important.

2. More generally, these results provide an empirical basis for inferring some of the properties of the speech production system. The neurophysiological aspects of these interpretations are loosely descriptive, and nothing more rigorous is intended. We have not presumed to formulate a neurophysiological theory of speech sequencing, but merely to specify some functional properties of the neurophysiological system which seemed to be implied by the output characteristics we have observed.

   A. The pivotal role of the tonic word in slips suggests that its phonological, syntactic and semantic prominence is matched by an analogous neurophysiological prominence, coded in the brain as a part of the articulatory programme. Note that the typical slip involves interference from the tonic word *before* it is uttered.

B. The fact that the span of interference in a slip is usually within one tone-group suggests that this unit is not simply a linguistic construct, but can plausibly be assumed to have behavioural properties as well.[4] In our view, the tone-group is handled in the central nervous system as a unitary behavioural act, and the neural correlates of the separate elements are assembled and partially activated, or 'primed', before the performance of the utterance begins. This state of affairs whereby target and origin are simultaneously represented in an interim assembly maximises the likelihood of interaction between them. This hypothesis also accounts for the observed fact that interactions across tone-group boundaries are fairly rare.

When slips do transcend tone-group boundaries, it will be recalled from Law C that the interaction is between the tonic words of the two tone-groups. In order to reconcile this fact with the above interpretation it is only necessary to add the not unreasonable assumption that the assembly of the next tone-group is already under way before the current one has been uttered and that the tonic syllable is the only element with sufficient neurophysiological prominence to break through the inhibitory forces holding the program in check.[5]

C. We have seen that there is an obedience to structural and metric laws in the segmental slip; that is to say, an initial segment in the target is likely to be interfered with by an initial segment in the origin, with the additional constraint that pairs of salient syllables or pairs of weak syllables are likely to interfere with one another as origin and target. This suggests that syllable structure and rhythm are also more than just linguistic constructs, and can be plausibly considered to be central aspects of the neural control program in speech.

Lenneberg (1967) has drawn together a number of lines of evidence concerning rhythmic phenomena in the brain, proposing, as had Lashley, a fundamental neural 'pacemaker' as a grid within which articulatory events are serially organised and integrated.

Suprasegmental features of structure and rhythm of units like the syllable are more relevant to the description of malfunctions in the sequencing control of speech than are narrowly segmental features of articulation. This suggests that a division of the speech-chain into segments is a more artificial exercise than is a division into these higher-order units. Segments would seem to have reality in neural coding only as modifications, nuclear and marginal, of more basic units such as the syllable, the foot and the tone-group. Or, to put the proposition more directly, segmental slips are the result of interaction, at the neural level, between higher-order units, even though the perceptual result of the slip may be apparently restricted to a change of segment-identity. That we perceive the result as involving segments rather than as involving properties of syllables, for instance, may be attributable to a perceptual 'set' given to us, as listeners, by our alphabetic culture, and, as linguists, by a phonemic approach to phonological analysis.

Additional Hypotheses

The tongue-slip laws presented above are supported by the main body of data, and are put forward with a reasonable degree of confidence. A number of less-supported ideas emerged in the course of the work, some of them deriving from only one or two instances of a phenomenon. These will be presented more tentatively, as no more than promising leads.

1. Accommodatory Adjustments

The following slip was made: '. . . a fairly compus . . . confusing pattern'
                                                  s   T   o
/ə fɛrli kəmpjuz . . . kənfjuzih patrŋ/. An optional accommodatory adjustment is involved, with an intended /n/ changing to /m/ as an accommodation to the following /p/ segment. This slip raises an interesting issue about the place in the speech process at which optional accommodation rules are applied. It suggests that they are applied to the performance string at some stage after the speech process has been initiated. This follows from the reasonable assumption that segmental replacement, as a neural event, occurs late rather than early in the speech process, that is, after an initial 'correct' neural program has been assembled. To place the event earlier is to require an additional assumption that the misplaced segment, here the /p/ in 'compus . . .', was undetected by the one or more stages of internal neural monitoring that must be postulated. If, then, an error of execution at a late stage is assumed, optional accommodatory adjustments of this sort must come into play at least as late, or even later, during the neuromuscular stage, and furthermore must be applied quite blindly and routinely. The bilabial accommodation in this instance was appropriate, if optional, even though the /p/ segment, to which the accommodation was made, was itself incorrect.

2. Determinants of Tonic Location

In another instance, a speaker intending to say 'how bád things were', said instead 'how thíngs bad were'. The words 'bad' and 'things' were inadvertently transposed. The tonic, however, was not transposed. It was applied to the correct position, which was occupied by an incorrect word. There are a number of similar examples in the corpus, and they raise the interesting possibility that the physiological determinants of the location of the tonic within the tone-group, whatever they may be, are programmed independently of the other articulatory features of tone-groups.

3. Atypical Origins

In some of our slips, the presumed origin is not represented in the utterance. Consider the following examples:

    (a) 'didn't bother me in the sleast . . . slightest' (SR (R))

    (b) 'what I . . . what she has given me to read . . . to read' (WR)

                                           /rɛd/   /rid/

    (c) 'separite . . . separating out the nucleuses' (SR)

In (a), 'slightest' was distorted, in fact nearly replaced, by 'least', which in this context is a synonym and a competing filler for the position. In (b), the ellipsis after 'I' represents a hesitation. In context, it seems highly probable that the speaker had intended to say /rɛd/. The utterance is syntactically revised at this point, and the verb in the new intention now has an altered grammatical and phonological form /rid/. In its place, however, the original form is substituted. In example (c), according to the report of the speaker (one of the authors) he had fleetingly considered, and rejected, the possibility of using the word 'nuclei', /njukliai/, instead of 'nucleuses'. Here, interestingly, the rejected word distorts not its successful competitor, as in the first example, but another word in the tone-group.

In these three examples (a), (b) and (c), the interactions that resulted in the slips can reasonably be assumed to have taken place in the earlier stages of formulation of the utterance, where syntactic and lexical decisions are being made. These examples are structurally similar to those published by Freud, in that the origin of the intrusion is not a part of the ultimate utterance, and it may be that a better understanding of these ordinary lexical slips would also illuminate the mechanics of Freudian slips.

Conclusion

Tongue-slips have been shown to be transient malfunctions of the sequencing system of the speech production process which obey stringent linguistic constraints. Neuropsychological hypotheses have been offered which suggest that tongue-slips may involve interactions at a number of different stages in the neural organisation of a speech act, from the earliest stages in the formulation of an utterance, when syntactic and lexical decisions are being made, to the final neuromuscular stages of executing the speech plan.[6] The data and interpretations are ordered to a speech unit, the tone-group or phonemic clause, which has both behavioural and formal linguistic properties.

The generalisations offered need to be tested and refined against larger corpora of slips in English. Beyond this, systematic studies of slips in other languages could conceivably expand the structure into a class of neurophysiologically-based language universals.

Not least, we hope to have supported our original contention that the study of the characteristic irregularities of actual speech can yield data which are relevant to linguistics, psychology and neurophysiology.

Notes

1. This research was carried out during the academic year 1966–7 at the University of Edinburgh, where the senior author was Honorary Lecturer in the Department of Phonetics at the kind invitation of Professor David Abercrombie.
2. Rulon Wells (Wells, 1951) first expressed this conclusion in his 'First Law' of tongue-slips: 'A slip of the tongue is practically always a phonetically possible noise'. By 'phonetically possible' he meant phonologically possible in the language concerned.
3. There were two exceptions to this: (a) sequences of voiceless fricatives seemed to encourage mistakes of place of articulation, and (b) alveolar consonants showed a slight tendency to interact. The instability of alveolar consonants in English has been noted before, in other aspects of connected speech such as assimilation, by A.C. Gimson (Gimson, 1960).
4. An initial formulation of the tone-group or phonemic clause as a unit with both linguistic and psychological properties was put forward by Boomer in a study of hesitation pauses (Boomer, 1965). For related evidence on the perceptual side, see Dittmann and Llewellyn (1967).
5. Karl Lashley's disciplined speculations concerning the relation between speech and brain events have provided the neurological framework within which we have ordered our data. In speaking of 'spoonerisms', he wrote, 'In these contaminations, it is as if the aggregate of words were in a state of partial excitation, held in check by the requirements of grammatical structure, but ready to activate the final common path, if the effectiveness of this check is in any way interfered with' (Lashley, 1951).
6. An article which came to our attention after the manuscript of this article had been written is Hockett (1967), in which he makes some interesting comments on the relevance of tongue-slip data for models of performance and for the distinction between the concepts of 'performance' and 'competence'.

References

Abercrombie, D. (1964) 'Syllable quantity and enclitics in English', in *In Honour of Daniel Jones*, Abercrombie, D. et al. (eds) Longmans, London.

Abercrombie, D. (1965) 'Conversation and spoken prose', in *Studies in Phonetics and Linguistics*, Oxford University Press, Oxford.

Bawden, H.H. (1900) 'A study of lapses', *Psychol. Rev. Monograph Suppl.* III, No. 4.

Boomer, D.S. (1965) 'Hesitation and grammatical encoding', *Lang. and Speech* 8, 148–58.

Cohen, A. (1966) 'Errors of speech and their implication for understanding the strategy of language users', 18th Int. Congress of Psychology, Moscow.

Dittmann, A.T. and Llewellyn, L.G. (1967) 'The phonemic cause as a unit of speech decoding', *J. Pers. Soc. Psychol.* 6, 341–9.

Freud, S. (1901) *Zur Psychopathologie des Alltagsleben (Psychopathology of everyday life*, Tyson, A. (trans.), Strachey, J. (ed.), Benn, E., London, 1966).

Fromkin, V.A. (1966) 'Some requirements for a model of performance', *University of California at Los Angeles Working Papers in Phonetics* 4, 19–39.

Gimson, A.C. (1960) 'The instability of English alveolar articulations', *Le Maitre Phonétique*, 119.

Halliday, M.A.K. (1963) 'The tones of English', *Archivum Linguisticum* 15, 1–28.

Hockett, C.F. (1967) 'Where the tongue slips, there slip I', pp. 910–36 in *To Honour Roman Jakobson*, Vol. II, Janua Linguarum, Series Maior XXXII, Mouton, The Hague.

Lashley, K.S. (1951) 'Serial order in behaviour', in *Cerebral Mechanisms in Behavior*, Jeffress, L.A. (ed.) Wiley, New York.

Lenneberg, E.H. (1967) *Biological Foundations of Language*, Wiley, New York.

Meringer, R. (1908) *Aus dem Leben der Sprache*, Berlin.

Meringer, R. and Mayer, K. (1985) *Versprechen und Verlesen, eine psychologischslinguistische Studie*, Vienna.

Oertel, H. (1901) *Lectures on the Study of Language*, New York.

Simonini, R.C. (Jnr) (1956) 'Phonemic and analogic lapses in radio and television speech', *American Speech* 31, 252–63.

Sturtevant, E.H. (1917) *Linguistic Change* (University of Chicago Press, 1961).

Sturtevant, E.H. (1947) *An Introduction to Linguistic Science*, Yale University Press.

Trager, G.L. and Smith, H.L. (1951) 'An outline of English structure', *Studies in Linguistics*: Occasional Paper 3, Norman, Oklahoma.

Wells, R. (1951) 'Predicting slips of the tongue', *Yale Scientific Magazine*, December, 9–12.

3 The Detection and Correction of Slips of the Tongue

Originally published as Laver, J. (1973) 'The Detection and Correction of Slips of the Tongue', in Fromkin, V.A. (ed.) *Speech Errors as Linguistic Evidence*, Mouton, The Hague (pp. 132–43)

Last year,[1] Donald Boomer[2] and I published an article in which we tried to show that the speech-errors that are called slips of the tongue are transient malfunctions of neural control programs in the speech production process, and that they obey stringent linguistic constraints (Boomer and Laver, 1968). That tongue-slips are so highly structured is in itself an interesting and important fact; but even more valuable is the fact that an examination of tongue-slips gives us a useful point of entry into speculation about the functional properties of the brain's control of speech.

In this article, I want to continue discussion of tongue-slips and cerebral functions, by exploring some of the implications which arise from the observation that slips of the tongue are usually detected and corrected by the speaker. In particular, I would like to offer some speculative comment on aspects of the neural function which allows this detection and correction to be achieved – the monitoring function.

The monitoring function is of course only one of the various functions in the brain's control of acts of speech performance, and I shall be obliged to say a little about the other functions and their relation to monitoring. Before I do so, however, I have to acknowledge that it is difficult to find a satisfactorily specific and adequate adjective to characterise such a functional model. The terms 'neurophysiological', 'neuropsychological' and 'neurolinguistic' would each reflect some characteristic of the model. Because the current state of research restricts us largely to a consideration of functions rather than of mechanisms, perhaps the least satisfactory of the possible labels is 'neurophysiological'. 'Neuropsychological' would be more acceptable, and would be sympathetic to a view recently expressed by Chomsky (1968: 1), where he suggests that linguistics is itself a branch of a branch of psychology, namely cognitive psychology. Personally, for the moment, I favour the most neutral term, 'neurolinguistic'.

If I may use this label, the construction of a neurolinguistic model of speech production has attracted a growing attention from phoneticians and linguists, and from other disciplines concerned with language. To name but a few workers in this area, Boomer, Fant, Fromkin, Fry, Hockett, Kozhevnikov, Ladefoged, Lamb, Lane, Lenneberg, Lindblom, Miller, Öhman and Tatham have all recently published material on neural aspects of speech production. (An interest in neural aspects of speech reception is of much longer standing, and is not under immediate consideration here.) The relevance for phonetics and linguistics of a neurolinguistic model of the brain's control of speech should need no emphasis, and it is significant that neurolinguistics is a field where the sub-disciplinary boundary between phonetics and linguistics (which has probably always been of doubtful validity) is largely disappearing. In providing a satisfactory model of the psychological processes which allow the brain to generate speech, neurolinguistics will contribute importantly to the development of a more comprehensive and unified linguistic theory. To assert this is to take the position that linguistics should accept, together with its other criteria for comparative evaluation of linguistic theories, a criterion of psychological veridicality. If it can be shown that the brain uses a particular psychological process in generating speech, then the linguistic theory which allows for such a process, in its performance component, is a better theory, in terms of accounting comprehensively for language-behaviour, than one which does not.

However, the development of a sufficiently comprehensive neurolinguistic model of the brain's control of speech is a very long way ahead. One major difficulty is the scarcity of persuasive evidence. To all intents and purposes, the healthy adult brain is not itself accessible to neurolinguistic experiment. This restricts us to a (widely accepted) research strategy which makes use of the fact that functional properties of unobservable control systems can be inferred from an examination of the output of those systems (Boomer and Laver, 1968: 3). This strategy can be applied both to the efficient, error-free output, and, as I indicated at the beginning of the article, to the output when malfunctions occur in the control systems. A third possible source of evidence is the output of the speech process while the control systems are being established and becoming skilled – the acquisitional stage of young children's speech.

I should emphasise that error-free speech should not be equated with 'normal speech' (Boomer and Laver, 1968: 2), nor should the malfunctions which occur in speech be considered necessarily the result of speech pathology. Spontaneous, normal speech is usually far from completely free of errors, and often contains ephemeral, non-pathological malfunctions such as slips of the tongue. Neither pathological malfunctions nor acquisitional speech will be discussed in this article, although they offer potentially valuable evidence for the construction of a neurolinguistic model of the normal adult brain.

Discussion in this article will be limited rather to slips of the tongue and their detection and correction.

Detection is a logical prerequisite to correction, and detection and correction together are taken to be evidence of a monitoring function in the speech-producing process. In distinguishing between detection and correction as aspects of the monitoring function, I am trying to lay the foundation of a view that I shall return to as my principal conclusion at the end of the article; namely, that the activities of scrutiny and revision are not the monopoly of the monitoring function, but an integral characteristic of all the brain's processes for constructing and controlling speech programs.

To show the similarity of underlying purpose in the monitoring and program-construction functions, it is necessary at this stage to say something about the different functions involved in the generation of any speech utterance. The outline I shall give is a very simplistic one, without commitment as to the actual mechanisms concerned; it is simplistic because I am conscious of the ferocious complexity of the problem, and feel the need to approach the complexity with the help of what may well turn out to be merely convenient fictions.

There seem to be four chief functions (Laver, 1968):
1. Ideation
2. Neurolinguistic program-planning
3. Myodynamic execution
4. Monitoring

1. Ideation

I make the fundamental assumption that the speaker has an initial idea, which he intends to communicate. In using the term 'idea', I am not seeking to imply that a high degree of cognitive complexity is necessarily involved; the idea consists of the approximate semantic content of any verbal message that the speaker wishes to communicate.

2. Neurolinguistic Program-planning

The next function is the construction of a neurolinguistic program for the expression of the idea – the organisation of a neural program for the lexical, grammatical and phonological characteristics of the message the speaker intends to communicate. This presumably involves the selection from long-term storage of lexical items and grammatical arrangements, together with their associated phonology, by criteria of semantic appropriateness to expression of the initial idea. So the planning function, in this convenient model, needs access to the initial idea, to lexical and grammatical storage, and to the phonology.

A major area of difficulty here is that of the relation between the idea and the neurolinguistic program planned to communicate that idea. It is a difficult area to conceptualise, because it is only possible to discuss ideas in terms of their expository linguistic programs. Miller et al. (1960) quote a passage from William James's 'The Principles of Psychology' (1890) which I think captures the nature of this difficulty with great clarity:

> And has the reader never asked himself what kind of a mental fact is his intention of saying a thing before he has said it? It is an entirely definite intention, distinct from all other intentions, an absolutely distinct state of consciousness, therefore; and yet how much of it consists of definite sensorial images, either of words or of things? Hardly anything! Linger, and the words and things come into the mind; the anticipatory intention, the divination is there no more. But as the words that replace it arrive, it welcomes them successively and calls them right if they agree with it, it rejects them and calls them wrong if they do not. It has therefore a nature of its own of the most positive sort, and yet what can we say about it without using words that belong to the later mental facts that replace it? The intention TO SAY SO AND SO is the only name it can receive. One may admit that a good third of our psychic life consists in these rapid premonitory schemes of thought not yet articulate.

Implied in this passage is the view that the planning function activates more items from storage than it finally selects for the neurolinguistic program. This is well supported by those slips of the tongue where the brain fails to complete its planning choice between competing alternatives before the speech program reaches the utterance stage. A lexical example would be:

didn't bother me in the sleast

with competition between *slightest* and *least* (Boomer and Laver, 1968). A syntactic example would be:

He behaved as like a fool

with competition between *like a fool* and either or both *as if he were a fool* and *as though he were a fool*.

A number of conclusions derive from the suggestion that more items are activated than are selected for inclusion in the final program. Firstly, the planning function must be able to scrutinise the various alternatives that have been retrieved from storage, and come to a decision about the relative appropriateness of the competing items for expressing the initial idea. Secondly, to allow the planning function to come to a decision about appropriateness of items, the idea itself presumably has some kind of semantic indexing, which serves as a predisposition towards choosing one rather than another of the competing alternatives. That such a choice seems often to be made is one theoretical justification, following William James, for treating ideation as a separate function from neurolinguistic program-planning, in opposition to the possible view that an idea is itself necessarily an associative linguistic response to a stimulus of some sort.

To separate the ideation function from the planning function is not to imply that the latter may not influence the former. It seems intuitively reasonable to assume that the specific restrictions and associations characterising particular items activated by the planning function may have the result of allowing the brain to reach a revised, and perhaps more precise, formulation of the original idea, which in turn may lead to a revision of parts of the neurolinguistic program.

The possibility of scrutiny and revision could thus be said to exist in both the ideation and the planning functions.

One of the conclusions that Donald Boomer and I reached in our article on slips of the tongue was that the brain pre-prepares stretches of speech, often of the extent of the tone-group (Halliday, 1963), before the utterance of the whole stretch begins. Pre-preparation was first suggested by Lashley, in his classic article 'Serial Order in Behavior' in 1951; he pointed out that a logical corollary is that the brain usually inhibits the stretch under preparation from being uttered until preparation is complete. A second implication is that the pre-prepared stretch has to be stored in short-term memory until its utterance, and a third implication would be that the planning function needs to make use of neural scanning of the preprepared stretch in order to be able to decide when preparation is complete and utterance can be allowed.

It is thus implicit in the concept of pre-preparation that the prepared stretch of speech is subjected to inhibition, short-term storage and scanning.

I make these points to emphasise that the planning function has many opportunities for revision of its programs, and for checking for program-errors which would lead to slips of the tongue.

I suspect that the Planner (to abbreviate its label) does sometimes detect program-errors before the utterance-stage. I feel that I have had the experience of being aware that a slip of the tongue was imminent, and reprogramming in time to maintain fluent speech. Hockett claims the same experience (1967: 936). It is interesting, though, that despite the multiple opportunities available to the Planner for checking for errors, some errors do get through to the utterance-stage. If an error does persist to the utterance-stage, then its detection and correction become the business of the monitoring function.

Before finally coming to a discussion of monitoring, I would like to make some brief comments about the myodynamic execution function, which so far I have been calling, rather loosely, the utterance-stage.

3. Myodynamic Execution

The neurolinguistic program constructed by the planning function is finally executed in the form of contractions of the muscles of the speech organs. It is important to emphasise that the myodynamic execution function is concerned exclusively with the contractions and movements of the muscles; all considerations of the neural control of those muscles are thus to be referred to the planning function and its various component sub-functions.

We know rather little at the moment about the detailed physiology of the vocal organs. Electromyography may eventually tell us a good deal, but the sheer complexity of the action of the different muscle systems used to manoeuvre the tongue, for example, is going to make progress rather slow. This is not to say that the electromyographic study of restricted numbers of muscles that is currently being carried out is not valuable, but rather that it seems likely to be a long time before a thoroughly well-founded and general theory of how such organs as the tongue move can be achieved.

However, when that time comes, one useful area of investigation may be the study of the degree of complexity and delicacy of adjustment of vocal musculature for different articulations; it seems logical to expect that the more complex and delicate the adjustments for a particular class of sounds, the greater the likelihood of members of that class being mutually involved in tongue-slips. One might expect, for example, that fricatives need more precise muscular control than plosives, and it certainly seems to be true that, in English, voiceless fricatives tend to interact in tongue-slips more frequently than plosives and other consonant-categories. This is reflected in the maximal difficulty of tongue-twisters like *She sells sea-shells on the sea-shore,* and *The Leith police dismisseth us.*

4. Monitoring

I have used the term 'monitoring' to refer to the neural function of detecting and correcting errors in the neurolinguistic program. I would like to make it quite clear at this point that in discussing this type of monitoring, I am not thinking of the use of sensory feedback to control speech-movements directly. Lashley (1951: 188) characterises this latter theory as assuming '. . . after a movement is initiated, it is continued until stopped by sensations of movement and position, which indicate that the limb has reached the desired position'. He suggests that such a theory is not applicable to every type of complex muscular action, and that a series of movements is not necessarily a chain of sensory-motor reactions. He points out, for example, that the execution of very rapid, accurate movements such as whip-cracking is often completed in a shorter time than the reaction time for tactile or kinesthetic reports to be made on what happened.

Speech, also, often involves very fast, complex movements, as in the articulation of an alveolar tap. It seems reasonable to suggest, following Lashley, that speech programs for such articulations can be pre-set for their muscular realisation, relatively independently of any sensory controls. In this connection, Ladefoged (1967: 170) cites Craik (1947) having shown that 'complex, comparatively long, muscular movements may be triggered off as a whole'. I think it follows, from these considerations and from the fact that the planning function pre-prepares stretches of speech, that much of speech performance may well be achieved by synergisms – skilled, well-practised routines, which, once started, can be left to run to completion without sensory information making a primary contribution to their control.

While sensory information may not be primarily important in controlling such speech performance directly, the information is nevertheless still available to the brain for use in monitoring as defined in this article. To put it explicitly, monitoring in this sense refers to the reception and processing of sensory reports on myodynamic execution for the purpose of detecting and correcting errors in the neurolinguistic program.

I have been careful throughout this article to speak of 'program-errors', rather than 'myodynamic errors' or 'utterance-errors', since, in the model I have offered, myodynamic execution, or utterance, consists of muscular actions, and any and every active muscular contraction is the result of a specific neural control program. When errors occur, they are thus to be attributed to incorrect programs.

It is important to consider by what criteria a program can be said to be 'incorrect' or to contain an 'error'.

One approach is to say that an incorrect program is one which in some detail does not correspond to the speaker's intention. This then transfers the problem to the nature of an 'intention', and this is conveniently thought of as the idea that the speaker is trying to communicate.

An incorrect program is therefore one which in some detail distorts the communication of the speaker's idea. It is striking that such considerations of program-errors lead us straight back into the heart of the language process – the relation I discussed above between an idea and the linguistic program constructed to communicate that idea.

There are two different sorts of errors that distort accurate communication of a speaker's idea:

(a) errors which result in a form not found in the language, such as

   didn't bother me in the sleast

and also

   Those frunds, funds are frozen (Boomer and Laver, 1968)

(b) errors which give linguistically permissible results, but which are semantically inappropriate for communicating the speaker's idea, such as

   Our queer old dean

for

   Our dear old Queen

(Lashley, op. cit.) and also

   Take it out to the porch – er – verandah

In this last example, suggesting that false starts (a revision of lexical choice, in this case), are errors which can be discussed in the same overall framework as other sorts of program-errors.

In the category of errors which give linguistically permissible results, it is often only the fact of correction that allows us, as observers, to know that an error has occurred.

In applying its detection apparatus to slips such as the above examples, the monitoring process can be seen as answering the question: 'Was the neurolinguistic program that was executed planned in all its details in such a way that it was capable of achieving communication of the intended idea?' To allow the posing and answering of this question, and the possibility of taking appropriate corrective action, the monitoring process needs four component sub-functions:

Peripheral Reception

The sensory information in the peripheral reception component of monitoring includes auditory and tactile exteroceptive reports, and positional and kinesthetic proprioceptive reports. In normal speakers perhaps the most important of the peripheral report systems for monitoring purposes is the auditory system.

Decoding

This sub-function gives the answer to two questions:
  (a) 'What was the neurolinguistic program that was executed?'
  (b) 'Was the program that was executed linguistically orthodox?'

There are two implications here: firstly, in decoding, it seems uneconomical to assume that the result arrived at would be expressed in terms different from the sort of neurolinguistic program used to produce speech – so that production and reception, in this special sense of reception, at least, seem likely to use the same neural units.

It is necessary to acknowledge here that the brain may well have additional information about the characteristics of the neurolinguistic program that was executed, from scanning its short-term memory of recent planning. If such neural scanning of short-term memory occurs, then I would still like to include the use of such information for the detection and correction of program-errors as part of the monitoring function, in this model. The definition of monitoring would have to be slightly enlarged to include the reception and processing of reports from the internal scanning of short-term memory of recent programming, as well as of sensory reports upon myodynamic execution.

The second implication of decoding as a sub-function of monitoring is that, to assess the linguistic orthodoxy of the program that was executed, access is needed to lexical and grammatical storage, and to the rules of the phonology.

Evaluation

This sub-function scrutinises the results of the decoding, to give the answers to two questions:

(a) 'Is any disobedience of lexical, grammatical or phonological constraints likely to distort communication?'

(b) 'Is the program that was executed, whether linguistically orthodox or not, likely to be semantically successful in communicating the speaker's idea?

An implication of the second question is that access is needed to the idea, which is presumably being held in short-term memory. A major point which arises at this juncture is that the Monitor, in this model, is seen as having the same needs as the Planner, for access to the idea, to lexical and grammatical storage, and to the rules of the phonology.

Action

This sub-function decides what to do about the results of the evaluation. There are two possibilities:

(a) 'Allow the myodynamic execution of the program to continue'

(b) 'Stop the myodynamic execution of the program; tell the Planner to revise the program, and restart the speech process at a pre-error stage'.

Access is needed, for this sub-function, to the speaker's motivation in trying to communicate. Some slips are detected and evaluated as likely to distort communication of the speaker's idea, but allowed to pass uncorrected, because the speaker is not highly enough motivated to take the trouble to correct the slip. Another possible explanation for the situation where a slip is detected, but not corrected, is where the speaker knows he made a slip, and knows the listener knows he made a slip, but the speaker believes that the general redundancy of the components of his message is sufficient to achieve satisfactorily accurate semantic communication.

When a slip is not corrected, and not commented on by the speaker, we have no means, as observers, of knowing whether the speaker detected the slip or not. There are thus two possible implications of failure to correct a slip: either the evaluation and action sub-functions of the Monitor decided to allow the myodynamic execution of the program to continue, or the Monitor failed to detect the slip.

This second possibility, of failure to detect a slip, is interesting. It is my impression that not many slips of the tongue are uncorrected, so it seems fair to assume that the Monitor maintains nearly constant surveillance, and is therefore an integral part of the speech-producing process. If it is possible for slips to get past the Monitor undetected, then this constitutes malfunction on the part of the Monitor. One explanation of the possibility of malfunction of monitoring is to posit attention as part of the Monitor's apparatus. It is useful to suggest that attention operates at all levels of the brain's control of speech, particularly in the Planner. Where slips are undetected, then perhaps attention is either momentarily elsewhere in the stream of speech, or is inefficient. Attention can be distracted, or its efficiency lowered, in a variety of ways, many of which are amenable to experimental manipulation. For example:

(a) when there are competing demands for attention

(b) under the influence of alcohol or drugs

(c) in the case of a marked degree of fatigue

(d) under the influence of psychological stress such as embarrassment, nervousness, anger, fear, et cetera.

This would certainly help to explain the informal observation that the incidence of uncorrected slips seems to be greater under these conditions, although the weakness in the argument remains – one cannot argue that because the slips are uncorrected, they were therefore undetected.

Before coming on to some general conclusions, I should say that of course attention is not the same as awareness. It is often the case that a speaker makes a slip and corrects it without either the speaker or the listener being aware that a slip has occurred. The conscious perception of speech in some sense regularises and idealises the actual data of speech (Boomer and Laver, 1968). Conscious awareness is thus not a necessary part of the monitoring process.

To offer some general conclusions, a point I have been leading up to is that on the one hand the Planner and the Monitor need access to largely the same areas, namely to the idea, to lexical and grammatical storage, and to the rules of phonology; and that on the other hand the Planner and the Monitor are involved in much the same sort of decisions. Both the Planner and the Monitor have to assess semantic appropriateness of programs for communicating ideas, for example. Also, the decision to stop an utterance, in order to allow revision and restart, is much the same sort of decision as the one to initiate an utterance. This implies that the Monitor's 'action' decisions, at least, are made, like many planning decisions, at a very central level.

Following on from this, I come to the most important general conclusion I want to offer – that planning and monitoring have so much in common, in terms of need for access, and level and type of decision, that it is economical to suggest that the two functions are merely different manifestations of a common major function.

Such a major function would be in the nature of a central control function, able to take decisions at the highest level, with access to the idea, to all types of long- and short-term storage concerned with speech production, and to all levels of the process of generating a particular utterance.

To postulate a common central control function underlying both planning and monitoring is to assert that there is a very considerable overlap of purpose in planning and monitoring. Following this up, it becomes possible to unify one's approach to the error-free and malfunctioning aspects of normal speech. I want to suggest that the purpose of the Monitor, and a large part of the purpose of the Planner, is to edit the initial program, and by continual scrutiny, and, where necessary, revision, to allow the central control function to achieve fairly continuously successful linguistic communication.

If 'necessary revision' is a shared purpose of the Planner and the Monitor, then the revisionary activities of the two systems can be equated. The revisionary activity of the Planner leads to error-free speech, because revisions are carried out before the myodynamic execution of the program; and the revisionary activity of the Monitor is reflected in the correction, after the myodynamic execution of the program, of overt errors. The difference between error-free speech, and speech containing overt errors, in this view, would be a fairly trivial difference of the point in time at which the central control function's revisionary resources were applied – before or after myodynamic execution of the neurolinguistic program. This is substantially the same conclusion as that reached by Hockett, who first formalised the notion of editing in this context, and who distinguishes between 'covert editing' and 'overt editing'. He writes: 'Editing in the internal flow is *covert editing* . . . In certain formal circumstances covert editing is thorough, and overt speech is unusually smooth. Much more typically, what is actually said aloud includes various signs of *overt editing*, . . . (Hockett, 1967: 936). I would equate covert editing with editing carried out by the Planner, and overt editing with editing initiated by the Monitor.

This is really a restatement of the view that I put forward at the beginning, that normal speech is not necessarily error-free speech, and, by extension, that errors are part and parcel of normal speech, and therefore worthy of study by linguists.

Notes

1. Reprinted from *Work in Progress* 3, Dept. of Phonetics and Linguistics, University of Edinburgh (1969). Most of the material of this article was originally presented in two conference papers: 'Aspects of the Monitoring Function in Speech', to the December 1968 meeting of the British Society of Audiology, and 'Speech and the Brain', to the March 1969 Colloquium of Academic Phoneticians of Great Britain.
2. I owe much to Dr Boomer, of the Laboratory of Psychology, National Institute of Mental Health, Bethesda, for early discussion of this area. Responsibility for the views expressed remains mine alone.

References

Boomer, D.S. (1965) 'Hesitation and Grammatical Encoding', *Lang. and Speech* 8(3), 148–58.

Boomer, D.S. and Laver, J. (1968) 'Slips of the Tongue', *Brit. J. Dis. Comm.* 3(1), 2–12.

Chomsky, N. (1968) *Language and Mind*, Harcourt, Brace and World, Inc., New York.

Craik, K.J.W. (1947) 'Theory of the Human Operator in Control Systems', *Brit. J. Psychol.* 38, 56–61.

Fant, G. (1967) 'Sound, Features and Perception', in *Proc. VIth Int. Congr. Phon. Sci.* (Prague).

Fromkin, V.A. (1965) 'Some Phonetic Specification of Linguistic Units: An Electromyographic Investigation', *Working Papers in Phonetics* 3, University of California, Los Angeles.

Fromkin, V.A. (1968) 'Speculations on Performance Models', *J. Ling.* 4(1), 47–68.

Fromkin, V.A. (ed.) (1973) *Speech Error as Linguistic Evidence*, Mouton, The Hague.

Fry, D.B. (1964) 'The Functions of the Syllable', *Zt. für Phon.* 17, 215–17.

Halliday, M.A.K. (1963) 'The Tones of English', *Archivum Linguisticum* 15, 1–28.

Hockett, C.F. (1967) 'Where the Tongue Slips, there Slip I', pp. 910–36 in *To Honour Roman Jakobson*, Vol. II (= *Janua Linguarum, Series Maior* XXXII), Mouton, The Hague.

James, W. (1890) *The Principles of Psychology*, Vol. I, Holt, New York.

Kozhevnikov, V.A. and Chistovich, L.A. (1965) *Speech, Articulation and Perception*, U.S. Dept. of Commerce, Joint Publications Research Service, Washington, D.C.

Ladefoged, P. (1967) *Three Areas of Experimental Phonetics*, Oxford University Press, London.

Lamb, S.M. (1966) 'Linguistic Structure and the Production and Decoding of Discourse', in Carterette, E.C. (ed.), *Brain Function*, Vol. III, University of California Press, Berkeley and Los Angeles.

Lane, H. (n.d.) 'On the Necessity of Distinguishing Between Speaking and Listening', mimeo.

Lashley, K.S. (1951) 'Serial Order in Behavior', in Jeffress, L.A. (ed.), *Cerebral Mechanisms in Behavior*, Wiley, New York.

Laver, J. (1968) 'Phonetics and the Brain', *Edinburgh University Department of Phonetics and Linguistics, Work in Progress* 2, 63–75.

Lenneberg, E.H. (1967) *Biological Foundations of Language*, Wiley, New York.

Lindblom, B. (1963) 'On Vowel Reduction', *Report No. 29*, Speech Transmission Laboratory, Royal Institute of Technology, Stockholm.

Miller, G.A., Galanter, E. and Pribram, K.H. (1960) *Plans and the Structure of Behavior*, Holt, Rinehart and Winston, Inc., New York.

Öhman, S. (1968) 'Peripheral Motor Commands in Labial Articulation', *QPSR* 4/1967, 30–63, Speech Transmission Laboratory, Royal Institute of Technology, Stockholm.

Öhman, S., Persson, A. and Leanderson, R. (1967) 'Speech Production at the Neuromuscular Level', in *Proc. VIth Congr. Phon. Sci.* (Prague).

Tatham, M.A.A. (1969a) 'Classifying Allophones', *Occasional Papers* 3, 14–22 (University of Essex Language Centre).

Tatham, M.A.A. (1969b) 'The Control of Muscles in Speech', *Occasional Papers* 3, 23–40 (University of Essex Language Centre)

Tatham, M.A.A. and Morton, K. (1968a) 'Some Electromyography Data

towards a Model of Speech Production', *Occasional Papers* 1, 1–24
(University of Essex Language Centre).
Tatham, M.A.A. and Morton, K. (1968b) 'Further Electromyography Data
towards a Model of Speech Production', *Occasional Papers* 1, 25–59
(University of Essex Language Centre).

4 Neurolinguistic Aspects of Speech Production

Originally published as Laver, J. (1977) 'Neurolinguistic Aspects of Speech Production', in Gutknecht, C. (ed.) *Grundbegriff und Hauptströmungen der Linguistik*, Forum Linguisticum, Hoffmann und Campe, Hamburg (pp. 142–55)

The traditional domain of phonetics has sometimes been considered to be the study of articulatory aspects of spoken language, together with, in a complementary but less primary way, the study of the auditory and acoustic correlates of articulation. The concentration of phonetic interest on articulation has led to the relative neglect by phoneticians of aspects of speech production upstream, as it were, from the movements of the peripheral speech apparatus. The study of articulation as such necessarily focuses attention on the activities of the vocal tract and its associated structures, and it is not surprising that this has tended until recently to exclude considerations of the control relations that exist between the brain and these peripheral structures.

The horizons of phonetics are expanding, however. This chapter is an attempt to explore one new perspective in phonetic theory – a developing interest in neurolinguistic aspects of speech production.

If asked to name the most highly skilled activity mastered by human beings, many people would perhaps choose the art of the concert pianist. But even this spectacular ability pales in comparison with a skill which every ordinary person uses every day – the ability to control his or her vocal tract to produce speech. It is fair to say that the problems of controlling the precise adjustment and temporal coordination of the very large number of muscles involved in speaking easily exceed in complexity all other voluntary human activities. A helpful first step in beginning to learn to understand the workings of such a complex system is to treat the problem as if speech were the final output of the activities of a series of analytically independent components. Thus, while certainly not urging the adoption of a thoroughgoing reductionist position, it is nevertheless useful to consider speech production from a cybernetic point of view, as an engineering system. In such a view, speech is seen as the product of the action of a complex effector system, whose component sub-systems are intricately coordinated under skilled temporal control by the brain. If we want to know how the brain works, we first have to establish in some detail the nature of the effector system, in order to infer the properties of the control system from the characteristics of effector operations.

In such a cybernetic model, the brain and the peripheral speech apparatus are unified as components of the total speech-producing system, but there are obviously domains of discussion that can be usefully differentiated. The most obvious distinction is the one already implied, between the effector system and its control. It is perhaps less obvious that there is not a one-to-one correlation to be drawn between the effector system and the peripheral speech apparatus, nor between the brain and the control system. Some aspects of the anatomy and physiology of the vocal tract will be seen to be more primarily concerned with the tactical control of speech than solely with the execution of control programs, for example.

Considering first the effector system and its different aspects, a number of domains can be further distinguished. Any neurolinguistic theory should be able to capitalise on the accepted structures of traditional phonetic theory. Even though, from a neurolinguistic point of view, articulation appears to be the superficial product of underlying muscular activities which might themselves be taken to be of more direct relevance, the phonetic metalanguage developed to describe articulation remains by far the richest source of observation of the operation of the speech-producing system. Supporting this stock of articulatory data are the research findings on the auditory, acoustic and aerodynamic correlates of articulation that make up the rest of general phonetic theory. The one major caveat that needs to be entered in considering established and widely accepted general phonetic categories for incorporation in an overall neurolinguistic theory of speech production is that the phonetic categories are based on no single analytic level. Very many ostensibly articulatory categories have an auditory element in their definition, for instance (Laver, 1974). The category 'fricative' would be an example, where the degree of articulatory stricture involved is specified in terms of correlation with 'audible friction'.

The next domain to be identified within the effector system is that of the anatomical structure of the apparatus. Within this, a distinction is often drawn between peripheral and central anatomy. The former includes the skeletal, muscular and sensory structures of the vocal tract and its related organs. The latter is made up of the neural networks of the brain, and the nerves connecting it to the peripheral anatomy. The peripheral anatomy might be thought to constitute the 'hardware' of the neurolinguistic system; the central anatomy is sometimes referred to as the 'wetware'. Together, the hardware and the wetware compose the apparatus exploited by the 'software' of the system, that is, by the control elements. Any thoroughly comprehensive neurolinguistic theory would have to include an account of all three aspects – 'hardware', 'wetware' and 'software'.

A different domain from the anatomy of the system is its physiology.

Included here are not only the detailed modes of operation of muscular contraction and the consequent movements of the vocal organs, but also such factors as the mechanisms and temporal characteristics of the transmissions of neural impulses along pathways within the brain, and along efferent and afferent nerves. Efferent nerves carry impulses from the brain to the muscles and afferent nerves carry impulses from the auditory, tactile and kinesthetic-proprioceptive sensors to the brain. The rapidly changing configuration of the vocal tract and its associated structures in speech is manipulated by the action of seven different major muscle systems. Their independence is a convenient analytic fiction, and they are more realistically seen as being anatomically interlinked and physiologically interdependent, with changes in one muscle system always being reflected in consequential changes in one or more of the others unless appropriate compensatory action is taken. The seven muscle systems are those respectively associated with the respiratory structures, the larynx, the pharynx, the soft palate, the tongue, the jaw and the lips. All these systems can be further sub-divided into more minor sub-components. As an illustration of the interactive relationship of the muscle systems, and in order to give some impression of the scale of the control problem that the brain masters in normal speech production, it may be profitable to consider for a moment the organisation of the muscles responsible for raising and lowering the soft palate (Hardcastle, 1976: 122 ff.).

A schematic diagram of some of the muscles concerned is shown in Figure 4.1: there are at least three muscles whose primary function is to help to lift the soft palate, or velum. The first of these is the palatal tensor. This is a paired muscle which is attached to the skull above and to the sides of the velum. It connects vertically downwards to a tendon, which then bends at right angles round a bony process, like a rope round a capstan, and continues inwards to insert horizontally into the sides of the velum. Contraction of the tensor tautens and spreads the body of the velum, and thus provides a fairly rigid band within the velum to which other muscles are attached and against which they can pull.

The second muscle is the paired palatal levator. This has its points of origin above and behind the velum. It passes downwards, forwards and inwards to insert laterally in the back upper surface of the velum, forming most of the velic mass. Contraction of the levator lifts the velum, which has been tensed by the tensor. (The bending of the velum to form the characteristic 'knee' shape may be helped by the contraction of the small uvular muscle, the azygos uvulae, which shortens the uvula.)

The third muscle is the superior pharyngeal constrictor, not shown in Figure 4.1. It is a tilted horseshoe-shaped muscle with its arms running forwards and downwards to the sides of the velum, pulling it up and back when it contracts. There are two muscles which pull the velum downwards to give velic opening. This opening process normally involves active

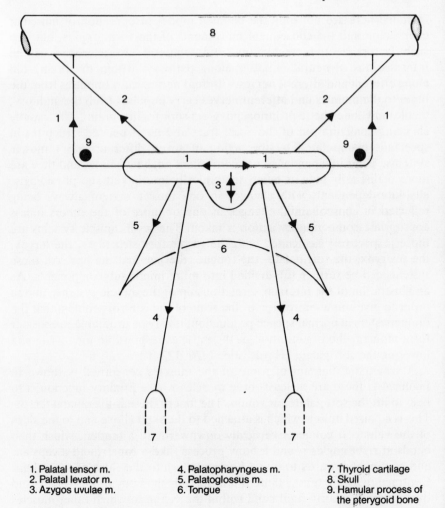

1. Palatal tensor m.   4. Palatopharyngeus m.   7. Thyroid cartilage
2. Palatal levator m.   5. Palatoglossus m.   8. Skull
3. Azygos uvulae m.   6. Tongue   9. Hamular process of
                                                             the pterygoid bone

Figure 4.1 A schematic diagram of the location and action of the muscles of the
soft palate.

muscular contraction. The first is the paired palatoglossus, which can be
seen at the back of the mouth as the forward pair of faucal pillars, or
arches. It runs from the body of the velum downwards to insert in the sides
of the back of the tongue.

The second palatal depressor is the paired palatopharyngeus, the rear set
of faucal pillars. This runs from the velum down the side walls of the
pharynx to insert on the top edge of the thyroid cartilage, which shields the
larynx and to which the front end of the vocal folds is attached.

The first coordinatory control problem to be coped with by the brain is
that all the muscles attached to the velum have to be programmed for an

appropriate state of contraction to achieve any velic position. A compensating balance must be managed, with all the muscles normally under active control; the situation is rather like that of adjusting the position of a tent-pole with guy-ropes. (Though it should be mentioned that this is not true of all speakers. Bell-Berti (1973) has shown that in nasalisation the palatoglossus shows no active contraction in some individuals.

Secondly, because the velum is attached to the tongue by the palatoglossus, each different position of the tongue will entail a different state of contraction of all the palatal muscles to achieve any given velic position. With the tongue being in almost continuous movement, this means that the dynamic and finely-adjusted control of velic position is an intricate problem.

From the point of view of the interaction of muscle systems, not only is the activity of the palatal muscles affected by that of the tongue muscles, but also of course vice versa. If the tongue body were not braced to some degree against the pull of the contracted palatoglossus, for example, then the tongue would be pulled slightly upwards and backwards in a velarising tendency. Similarly, contraction of the palatoglossus will tend to pull the larynx slightly upwards. Even if the larynx is braced against this pull, the fine detail of the mode of vibration of the vocal folds in phonation is inevitably affected.

Appropriate control of the velic musculature, and of harmonisation with the activities of other linked muscle systems, can thus be seen as a formidable programming problem. The scale of the general problem can perhaps be better appreciated in the light of the fact that the velic system is probably the simplest of all the muscle systems, standing in sharp contrast to the multiplicities of interacting and interlaced muscular sub-systems within the tongue, for instance.

In discussing the physiological properties of the effector system, we begin to approach considerations of control. There is, however, one area in the relationship between the effector system and the control system where the distinction between them becomes very clear. This is the matter of the constraints imposed on the control system by the nature of the effector system. These constraints set the bounds within which the control system can exercise its options. Intrinsic constraints deriving from the physical make-up of the speech-producing system have both mechanical and neural origins. Mechanical constraints limit the maximum velocity at which vocal structures such as the jaw or the tongue can be made to move, because of the relationship between the inertia of particular masses and the muscular force at the disposal of the control system. Other mechanical constraints derive from the specific anatomy of organs such as the tongue, in terms of the particular spatial disposition of the muscles involved. Although the tongue can assume a surprising variety of shapes, in fact the range is quite strongly limited by the available combinations of muscular contractions.

Neural constraints derive partly from such factors as the limit on the maximum rate of transmission of neural impulses set by the chemical nature of their propagation. It has also been suggested that neural anatomy may set constraints of a different sort, because of the fact that different parts of the peripheral effector system are supplied by nerves of very different lengths, and hence, other things being equal, of different overall transmission times ('innervation times'):

> the anatomy of the nerves suggests that innervation time for intrinsic laryngeal muscles may easily be up to 30 msec longer than innervation time for muscles in and around the oral cavity. Considering now that some articulatory events may last as short a period as 20 msec, it becomes a reasonable assumption that the firing order in the brain stem may at times be different from the order of events occurring at the periphery . . . It is clear that there must be considerable precision in timing if laryngeal mechanisms are to be integrated with oral ones. In addition, there are hundreds of muscular adjustments to be made every second (that is, a new neuromuscular event every few milli-seconds), from which we begin to see the magnitude of the timing-ordering problem. (Lenneberg, 1967: 96 f.)

These intrinsic constraints, as part of the properties of the actual effector system, are quite distinct from another type of constraint, which we might call extrinsic constraints, and which reflect aspects of the use of the control system. Extrinsic constraints are the habitual limits on performance established in the characteristic control of the apparatus. There is a hierarchy of constraints of this sort. The longest-term constraint involves so-called 'articulatory settings' (Honikman, 1964; Laver, 1968) of the vocal musculature. These are tendencies throughout the speech production of the individual speaker to maintain the vocal tract in a particular con-figuration, lending the general quality of his voice a particular auditory colouring. An example would be the tendency to hold the lips, say, in some given posture throughout the speech; another would be the use of persistent nasality as a feature of voice quality. Similar tendencies are seen in laryngeal control, where a person will habitually use some particular type of phonation. Whispery voice, where this was not merely the consequence of a pathological state but rather the product of habitual voice control, would be a not uncommon instance. Other extrinsic constraints on laryngeal behaviour include the habitual choice, within the extreme limits set by intrinsic constraints of the actual apparatus, of a particular pitch-range and loudness-range.

The paralinguistic communication of attitude can also be seen as being achieved through the superimposition on the control of the speech apparatus of constraining tendencies, though of shorter duration than the quasi-permanent speaker-characterising behaviour discussed immediately above. Speaking while smiling, for example, sets an obvious constraint on the activities of the lips in the articulatory production of the more momentary consonant and vowel segments. One might extend this notion of constraints on the control of the speech apparatus a stage further. The performance of the individual consonant and vowel segments of the language could be thought of as being obedient to a particular type of constraint, in that there are discernible limits on the range of articulatory variability allowed by the language for the production of any given segment.

The brain's task in designing a control program for the production of even a single articulatory segment is thus impressively complex. Firstly, account has to be taken of relevant intrinsic constraints. Then allowance has to be made for the constraining effect of volitional elements of voice quality, and of characteristic pitch- and loudness-ranges. Then the paralinguistic colouring superimposed on the overall stretch of speech concerned must be included. Finally, the program of muscular contractions for the characteristic production of the segment itself must be planned, incorporating not only the anticipation of the effects of interaction of the different muscle systems involved, but also the appropriate accommodation to the contingencies of the muscular performance of preceding and succeeding segments. It may be reasonable to think that the brain plans the three levels of speech performance (extralinguistic voice quality, paralinguistic communication of attitude and linguistic segments) separately in some way, in a layered hierarchy of planning, but eventually the muscle systems have to be given specific commands, and any given neuromuscular command will necessarily reflect the composite effect of planning at all different levels.

While phonetics can contribute much of the necessary information about the effector system, together with some of the details of lower levels of the control system, the construction of an overall neurolinguistic model of speech production obliges us to move, for an outline of the higher strategic levels of the control system, into a field more akin to cognitive psychology. It would also be necessary, much later in the future, to incorporate a strictly neurophysiological element dealing with such matters as the possible localisation of particular neurolinguistic control functions in specific parts of the brain. But such detailed neurophysiology seems premature in thinking about a neurolinguistic model of speech production, and it is thought sufficient here to restrict discussion of strategic control to considerations of logical relations between the different control functions that need to be posited.

The discussion that follows will be directed first to questions of high-level strategic control of functions such as ideation, abstract linguistic planning and abstract motor planning, and then to matters of low-level tactical control, in the conversion of abstract plans to actual programs of muscular contractions. Monitoring of the progress and success of neurolinguistic activity will be shown to involve both the strategic and the tactical levels of control.

The objective of the neurolinguistic system is to construct and execute a linguistic program in some specific motor medium, usually speech or writing, which is semantically appropriate to the expression of a specific idea (Laver, 1969).

The process of ideation is seen here, following William James (1890), as completely distinct from the processes of constructing an expository linguistic program. It is difficult to see on what other basis the mental editing of linguistic programs could be achieved. The notion of editing is the procedure where a tentative linguistic program is mentally rejected as not quite appropriate for the expression of a particular idea, and an alternative linguistic program is accepted. It is difficult to prove that such editing takes place, but it must be one of our most confident introspections that we each often mentally consider the suitability of competing alternative formulations of an idea before finally selecting one for eventual utterance. An editing procedure of this sort seems to be a very important part of thinking. As William James (1890) comments: 'One may admit that a good third of our psychic life consists in these rapid premonitory schemes of thought not yet articulate'.

Accepting that ideation is a separate process from neurolinguistic programming, though probably the two elements are highly interactive, the internal structure of the ideational process is left unexplored as the most difficult problem one can conceive in cognitive psychology today.

A certain amount of recent research has been addressed to the question of the nature of the neurolinguistic units, at a variety of levels, that must be posited as being held available in long-term memory for retrieval and organisation into expository programs. This research, together with a brief account of evidence about the way in which these neurolinguistic items might be arranged in memory, in terms of an addressing system, is described in Laver (1970). From the point of view of this general discussion of control aspects of the neurolinguistic system, perhaps it is sufficient to take the existence of neurolinguistic units for granted, whatever their actual nature.

One interesting discovery about the way in which the neurolinguistic control system goes about its business of constructing a program for articulation was established by Boomer (1965), in a study of the distribution of pauses in speech, and by Boomer and Laver (1968), analysing slips of the tongue. This research confirmed the idea that

> the preparation and articulation of a speech program is not performed on a sound-by-sound, or even on a word-by-word basis. It is much more likely that neural elements corresponding to much longer stretches of speech are assembled in advance, and then allowed to be articulated as a single continuous program' (Laver, 1970: 68)

The typical stretch of speech that seems to be pre-planned in this way in English is an intonationally and rhythmically marked unit which Halliday (1967) calls the 'tone-group', and Trager and Smith (1951) the 'phonemic clause'. The tone-group in English is characteristically about seven or eight syllables long.

The assumption is thus made in the discussion that follows that the neurolinguistic control system manages its task of producing speech by assembling molar programs corresponding to tone-groups. A useful framework for a consideration of the activity of the neurolinguistic control system is to examine, in a speculative way, some aspects of the evolution of the planning and execution of one such molar program. Reference has been made to four different control functions in the neurolinguistic system: linguistic planning, motor planning, the neuromuscular conversion of the motor plan to actual commands to the muscles, and monitoring of the appropriateness of all these activities. The progression of the molar program through the first three levels can be seen as a series of mapping operations from one code to another, with the monitor assessing the ideational adequacy of the linguistic program, the linguistic adequacy of the motor program, and the motor adequacy of the neuromuscular program. The function of the monitor is then not only to assess the suitability of a program at one level for expression of the program at the next-highest level, but also to take decisions about whether the seriousness of any detected unsuitability is such as to require reprogramming, and then to recycle the program to the relevant reconstructional level. In a cybernetic model of the sort being discussed here, unsuitability constitutes error, and the monitoring operation is essentially a comparator function carried out on an equation where one side of the equation can be translated to terms compatible with the other side. Monitoring is thus an absolutely integral part of any editing facility, and has to be attributed decoding abilities of considerable power. Unsuitability can be regarded as error in the sense that it reflects a discrepancy between intended performance and actual performance. The comparison of actual performance with intended or ideal performance, and the contingent modification of actual performance, is a perfect illustration of the cybernetic concept of 'feedback'. Feedback is posited here, therefore, as a major constituent of the monitoring process. This view espouses Norbert Wiener's 'cybernetic hypothesis', characterised by Miller, Galanter and Pribram (1960: 26–7) as the notion that 'the fundamental building block of the nervous system is the feedback loop'. Of equal importance in considerations of editorial monitoring is the notion of information about a plan being fed forward from some earlier neurolinguistic level to the point in time when it is necessary to compare the plan with some actualisation of it at the later level.

Speculatively, the progression of the continually monitored programming for the utterance expressing the original idea might be as follows. The first stage involves the retrieval from long-term memory of a number of neurolinguistic items, both lexical and grammatical in nature, which are associatively linked to the idea in varying degrees of strength. More such candidates are activated than will eventually be chosen for the final speech program, and the immediate task is to decide which of the neurolinguistic candidates are the most suitable for expressing the idea. Once the candidates have been arranged in a number of permutations, the monitoring function compares each tentative program with the idea, and arranges them in a hierarchy of goodness of semantic fit. It then examines the program selected as the best of the hierarchy to see if the best is in fact good enough, in which case the others will automatically be regarded as even worse, and it will be necessary to start the cycle of the original procedure once again. This process will continue until the monitoring function is satisfied that the best program constructed is in fact semantically adequate, and the linguistic program is then accepted.

That more candidates are activated than are finally selected is a view supported by actual slips of the tongue where, as a result of a failure on the part of the monitoring function, an error reaches public utterance in which a blend can be seen of two equally likely candidates. An example is a slip recorded by Fromkin (1971: 40)

'importance of adjoicent rules' ('adjacent' + 'adjoining').

All slips which reach the level of public utterance would thus be taken to involve failure on the part of the monitoring component whose purpose it is to intercept such errors at earlier stages of programming. At least two additional causes of errors can also be imagined. The first is straightforwardly where the relevant program-construction component malfunctions and produces a wrongly-retrieved item or a mis-ordered sequence. The second is the interesting possibility that in the finite amount of time taken to construct a linguistic program to match the idea, the idea might itself, for a variety of reasons, have changed. The monitoring function would normally intercept either type of error and deal with it by the same technique of recycling erratic programs until semantic adequacy is reached.

Given that the linguistic program is now judged by the monitoring function to be satisfactory, the next stage concerns the construction of a program of abstract motor plans for the appropriate realisation of the linguistic program just constructed. The separation of the linguistic level of programming from the motor level in this model reflects the view that it would be uneconomical to set up independent complete control systems for both speaking and writing. Here the linguistic element common to spoken and written language is seen as the responsibility of a single control function, with speaking and writing each being managed thereafter by separate medium-specific motor-control elements.

The structure of the motor programming level is rather similar in sequence to the earlier linguistic programming level. Once the linguistic program has been accepted by the monitoring function as semantically adequate, it is taken for granted by the motor programming function and not questioned further. A program of abstract motor 'targets' is put together to correspond to the linguistic program, and examined by the monitoring function for appropriateness. Errors of serial order, such as 'whipser' for 'whisper', when detected by the monitor, similarly result in a recycling of the constructional procedure. When the monitoring function is satisfied (and it may be so at even the first examination, in much of speech production), the motor program is accepted.

The next stage is for the abstract motor program to be converted to actual sequences of neuromuscular commands, and transmitted to the muscle systems for execution. It is clear that these two rather different levels of motor performance are necessary. It is out of the question that the brain could keep blueprints for all the actual neuromuscular commands used in speech in long-term memory, and incorporate them in the production of every utterance the speaker produces. The number of separate neuromuscular commands involved is astronomically high, and well outside the storage capacity even of the 10,000 million nerve cells contained in the brain (Eccles, 1973). The total number of neuromuscular commands the brain uses in speech is greater than this largely because of the very wide range of different conditions under which speaking is achieved. To control all the individual motor units of all the components of all the muscle systems used in the performance of a given language, as spoken in a given style, at a given rate, pitch-range, loudness-range, in a single tone of voice, would itself be an enormous undertaking if all the neuromuscular commands had to be kept available in permanent storage. To multiply the size of this task by the number of all the variations of style, rate, tone of voice, etc., makes it an impossible storage problem.

At the level of the vocal tract, the problem is that rather a small number of nearly unique articulatory states have to be reached from a potentially almost infinite number of different starting-points, depending on the momentary spatial disposition of the vocal organs. A good discussion of this problem appears in MacNeilage (1970: 186), where he writes:

> Although it has been neglected by linguistically oriented models of speech production, the problem of accounting for 'a variability of specific muscular responses, with circumstance, in such a way as to produce a single result' has been recognised by some psychologists as 'a ubiquitous fundamental psychological problem' and the phenomenon has been termed 'motor equivalence'. (Hebb, 1949: 153–7)

The problem of motor equivalence thus obliges us to reject the notion that blueprints for all possible motor events are held in long-term memory. The alternative is to believe that we keep a more limited number of more 'abstract' forms in long-term memory, together with strategies for taking account of the current muscular status of the vocal apparatus and for designing appropriate series of neuromuscular commands to move the apparatus to the next desired configuration or trajectory. This strategic ability to achieve a context-dependent modification of the events specified by the abstract blueprints reduces the scale of the storage problem to manageable proportions.

It may be interesting to consider for a moment the possible nature of these abstract blueprints held in storage. It might be taken from the discussion immediately above that the relationship envisaged between the blueprint and the eventual motor commands is relatively simple and direct, involving consideration chiefly of efferent neural command activity. Research into the motor equivalence problem, however, suggests that the relationship may be somewhat more indirect, with an afferent sensory component making a fundamental contribution to the relationship. The simplistic position is that the elements held in long-term memory are merely patterns of muscular commands, in some abstract representation, which can be contingently modified for actual programs of muscular contraction for a particular utterance. The more complex, but more satisfactory, alternative is that the most basic elements held in long-term memory are not the abstract representations of motor command patterns as such, but rather spatio-temporal 'states' or 'target configurations' of the vocal apparatus, specified within the parameters of a space coordinate system built up from a lifetime of sensory experience. In order to progress from one target configuration to another, the motor command system would have to utilise peripheral sensory information to be able to program the necessary context-dependent modifications of on-going control of motor activity. Implicit in this ability to exercise tactical control of motor activity is the maintenance by the sensory system of a running plot of the state of the vocal apparatus, providing continuously updated information for feedback purposes.

The sensory system thus plays a double role in motor performance. It is basic to the establishment and maintenance of a space coordinate frame of reference within which target configurations can be specified, and it contributes essential on-going feedback information to enable the motor control system to reach those target configurations.

If the sensory system is seen as part of the overall monitoring function, then the latter, far from being a parasitic appendage on the main speech-producing system, has to be regarded as an entirely integral element without which the overall system would be completely unable to achieve adequate performance.

In converting the abstract motor program to actual neuromuscular commands, a potent opportunity for error arises. Given the validity of the assumption that the brain programs speech performance in the form of molar plans for tone-groups, it is highly likely that planning and articulating are carried out asynchronously, at different speeds. Because articulation is relatively slow, a number of tone-groups may have been completely or partially planned before the first tone-group to be uttered has been articulatorily completed. The result is that the plans for successive tone-groups, specified to the abstract motor level, have to be put into short-term memory. When the time comes for the plan for a particular tone-group to be converted to appropriate neuromuscular commands, the plan has to be retrieved from short-term memory, and the process of storage and retrieval from short-term memory is notoriously fallible. The large number of psychological experiments that have been carried out on short-term memory are relatively unanimous in showing that confusions tend to occur between items co-present in storage which share characteristics. The tendency is summarised by the maxim 'Similars interact', and it holds true for the errors which occur in speech programs just as well as for the digits etc. that are the more usual content of psychological experiments on memory. When segmental transpositions occur within a single tone-group, they tend to involve articulatorily similar elements. At the level of the individual segment, voiceless fricatives are often mutually confused, as in a slip like 'alsho share' for 'also share' (Fromkin, 1971: 30); approximants interact, as in 'blake fruid' for 'brake fluid' (Fromkin, 1971: 31); and vowels metathesise, as in 'fash and tickle' for 'fish and tackle' (Fromkin, 1971: 31). At the level of the syllable, segments at the same place in their syllables interact; initial segments replace initial ones, medial replace medial and final replace final (Boomer and Laver, 1968: 7). There is a tendency for the syllables containing segments which interact to be similar in their stress status; either both are stressed syllables, or both are unstressed, and it is rather less common for a stressed and an unstressed syllable to interact (Boomer and Laver, 1968: 7).

Because the situation sometimes arises where the plan for more than one tone-group is being held in short-term memory, slips sometimes occur where elements of two tone-groups interact. When this happens, the interaction tends to be between elements of similar status within their respective tone-groups. The two tonic syllables, for example, are the most likely to be involved in the interaction (Boomer and Laver, 1968: 7).

As soon as the neuromuscular commands are executed by the muscle systems, the utterance reaches its public stage, where any errors are overt. Most slips are corrected very quickly, though often the fact of their correction escapes the conscious attention of both listener and speaker. In order for overt slips to be corrected, the monitoring function has to compare the performance which was actually achieved with the performance that was intended, at each of the major constructional levels where the opportunity for the occurrence of error arises (Laver, 1969).

To achieve the most economical re-programming solution to the problem of any detected error, the monitoring function must first establish the point in the constructional process where error in fact occurred. Cybernetically, this is a fairly simple problem, in that information is already available in every case about the nature of the intended performance, from those points in the neurolinguistic process where a program at a particular level was accepted as an adequate actualisation of the program at the preceding level. This information can therefore be fed forward to allow the monitoring function to compare it with monitoring reports on the actual performance. To register the details of the actual performance, the monitoring function must first calculate, from sensory reports, what the abstract motor program would be that would be taken to underlie the articulatory activity produced by the patterns of muscular contraction that in fact took place. If this inferred abstract motor pattern is different from the intended motor program, then clearly an error must have been introduced after the acceptance of the intended motor program, at the stage of its retrieval for neuromuscular conversion. Identifying the location of error in the neurolinguistic process allows the monitoring function to restart corrective programming at the lowest necessary level, in this case at the level of neuromuscular conversion.

The monitoring function must then calculate the linguistic program that would be taken to underlie the inferred motor program – the 'performed' linguistic program. If the comparison of the performed and the intended linguistic program shows a discrepancy, while the comparison of the performed and the intended motor programs shows none, then logically the error that was introduced must have occurred after acceptance of the linguistic program and before acceptance of the motor program, during the construction of the motor program itself. Appropriate recycling can then be arranged.

Finally, the monitoring function must establish the ideation that would be taken to underlie the inferred linguistic program – the 'performed' ideation. If the comparison of the performed and the intended ideation reveals a discrepancy while none of the lower-level comparisons reveals any, then the introduced error must have occurred during the construction of the linguistic program. Only in this case need the monitoring function initiate re-entry to the neurolinguistic process at the highest level, and restart the whole procedure.

An interesting point here is that ideational discrepancy need not solely be the result of malfunction of the neurolinguistic system. It may be that by the time a linguistic program has been constructed, transformed to a motor program, converted to neuromuscular commands and articulated, the original ideation may itself have changed. Changes of mind (literally) at the ideational level, can thus be treated in exactly the same way as the errors which arise from constructional malfunctions (Laver, 1970: 74).

Occasionally, manifest errors are not corrected. This does not constitute an argument for maintaining that the error was not detected. We must all have had the experience of making an error, recognising the fact and nature of the error, and deciding that in the social or linguistic context in which the error occurred, it was unnecessary to correct it. In order to make judgments of this sort, the monitoring function must have an appreciation of the degree of motivation the speaker has to communicate precisely, and knowledge of linguistic redundancy.

This chapter has offered some discussion of the capacities the brain must have, as a control system, to produce semantically adequate acts of speech performance. It is not accidental that the data supporting the presentation of the brain as a cybernetic model should be taken chiefly from research on speech errors. But many other domains of evidence for inferring the properties of the control system suggest themselves as likely to provide valuable contributions. A major possibility that has emerged in phonetic research in the last decade is evidence from the study of temporal coordination in normal speech, and of articulatory dynamics (MacNeilage, 1972). Another field is the process of learning and forgetting speech, in acquisition and pathology. A third possible type of evidence comes from experimental intervention in the normal process of speech, using such techniques as selective anaesthesia of different sensory receptor systems to establish their particular contribution (Ladefoged, 1967: 163).

The broadening of phonetic interests to include the neurolinguistic system responsible for controlling the activities of the vocal apparatus has its own justification within the subject, in making phonetic theory more comprehensive and more explanatory. But a wider justification is perhaps to be found outside the discipline of phonetics itself. In a famous article, Lashley (1951) suggested that, because of its disproportionate complexity, the study of speech could profitably be taken as a paradigm for the study of all other skilled cerebral activity. Phonetics, in learning more about the production of speech, may be able to tell us more about one of our ultimate mysteries, the brain.

References

Bell-Berti, F. (1973) 'The velopharyngeal mechanism: an electromyographic study', *Status Report on Speech Research* (supplement), Haskins Laboratories, New York.

Boomer, D.S. (1965) 'Hesitation and grammatical encoding', *Language and Speech* 8, 148–58.

Boomer, D.S. and Laver, J. (1968) 'Slips of the tongue', *British Journal of Disorders of Communication* 3, 2–12 (reprinted in Fromkin (1973), pp. 120–31).

Eccles, J.C. (1973) *The Understanding of the Brain*, McGraw-Hill, New York.

Fromkin, V.A. (1971) 'The non-anomalous nature of anomalous utterances', *Language* 47, 27–52 (reprinted in Fromkin (1973), pp. 215–42).

Fromkin, V.A. (1973) *Speech Errors as Linguistic Evidence*, Mouton, The Hague.

Halliday, M.A.K. (1967) *Intonation and Grammar in British English*, Mouton, The Hague.

Hardcastle, W.I. (1976) *Physiology of Speech Production*, Academic Press, London.

Hebb, D.O. (1949) *The Organization of Behavior: a Neuropsychological Theory*, Wiley, New York.

Honikman, B. (1964) 'Articulatory settings', pp. 73–84 in Abercrombie,D., Fry, D., MacCarthy, P.A.D., Scott, N.C. and Trim, J.L.M. (eds) *In Honour of Daniel Jones*, Longman, London.

James, W. (1980) *The Principles of Psychology*, Vol. 1., Rinehart and Winston, New York.

Ladefoged, P. (1967) *Three Areas of Experimental Phonetics*, Oxford University Press, Oxford and London.

Lashley, K.S. (1951) 'The problem of serial order in behaviour', pp. 112–46 in Jeffress, L.A. (ed.) *Cerebral Mechanisms in Behaviour*, Wiley, New York.

Laver, J. (1968) 'Voice quality and indexical information', *British Journal of Disorders of Communication* 3, 43–54 (reprinted in Laver, J. and Hutcheson, S. (eds) (1972), pp. 189–203).

Laver, J. (1969) 'The detection and correction of slips of the tongue', *Work in Progress* 3: 1–12 (Department of Phonetics and Linguistics, University of Edinburgh), (reprinted in Fromkin (1973), pp. 132–43).

Laver, J. (1970) 'The production of speech', pp. 53–75 in Lyons, J.(ed.) *New Horizons in Linguistics*, Penguin Books, Harmondsworth.

Laver J. (1974) 'Labels for voices', *Journal of the International Phonetic Association* 4, 62–75.

Laver, J. and Hutcheson, S. (eds) (1972) *Communication in Face-to-Face Interaction*, Penguin Books, Harmondsworth.

Lenneberg, E.H. (1967) *Biological Foundations of Language*, Wiley, New York.

MacNeilage, P.F. (1970) 'Motor control of serial ordering of speech', *Psychological Review* 77, 182–96.

MacNeilage, P.F. (1972) 'Speech physiology', pp. 1–72 in Gilbert, J.H. (ed.) *Speech and Cortical Functioning*, New York.

Miller, G.A., Galanter, E. and Pribram, K.H. (1960) *Plans and the Structure of Behavior*, Holt, Rinehart and Winston, New York.

Trager, G.L. and Smith, H.L. (1951) *An Outline of English Structure*, Studies in Linguistics, Occasional Paper No. 3, Norman, Oklahoma.

5 Monitoring Systems in the Neurolinguistic Control of Speech Production

Originally published as Laver, J. (1979) 'Monitoring Systems in the Neurolinguistic Control of Speech Production', in Fromkin, V. (ed.) *Errors of Linguistic Performance*, Academic Press, New York (pp. 287–305)

The chief benefit of the past decade of research into slips of the tongue is that it has provided a fresh approach to the question of how the brain controls the production of spoken language. It might seem reasonable to expect a synthesis to emerge, bringing together ideas from linguistics, psychology, and neurophysiology. The distance still seems formidable, however, between the cognitive modelling undertaken by psychologists and linguists on the one hand, and the more directly empirical standpoints of researchers investigating neurophysiological mechanisms. To take one example: Miller, Galanter, and Pribram (1960: 26–7) characterise Norbert Wiener's 'cybernetic hypothesis' as asserting that 'the fundamental building block of the nervous system is the feedback loop'. Fromkin's 'utterance generator', described in one of the best articles on slips of the tongue (Fromkin, 1971: 50), contains no feedback loops at all.

The problem lies at least partly in the descriptive metalanguages used in the modelling. The metalanguage of formal linguistics does not necessarily lend itself effectively to the task of facilitating the making of complementary statements in the metalanguage of neurophysiology. If linguistic models of the brain's control of speech performance are to court not only psychological validity but also potential neurophysiological realisations, eventually, then the adoption of a suitable metalanguage is clearly desirable.

A very useful lead toward a 'neurolinguistic' metalanguage, which could permit compatible statements by linguists, psychologists and neurophysiologists, was given a number of years ago, in neurophysiology itself, by McCulloch and Pitts (1943). They discussed the description of the activity of neuronal networks in terms of the logic of propositional calculus:

> The 'all-or-none' law of nervous activity is sufficient to insure that the activity of any neuron may be represented as a proposition. Physiological relations existing among nervous activities correspond, of course, to relations among the propositions; and the utility of the

representations depends upon the identity of these relations with those of the logic of propositions. To each reaction of any neuron there is a corresponding assertion of a simple proposition. This, in turn, implies either some other simple proposition or the disjunction, or the conjunction, with or without negation, of similar propositions, according to the configuration of the synapses upon and the threshold of the neuron in question. (McCulloch and Pitts, 1943: 117)

Propositional logic is thus a suitable metalanguage for discussing the activity of any given neuron, in the sense that for any given firing threshold, the state of the neuron is completely accounted for by a statement of the condition of all neurons whose activities are prerequisites for that state. McCulloch and Pitts developed this argument further, and made it clear that wider psychological operations, because of their necessary dependence on the neuronal make-up of their underlying neurophysiological mechanisms, could also suitably be discussed in terms of propositional logic:

To psychology, however defined, specification of the net [namely, the neuronal network concerned in any particular cognition, perception, or state] would contribute all that could be achieved in that field – even if the analysis were pushed to ultimate psychic units or 'psychons', for a psychon can be no less than the activity of a single neuron. Since that activity is inherently propositional, all psychic events have an intentional, or 'semiotic' character. The 'all-or-none' law of these activities, and the conformity of their relations to those of the logic of propositions, insure that the relations of psychons are those of the two-valued logic of propositions. Thus in psychology, introspective, behavioristic or physiological, the fundamental relations are those of two-valued logic. (McCulloch and Pitts, 1943: 131–2)

This chapter briefly presents a model of the speech-producing system based on findings from research on slips of the tongue, which makes use of a descriptive metalanguage embodying the concepts of propositional, Boolean logic. The logical relations posited to obtain between the various neurolinguistic functions, and between their component sub-functions, will be those of simple propositions, conjunction, inclusive and exclusive disjunction, and negation. By linking the different neurolinguistic functions in a relational network, it is possible to emphasise the specification of the relations between any given function and the logically prior functions that supply the prerequisite conditions for its operation. Control strategies of the brain are thus accounted for, in the discussion offered in this chapter, as the ways in which interaction between the posited neurolinguistic functions is either facilitated or limited by the hypothesised network of logical relations.

A major focus of this chapter is the nature of the monitoring systems for the detection and correction of errors in program construction and execution. The choice of such terms as 'monitoring', 'detection', 'correction', and 'error', with their strongly cybernetic flavour, is not accidental: the interesting problems of neurolinguistic performance are those of control. Cybernetics, as the science of all possible control systems, has a number of concepts of special relevance to the discussion of these problems. Among the most useful cybernetic concepts applicable here are the notions of the feedback loop and the feedforward link, together with the notion of error as a discrepancy between desired action and performed action.

This cybernetic conception of error will be particularly valuable in modelling neurolinguistic performance. Such a definition is wider than that usually used in research on slips of the tongue. The literature on tongue-slip data characteristically discusses slips that either result in non-existent linguistic forms or that substantially distort the semantic sense of the utterance. Slips of this sort certainly fall within the wider definition of a discrepancy between desired and performed action; but also included would be, say, choices of lexical candidates that are only slightly imprecise in terms of the speaker's cognitive intention. A listener would have no evidence of any inadequacy of performance on the part of the speaker if such an 'error' were not corrected. The virtue of the broad cybernetic definition of error is that processes of mental editing, where the degree of semantic appropriateness of a linguistic candidate is used as a criterion for its inclusion in or exclusion from a linguistic program, can be shown to be exploiting exactly the same monitoring mechanisms as are used for the detection of incipient slips of the tongue in the more customary definition. Broadening the definition of error to mean 'inadequate performance' thus unifies normal language-processing and tongue-slip detection in a single system.

In order to capitalise upon relevant cybernetic ideas, the logical relations of the control systems that make up the neurolinguistic model are symbolised by a diagrammatic cybernetic network, rather than by the conventional algebra of propositional logic. The two representations are notationally equivalent, but the cybernetic network is not only mnemonically easier to understand, but it also conveniently allows a global statement to be made of the overall relationships of the model assembled in a single diagram.

Four principal neurolinguistic decision-making functions are posited. These are IDEATION, LINGUISTIC PROGRAMMING, MOTOR PROGRAMMING and MONITORING (Laver, 1969; 1970; 1977). An initial indication of their serial relationship is shown schematically in Figure 5.1.

In Figures 5.3 to 5.7 the neurolinguistic functions are diagrammed in networks as 'boxes' (of largely unknown internal strategy) connected to each other by lines, either directly or (more often) through one or more

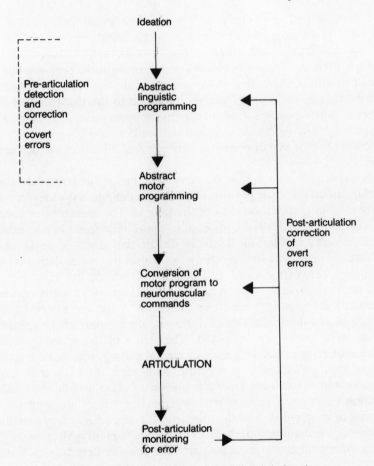

Figure 5.1 Schematic outline of neurolinguistic functions.

'gates'. The gate symbols – the AND gate, the INCLUSIVE OR gate, and the EXCLUSIVE OR gate – specify the logical relations between the boxes they connect. The inputs to each gate represent the prerequisite conditions that must logically obtain before the box to which the gate supplies the input can carry out its prescribed function. Conventions for interpreting the gate symbols, and line-junctions, are given in Figure 5.2. Such symbols are often used for representing two-valued Boolean relations in electronic circuitry, for instance, and are thus particularly suitable for incorporation in a cybernetic network of this sort. They have been used in linguistic notation before, in writings on stratificational grammar. Equivalent devices are also used in writings on systemic grammar.

For convenience of exposition, the diagram of the total perform-ance process has been initially broken down into four sections. These will be briefly discussed in turn as follows: Figure 5.3 shows the linguistic

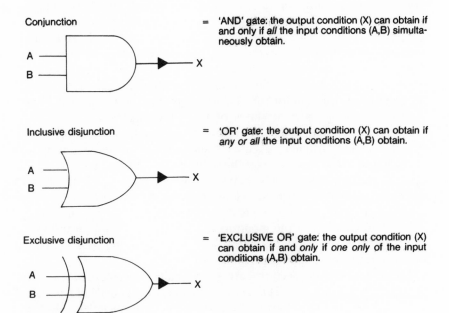

Conjunction

= 'AND' gate: the output condition (X) can obtain if and only if *all* the input conditions (A,B) simultaneously obtain.

Inclusive disjunction

= 'OR' gate: the output condition (X) can obtain if *any or all* the input conditions (A,B) obtain.

Exclusive disjunction

= 'EXCLUSIVE OR' gate: the output condition (X) can obtain if and *only* if *one only* of the input conditions (A,B) obtain.

(1 = condition obtains; 0 = condition does not obtain.)

Conjunction			Inclusive disjunction			Exclusive disjunction		
Inputs		Output	Inputs		Output	Inputs		Output
A	B	X	A	B	X	A	B	X
1	0	0	1	0	1	1	0	1
1	1	1	1	1	1	1	1	0
0	1	0	0	1	1	0	1	1
0	0	0	0	0	0	0	0	0

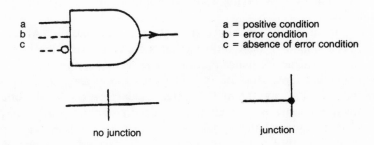

a
b
c

a = positive condition
b = error condition
c = absence of error condition

no junction   junction

Figure 5.2 Symbol convention for Boolean network of logical relations.

programming section, whose function is to construct an abstract linguistic program suitable for expressing the cognitive structure of the ideation concerned. Figure 5.4 shows the initial stage of the motor programming section, where a motor program of abstract motor schemata is produced, designed to express the linguistic program just constructed. Figure 5.5 shows the final stage of the motor programming section, where the program of abstract motor schemata is converted, in the light of sensory information about current states of the vocal apparatus, to the actual neuromuscular commands that result in the public articulatory performance audible to listeners. Figure 5.6 shows the stage where a component of the monitoring function scans the published performance for any error – that is, for any discrepancy between the intended utterance and the utterance actually performed. Monitoring for error in the pre-utterance stages of program construction is shown as an integral part of those stages. All sub-components of the monitoring function are shown on the various diagrams as boxes printed in black, with white lettering. Associated gate symbols are printed similarly.

The four different sections are then finally combined in an overall diagram, in Figure 5.7. This shows not only the global and individual relationships of the different functions, but also includes the logical network utilised by the monitoring function in recycling detected overt errors to the lowest appropriate program construction level for correct reprogramming.

A number of preliminary points need to be made before embarking on the exposition of the model. First, following William James (1890), it is assumed that ideation is to be distinguished from the linguistic resources that are exploited to construct expository linguistic programs. If this were not so, it would be difficult to understand how one linguistic program could be judged as semantically more appropriate for the expression of a given cognitive apprehension than a different but fairly similar program. This is not to oppose a potentially high degree of interaction between the two functions, but no provision is made in the model offered here for the possible influence of the linguistic programming function on the ideational function.

Second, a distinction between LANGUAGE and MEDIUM (Abercrombie, 1967) is assumed. That is, a distinction is drawn between those features of neurolinguistic performance that should be seen as common to all media of language and those that are specific to the motor aspects of a particular medium. In this way, the model preserves its relevance for the operations involved not only in speaking, but also in writing, and in any other linguistic medium. Pathological data supports this position in that patients who can write but not speak, or speak but not write, demonstrate the retention of their linguistic ability in the absence of a medium-specific motor ability.

Third, the neurolinguistic operations suggested are seen as relevant to the performance of a single molar program of spoken communication. Previous work has shown, using evidence from the distribution of pauses (Boomer, 1965) and speech errors (Boomer and Laver, 1968; Fromkin, 1971), that molar programming, where a stretch of speech 'is handled in the central nervous system as a unitary behavioural act, and the neural correlates of the separate elements are assembled and partially activated, or "primed", before the performance of the utterance begins' (Boomer and Laver, 1968: 9), is very probable. The tone-group, or phonemic clause, often coterminous with the syntactic clause, seems the best candidate for such molar programming, on the evidence of the preceding articles.

Fourth, a number of basic resources of the neurolinguistic system have been left out of the diagrams, partly for legibility. For example, every level of performance needs access to either or both long-term memory and short-term memory. Similarly, ATTENTION and MOTIVATION could be thought to have a potentially universal influence on the components of the network. Appeal could be made to these two factors to explain variability in the efficiency of components. If attention is acceptable as a viable concept, then fluctuations in the degree of attention devoted to the operation of given components on different occasions could be responsible for some erratic performance. Also, variability in the efficiency of monitoring components might sometimes be attributable to changes in their operational thresholds, brought about by variations in the degree of motivational pressure felt by the speaker to communicate with his or her listener in a precise manner. Factors of social context would presumably be influential in this way. Access to memory, attention, and motivation is assumed throughout, although not explicitly diagrammed.

Finally, it may be helpful to summarise the basic rationale underlying the construction of a model concerned at least partly with the covert correction of covert errors. The incidence of overt errors in speech seems surprisingly low, given the large volume of speech we each produce every day. The assumption is made here that the neurolinguistic speech production system is subject to more frequent inadequacies of performance, and that it has an integral monitoring system for the detection and correction of still covert errors in programming, which is efficient enough for such errors only occasionally to reach the level of overt articulatory performance. The assumption is buttressed by the notion of linguistic performance as a skilled and creative activity. That linguistic performance, particularly of cognitively novel and precise formulations, is creative is indisputable. That skill should be the partner of creativity in the continual, progressive refinement, before articulation, of expository linguistic programs seems highly plausible. One might say that skill can be defined as behaviour that is prone to error where error is quickly detected and corrected. The highest degree of skill is then seen in the situation where error is normally intercepted and corrected while still covert, in the programming processes prior to the overt, public stages of performance. That such behaviour can be identified by the observer as skilled, rather than as automatic and incapable of error, will reside in the fact of a slight but necessary and publicly visible fallibility. A small number of errors must occasionally elude the internal monitoring mechanisms that have to be posited, and become overt. Their subsequent overt correction, and logically prior detection, then constitute the empirical data that support the formation of explanatory hypotheses about the characteristics of the covert programming and monitoring processes whose normal functioning successfully reduces the incidence of overt errors in everyday speech to a low level.

The Descriptive Model
The Linguistic Programming Section (Figure 5.3)

The first posited responsibility of this section, once the output of the ideation process has been established by Box 1 and stored in short-term memory, is to activate a number of linguistic candidates of tentative semantic suitability for the expression of the ideation. It is the function of Box 2 to do this, and the function of Box 3 to arrange them in a number of tentative linguistic programs. We know that more candidates are activated than are finally spoken, from blending errors widely reported, such as Fromkin's (1971: 40):

> *the importance of adjoicent rules*   ('adjacent' + 'adjoining')

and Laver's (1970: 67):

> *he behaved as like a fool* ('like a fool' + 'as if/though he were a fool').

For Boxes 2 and 3 to perform their function, prerequisite information is not only the cognitive structure of the ideation, supplied by Box 1, but also the fact that the performance is intended eventually to be spoken rather than written. The implications of choice of medium will be more substantial later in the performance process, but even at the level of linguistic programming, the choice is influential – the language of speaking is, after all, not the same as the language of writing. The necessary conditions for Boxes 2 and 3 starting to work are symbolised by gate A1 – the 'absence of error' input is explained in the following section. When the conditions at A1 are satisfied, gate B will operate on a single input.

The next task is the first editorial task: It is necessary to decide which of the constructed linguistic programs is most suitable for expressing the idea. The function of Box 4 is to assess the semantic suitability of each of the tentative programs, and arrange them in a hierarchy of goodness of fit. To do this, Box 4 has to be attributed major decoding and comparator powers. It also has to have access to the output of Box 1. The function of Box 5 is

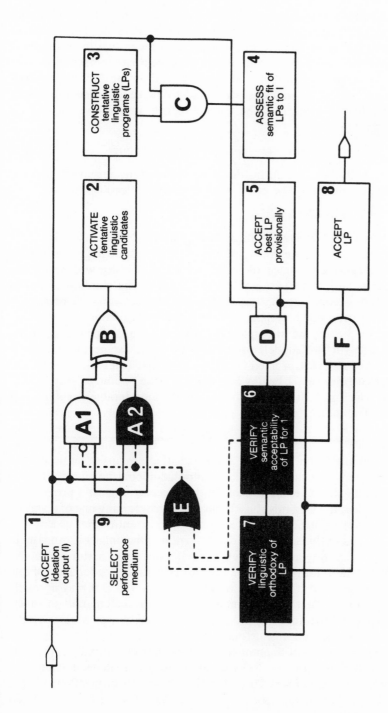

Figure 5.3 Schematic outline of the abstract linguistic programming section of the speech performance process.

merely to pick the most highly valued program from the top of the hierarchy established by Box 4. That this program is the most suitable program so far constructed does not necessarily mean that the program is adequate by whatever criteria the standards of the occasion of conversation impose. It is the responsibility of Boxes 6 and 7, the first of the sub-components of the monitoring function, to make the decision about adequacy. Mistakes such as the spatiotemporal confusion reported by Nooteboom (1967: 14):

the two contemporary, er – sorry, adjacent buildings

would normally be rejected by Box 6 as semantically unsuitable for the expression of the idea. The error reported in the preceding section:

he behaved as like a fool

would normally be rejected as linguistically unorthodox by Box 7. In either case of unsuitability, an error signal would be sent through gate E to gate A1, the necessary 'absence of error' condition for A1 would become inapplicable, and as an AND gate it would block. The conditions for A2 would then become applicable, however, and it would become the alternative entry for recycling, allowing the constructional process of Boxes 2 and 3 a second attempt to provide an adequate program, in the first example, in this model, of a feedback loop. (Some mechanism is needed here, not yet specified, for arranging that when A1 blocks, the serial output from Box 1 begins again at its starting point.)

Box 6, which like Box 4 must be attributed considerable decoding and comparator abilities, may reject programs for a variety of reasons: the candidates may be semantically nearly right, but on the occasion not precise enough; or the program accepted by Box 5 may be a miscon-structed program unacceptably distorting the semantic sense of the communication. But there is an interesting additional possibility (Laver, 1977: 150). In the finite time taken to construct a linguistic program to match the idea, the idea might itself have changed, for any one of a variety of reasons. Given that Box 6 has access to the current output of Box 1, a change of mind of this sort will lead to rejection of the linguistic program in exactly the same way as with other types of inadequate performance.

When the monitoring function is satisfied with the adequacy of the linguistic program for the expression of the ideation (and it may normally be satisfied on the first pass, on many occasions of undemanding conver-sational speech), the linguistic program is accepted by Box 8, through the AND gate F, and stored in short-term memory.

One of the features of the model presented here is that once a linguistic program is accepted by Box 8, its suitability is not challenged again until after the fact of articulation. This is possibly an unrealistic position, and is a consequence of the mainly serial flow of the model. In reality, one might prefer to believe that parallel access is more likely, and that decisions once taken are potentially subject to rescrutiny.

The Motor Programming Section (Figure 5.4)

The operation of this section is straightforward. The task of Box 10 is to construct a program of abstract motor schemata, in the appropriate performance medium, for the expression of the chosen linguistic program. The relevant information comes to Box 10 through gates G1 and H. Box 11 checks on the suitability of the constructed motor schema program and rejects it if inadequate. When error is registered by Box 11, G1 blocks and gate J permits re-entry to the program construction process. Errors of serial order, such as Fromkin's (1971:39):

Ralebais for 'Rabelais'

may be thought likely to arise here. However, it would not be appropriate to conclude that all errors involving only consonant- or vowel-sized segments are necessarily attributable to this section. For instance, one tongue-slip reported by Fromkin (1971: 41) was:

a kice ream cone for 'an ice cream cone'.

It is clear that a morphophonemic adjustment took place here after the malfunction that caused the misplacing of the segments. Since such a morphophonological process must be applied in the linguistic programming section, then, logically, the misordering of the segments took place there also. We are thus faced with the situation, in trying to use data from speech errors to construct a model of the speech generation process, of a given symptom of malfunction having multiple potential causal locations.

Once Box 11 is satisfied, then Box 12 accepts the motor schema program and stores it in short-term memory. The same comments apply to the 'non-challengeability' of acceptance of a program by Box 12 as applied to the case of Box 8.

The Neuromuscular Conversion Stage of the Motor Programming Section (Figure 5.5)

The function of this stage is to design and execute a program of neuromuscular commands to the articulators that will embody the motor sequence specified by the preceding section. To do this, three types of information are needed by Box 15. The first, available from Box 12, is the specification of the motor schema program. The second is that the neuromuscular sequence for the preceding molar neurolinguistic program has been completed – this information is available from Box 14. The third is information from continuous auditory, tactile, and kinesthetic-proprioceptive reports about the current disposition of the vocal apparatus, from Box 13.

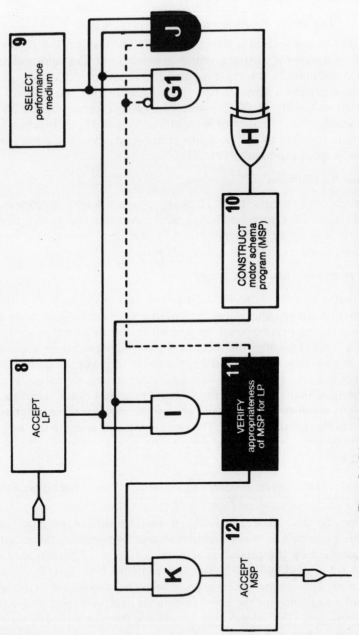

Figure 5.4 Schematic outline of the initial stage of the motor programming section of the speech performance process, which constructs a program of abstract motor schemata to match the linguistic program which is the output from Figure 5.3.

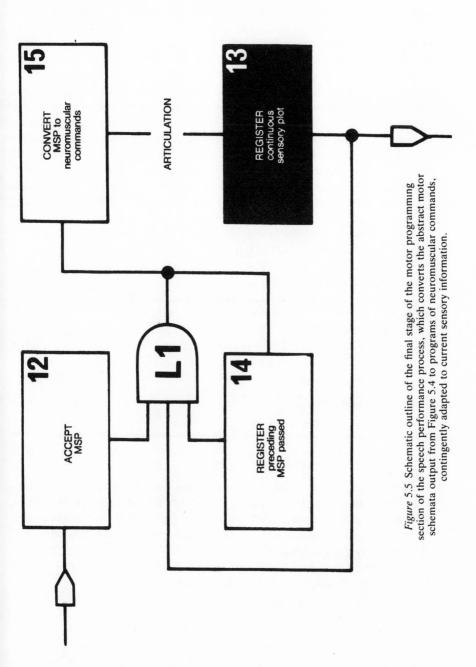

Figure 5.5 Schematic outline of the final stage of the motor programming section of the speech performance process, which converts the abstract motor schemata output from Figure 5.4 to programs of neuromuscular commands, contingently adapted to current sensory information.

When all three conditions for gate L1 are satisfied, Box 15 operates; and, retrieving the stored motor schema program from short-term memory, produces the neuromuscular commands that give rise to the audible articulatory performance of the utterance.

It is necessary to distinguish between this neuromuscular stage and the earlier abstract motor planning stage. The problem of motor equivalence, where a small number of nearly unique articulatory states have to be reached from a potentially almost infinite number of starting points, depending on the momentary spatial disposition of the vocal organs, makes it quite impossible for the brain to store all the necessary varieties of neuromuscular command patterns. It seems plausible that we store a more limited number of more abstract forms in long-term memory, together with strategies for taking account of the current muscular status of the vocal apparatus and for designing appropriate series of neuromuscular commands to move the apparatus to the next desired configuration or trajectory (MacNeilage, 1970: 186; Laver, 1977: 151).

In retrieving the motor schema program from short-term memory, the operation of Box 15 may be a fertile source of error. The large number of psychological experiments that have been carried out on short-term memory are relatively unanimous in showing that confusions tend to occur between items co-present in storage that share characteristics (Laver, 1977: 152). Fromkin (1971: 30–1) shows that voiceless fricatives interact as in

alsho share for 'also share',

as do approximants:

blake fruid for 'brake fluid'

and vowels:

fash and tickle for 'fish and tackle'.

Boomer and Laver (1968: 7) showed that the interaction of similars is effective in terms of syllable place, in that initial segments replace initials, medials replace medials, and finals replace finals. They also showed that stressed syllables interact with other stressed syllables, as a tendency, and that unstressed syllables preferentially affect other unstressed syllables.

The confusion of articulatory features reported by Fromkin (1971: 36) may also be attributable to this source of error, as in

tebestrian for 'pedestrian'

The Post-utterance Monitoring Function (Figure 5.6)

It is the function of this component of the monitoring function to establish what utterance was actually performed, and to assess whether any discrepancy exists between the actual performance and the one that was intended.

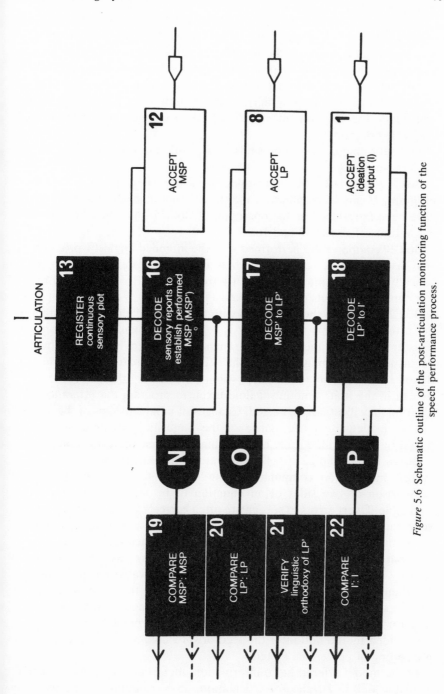

Figure 5.6 Schematic outline of the post-articulation monitoring function of the speech performance process.

Since adequate performance cannot be taken for granted, the monitoring function has to operate on the basis of sensory information supplied by Box 13 about the details of the articulatory performance. Boxes 16, 17, and 18 successively establish the performed motor schema program (that is, the motor schema program that would be taken to underlie the actually performed articulatory program); then the performed linguistic program; and finally the ideation that would be taken to underlie the performed linguistic program.

The neurolinguistic system is now in a position to establish the fact and level of any error.

Box 19 compares the performed with the intended motor schema program. If any discrepancy is registered, then logically the error must have been introduced by the operation of Box 15, since Box 19 compares the outputs of Boxes 12 and 16.

Box 20 compares the performed with the intended linguistic program. If any discrepancy is registered, when Box 19 registers no error, then logically the error must have been introduced by Box 10, since Box 20 compares the outputs of Boxes 8 and 17.

Box 22 compares the performed with the intended ideational content of the utterance. If any discrepancy is registered, when Boxes 19 and 20 register no error, then the error must have been introduced by the linguistic programming section, since Box 22 compares the outputs of Boxes 1 and 18. The additional possibility exists here that, as earlier with Box 6, in the finite amount of time taken to program the utterance, the ideation may itself have changed. Changes of mind and slips of the tongue due to inadequate performance of the linguistic programming section would be treated identically by the monitoring system at this point.

Boxes 19, 20, and 22 are all comparator functions. In any such function in this model, the computation time needed to allow the necessary comparison of two sides of an equation to be made is unlikely to be negligible. Overt errors in speech are often corrected (and hence detected) very quickly indeed. This prompts speculation about possibilities of economising on post-utterance monitoring latencies. If none of the necessary computation for post-utterance monitoring was able to start until sensory information about the actual articulation was available from Box 13, then it would be difficult to understand how the brain manages to correct some overt slips so rapidly, as there does not seem to be enough time for all the computation to be carried out. One possible time economy is provided by the notion of the feedforward link, and by the concept of pre-setting of perceptual systems.

In the model offered here, information about intended performance is available well in advance of articulation, at every point in time where a program is accepted and put into short-term memory storage. The output of Boxes 1, 8, and 12 is thus available to be fed forward to Boxes 22, 20, and 19 respectively, well ahead of the point in time when the actual comparisons will be made. Any necessary decoding, or reading-off of indexation, that might be involved can therefore proceed in advance of the arrival of the later information about the articulated performance.

The time economy envisaged in this discussion concerns operations of a fairly high degree of cognitive complexity: pre-setting any cognitive system to expect to perform on an anticipated set of data is likely to abbreviate the computation time necessary for that cognitive task. Pre-setting can be achieved at a lower perceptual level as well, however. It seems not impossible that another degree of time economy might be achieved by pre-setting the perceptual detectors involved in the earliest registration of the articulatory performance.[1] The network suggested here would have to be amended to include a link from Box 12 to Boxes 13 and 16 to incorporate this possibility.

Box 21 is the counterpart, in the post-utterance monitoring section, of Box 7. Errors of linguistic unorthodoxy, such as the slip mentioned earlier

he behaved as like a fool

that had eluded the attention of Box 7, would presumably normally be caught by Box 21.

Post-utterance Error Correction (Figure 5.7)

If Boxes 19 to 22 each produce a positive 'no error' output, then all the conditions for the AND gate Q are satisfied, and articulatory performance continues. However, if even one of those boxes registers an error, then gate Q blocks, and the alternative route through gate 5 to Boxes 23 and 24 has to be traversed before the decision to continue articulatory performance or to halt it can be taken.

The function of Box 23 is to assess the degree of degradation the communication is likely to suffer as a result of the registered error. Box 24 then decides whether it is desirable to take any corrective action, in the particular circumstances of the occasion of conversation, about the error. If the decision is to allow the slip to pass without correction, then articulatory performance continues. So failure to correct a slip is not to be equated with failure to detect the slip (Laver, 1969: 41). If it is decided that the slip should be corrected, then the first consequence is that the resultant 'error' signal from Box 24 blocks gate L1, where 'absence of error from Box 24' is a necessary condition. This is the articulation-halting mechanism.

When it is decided to correct an error, all the information for redirecting entry to the lowest necessary level of program-construction is already available in the differential decisions of Boxes 19 to 22.

If Box 19 is the only one to register an error, then re-entry is

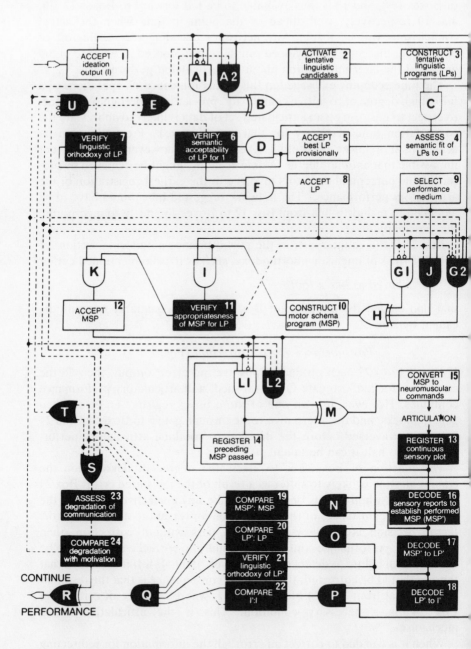

Figure 5.7 Global diagram of the logical networks for generating neurolinguistic and neuromuscular programs for speech, for monitoring the output of those networks for error, and for re-cycling detected errors to an appropriate re-programming stage.

automatically directed through gate L2. Since registration of error by Box 19 means that the error was introduced by Box 15 (or that Box 13 gave false information, as in anaesthetic intervention experiments), re-entry through L2 will allow re-use of the adequate motor schema program previously accepted by Box 12, and will allow Box 15 another opportunity to achieve a satisfactory performance. The crucial effect of a delay of 180 msec in delayed auditory feedback experiments may be partly a reflection of the fact that when Box 13 gives misleading auditory information, and the brain establishes through the monitoring function that the apparently inadequate articulatory performance was due to an error being introduced after Box 12, then this is the typical latency for the lowest-level error-detection and articulation-halting mechanism to operate. The apparent stammering that often results from delayed auditory feedback would then reflect the repeated transmission of an adequate motor schema program from Box 12 through the remainder of the neuromuscular conversion section.[2]

If Box 20 registers an error while Box 19 shows no discrepancy, then re-entry is directed through G2 to Box 10. If, on reconstructing the motor schema program, another error is created and detected by Box 11, then the feedback loop through gate J is used, and recycling occurs locally until Box 11 is satisfied.

If either Box 21 or Box 22 registers an error, then re-entry is directed through gates T, U, E and A2 to the beginning of the linguistic programming section.

Conclusion

The questions that this model provokes are interesting. For example, are errors that have their source at different levels corrected at different latencies? If slips of the tongue are the result of ephemeral malfunctions of some particular part of the model, does the permanent malfunction of that part of the model plausibly cause a recognisable speech pathology? Is it possible to manipulate experimentally the thresholds of the sub-components of the monitoring function? Would one gain more extensive insight into the speech-producing system by attempting to rewrite the model as a computer program?

Modelling of this sort is valuable to the extent that it provides a framework for research, generates further hypotheses, and encourages complementary statements from related research and related disciplines. The descriptive metalanguage used in this chapter is possibly over-powerful for the data it is called upon to handle, at present. It does have the virtue of demanding a degree of explicitness that a prose statement sometimes fails to compel. At the least, it holds some promise as a possible unifying metalanguage that might encourage the synthesis of some ideas in linguistics, psychology and neurophysiology.

Notes

1. I am indebted to Professor Robert Hanson, of the University of California at Santa Barbara, for this hypothesis.
2. This idea also emerged from discussion with Robert Hanson.

References

Abercrombie, D. (1967) *Elements of General Phonetics*, Edinburgh University Press, Edinburgh.

Boomer, D.S. (1965) 'Hesitation and grammatical encoding', *Language and Speech* 8, 148–58.

Boomer, D.S. and Laver, J. (1968) 'Slips of the tongue', *British Journal of Disorders of Communication* 3, 2–12.

Fromkin, V.A. (1971) 'The non-anomalous nature of anomalous utterances', *Language* 47, 27–52.

James, W. (1890) *The Principles of Psychology* (Vol. 1) Holt, Rinehart and Winston, New York.

Laver, J. (1969) 'The detection and correction of slips of the tongue', *Work in Progress* 3, Department of Phonetics and Linguistics, University of Edinburgh.

Laver, J. (1970) 'The production of speech', pp. 53–75 in Lyons, J. (ed.), *New Horizons in Linguistics*, Penguin, Harmondsworth.

Laver, J. (1977) 'Neurolinguistic aspects of speech production', pp. 142–55 in Gutknecht, C. (ed.), *Grundbegriffe und Hauptströmungen der Linguistik*, Hoffmann und Campe, Hamburg.

MacNeilage, P.F. (1970) 'Motor control of serial ordering of speech', *Psychological Review* 77, 182–196.

McCulloch, W.S. and Pitts, W. (1943) 'A logical calculus of the ideas immanent in nervous activity', *Bulletin of Mathematical Biophysics* 5, 115–33.

Miller, G.A., Galanter, E. and Pribram, K.H. (1960) *Plans and the Structure of Behavior*, Holt, Rinehart and Winston, New York.

Nooteboom, S.G. (1967) 'Some regularities in phonemic speech errors', *Annual Progress Report* 2, Instituut voor Perceptie Onderzoek, Eindhoven, The Netherlands.

Slips of the Tongue as Neuromuscular Evidence for a Model of Speech Production

6

Originally published as Laver, J. (1979) 'Slips of the Tongue as Neuromuscular Evidence for a Model of Speech Production', in Dechert, H.W. and Raupach, M. (eds) *Temporal Variables in Speech*, Mouton, The Hague (pp. 21–6)

In 1951, Rulon Wells put forward three descriptive laws for slips of the tongue. He suggested the First Law in the following terms:

A slip of the tongue is practically always a phonetically possible noise. The notion of phonetic possibility is most easily explained by examples. There are lots of noises that could perfectly well be English words, though they are not: 'scrin', 'scring', 'scrill', 'scriffly', 'sny', 'mip', and so on. Then there are a lot of noises that could not be English words, either because they contain un-English sounds (e.g. 'loef' – with 'oe' pronounced as in French 'l'oeuf' or German 'Löffel') or because they contain English sounds but in un-English combinations (e.g. 'ktin', 'pmip', 'ksob', where none of the letters are silent). [. . .] A few exceptions to this First Law have been recorded; but exceptions are so exceedingly rare that in the present state of linguistics they may be disregarded. (Wells, 1951: 26)

It is thus clear that by 'phonetically possible' Wells meant 'phonologically possible in the language concerned'. The exceptions to his First Law are either sub-phonemic errors which break orthodox phonetic realisation rules, or they are structural errors that violate constraints on segmental sequence. Discussion here will be limited to this first, sub-phonemic type of error. We must also leave unresolved Wells' contention that such errors seem to be very rare in spontaneous speech. It may be that their apparent rarity is actually an artefactual product of the observer's perceptual system, in that listeners tend to edit the speech they hear into canonical form, sometimes to the point of not being consciously aware of even quite blatant errors by the speaker (Boomer and Laver, 1968: 3).

Sub-phonemic errors do sometimes occur, however, and they can give us important insights into the nature of neurolinguistic units in speech production, and of strategies of neuromuscular execution of speech programs. It would take an inconveniently long time to collect a reasonable corpus of these errors from spontaneous speech. This paper describes an

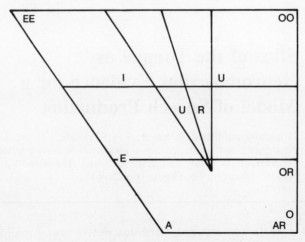

Figure 6.1 Cardinal vowel diagram of the articulatory position of the ten
stimulus-vowels PEEP, PIP, PEP, PAP, PARP, POP, PORP, PUP, POOP and
PURP.

experiment designed to provoke sub-phonemic errors of vowel quality in a
laboratory situation, and offers some initial conclusions about the relationship between the neurolinguistic representations of vowels and the muscle
systems available for their implementation. The following account gives a
brief outline of the preliminary analysis of the results of the experiment.

PUSS (Programming Unit for Stimuli Sequencing) is an electronic device
built in the Phonetics Laboratory of the University of Edinburgh, the
principle of whose design was suggested by Donald Boomer. PUSS controls
the random sequencing of two stimuli, and the durations and intervals of
their presentation to subjects. The stimuli in this case were two lights,
below each of which was a stimulus-word of the form P——P, with a medial
vowel taken from the list of stressed vowels in Received Pronunciation of
British English (Jones, 1962). This gave a set of ten words (the retracted
half-open central vowel found in 'cup' was omitted) as follows: PEEP, PIP,
PEP, PAP, PARP, POP, PORP, PUP (with the vowel found in 'push'), POOP and
PURP. Articulatory positions for these ten vowels are given in Figure 6.1.
The subject's task was to pronounce the stimulus-word as accurately as
possible immediately on presentation of the corresponding stimulus-light.
The rationale of the experiment was to push the subjects just beyond the
limits of their accurately-controllable performance, in order to explore any
regularities in the consequent effect on accuracy of vowel production. The
hypothesis underlying the experiment was that the incidence of error
should reflect neuromuscular dissimilarity in the production of the vowels
concerned.

The material for the experiment was made up as follows: the words were arranged in forty-eight pairings, six consisting of PIP-PEEP, PEEP-PIP, PUP-POOP, POOP-PUP, POP-PORP and PORP-POP. The remaining forty-two consisted of all possible pairings of PEEP, PEP, PAP, PARP, PORP, PURP and POOP, with any left-right reading effect being cancelled by having both possible sequences of each pairing. The forty-eight pairs were then divided into six groups of eight pairs, with each group including one pair from the first six mentioned and seven pairs from the last. Each group of eight pairs was then presented, after two practice trials, to one of six adult male speakers of Received Pronunciation. Each pair of words formed the material for a 30-second trial, with the stimuli being presented by PUSS initially for 0.3 seconds each, with an interval between stimuli of 0.3 seconds. After 15 seconds, the presentation rate was increased, with each stimulus lasting for only 0.2 seconds, with an inter-stimulus interval of 0.2 seconds. Each subject's performance was tape-recorded under studio conditions on a Revox A77 recorder, and analysed auditorily, spectrographically and oscillographically.

In addition to the main experiment, a supplementary group of seven pairs of words was presented to one of the same subjects, to check on the possible interaction of short vowels, both with each other (PIP-POP, PIP-PUP and POP-PUP), and with other vowels (PIP-PEP, PIP-PARP, PORP-PUP and PUP-PARP).

The P——P frame was chosen for the stimulus-words in order to facilitate segmentation, to minimise formant-transitions for convenience of spectrographic analysis, and to allow ease and speed of performance by the subjects, for whom the lingual gesture for the vowel would thus be articulatorily uncontaminated by consonantal requirements.

Most of the subjects were able to maintain adequate performance of vowel quality during the first 15 seconds of each trial. The increased presentation-rate of the last 15 seconds of the trial produced a number of errors. These fell into four categories: two sorts of diphthongs, one in each direction between the target-vowels (thus competition between PEEP and PARP gave rise to both 'PIPE' and 'PIARP', as it were); a monophthong of a quality intermediate between the two targets – often of a quite un-English quality; and a monophthong of the right articulatory quality but the wrong phonological length. Figure 6.2 gives examples of the articulatory correlates of some of these errors.

Errors were often shorter than either target would have required, of lower loudness, with inefficient (breathy, whispery or creaky) phonation, and with a longer voice onset time for the initial plosive. The support which such findings give to notions of internal monitoring of the pre-articulation stages of neurolinguistic programming (Laver, 1970; 1977) is strong.

All errors, together with sample target vowels performed by the same speaker, were edited onto a data-tape with an electronic segmenter. The auditory quality of all vowel-errors was then plotted on Cardinal Vowel

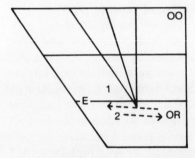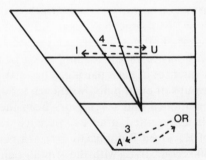

Figure 6.2 Cardinal vowel diagrams of the articulatory positions of some target vowels and errors. 1 = labialised front vowel produced by competition between PEP and POOP. 2, 3 and 4 = diphthongal errors produced by competition between PEP and PORP, PAP and PORP, and PIP and PUP respectively.

diagrams (Jones, 1962), and broad-band 4 KHz spectrograms were made. An oscillographic print-out of the speech waveform of the subject's recording was made, on which was also included a synchronised recording of the PUSS output controlling the two stimulus-lights, to allow measurement of response-latencies. The discussion that follows is based on the auditory analysis that was performed.

Because the purpose of the experiment was to examine the characteristic degradation of performance when the required task was beyond the comfortable attainment of the subjects, it is important to make clear the definition of 'error' used here. With stimuli following each other so fast, it was not possible to be sure which was the stimulus to which the subject was currently responding. This difficulty was compounded by the tendency of subjects to stop momentarily after detecting (and often trying to correct) an erroneous response. In the analysis of the recorded tapes, many wrong responses may well have escaped notice, so long as the performed vowel was a satisfactory version of either of the target vowels, regardless of whether it was in fact a 'correct' response or not. 'Errors', therefore, are to be understood here as meaning any performance of a vowel other than one of the two prescribed target vowels, either in terms of vowel quality or of vowel quantity.

Nearly all pairs of vowels interacted to produce errors. Subjects regarded the experimental procedure as a challenge to their articulatory skill, and devoted considerable effort and concentration to avoiding error, so that the overall error-rate was low. Each subject was exposed to approximately 560 stimuli, over the eight trials per subject. Total numbers of errors varied between subjects, from six to twenty-one. The most erratic performance on a single 30-second trial yielded six errors, in response to the seventy or so stimuli of the trial. The differential results for the various vowels are therefore not strong. They are, however, provocative. Out of the fifty-five trials, only seven pairs of vowels failed to produce errors of vowel quality. These seven were: PEEP-PIP, PIP-PEEP, POOP-PUP, PUP-POOP, PORP-POP, POP-PORP and PUP-POP. The first six of these, strikingly, are pairs involving long-short vowel contrasts of considerable articulatory similarity, with their order of presentation balanced to prevent a left-right reading effect. The zero-error finding is made stronger in these instances by the fact that in no case were the two pairs concerned in the same long-short contrast presented to the same subject.

Leaving out of account PUP-POP (and noting that POP-PUP was not tested), we can ask the question: 'Of all the competing pairings of vowels, why should only PEEP-PIP, POOP-PUP and PORP-POP (ignoring their order of presentation) resist what Hockett (1967) would have called this tendency to blend?' The physiological conclusion that comes to mind is couched in terms of the neuromuscular control of vowel articulation. If we consider what muscle systems might be responsible for the production of particular vowels, then the vowels in PEP and POOP, for example, are obviously performed by largely different systems. If, in indecision, the speaker issues simultaneous neuromuscular commands to both systems, then some intermediate vowel will be the consequence, as the mechanically-joint product of their simultaneous muscular contraction. This is plausibly what happened in this experiment, where hesitating between PEP and POOP, the speaker pronounced 'POEP', with a vowel similar to that in French 'peu'. The finding that a diphthong is sometimes the outcome is then explicable as a matter of the time-course of the issuing of the commands to the different muscle systems concerned. If the command for PARP, for instance, precedes very slightly that for PEEP, then 'PIPE' will be the result; if the reverse happens, then 'PIARP' will be pronounced. The alternative explanation for such diphthongs would be that an error of wrong vowel-choice is detected sensorily and very quickly corrected in mid-syllable. This would, however, fail to explain the monophthongal mistakes of intermediate qualities between the target vowels.

If we consider the three vowel-pairs that resisted erratic performance, PEEP-PIP, POOP-PUP or PORP-POP, then it is not implausible to suggest that each of the members of any of these pairs is performed essentially by the same muscle system as the other member of the pair, the muscles being contracted merely to a different degree. POOP and PUP, for instance, are reasonably thought of as being executed by a muscle system in which the styloglossus muscle is the chief protagonist component (see Figure 6.3; cf. Figure 6.1).

The muscular responsibility for PEEP and PIP is more complex, but although more muscles are probably involved, their cooperative effect is to distinguish between the two vowels in terms of greater or less movement along the same oral radius. To some extent, this is also true of PORP and POP. In this hypothesis, blending errors of these vowel pairs would not normally occur, because it is improbable to think of the brain as sending

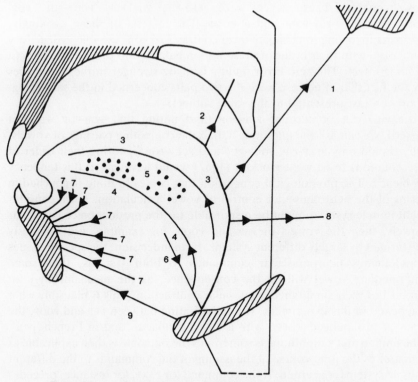

Figure 6.3 A schematic diagram of the location and action of some of the
muscles responsible for vowel production.

1. Styloglossus m.	6. Hyoglossus m.
2. Palatoglossus m.	7. Genioglossus m.
3. Superior longitudinal m.	8. Middle pharyngeal constrictor m.
4. Inferior longitudinal m.	9. Geniohyoid.
5. Transverse lingual m.	

out simultaneous but contradictory neuromuscular commands to the same
muscles.

The findings described here lend some support to a view of vowels
having primarily a motor representation, and minimise the role played in
vowel production by auditory feedback control.

The hypothesis that multiple muscle systems are active in the production
of blending errors of the sort discussed above is clearly amenable to testing
by electromyographic techniques. But if electromyographic experiment
sustains the hypothesis, and if replication experiments uphold the differential error-results, then here is an interesting example of a finding from
speech-error data enriching general phonetic theory. The principle being
put forward, of neuromuscular compatibility in the production of different
speech segments, would be applicable to many other areas of phonetic
interest. These include the study of coarticulatory phenomena, of natural

classes in phonology, of physiologically-motivated sound-change, and of physiologically-based constraints on the progression of language-acquisition and of second-language-learning.

References

Boomer, D.S. and Laver, J. (1968) 'Slips of the tongue', *British Journal of Disorders of Communication* 3, 2–11 (reprinted in this volume as Chapter 2).

Jones, D. (1962) *An Outline of English Phonetics*, (9th edition), Heffer, Cambridge.

Laver, J. (1970) 'The production of speech', pp. 53–75 in Lyons, J. (ed.) *New Horizons in Linguistics*, Penguin, Harmondsworth (reprinted in this volume as Chapter 1).

Laver J. (1977) 'Neurolinguistic aspects of speech production', pp. 142–55 in Gutknecht, C. (ed.) *Grvndbegriffe und Hauptströmungen der Linguistik*, Hoffmann und Campe, Hamburg (reprinted in this volume as Chapter 4).

Lyons, J. (ed.) (1970) *New Horizons in Linguistics*, Penguin, Harmondsworth.

Wells, R. (1951) 'Predicting slips of the tongue', *Yale Scientific Magazine* December, 9–12.

7 Cognitive Science and Speech: a Framework for Research

Originally published as Laver, J. (1989) 'Cognitive Science and Speech: a Framework for Research', in Schnelle, H. and Bernsen, N.-O. (eds) *Logic and Linguistics*, Vol. 3: 37–69, in Bernsen, N.-O. (ed.), *Research Directions in Cognitive Science: European Perspectives* (5 vols), published by Lawrence Erlbaum Associates, Hillsdale, NJ, and Hove and London, for the European Commission's Directorate XII (Forecast and Assessment in Science and Technology) and Directorate XIII (European Scientific Programme for Research in Information Technology)

1. Introduction

The objective of this chapter is to offer a framework within which the contribution to the cognitive sciences of research on fundamental aspects of speech can be placed, and to identify some major strategic research problems within a cognitive approach to speech. Companion chapters in the source-volume of this chapter cover higher-order aspects of language relevant to speech such as syntax and morphology (Klein), semantics (van Benthem), discourse (Guenthner), linguistics and parallel processing (Schnelle), and applied aspects of natural language processing (Wahlster). Chapters in other volumes of the series cover other interests which are directly relevant to the study of speech, such as psycholinguistics (Noordman) and auditory processing and recognition of speech (Patterson and Cutler). The choice is therefore made in this chapter to focus chiefly on questions of speech production, with some brief discussion of phonology, and some more extended comments on the use of speech technology as a test-bed for theories about speech production, perception, and understanding.

The long-term goal of cognitive science is to understand the integrated nature of the complex of neural, muscular and sensory systems that mediate our cognitive interpretation of the physical and social world. Spoken communication, with its three elements of production, perception and understanding, offers one of the most accessible examples of the workings of this complex of systems. Furthermore, it seems reasonable to insist that a comprehensive view of the human cognitive system would be radically incomplete without an accompanying understanding of the relationships between the production, perception and understanding of speech. Spoken communication thus deserves the concentrated attention of the cognitive sciences.

The sub-systems integrated in the overall process of spoken communication range from the ideational creation of the message to be transmitted, through the neurolinguistic, neuromuscular and neurosensory mechanisms of the speaker, through the acoustic characteristics of the transmission phase, to the sensory, perceptual and interpretive mechanisms exploited by the listener to reach an understanding of the content of the message transmitted. The integrated sub-parts can be thought of as making up a cognitive, biological and physical chain that links the speaker's mind to the hearer's mind. (A similar integrated approach is applicable to the cognitive, biological and physical systems for achieving linguistic communication through writing and reading.) An adequate description of the production, perception and understanding of speech is thus obliged to invoke strata at very many levels, from ideation to production, through acoustic transmission, and on through perception to semantic interpretation of the message. Some parts of this continuum of levels are normally considered primarily from a cognitive perspective, others from a biological or a physical perspective. A full appreciation of the task faced by the cognitive functions involved in planning, executing, decoding and understanding speech will come only from a clear understanding of the biological and physical machinery with which the cognitive system has to mesh. I shall therefore refer from now onwards to an integrated cognitive, biological and physical model of the human communication system as 'a unified cognitive model'.

There can be no doubt that we are at present a very long way from any such unified cognitive model for language performance in either the spoken or the written medium. The gap which is currently visible between high-level cognitive psychology and the lower-level neuromuscular and neurosensory systems is a very broad chasm across which all the different disciplines concerned must somehow build a scientific bridge. The necessary continuity of the bridge does not mean, nevertheless, that each different discipline should expect all collaborators to use a common set of methodological tools. This problem has been elegantly characterised by Smolensky, in his discussion of the potential contribution to cognitive science of the parallel distributed processing (PDP) paradigm applied to perceptual processing:

> The vast majority of cognitive processing lies between the highest cognitive levels of explicit logical reasoning and the lowest levels of sensory processing. Descriptions of processing at the extremes are relatively well-informed – on the high end by formal logic and on the low end by natural science. In the middle lies a conceptual abyss. How are we to conceptualise cognitive processing in this abyss?

The strategy of the symbolic paradigm is to conceptualise processing in the intermediate levels as symbol-manipulation. Other kinds of processing are viewed as limited to extremely low levels of sensory and motor processing. Thus symbolic theorists climb down into the abyss, clutching a rope of symbolic logic anchored at the top, hoping it will stretch all the way to the bottom of the abyss.

The sub-symbolic paradigm takes the opposite view, that intermediate processing mechanisms are of the same kind as perceptual processing mechanisms. Logic and symbol-manipulation are viewed as appropriate descriptions only of the few cognitive processes that explicitly involve logical reasoning. Sub-symbolic theorists climb up into the abyss on a perceptual ladder anchored at the bottom, hoping it will extend all the way to the top of the abyss. (Smolensky, 1986: 197)

The relevance for a unified cognitive model of these comments on what we might call the 'Smolensky Gap' is not that identical mechanisms and modes of description must be proposed for every stratum of the model, but rather that a multi-layered, unified, cognitive model must display a proposed continuity from the lowest to the highest layer (and vice versa), with explicit connectibility between adjacent layers. Each stratum will have mechanisms and modes of description whose nature may in principle be unique to the stratum. But the essence of a unified model involving multiple strata is that the methodology particular to the description and explanation of a given stratum must be compatible with the methodologies of at least its neighbouring strata. The search for commonalities thus has to be given priority, here as in all science, as a standard objective of scientific method. Given that the cognitive sciences currently have only a very tenuous understanding of many of the intermediate strata in the overall model, a comprehensive understanding of the continuities throughout the model is bound to take many years and much fundamental research to be achieved.

More immediately, practicable goals might consist of putting theories of sub-parts of the overall system to effective test in working simulations. In the case of speech and natural language processing, these simulations could be incorporated and tested in the computer-based systems for natural language synthesis, generation, recognition and understanding of the next fifteen years.

The structure of the chapter will be to look first at three perspectives on the human system for speech production and perception – a semiotic perspective, a biological perspective and a physical perspective. Then some recent developments in phonological theory will be briefly discussed. The chapter concludes with a discussion of the ways in which knowledge of functional characteristics of the human speech production and perception system, and about the acoustic characteristics of speech transmission, can offer design principles for machines which can produce and recognise speech, and which in their turn can act as test-beds for the theories they embody.

2. Perspectives on the Human System for Speech Production and Perception

2.1 The Semiotic Perspective

The first perspective on speech to be discussed is the semiotic perspective, where the process of communication is analysed in terms of the information conveyed between speaker and listener. This perspective comes from the general theory of signs, and an important distinction here is that between two types of semiotic function in speech – the *symbolic* function (which serves the communication of semantic information, and which is sufficiently familiar that further explanation can perhaps be dispensed with), and what we shall call (in the spirit of C.S. Peirce, the nineteenth-century American pragmaticist philosopher) the *evidential* function. In order to explain the evidential function, some brief preliminary comments should be made.

It is convenient within a semiotic approach to linguistic theory to draw a distinction between language and the medium exploited by the producer of linguistic acts of communication: language lies in the patterns formed by the medium, and not in the physical events as such, or the artefacts, of the medium (Abercrombie, 1967). A linguistic pattern is said to be distinct from its material embodiment (or manifestation, or implementation) so that where language is *form*, the medium is *substance*. Formal aspects are of two types: phonological and grammatical. These two aspects combine to show a dual patterning of structure in the speech code, which has variously been called 'double structure', 'double articulation' or 'dual structure' (e.g. Lyons, 1968: 45). The relatively small number of phonological units (including, but not only, consonant and vowel phonemes) have the sole linguistic function of being combinable and permutable, within narrowly defined structural constraints of sequence, to give distinctive shape to the very large number of grammatical units (words) whose identity and sequence in their turn make up the lexical and syntactic patterns of the language. The meaning of these lexical and syntactic patterns constitutes the semantic level of language, which is of prime cognitive relevance.

However, it deserves emphasis that insisting on the differences between form and substance offers the risk of blurring an important issue in cognitive science – the bridging of the Smolensky Gap between high-level, abstract, formal, cognitive categories and the substantial events of the observable, manifestatory surface. The major issue in cognitive science, in the concerns of this chapter, is the nature of this link between cognitive form and manifestatory substance.

Although it is essential that the spoken medium is capable of being formed into abstract symbolic patterns which carry language and have semantic meaning, the medium has other properties as well. Because the substance of the medium is an artefact, such artefacts inevitably carry evidence of the handiwork of the artisan who created them. This then is an evidential property of the medium. Among the different evidential properties of the medium, it is possible to distinguish social, psychological and physical markers of identity of the speaker (Laver and Trudgill, 1979). The cognitive perceptual work of the hearer, on listening to speech, is thus not only to register the formal, symbolic content of what was said, but also to reach conclusions about the identity and attitudinal state of the speaker. The continuing registration of the speaker's changing attitudinal state is a skill that is extremely important to the due conduct of a conversational interaction, and involves no little cognitive effort.

A further semiotic distinction can be drawn between 'communicative' and 'informative' aspects of vocal signals. A signal is communicative if 'it is intended by the sender to make the receiver aware of something of which he was not previously aware'. A signal is informative if '(regardless of the intentions of the sender) it makes the receiver aware of something of which he was not previously aware' (Lyons, 1977: 33). A unified cognitive model will need to give a comprehensive account of both communicative and informative traffic between speakers and listeners.

Finally, we should distinguish three sorts of information carried by speech: *linguistic, paralinguistic* and *extralinguistic* information. Symbolic linguistic information in speech is fully communicative, in the terms offered above, and is coded by the segmental and suprasegmental (metrical and prosodic) elements of phonology. It is important to note, however, that artefactual aspects of the speech substance used to convey communicative, symbolic contrasts also have evidential properties of accent which serve an informative role in marking regional or social affiliation.

Paralinguistic information is conveyed by what is generally called tone of voice. An example would be the whispery phonation adopted in English when the communication is intended to be conspiratorially confidential. Paralinguistic communication tends to exploit phonetic features which have a longer time-base (such as a whole phrase, or whole utterances) than the use of those same features for linguistic communication, and is a psychological marker of the speaker's attitude or mood. Such features are *para*linguistic in the sense that they form a communicative code subject to cultural convention for its interpretation; but they are not fully linguistic in that paralinguistic communication involves no possibility of the creation of meaningful sequential structures. Unlike language, where the semantic interpretability of the messages communicated relies in part on the structural sequence of the phonological and grammatical units involved, the sequence in which particular paralinguistic features are expressed carries with it no superordinate value of interpretability. Paralinguistic communication has only a vocabulary, as it were, and no syntax. The semiotic function of paralinguistic features is hence more evidential than symbolic.

Extralinguistic features in speech are those properties of vocal artefacts, such as the habitual quality of the speaker's voice, which carry neither linguistic nor paralinguistic communicative functions. They are solely informative, and solely evidential. They often have a powerful role as physical and social markers of individual identity (Laver, 1980; Nolan, 1983). They arise from such physical origins as the length and geometry of the individual speaker's vocal tract and larynx, and from phonetic, learnable origins (acquired through a lifetime's experience of speaking) such as the linguistically irrelevant aspects of detailed pronunciation that mark a speaker's accent as personally idiosyncratic.

Much work on speech has historically concerned itself with an idealised speaker, choosing to ignore as irrelevant the wide range of anatomical and physiological differences between speakers. An acceptance of the responsibility for accounting for extralinguistic facts about speakers would mean that a broader scope would have to be pursued. Failure to provide an adequate theoretical model for such extralinguistic facts as inter-speaker variability of acoustic output would mean, for example, that ambitious automatic speech-recognition systems would be deprived of the possibility of effective knowledge-based speaker-adaptation components.

The comments offered above about paralinguistic and extralinguistic features in speech concentrate on the surface realisations of such features. But obviously very many such features are the consequence of both high-level and low-level neurophysiological actions which are not very different in complexity from those that underpin linguistic communication. Indeed, there is a more immediate relationship in some cases where it becomes possible to say that paralinguistic and extralinguistic evidential features are themselves directly relevant to symbolic linguistic interests. This is because many of the same manifestatory phonetic features are exploited in all three cases, typically differing chiefly in their time-base. They constitute a background, or baseline, against which the linguistic articulations can achieve their perceptual prominence. An example would be the medium-term paralinguistic action of smiling, where the phonetic perception of linguistic events has to allow for the systematic phonetic distortion introduced by the spreading of the lips. If such perceptual adjustment is thought of as a normalising process, something of the same type of normalisation is necessary to recover the intended linguistic communication from longer-term extralinguistic perturbations, such as habitual nasalisation as a speaker-identifying feature.

A unified cognitive model should therefore account for the generation, transmission, reception and interpretation of all informative and communicative aspects of speech, and should thus address all three types of features – linguistic, paralinguistic and extralinguistic.

2.2 The Biological Perspective

The second perspective to be explored is the biological perspective, where the speaker and the listener are regarded as organic entities to be described in terms of anatomy, physiology and neurology. There are three planes of study that intersect in this perspective: the study of the normal, adult system for producing, perceiving and understanding speech and language; the study of the acquisition of speech and language by the child; and the study of speech and language 'in dissolution', or the study of speech and language pathology.

One of the benefits of studying acquisition and pathology is that while the details of the operational design and function of the normal, established adult system tend to be very opaque, an examination of the errors which are characteristic of the system during acquisition and breakdown tends to be much more revealing of functional design principles. The study of pathology, valuable in its own right, is particularly profitable, potentially, for its contribution to knowledge about the normal, adult system at the neurolinguistic and neurophysiological levels.

Caplan's (1987) recent book, which explores neurolinguistics and linguistic aphasiology, is relevant for a unified cognitive model. Caplan characterises the chief goal of these two subjects as:

> a study of the relationship between two theories: that of language structure and processing, and that of neural tissue and its functioning. Linguistic aphasiology is partly a domain of its own, and partly a source of data on which neurolinguistic theories are constructed. (Caplan, 1987: 15)

He suggests that three basic theoretical questions in neurolinguistics and linguistic aphasiology are as follows (Caplan, 1987: 12–14):

1. Is language breakdown related in natural ways to the structure of normal language?
2. Does language disorder parallel language development in reverse?
3. Can the brain support language in many different ways, or can it do so only in one or in a limited number of forms?

This last question is especially important for a unified model, in that, while the discovery of what

> neural elements and organisational features are responsible for language [is highly problematic], . . . the existence of regular patterns of breakdown – if they exist – would indicate that the ways in which neural tissue supports language are restricted, even when neural tissue is incomplete, damaged, and partially self-repaired. (Caplan, 1987: 24)

The remaining comments in this section will be addressed chiefly to the study of the normal process itself.

One of the underlying issues in a complete model of the role of speech in cognitive performance is the question of whether the brain integrates the performance of a plurality of biologically more primitive functions to serve the singular purposes of speech, or whether it is more valid to propose that speech (and, more generally, language), has its own biology.

Alvin Liberman (1984), the distinguished American experimental phonetician, characterises his earlier work on speech synthesis and the perception of speech as espousing the non-specialised view, for which he suggests the metaphor of a 'horizontal' organisation:

> As applied to language, the metaphor is intended to convey that the underlying processes are arranged in layers, none of them specific to language. On that horizontal orientation, language is accounted for by reference to whatever combination of processes it happens to engage. Hence our assumption, in the attempt to find a substitute for speech, that perception of phonological segments is normally accomplished, presumably in the first layer, by processes of a generally auditory sort, by processes no different from those that bring us the rustle of leaves in the wind or the rattle of a snake in the grass. To the extent that we were concerned with the rest of language, we must have supposed, in like manner, that syntactic structures are managed by using the most general resources of cognition or intelligence . . . But all the processes we might have invoked had in common that none was specialised for language. We were not prepared to give language a biology of its own, but only to treat it as an epiphenomenon, a biologically arbitrary assemblage of processes that were not themselves linguistic. (Liberman, 1984: 171)

In his more recent work, Liberman has abandoned the epiphenomenal view, in favour of an approach to speech and language as a specialised biological system:

> The opposite view – one towards which I now incline – is, by contrast, vertical. Seen this way, language does have its own biology. It is a coherent system, like echo-location in the bat, comprising distinctive processes adapted to a distinctive function. The distinctive processes are those that underlie the grammatical codes of syntax and phonology; their distinctive function is to overcome the limitations of communication by agrammatic means. . . . What the processes of syntax and phonology do for us . . . is to encode an unlimited number of messages into a very limited number of signals. In so doing, they match our message-generating capabilities to the restricted resources of our signal-producing vocal tracts and our signal-perceiving ears. As for the phonetic part of the phonological domain . . . I suggest that it,

too, partakes of the distinctive function of grammatical codes, and
that it is, accordingly, also special. (ibid.)

Liberman's current view that speech is supported by integrated, specialised
biological sub-systems is shared by many (perhaps most) workers in the
field today. But the extract from Liberman is quoted here at some length to
allow me to offer the following major reservation about the issue of
biological specialisation of speech: such specialisation as might exist does
not lie notably at the periphery of the system.

We can consider first the vocal apparatus for the production of speech.
In talking about the vocal apparatus, we make an arguable assumption. It
already implies that the organs used for the production of speech can be
thought of as biologically specialised for this purpose. It could be argued,
for instance, that the evolution of the physiological capacity for speech
gave mankind a biological advantage that promoted our social and
cognitive development to such an extent that the very nature of this
sociocognitive organisation is a biologically unique characteristic of the
species. Against such a view, however, is the opinion that not one
anatomical aspect of the so-called 'vocal' apparatus can be singled out as
specialised for the purposes of producing speech as such, apart perhaps
from some aspects of the neuroanatomy of the brain. Every action of the
apparatus that is involved in speaking could be claimed to exploit the
physiological capabilities (neural and muscular) of a architecture whose
primary biological functions are other than articulate speech – breathing,
sucking, biting, chewing, swallowing, licking, spitting, sniffing, clearing the
throat, coughing, yawning, lifting and straining, and phonating while
laughing, crying, threatening, and shouting (Laver, 1992).

There thus seems to be no evidence yet that the peripheral apparatus for
speech production is specialised for speech. It is true that the capacity of
the peripheral speech production apparatus to generate signals is limited,
and it may well be true that spoken language evolved in such a way as to
take account of this limitation. Considering now the perception of speech,
there seems to be no corresponding limitation of the peripheral auditory
system that is governed by criteria relevant to speech as such. Playback of
speech-recordings can be accelerated to a rate well beyond the maximum
articulatory rate without losing its intelligibility, for example.

The specialisation of the biological systems supporting speech, to the
extent that such specialisation exists, is better thought of as located
upstream from the peripheral apparatus, in the stages of neural processing.
This argument becomes clearer if we examine the analogy that Liberman
himself invokes as a parallel in the perceptual domain – that of echo-
location in the bat.

As Roy Patterson pointed out to me in a review of a draft of this chapter,
it is true that the bat's echo-location system is a coherent biological system,
as one might concede speech to be. But there the parallel ends, in that the

bat is an animal which once 'learned', in a cognitive sense, to make some rudimentary use of reflected sound, and which then progressively evolved a peripheral physiological structure to take over the responsibility for this cognitive processing, reducing the load on neural processing. There seems to be no evidence that the peripheral auditory system in man has been evolutionarily modified to reduce the cognitive burden of speech processing. The more apt analogy would have been the dolphin and other cetaceans, where elaborate echo-location systems exist with a minimum of peripheral specialisation and a maximum of specialisation at the level of neural processing.

2.2.1 THE PRODUCTION OF SPEECH

The anatomy of the vocal apparatus is an intricate assembly of different physical materials. The materials include a number of cartilages and bones, motor nerves carrying control messages from the brain, sensory nerves carrying information back to the brain, and a fairly large number of muscles, together with associated tendons, ligaments and membranes. The muscles are mostly rather small and fast-acting, and their dynamic, interlinked actions give rise to the continually changing patterns of articulation. They contract in obedience to neural commands and change the configuration of the vocal apparatus. In order for the vocal apparatus to take up a given configurational state, the different muscles have to be made to collaborate with each other in an appropriately cooperative way.

A slightly extended account of the scale of the neuromuscular control problem, for the solution of which a comprehensive unified cognitive model will have to be able to offer an explanatory account, is appropriate here. A convenient assumption is that the anatomy and physiology of the vocal apparatus can be described as if the muscles of the vocal apparatus acted in cooperative groups, or muscle systems (Laver, 1992). The benefit of making this assumption is that it allows attention to be focused on the strategic targets of cooperative muscular action, and the notion of a muscle system will therefore be discussed as if the muscles which made up the system were members of a conspiracy to achieve the articulatory, phonatory, or respiratory objectives attributed to the system. Eight functional groupings of muscles into major muscle systems can be suggested. These make up the respiratory, phonatory, hyoid, pharyngeal, velopharyngeal, lingual, mandibular and labial systems. It is further possible to isolate a number of smaller functional sub-systems within these major systems. It is also possible for a given muscle to participate in more than one muscle system or sub-system.

Another assumption, closely related to the previous one, is that the consequence of the contraction of a single muscle for the configuration of the vocal apparatus can usefully be discussed in isolation, when considering the contribution of these individual muscles to their muscle systems. In reality, of course, the muscular fabric of the vocal apparatus is densely interwoven. Any change in the length of one muscle will inevitably change the degree of passive tension in all other muscles to which it is anatomically connected. This holds true not only for the other muscles in the same muscle system, but for all other muscle systems to which a pathway of physical connection exists. The states of such passive tension, and the consequent geometry of the vocal apparatus, are then variables that the brain has to take into account in designing and executing a program of neural commands to control the contraction patterns of the active muscles, to reach a given target configuration.

In performing any movement of the human body, some muscles play a primary, protagonist role. When the protagonist role is played by multiple muscles, the primary contributors are sometimes called the prime movers, with the assisting muscles being called synergists. But two other potentially active roles can also make a crucial contribution to the success of the overall performance. The first of these is a permissive role, played by muscles acting in an opposing, antagonist function. Antagonist muscles can be either passive or active. When passive, they are inhibited from actively opposing the effort of the protagonists. When active, their part in the performance is to offer exactly the amount of checking resistance that will allow the protagonist muscles to bring the vocal apparatus to the planned configuration and no further. Reaching an articulatory target is hence often a finely graded balancing of the opposition between protagonist and antagonist forces, with collaborative action of this sort facilitating the delicately controlled precision of the overall performance. Other muscles can play a more minor role, giving support by fixating and bracing the structures on which the protagonists and antagonists are operating. From an analytic point of view, a given muscle may simultaneously be called on to play different roles, e.g. as a protagonist in the actions of one muscle system, while also performing a bracing role in the actions of another muscle system of which it is recruited as a member, and an antagonist role in another.

A general word of caution is necessary here. Many textbooks on the anatomy and physiology of speech describe the functions of individual muscles as if they were clearly understood and widely agreed. This is perhaps acceptable when relatively simple manoeuvres are being described, and to the extent that the given muscle can be thought of as acting in isolation. But as the discussion above emphasises, muscular action is typically collaborative, with complex mechanical consequences throughout the network of linked muscle systems. The detailed repercussive nature of such collaborative action in speech is still not well understood, and constitutes a major potential research area, especially in the context of synchronised inter-articulator programming.

There are nearly eighty different muscles in the vocal apparatus, most of them arranged in pairs, which can plausibly be thought of as being directly involved in the different neuromuscular strands of speech production. The process of speaking requires virtually continuous changes of tension and position of all of these muscles, with the result that the configurational state of the vocal organs is constantly in transition. One can view the changes of muscular tension and position as trajectories through the possible space of such configurations. The navigational course of every such trajectory through this space has to be planned and monitored, and the actual muscular performance that takes place has to fulfil, within acceptable limits, an intricately detailed timetable. The scale of the navigatory and coordinatory problem of physiological control that the brain has somehow to deal with in producing speech is thus immense. The gap between our present understanding and a comprehensive model is difficult to exaggerate, and the importance for a unified cognitive model of closing the gap difficult to over-emphasise.

An important debate on the nature of physiological control in speech is that between the approach that has been dubbed 'Translation Theory', and its critics who support 'Action Theory'. This debate has been succinctly and effectively reviewed by Nolan (1982). The essence of the Translation Theory approach, according to Nolan, is that:

> a translation theory is one in which a representation in terms of discrete primes, taken usually from linguistic theory, is considered as input to the speech mechanism; the problem is then defined as how these primes (abstract in that they are discrete, invariant, and lacking a time dimension) are implemented as, or TRANSLATED into, the continuously varying flow of speech articulation taking place in time. . . .
>
> Two separate questions can be distinguished which arise in work in the translation theory mould: first, what are the primes, the 'building blocks' out of which utterances are constructed? And second, what are the organisational structures within which the primes are concatenated? (Nolan, 1982: 289)

Translation Theory of the sort described above is overwhelmingly the most common type of theory of the study of speech production to date. Many primes have been postulated, almost all familiar from linguistic theory. They include the individual consonant and vowel phoneme, the syllable, the rhythmic unit called the foot, and prosodic intonational units. Many investigations have found evidence that such postulated primes indeed appear to be concerned in the organisation and control of speech. For example, Boomer and Laver (1968) found that all the above-mentioned primes play a statable role in the empirical data of speech errors, such that prosodic and metrical units to do with intonational, rhythmic and syllabic structure appear to act as organising constructs in the neuromuscular planning and execution of the performance of individual vowel and consonant phoneme segments. Unfortunately, a vicious degree of circularity is involved (probably inevitably) in arguments in favour of such 'discoveries'. Given that the search for organising entities is conducted with the help of these primes as basic descriptive tools, it is hardly surprising that the entities discovered might then be describable in terms of those *a priori* units of description. At the limit, the best that one could say on the basis of such work would be that the proposed primes were not inconsistent with the cognitive structure being investigated. A further problem has been that the involvement of the major primes has not been able to be demonstrated on a simple, straightforward and unequivocal basis, without somewhat debilitating qualifications and assumptions almost always having to be made.

One of the most general research problems in the area of the control and coordination of speech is that of the variability of speech. This is a problem that has exercised translation theorists for many years, and it may be helpful here to give a brief account of the four main types of variability that normally occur within the speech of a single speaker.

No two repetitions by a single speaker of a given phrase spoken at the same tempo are ever fully identical, at the level of articulatory and temporal microstructure. There is a type and degree of articulatory and temporal microvariability which seems to be describable only on a stochastic, quasi-random basis. This is observable, particularly in fast speech, in the area of the synchronisation of inter-articulator programming, where the movements of one articulator relative to those of another are not precisely time-locked, even though their coordination has to satisfy some necessary and demanding acoustic and auditory temporal constraints. As Kent comments:

> in the case of speech, fluent motor execution and a high event rate may depend on overlapping of movements rather than synchronisation of movements. I do not mean to imply that synchronised movements are unnecessary or undesirable, but only that exclusive reliance on the principle of 'everything moves at once' does not seem to be the plan of speech articulation. Synchronous patterning may be a default principle that is overridden by phonetic and motor learning to yield the highly overlapping patterns that characterise rapid, fluent motor execution. (Kent, 1983: 70)

An example of this would be the observable variability of timing of movement of the soft palate with respect to the tongue in the production of a nasalised vowel in repetitions of the same word at a standard rate.

Secondly, the articulatory and temporal phonetic manifestation of a given (supposedly invariant) phonological prime varies according to the phonological context in which it finds itself. Two sets of factors contribute to this contextually conditioned variability, whose articulatory aspects are usually given the label of 'coarticulation' (Kent, 1983). The first is the complex of biomechanical factors, which by definition lie beyond the possibility of control, that constrain the physical realisation of the articulation as part of a continuous muscular performance – factors of inertia, elasticity and muscle geometry. The second is the complex of phonetic factors of volitional control that the speaker has learned to prefer, as part of his habitual accent, for the pronunciation of the given phonological element in the particular sequence in which it finds itself. The coarticulatory influence of one phonological element over another adjacent or nearby element tends to be more powerful when the direction of influence is anticipatory – that is, the influence of elements yet to be pronounced on those currently being articulated tends to be more powerful than the perseveratory influence of elements pronounced earlier in the string. In English, the span of coarticulatory influence in a phrase of informal, continuous speech such as 'they strewed flowers in her path', shows itself more powerfully in the way in which the rounded lip-position for the /uu/ vowel in 'strewed' is anticipated as early as the initial /s/ of the word, while its influence typically disappears during the /f/or the /l/of 'flowers'. Such anticipatory influence on current muscular contraction patterns by events that have at that moment only a neural representation is a pivotal piece of data to be accounted for by neurophysiological models of speech control.

The third type of articulatory variability lies in the changes in speech patterns that characterise different rates of speaking. Speaking faster is not simply a matter of a linear acceleration of a standard chain of muscular activities. First, the formal phonological content of the message typically changes, with the structure of individual syllables changing (usually tending to reduce in complexity at faster rates by deleting individual consonants and/or vowels). In addition, unstressed peripheral vowels have the option of changing to a more central vowel phoneme. Examples of both a structural and a vowel change of this sort would be the reorganisation of the phrase 'Do you know a good solicitor?' from the slow, careful pronunciation represented in (1) (in the machine-readable transcription of British English developed at CSTR Edinburgh for work on speech technology, where the symbol '*' means a word boundary, and the symbol '@' stands for a central schwa vowel) to the more informal, faster pronunciation shown in (2):

(1) /d uu * y uu * n ou * @ * g u d * s @ l i s i t @*/
(2) /d * y @ * n ou * @ * g u d * s l i s t @*/.

In such circumstances, unstressed vowels in English tend also to reduce both their duration and their peripherality in vowel space, as a phonetic phenomenon without change of phonemic identity, selecting more central locations. As an aspect of the time-course of articulatory events, vowel reduction of this sort can be envisaged as an undershooting device to minimise articulatory effort (Lindblom, 1983). Undershoot of navigatory targets can thus be seen as a smoothing device, allowing the tongue (and jaw and lips) to economise on the range of articulatory displacement needed to achieve the vowel performances. However, Lindblom points out that undershoot of this sort is not simply an inevitable mechanical consequence of shorter duration. He cites Kuehn and Moll (1976) as interpreting the results of their cineradiographic work on articulatory velocities at rapid speaking rates to mean that ' "speakers have the option of either increasing velocity of movement or decreasing articulatory displacement". In other words, undershoot can be, and sometimes is, avoided by making more rapid approaches to targets' (Lindblom, 1983: 229). This emphasises that adjustments of articulatory velocities for rate are not able to be described simply as linear adjustments (Kuehn, 1973).

The fourth type of variability is at the phonological level, where the sequence of phonological primes that represent the lexical items of the phrase may differ according to the choice of formal versus informal style made by the speaker. Vowel reduction, at both the phonological and the phonetic levels, also applies as a typical process in moving from a more formal to a more informal style. There are thus obvious correlations between rapid and informal speech, and between slow and formal speech. The example of syllabic reorganisation given immediately above in fact included some phenomena of style-change, in that the pronunciation of 'solicitor', characterised above as /slist@/, is much more typical, for example, of an informal style than a formal style. A similar example[1] would be the word 'actually', which a British English speaker with an educated accent from the South of England speaking in the most formal possible style might pronounce as:

/a k t y u@ l i/.

However, if the speaker's pronunciation becomes more informal, the forms of this word could vary from the still quite formal:

/a k ch u@ l i/

through

/a k ch u l i/
/a k ch @ l i/
/a k ch l i/
/a k sh l i/

to the most informal possible pronunciation

/a sh l i/.

On average, English words have between two and three reorganised forms of this sort for informal pronunciations, though some can have very many more alternatives. However, there are other reorganisational phenomena that are typical of informal speech in addition to syllabic reorganisation. These include assimilatory phenomena, where the segments at the margins of adjacent words can optionally change in type to become more similar in some phonological respect to their neighbour. The formal pronunciation of the phrase 'Horseshoes can bring you luck' is:

/h oo s * sh uu z * k a n * b r i ng * y uu * l uh k/.

A more informal pronunciation of the same phrase would be:

/h oo sh * sh uu z * k @ m * b r i ng * y u * l uh k/

where assimilatory influence has worked (anticipatorily) on both the /s/ of 'horse', and the /n/ of 'can', to make them more like their immediately following neighbour, in terms of a feature-copying process involving the contextually controlled revision of the specification of their place of articulation. In addition, the /a/ of the formal pronunciation of 'can' has been reduced to the more central vowel /@/, as has the /uu/ of 'you' to /u/.

The phenomena of variability are thus far from explainable simply at a relatively peripheral level of phonetic processing, making appeal solely to ideas of articulatory economy of implementation. They involve some of the most central aspects of phonological planning and execution. It is, however, the more phonetic aspects of variability such as coarticulation and rate-related phenomena that have given the translation theorists the most trouble, and which Action Theory claims to be able to handle better. Nolan leads in to his discussion of Action Theory with the following comments:

> The failure of the [translation theory] models . . . to uncover simple regularities underlying speech production has led a number of researchers to question not (merely) the elements of such model – the primes, and the organisational structures – but also the fundamental concept of the translation of abstract representations into physical articulations which is the presupposition behind these models. It is this duality – between phonetic plan and execution – which critics see as misguided, and the origin of problems which may turn out to be merely artefacts of the models. (Nolan, 1982: 291–2)

Action Theory is a model that has been extended to speech from its sources in the general physiological study of the muscular control of cyclic events such as walking. Its main proponents are associated with Haskins Laboratories in New Haven, Connecticut (e.g. Fowler et al., 1980; Kugler et al., 1980; Scott Kelso, Holt, Kugler and Turvey, 1980; Scott Kelso, Tuller and Harris, 1983; Scott Kelso and Tuller, 1984; Tuller, Harris and Scott Kelso, 1982; Tuller, Scott Kelso and Harris, 1982). It is a more neurophysiologically informed approach than that taken by most translation theorists, and it attempts to provide an action-oriented, physiological description of speech which expresses intentions and muscular actions in compatible vocabulary. One of the most characteristic constructs of this approach is that of the 'coordinative structure', which consists of a 'group of muscles marshalled to act together, the degrees of freedom of the group being constrained so that together they produce activity of a specific type' (Nolan, 1982: 300). This development of the notion of a coordinative structure gives more precise shape to the general concept described earlier in this chapter of a 'muscle system' or 'sub-system'.

The idea of a coordinative structure derives from earlier concepts of neuromuscular coordination in neurophysiology, such as 'synergy', from the Soviet school influenced by Bernstein (1967), a 'collective' (Gel'fand, Gurfinkel, Tstetlin and Shik, 1971), or a 'linkage' (Boylls, 1975). Boylls, cited by Scott Kelso and Tuller (1984: 322), defined a linkage as being 'a group of muscles whose activities covary' as a result of shared efferent and/ or afferent signals, deployed as a unit in a motor task. Synergistic linking of individual muscles into cooperative systems was proposed by Bernstein (1967) as a solution to one of the basic problems of control and coordination, to which Nolan alludes in the comment quoted directly above, namely that of the multiplicity of potential degrees of freedom enjoyed by the skeletomuscular apparatus. Given that volitional muscular actions seem typically to be designed to reach relatively standard goals from innumerably different starting positions (the 'motor equivalence' or 'equifinality' problem), the linking of different parts of the apparatus in such a way that the collective degrees of freedom are minimised by mutual compensation results in a reduction of the number of control decisions needed (Scott Kelso and Tuller, 1984: 325).

The concept of a coordinative structure of linked muscles is very helpful, for example, in providing the explanatory basis for the tendency of many speakers to put a consistent bias on their articulatory activities as a recurrent aspect of their characteristic voice quality, such as a tendency to keep their lips in a rounded position throughout speech, or to use a habitually whispery mode of phonation (Laver, 1980).

One property of a coordinative structure is said to be that it is 'modulable', to support changes of rate. However, while the notion of a coordinative structure is of relevance in considerations of cyclic, auto-mated activities such as walking, where rate-changes can perhaps plausibly be seen as open to modulation of the overall structure, the complex and non-linear physiological changes in the organisation of speech at different rates are much less clearly captured by such notions. Furthermore, since a given muscle must necessarily be able to be marshalled to participate in different coordinative structures for different activities, it is hard to see how the concept of control of such marshalling is not subject to uncon-strained theoretical regress to ever-higher levels in the neurophysiological system, eventually obliging the analyst to make appeal to a type of translation theory. Given that eventual appeal to a concept of an interface between symbolic representation and neuromuscular implementation is necessary, even though Action Theory as applied to speech developed out of discontent with a Translation Theory approach, it could be argued that the two approaches are complementary rather than incompatible. The competitive issue between the two approaches then reduces to the question of the location in the unified cognitive model of the interface between the symbolic and the implementational components of the model. It also has to be said that the Translation Theory approach has been made much more explicit and systematic than has the Action Theory approach, where discussion is still focused more on mechanisms than on a complete model.

Action Theory depends heavily (and not unreasonably) on the notion that general (non-speech) mechanisms of physiological control can be extended to explain the modes of speech control. To the extent that Action Theory adopts this approach of invoking general mechanisms of physiological control to explain the physiology of speech, it commits itself to the view that speech and language do not have their own biology. While this is a parsimonious approach, it also deserves saying that speech is by far the most complex muscular skill that human beings ever achieve, and that the scale of the co-ordinatory task is almost certainly more demanding in precision and variety than is the case in other spheres of skilled neuromuscular activity. If Liberman, cited earlier, is correct in believing that speech and language have their own biology, then the modes of neuromuscular coordination observable in speech may not be able to be accounted for simply by generalisation from the control of other activities.

Of the current models of speech production, Action Theory is nevertheless among the more immediately appealing for integration in a unified cognitive approach, not least because of its close attention to neurophysiological underpinnings. It is potentially compatible, for example, with the neural network simulations of the parallel distributed processing paradigm promoted by Rumelhart and McClelland and their colleagues (1986). A Translation Theory approach, on the other hand, is eminently suitable for the representation of phonetic, phonological and linguistic knowledge in machine systems for speech synthesis and recognition, not least because virtually all the explicit rules that have been written by phoneticians, phonologists and linguists about spoken language are couched in a Translation Theory framework. Its explicitness lends itself well to current efforts to find suitable modes of knowledge representation in computer-usable form for speech technology purposes.

2.2.2 THE PERCEPTION OF SPEECH

If we turn briefly now to the perception of speech, it is useful to distinguish between the peripheral auditory apparatus that accomplishes the transformation of the incoming acoustic signal into neural signals, and the more central recognition system that processes this neural product. The more peripheral element of this chain is relatively well understood, and is well described (e.g. Carlson and Granström, 1982; Dickson and Maue-Dickson, 1982; Møller, 1983; Pickles, 1982; Schroeder, 1975). The peripheral auditory system consists of a complex biological series of mechanical and transducing elements, elegantly and simply described by Allen (1985) and Cooke (1985). In addition to its transducing function, the peripheral auditory system supplies data to achieve the functions of sound-source localisation and reverberation echo of compensation. A more detailed account of the psychophysics of the peripheral auditory system is given by Patterson and Cutler (Volume 1 of the source-volumes of this chapter, Chapter 3).

The more central element of speech perception (from the transduced neural signal to the symbolic phonological level of representation) is much less well understood at present. The identity of the individual auditory features that are exploited in speech recognition by human listeners, and the neurocomputational strategies whereby they are treated as evidence of phonological features, is the subject of a good deal of current research (Moore, 1982). It is far from clear, for example, that different listeners typically exploit the same set of temporal and spectral features, or even that a given speaker habitually relies on a standard set of features for listening to different speakers, or even to the same speaker in different ambient noise conditions. One of the topics that cognitive research will have to address is the variability of perceptual strategies both within a single listener and between a wide range of listeners.

The general psycholinguistic issues of speech perception at the phonological level are discussed by Patterson and Cutler (*ibid.*) The higher psycholinguistic levels of morphological, lexical, syntactic and semantic processing are beyond the scope of this chapter. A detailed discussion is offered by Noordman (Volume 1 of the source-volumes of this chapter, Chapter 6). An outline is also offered in Myers, Laver and Anderson (1981).

A general point about the relationship between speaking and listening is relevant at this stage. Accepting a translation model as a framework, and leaving aside the question about the nature of the units in which speech perception is centrally represented, it is interesting to consider the relation between units of perception and units of production. Are listeners' abilities to decode and recognise the speech of other speakers based in part on knowledge about transformations which map their own articulatory activities onto auditory space? And, conversely, do speakers organise and control their speech on directly auditory criteria? It is notable that human languages exploit only part of the articulatory space potentially available to the vocal apparatus (Maddieson, 1984); have these constraints developed, as Stevens (1972) suggested in his 'quantal' model of speech, in response to the differential ability of the vocal apparatus in different articulatory zones to make auditorily noticeable changes?

2.3 The Physical Perspective

In the third perspective, the speaker/hearer is modelled as a physical system, and appeal is made to a biocybernetic point of view. The speech production system can be described in terms of physical properties of the apparatus such as its three-dimensional geometry, its inertial parameters, the elasticity of muscles, the interdigitation of the muscles of the vocal apparatus and the complex mechanical consequences of contraction of a given muscle or muscle system for the other muscle systems to which it is physically connected, and limitations on the type and rate of mechanical adjustments. Also included in this approach is the cybernetic modelling of feedback and feedforward as elements of a control system.

The physical properties of the speech perception system have to take into account the biomechanical properties of the peripheral auditory system, particularly in terms of limitation of perceptual acuity by phenomena such as masking, and of enhancement processes such as lateral inhibition, and of difference thresholds for spectral and temporal resolution.

The physical perspective also addresses the acoustic link through which speech is transmitted from the speaker to the listener. The acoustics of the transmission phase, very comprehensively covered by Fant (1960; 1973) and the wealth of texts in speech signal processing, such as Oppenheim and Schafer (1975) and Rabiner and Schafer (1978), serve as the public, manifestatory link between the biological and the semiotic perspectives.

The generally accepted model of speech acoustics, for whose development Fant himself deserves much of the credit, is the so-called 'source-filter' model. This seeks to separate excitatory source phenomena from resonant filter phenomena, so that a basic analytic task in speech acoustics is how to deconvolve the relative contributions of these two components from the fully convolved time/amplitude speech waveform. The analytic theory of their deconvolution is reasonably well understood, but a major problem that speech technology has inherited from this theoretical work is that a model of speech acoustics has been worked out in great detail only for an idealised vocal apparatus which corresponds to a notional adult male speaker with a vocal tract length of 17.5 cm. The typical vocal anatomy of adult female speakers is not simply a scaled-down version of the typical male vocal tract, being different in the length-ratio of the pharyngeal component to the mouth component. The vocal apparatus of children approximates more closely, on a scalar basis, to female adult geometry than to male geometry. So we know less than is useful, from an acoustic point of view, about both adult females and children, compared to our knowledge about adult males. On a more general basis, the concentration on an idealised vocal apparatus has left us relatively ignorant about the acoustic differences between speakers which are due to anatomy rather than to accent.

A particularly crucial aspect of the acoustic characteristics of speech, for the automatic recognition of speech, lies in their variability. As pointed out earlier, no two speech events, even from the same speaker pronouncing exactly the same phrase, are ever fully identical; apparently random variation, within a distribution whose characteristics are not yet fully established for any class of speech sounds in any language, ensures that there is never any one-to-one correspondence between any given phonological prime and its detailed acoustic manifestation. Variation due to context then creates even more variability in the signals corresponding to different messages. Hypothesising the invariant (symbolic) primes represented by the randomly and contextually variable signal is the main problem of speech recognition (Perkell and Klatt, 1986). The human perceptual system copes with this inter-speaker and intra-speaker variability very well indeed: in the speech technology world, acoustic variation between speakers is a problem that is of the same order as the recognition of spoken messages from continuous speech, and variation within a single speaker is itself a major part of the speech recognition task. It is almost certain that the problem of successful recognition of continuous speech from a single speaker using a large vocabulary will be solved long before the solution is found to the problem of adequate adaptation to new speakers of different accents.

3. Recent Developments in Phonological Theory

Phonology, whose function it is to define and relate phonetic events to the segmental, suprasegmental, morphological, lexical, syntactic and semantic levels of language, is a very large and active field. General introductions to phonology can be found in Chomsky and Halle (1968) (for English), Anderson (1974) and Fischer-Jørgensen (1975). Some recent developments, particularly in suprasegmental phonology, can be pursued in Aronoff and Oehrle (1984), Beckman (1986), Clements and Keyser (1983), van der Hulst and Smith (1982), Kiparsky (1982), Ladd (1980), Liberman (1975), Liberman and Prince (1977) and Selkirk (1984). An interesting account of psychological reality in phonology is Linell (1979), and a view of the relevance of phonology to the cognitive representation of speech can be found in Myers, Laver, and Anderson (1981). This section on recent developments in phonology will be limited to some brief comments on two modern theories – Autosegmental Phonology and Metrical Phonology.

One of the principal issues in a cognitively oriented view of phonology is that of integration of subordinate parts into their superordinate structures, and the way that this integrational relationship can be represented theoretically. Recent phonological theories have taken issue with traditional approaches to this question. Van der Hulst and Smith explain the inadequacy of what they call the 'strict segmental theory' in the traditional approach in these terms:

> In the standard theory phonological representations consist, at every level, of a linear arrangement of segments and boundaries. Segments are conceived of as unordered sets of features (with a feature-specification). The boundaries interspersed between the segments are, with respect to their 'nature' and location, dependent on morphological and syntactic structure. They partition the string of segments into sub-strings that constitute possible domains for phonological generalisations (van der Hulst and Smith, 1982: 3).

(For the purpose of this chapter, the notion of 'segments' here corresponds more or less to the familiar concept of consonant and vowel phonemes.)

The standard view of generative phonology that van der Hulst and Smith are criticising is sometimes called a one-tiered approach. One recent development in phonological theory is autosegmental phonology, which proposes a multi-tiered approach, where individual tiers of organisation, consisting of linear arrangements of elements, are autonomous (Halle and Vergnaud, 1981; 1982; van der Hulst and Smith, 1982: 1–46). The benefit of proposing multiple tiers, where individual elements on different tiers are linked to each other by association lines subject to rule-governed 'association principles', is that separation of types of elements into different tiers allows certain phonological generalisations to be more easily handled. An example of this facilitation is the case where the domain of a phonological rule applies to the internal substructure of an individual complex segment (not expressible in the standard theory where segments are indivisible entities). Another example is where the domain of a phonological (or morphological or syntactic) rule is a suprasegmental aspect of the speech stream, and where the suprasegmental phenomenon is separable from any direct notion of a fixed segmental 'carrier'.

Proposing a phonological representation which consists of independent segmental and suprasegmental tiers promotes the question of the nature of the neurolinguistic control mechanisms whereby these autosegmental tiers might be coordinated and synchronised (Halle and Vergnaud, 1982: 65). This question is relevant for a cognitive model, and would have been more difficult to pose in the standard generative theory of phonology.

Another recent development in phonological theory is metrical phonology, which has grown from original proposals by Mark Liberman (1975) and Liberman and Prince (1977). As its name suggests, metrical phonology is concerned chiefly with suprasegmental (or 'prosodic') phonology. It proposes a hierarchy of phonological units in which segments are grouped into syllables, syllables into rhythmic 'feet', and feet into phonological words. Metrical properties of interest include stress and length, and metrical phonology today is 'a theory about this phonological hierarchy, its internal organisation, its role in the application of phonological rules, and its relation to the morpho-syntactic hierarchy' (van der Hulst and Smith, 1982: 30). The morpho-syntactic hierarchy referred to here is the one where segments are composed into morphemes, morphemes into words, words into phrases, and so forth.

Metrical phonology, like autosegmental phonology, is designed partly to escape from the constraint of segmental unilinearity suffered by the standard theory of phonology. Both metrical phonology and autosegmental phonology are multi-level theories, and can be regarded as largely complementary, though recent work has sharpened the debate about apparent competition between them. Leben (1982: 189) suggests that in fact autosegmental phonology can be regarded as a special case of metrical phonology. Both have encouraged a surge of work on suprasegmental phenomena, and have brought the issue of integration of the different segmental and suprasegmental levels of phonological representation to the forefront of current research in phonology. A good introduction to metrical phonology is Hogg and McCully (1987).

4. Perspectives on the Machine Systems for Automatic Speech Synthesis and Recognition

We can now return to the suggestion made in the introduction to this chapter – that the more practicable goals of research addressing a unified cognitive model of speech might consist of putting theories of sub-parts of the overall system to effective test in working simulations, in computer-based systems for natural language synthesis, generation, recognition and understanding. The simulations would consist of models of the functionality of the human system, and an important practical question is whether we already know enough about speech to make the effort of simulation worthwhile from the point of view of speech technology. An important question here is whether the simulated speech functionality is better supported by explicit knowledge-based rules from a unified cognitive theory, or by tacit knowledge developed by allowing the computer system to learn the knowledge structures for itself through automatic learning algorithms.

Automatic learning of relevant knowledge is becoming possible in the parallel distributed processing paradigm, where systems simulating neural networks can learn the necessary weightings between the elements of the network by exposure to exemplar material (Rumelhart et al., 1986). However, the ceiling of achievement in such automatic learning, though impressive, is still quite low, and it seems likely that advances of a significant order in speech technology using such techniques will only be made when a method is found of injecting explicit rule-formulated knowledge into the performance of the learning algorithms. So the answer to the question, for many years ahead, is likely to be that even from the perspective of the usefulness of applying explicit phonetic and linguistic knowledge to speech technology, it is desirable and profitable to test a unified cognitive theory by machine simulation.

Benefit also flows in the other direction. Indeed, as Miller and Gazzaniga (1984: 8) insist, 'the study of nervous systems promises to reveal important new design principles for artificial cognitive devices'. In the interests of drawing connections between speech technology and cognitive processing, the discussion that follows of automatic speech recognition will concentrate on systems which attempt to implement what is known about human performance, rather than on the solely statistical model-based systems for Hidden Markov Modelling and the like which currently dominate the commercial marketplace, and which are relatively free from explicit knowledge about speech.

4.1 Automatic Speech Recognition Systems

The attempt to develop automatic large-vocabulary systems for phonetic feature-based speaker-adaptive recognition of continuous speech is currently a major research effort in a number of institutions, in both the United States and in Europe. The process of trying to build such a system is mutually illuminating for both speech technology and cognitive science.

In phonetic feature-based automatic speech recognition, four serious problems exist. The first is straightforwardly the problem of how to extract enough information from the time/amplitude speech waveform to hypothesise plausible linguistic utterances, in the interpretive light of a rich knowledge-base of phonetic and linguistic rules. The second is the need to overcome the variability of speech patterns that has been described above as occurring within the same speaker and between different speakers. The third is the problem of how to reduce the contaminating effects of environmental and other sorts of noise. The fourth, because we are now beginning to deal with machines endowed with a certain amount of linguistic knowledge-based intelligence, is how to design a recognition system that fits as naturally as possible into the human user's cognitive world, without forcing the user into unnaturally constrained modes of cognitive behaviour. We can discuss each of these problems briefly in turn.

First, in automatic speech recognition, a distinction can be drawn between a *selective* approach, that seeks to extract conclusions about linguistic structure from the speech waveform in a bottom-up process, and an *instructional* approach, that compensates for the impoverished nature of the linguistic material represented in the speech waveform by inserting amplifying hypotheses based on top-down knowledge of linguistic expectations.[2] A basic attitude in linguistic knowledge-based approaches to automatic speech recognition is that a solely selective method will never succeed in the objective of recognising large vocabularies of continuous speech from multiple speakers of different accents. The human listener brings a wealth of knowledge to bear on the interpretation of the speech signal. This allows the listener to generate hypotheses not simply in a selectional, detection mode based only on surface evidence, but also in a creative, instructional manner illuminated by the empathetic ability to predict what the speaker is most probably intending to say. It will be a very long time before we succeed in making machines with a capacity for automatic learning that will emulate the scale and richness of linguistic knowledge that the human listener brings to bear on the task of speech recognition.

Secondly, as well as incorporating the necessary linguistic knowledge to recognise speech, machines will have to deploy a capacity to compensate for differences within and between speakers. Differences within a single speaker form an inherent part of the main speech recognition task. This is because linguistic hypotheses can only be deployed efficiently by taking such variability into account, by exploiting knowledge about the distribution in acoustic space of the speaker's typical performance. A successful automatic recognition system will have to be able not only to compensate for intra-speaker variability of this sort, but will also have to become speaker-adaptive, progressively moulding its own performance over time to the analysed characteristics of the speaker to whom it is attending.

In order to deal with inter-speaker differences, techniques for speaker-normalisation are necessary to reduce the more gross differences between speakers of the same accent that derive from such factors as differences of vocal tract length, especially between men and women, that have been commented on earlier. Such techniques are increasingly based on auditory modelling approaches.

Human listeners seem able to adjust to new accents fairly efficiently. For automatic speech recognition systems based on an explicit phonetic and linguistic rule-based approach, this constitutes one of the most severe problems in the whole domain. The worst problem of all for explicit linguistic knowledge-based systems is that the inventory of consonants and vowels differs in different accents and, therefore, the phonemic specification of pronunciation in a recognition system's dictionary has to be rewritten for every new accent, if possible on an automatic basis. It would not be so serious if the correspondences between accents were one-to-one, with every instance of one sound in one accent being able to be replaced with a different but standard pronunciation in the other. An example where this does happen is the case where speakers of an educated Southern English accent pronounce a diphthongal vowel of changing quality in words such as 'day', whereas speakers from most parts of Scotland pronounce such words with a monophthongal vowel of unchanging quality. In most cases of comparison of two accents of English, however, the specification of vowels is chosen from a list (or 'vowel-system') which varies in number between the two accents. This means that there are many cases where two distinct words in one accent cannot be distinguished in the other, and vice versa. An example of this is that where almost all accents of England distinguish between the words 'tot' and 'taught', Scots accents typically make no distinction. Similarly, 'pull' and 'pool' are not distinguished by many Scots accents. On the other hand, Scots distinguishes between 'tide' and 'tied', whereas many English accents do not. The mapping of the one accent onto the other is thus partly unpredictable, and the system dictionary's pronunciation element has to be written anew for each new accent.

A related problem of speaker-adaptation concerns the question of vocabulary size. Training of the recognition system by the new speaker on every single word of the vocabulary is impracticable once the vocabulary exceeds some 1500–2500 words (for reasons of sheer tedium for the user). Such systems therefore have to be constructed to be intelligently adaptive to the style of pronunciation of the new speaker, often by extrapolating from partial information about one aspect of the speaker's pronunciation to a prediction of the anticipated pronunciation of another aspect. Some progress is being made in this area, but the issue of how to make knowledge-based speech recognition systems successfully speaker-adaptive is one of the most challenging problems in speech technology today.

Thirdly, to achieve practical success, a sophisticated automatic speech recognition system will have to be able to perform a number of tasks such as noise reduction, and spatial localisation of the speaker. Noise reduction relevant to machine (and human) recognition of speech is of three types: the cancellation of noise of relatively stationary spectral and temporal characteristics, such as the 50–60 Hz hum from fluorescent lights, or air-conditioning noise; the identification and filtering of more dynamic types of noise that contaminate the speech signal, such as passing traffic, doors slamming, or telephones ringing; and, most difficult of all, the compensation for the sound of competing speech from other speakers that the listener would prefer to ignore. This last is the 'cocktail party' problem, and it is interesting to consider what resources the human listener requires to cope with the last and most severe of these types of noise.

Stereophonic exploitation of phase differences in the signal may allow the listener to localise the chosen speaker in space, in a horizontal plane (Blauert, 1983). This can be simulated in an automatic speech recognition system by means of a microphone array. Secondly, the ability to minimise the effects of competing voices (or of competing, dynamic non-human noise) depends on the listener's knowledge of the characteristic statistical properties of such signals. This is much harder to simulate on a machine, because a prerequisite is a typology of signals that distinguishes between human speech and non-speech, and, even more challenging, a knowledge-base which would allow the listener or the machine to track an individual speaker's voice partly on the basis of statistical coherence of the data from that speaker's voice versus the data from the voices of other competing speakers.

Fourthly, there is the task of ensuring a comfortable fit between the machine's capabilities and the user's cognitive world. One of the problems that naive users are likely to have with apparently intelligent machines is that they are likely to overestimate both the intelligence and the world-knowledge internalised within the machine. A lay user encountering for the first time a database query system using speech input and output for the human/computer interface may be misled into attributing to the system more world-knowledge than the machine actually has. The more fluent the working of the natural language interface, the more the lay user may have the impression that the human quality of the interface is matched by a human scale of understanding of the real world. One of the ergonomic problems in this area is, therefore, the education of the user-population about the limitations that currently remain on the capacity of machines to 'know' about the world on any truly intelligent basis. Part of this education will have to focus on the efficient identification to the user of constraints on the domain of knowledge of the machine: how to offer the user an understandable and usable model of the machine's knowledge of the world is itself a difficult ergonomic research problem.

Other ergonomic problems that will have to be addressed are, first, the question of maintaining, in the face of restrictions of vocabulary size, some sensible and natural principles of vocabulary selection. Second, in the same vein, any attempt to constrain the grammatical characteristics of the speech material input to the system will be counter-ergonomic. Third, it will be essential to develop mechanisms for the easy extension of the system's vocabulary, to the user's requirements. Finally, it is certain that the recognition systems of tomorrow will continue to make mistakes. Indeed, it is equally certain that they will always make mistakes, just as humans make perceptual mistakes. Only the scale of error, and perhaps the nature of error, will change. But it is going to be very important for the ergonomic acceptability of recognition systems that a simple, comfortable and effective method of error-correction is devised.

4.2 Text-to-Speech Synthesis Systems

In the area of speech synthesis and text-to-speech conversion systems, although the speech technology is perhaps somewhat more advanced than in the case of automatic recognition systems, it is noteworthy that no synthesis system yet exists which could be said to have a fully natural quality. This is a reflection of the fact that we do not yet know enough about the acoustics either of speech or of speakers. Similarly, no text-to-speech conversion system yet exists which knows enough about patterns of intonation and rhythm relevant to the discourse structure of the messages of the text to perform the task of reading aloud with a degree of discourse control comparable to that of a human reader. What this reflects is that we do not yet know enough about our cognitive strategies for understanding written language to be able to make a machine simulate our ability. Despite this idealistic criticism, it should be said that the most ambitious of the text-to-speech systems available today show considerable linguistic sophistication and an impressive ability to generate continuous speech of a degree of intelligibility that is close to complete (Allen, Hunnicutt and Klatt, 1987). The next phase of research will need to address two massive problems: how to make the systems sound more naturalistic rather than simply intelligible, and how to give them the ability to make their prosodic performance relevant to the discourse structure of the messages which they seek to communicate.

A valid criticism of modern research on synthesis is that, in the search for intelligibility, the pursuit of naturalness has been unduly overlooked. All commercial synthesis systems available today have voice qualities that are transparently mechanical, and not one would pass the test, over any length of time, of being taken for a genuine human voice. This is acceptable in some applications, provided that intelligibility is achieved. But to expand the field of applications of synthesis to its full potential range, it will be essential not only to guarantee intelligibility, but also to equip synthetic voices with substantially more natural, human-like qualities than is the case at present. The reason for this is not simply that in some applications it may be desirable for the synthetic voice to pass for human (though this is controversial), but that the unnatural quality of present synthesis is ill-designed for the human perceptual system to process efficiently.

Pisoni, Nusbaum and Greene (1985) have shown that the perception of synthetic speech imposes a severe load on the cognitive processing capacity of listeners. This has many thoroughly undesirable consequences for the use of synthetic speech in the human/computer interface: synthetic speech loses full comprehensibility when listened to over any long period, with the attention of listeners tending to oscillate between 'tuning in' and 'fading out'; it is distinctly tiring to listen to for any length of time; it rapidly loses intelligibility in ambient noise or channel noise; and worst of all, because of the high cognitive loading, current synthetic speech is often unsuitable for use in applications where a competing demand for the listener's cognitive capacity exists. Pisoni et al. (1985: 1675) comment that 'the presentation of a synthetic message might not be detected at all under very demanding or life-critical conditions in severe environments'. The use of synthetic speech in current military aviation applications, or noise-contaminated factory applications, for example, is far from free of these problems.

One way to improve this situation is to enhance the naturalness of synthetic speech, and bring the attributes of the signal closer to those to which the human cognitive process is presumably evolutionarily optimised to attend with ease and efficiency. There are signs that research into synthetic speech is beginning to move in this direction.

Another enhancement of the perceived naturalness of synthetic speech, though this time in the area of prosodic control of intonation and rhythm, would be the ability to signal the discourse structure of the message. To do this, a level of rule-based linguistic control is necessary which takes into account structural relations between phrases and sentences in the same paragraph, and preferably in the same overall text. Unfortunately, the very large majority of current text-to-speech systems are limited to controlling prosodic relations between linguistic units within the span of a single phrase or simple sentence. Almost all state-of-the-art text-to-speech systems pronounce phrases and sentences as if they were isolated from their co-text, and as if knowledge about the grammatical and phonetic aspects alone of the individual words was sufficient. In many neutral instances, this is possibly satisfactory, and none of the intended sense of the message is lost. But even if it were simple (and it is not) to incorporate structural knowledge about items that have already been mentioned in the earlier co-text, some other types of knowledge about discourse are needed before a text-to-speech system could approach a human speaker's level of competence in this area. The prosodic structure of normal discourse often reflects knowledge about the semantic structure of the real world. In order to construct an appropriate prosodic structure for the pronunciation of the phrases and sentences which make up a given text, the system therefore sometimes has to know something about the semantic relationship between the objects and concepts mentioned in those phrases and sentences.

Few text-to-speech systems currently include any except the most rudimentary representation of semantic information. When the appropriate pronunciation of the sentence demands knowledge of such real-world semantics, then control of the relevant intonational and rhythmic performance is deficient. This can be seen in the following example. Almost all text-to-speech systems currently available would pronounce the sentence

These are VAXes, not microcomputers

wrongly, as

These are +VAXes, not microcom+puters

where the symbol '+' indicates the beginning of the syllable showing the auditorily most prominent intonational peak, by appeal to a standard rule which locates the prominence on the last lexical form of the phrase, on a syllable identified by the dictionary as the main accented syllable of the word concerned. A future system displaying appropriate knowledge of real-world semantics would place the intonational peak differently, as in

These are +vaxes, not +microcomputers.

This pronunciation would reveal the fact that the system, like a human reader, knew the semantic fact that a vax is a computer, but that its type is not that of a *micro*computer. In other words, it would be able to communicate the opposition that the writer had intended to convey, namely between a vax as a type of minicomputer and smaller systems called microcomputers.

A further area where the design of text-to-speech systems could be much enhanced by adequate knowledge of a comprehensive model of the corresponding human domain is the extralinguistic and paralinguistic area of speaker attributes and voice-typing. A number of currently available text-to-speech systems provide a facility for changing the voice type of the system. The usual facility is to offer a range of voices from which to choose (male/female, same accent), and/or to allow the user to change the voice type of the given speaker, changing the apparent personality of the speaker. Tempo and pitch-range can also sometimes be altered by the user.

Options of this sort are the vestigial beginnings of a range of facilities that will become increasingly important as text-to-speech output becomes more natural. At the moment, guaranteed intelligibility is difficult enough to achieve. But as synthetic speech of an acceptably natural quality becomes accessible, there will be an increasing realisation that the voice-type of a text-to-speech system needs to be able to be adjusted to suit the communicative and informative function to which it is being applied. The voice-type needed for an application in a primary school teaching-support role is very different from that needed in an aircraft avionics emergency alert application. More subtly, the voice of persuasion is phonetically different from that of the voice of neutral reporting, even in the same speaker.

There are four layers of voice-typing involved. The first concerns the vocal consequences of physical factors of sex, age and individual anatomy. The second involves accent factors due to the regional and social milieu of the speaker. The third is to do with the reflection of a speaker's personality in the general quality of his voice, to the extent that such a connection exists. The fourth is a matter of the more momentary changes in the individual speaker due to ephemeral variations of mood and attitude. All these factors are potentially capable of systematic description, and are thus candidates for inclusion in the sophisticated vocal engineering systems of the future. Because the voice is such a rich vehicle for evidence about the characteristics of its owner, any speech technology system that is able to control its presentation of vocal attributes of the apparent speaker in a way convincing to its human listeners, and appropriate to its intended communicative function, will be radically more plausible as an interlocutor in any conversational interaction.

Vocal engineering may look to phonetics and social psychology for a suitable descriptive model for different voice types, and for the link between given voice types and the perception of particular speaker attributes (in the terms mentioned above of the physical, social and psychological attributes of speaker identity, as well as shorter-term attributes of mood and attitude). But, unfortunately, it will look largely in vain. Descriptive theories linking voice-type and speaker attributes constitute a neglected area of research in both phonetics and social psychology. Some of the limited research that has been done in the last decade is reported in Laver (1980), Laver and Trudgill (1979), Laver and Hanson (1981), Scherer (1982), Scherer and Giles (1979) and van Bezooyen (1984). The requirements of speech technology might give this area some of the needed research impetus.

4.3 Basic Versus Pre-competitive Research

There are many technical problems that will have to be solved before speech technology can reach some of the ambitious goals for which it is striving. These technical problems often pose very serious challenges to the technical competence and imagination of the speech technology community. The recognition of continuous speech by the acoustic-phonetic feature approach, for example, calls for an advanced and complex system design, particularly because the adequate representation and deployment of the necessary phonetic and linguistic knowledge-base in a computer-usable form still lies out in the twilight zone just beyond our present competence. Similarly, the generation entirely by rule of synthetic speech of a truly naturalistic human-equivalent quality is just beyond our present reach. But many of the future advances desired will only be possible if basic research into the characteristics of natural language and speech is vigorously pursued.

The discussion about the relationship between speech technology and cognitive research may be sharpened at this point by drawing a distinction between basic research and relatively shorter-term pre-competitive, industrially-oriented research. The European programmes which currently support advanced research and development in information technology, such as the European Community's ESPRIT Programme, and the national programmes such as the United Kingdom's Alvey Programme, typically support pre-competitive research in speech and natural language processing which is aimed directly, if not necessarily in the shortest term, at industrial exploitation. As such, the major activity in such pre-competitive research is enabling current scientific knowledge to be expressed in a way that it is usable for computer-based speech technology purposes close to the potential marketplace. The research supported seldom addresses basic theoretical issues, and most often is limited, apart from issues of usability, to ones of comprehensiveness of coverage. The balance of emphasis has tended therefore to be more on the consolidation of present knowledge than on making the major theoretical advances which will constitute future knowledge: by definition, it has been concerned more with technology and engineering than with advancing science as such.

The speech and natural language processing technology that lies at the end of the present development cycle thus stands on a platform of current scientific understanding made available to industry by pre-competitive and enabling research. In the domain of the cognitive sciences, the range and degree of this scientific understanding is still rather limited. For future generations of speech and natural language processing products to continue to evolve, and to maintain economic competitiveness in an international market, it is clear that major advances in our basic understanding of the human processes of speech and language production, perception and understanding are essential. Underlying this assertion, it has to be declared, is the assumption that the design of machines in this area is best illuminated by functional principles of human cognitive operation.

A stringent test of the adequacy of basic theoretical models of human cognition is an attempt to build working versions of such models through computer simulation, as indicated earlier. These simulations can be viewed not only as theoretical test-beds, but also as software prototypes of potential machines in speech and natural language processing technology. The effort to achieve a unified cognitive model and the effort to build advanced speech technology machines are hence mutually supportive and mutually relevant. Each needs the other to succeed.

5. Summary Conclusions: Avenues for Research

It would seem appropriate to conclude this survey of the place of speech research in cognitive science by summarising some of the avenues along which promising and relevant advances may be made towards the goal of a unified cognitive model for speech.

The most fundamental issue in a cognitive approach to speech is the nature of the linkage between linguistic form and speech substance. This problem can he approached through an examination of the production, perception and understanding of speech, during acquisition, normal use or pathology, and through the relation between these and speech acoustics.

In speech production, the most general issue is the nature of the central units of cognitive representation, and the strategic and tactical aspects of control. The issue surfaces in such areas as the control of sequence and serial order, the temporal control of durational and rhythmic activity, the control of inter-articulator synchronisation, the study of coarticulatory phenomena, the reorganisation of articulatory and acoustic performance in changes of rate and style, and the nature of compensatory strategies to reach relatively standard goals from contextually different starting-points.

Over-arching questions in speech production concern the validity of generalisation from and to other motor skills than speech, and whether speech and language have a specialised biology. Another important avenue is the general issue of integration. This includes the general physiological question of how sensory feedback (of auditory, touch, contact pressure, muscle-tension and joint-position information) participates in on-going control. It also includes the strategic question of how superordinate structures integrate their subordinate elements (e.g. how metrical units of rhythm in speech integrate their syllabic constituents, or how syllabic structures integrate their segmental elements).

In speech perception and understanding, a major issue is the question of how the listener exploits prosodic information in the stream of speech to reach a hypothesis about the pragmatic value and the relevance to discourse structure of the speaker's utterances. In order to do this, the listener has to call on knowledge about the context of the conversation, on the knowledge the speaker can be assumed to possess, and in particular on the knowledge that the speaker and the listener can be assumed to share. Perhaps the broadest of all the topics in this area is the problem of how a speaker and a listener successfully collude in the progressive development of the cognitive structure of a conversation.

The general topic of research methodology is itself an issue. Much valuable research can be and has been done by studying the activities of the normal brain controlling the normal apparatus in normal speech production and perception. But it is worth reminding ourselves of the value of trying to penetrate an opaque system through an examination of its characteristic malfunctions. The study of neurolinguistics, aphasiology and other topics in speech pathology, worthwhile for its own sake, offers some unusual opportunities for establishing the operational characteristics of the normal, healthy system. A similar argument can be made for the study of speech and language acquisition, as a window on otherwise hidden processes in the adult production, perception and understanding of speech and language.

In keeping with the more comprehensive approach to semiotic behaviour that was urged earlier in this chapter, the value of paralinguistic research into cognitive aspects of affect and emotion is worth underlining. It may be plausible to assert that speech and language have their own biology, but it is unlikely in the extreme that such relatively young systems, phylogenetically speaking, are completely divorced from their antecedents in more ancient structures.

In the widest semiotic perspective on the study of speech and language, a necessary contribution to the creation of a cognitive model of speech and language that is fully general to human beings is the development of an adequate understanding of the extralinguistic factors specific to individual speakers and hearers. The aspect of speech and language production and perception that is idiosyncratic to the individual, and that which is general to the individual's speech community, are figure and ground to each other. Neither can be fully understood in the absence of an understanding of the other.

From the point of view of research on speech and language, a unified cognitive model should thus try to account for the generation, transmission, reception and interpretation of all informative and communicative aspects of speech, and should therefore address all three types of semiotic features mentioned earlier – linguistic, paralinguistic and extralinguistic features. Such a model is not only more comprehensive from a unified cognitive point of view, but is also of more general semiotic relevance than one which allows the inclusion of only linguistic features.

This chapter has argued that the aim of establishing a unified cognitive model, where there is an unbroken succession of links in the chain of implementation from ideation through to speech production and speech acoustics, and from auditory perception through to semantic interpretation, is no longer a wildly quixotic ambition. This is not to suggest that such an unbroken chain can be welded together in the near future; it will take generations of basic research before a convincingly integrated model is fully achieved. But a long-term drive towards a unified cognitive model now seems more practicable, in the sense of a growing readiness on the part of the disciplines concerned to accept an organising framework for research which is as wide as the cognitive sciences themselves, in which the individual subjects can pursue a unifying theme of mutual relevance.

Notes

1. I owe this example to Jonathan Harrington.
2. This distinction was first brought to my attention by Henry Thompson of the Department of Artificial Intelligence at the University of Edinburgh.

References

Abercrombie, D. (1967) *Elements of General Phonetics*, Edinburgh University Press, Edinburgh.

Allen, J.B. (1985) 'Cochlear modelling', *IEEE ASSP Magazine* (January), 3–29.

Allen, J., Hunnicutt, M.S. and Klatt, D. (1987) *From Text to Speech: The MITalk System*, Cambridge University Press, Cambridge.

Anderson, S.R. (1974) *The Organisation of Phonology*, Academic Press, San Diego.

Aronoff, M. and Oehrle, R.T. (eds) (1984) *Language Sound Structure: Studies in Phonology Presented to Morris Halle by his Teacher and Students*, MIT Press, Cambridge, Mass.

Beckman, M.E. (1986) *Stress and Non-stress Accent*, Foris Publications, Dordrecht.

Bernsen, N.-O. (ed.) (1989) *Research Directions in Cognitive Science* (5 vols.), Lawrence Erlbaum Associates, Hillsdale, NJ.

Bernstein, N.A. (1967) *The Coordination and Regulation of Movement*, Pergamon Press, London.

Bezooyen, R. van (1984) *Characteristics and Recognisability of Vocal Expressions of Emotion*, Foris Publications, Dordrecht.

Blauert, J. (1983) *Spatial Hearing*, MIT Press, Cambridge, Mass.

Boomer, D.S. and Laver, J. (1968) 'Slips of the tongue', *British Journal of Disorders of Communication* 3, 2–12.

Boylls, C.C. (1975) 'A Theory of Cerebellar Function with Applications to Locomotion: II. The Relation of Anterior Lobe Climbing Fiber Function to Locomotor Behavior in the Cat', *COINS Technical Report 76–1*, Department of Computer and Information Science, University of Massachusetts.

Caplan, D. (1987) *Neurolinguistics and Linguistic Aphasiology: An Introduction*, Cambridge University Press, Cambridge.

Carlson, R. and Granström, B. (eds) (1982) *The Representation of Speech in the Peripheral Auditory System*, Elsevier Biomedical Press, Amsterdam.

Chomsky, N. and Halle, M. (1968) *The Sound Pattern of English*, Harper and Row, New York.

Clements, G.N. and Keyser, S.J. (1983) *CV Phonology: A Generative Theory of the Syllable*, MIT Press, Cambridge, Mass.

Cooke, M.P. (1985) 'A computer model of peripheral auditory processing', *National Physical Laboratory Report*, Division of Information Technology and Computing, No. 58/85. Teddington, England.

Dickson, D.R. and Maue-Dickson, W. (1982) *Anatomical and Physiological Bases of Speech*, Little, Brown and Company, Boston.

Fant, G. (1960) *Acoustic Theory of Speech Production*, Mouton, The Hague.

Fant, G. (1973) *Speech Sounds and Features*, MIT Press, Cambridge, Mass.

Fischer-Jørgensen, E. (1975) *Trends in Phonological Theory*, Akademisk Forlag, Copenhagen.

Fowler, C., Rubin, P., Remez, R.E. and Turvey, M.T. (1980) *Implications for Speech Production of a General Theory of Action*, in Butterworth, B. (ed.), *Language Production*, Vol. 1. Academic Press, London and San Diego.

Gel'fand, I.M., Gurfinkel, V.S., Tstetlin, M.L. and Shik, M.L. (1971) 'Some problems in the analysis of movement', in Gel'fand, I.M., Gurfinkel, V.S., Fomin, S.V. and Tstetlin, M.L. (eds), *Models of the Structural-functional Organisation of Certain Biological Systems*, MIT Press, Cambridge, Mass.

Halle, M. and Vergnaud, J.R. (1981) 'Harmony processes', pp. 1–23 in Klein, W. and Levelt, W. (eds), *Crossing the Boundaries in Linguistics*, Reidel, Dordrecht.

Halle, M. and Vergnaud, J.R. (1982) 'On the framework of autosegmental phonology', pp. 65–82 in van der Hulst, H.G. and Smith, N. (eds) *The Structure of Phonological Representations* (2 Vols), Foris Publications, Dordrecht.

Hogg, R. and McCully, C.B. (1987) *Metrical Phonology: A Coursebook*, Cambridge University Press, Cambridge.

Hulst, H.G. van der and Smith, N. (1982) 'An overview of autosegmental and metrical phonology', pp. 1–46 in van der Hulst, H.G. and Smith, N. (eds), *The Structure of Phonological Representations* (2 Vols), Foris Publications, Dordrecht.

Kent, R.D. (1983) 'The segmental organisation of speech', pp. 57–90 in MacNeilage, P.F. (ed.), *The Production of Speech*, Springer-Verlag, New York.

Kiparsky, P. (1982) 'From cyclic phonology to lexical phonology', pp. 131–76 in van der Hulst, H. and Smith, N. (eds), *The Structure of Phonological Representations* (2 Vols), Foris Publications, Dordrecht.

Kuehn, D.P. (1973) 'A cinefluorographic investigation of articulatory velocities', unpublished doctoral dissertation, University of Iowa.

Kuehn, D.P. and Moll, K.L. (1976) 'A cinefluorographic study of VC and CV articulatory velocities', *Journal of Phonetics* 4, 303–20.

Kugler, P.N., Scott Kelso, J.A. and Turvey, M.T. (1980) 'On the concept of co-ordinative structures as dissipative structures: I. Theoretical lines of convergence', pp. 3–47 in Stelmach, G.E. and Requin, J. (eds), *Tutorials in Motor Behavior*, North-Holland, Amsterdam.

Ladd, D.R. (1980) *The Structure of Intonational Meaning: Evidence from English*, Indiana University Press, Bloomington.

Laver, J. (1980) *The Phonetic Description of Voice Quality*, Cambridge University Press, Cambridge.

Laver, J. (1992) *Principles of Phonetics*, Cambridge University Press, Cambridge (in press).

Laver, J. and Hanson, R. (1981) 'Describing the normal voice', pp. 51–78 in Darby, J. (ed.), *Speech Evaluation in Psychiatry*, Grune and Stratton, San Diego.

Laver, J. and Trudgill, P. (1979) 'Phonetic and linguistic markers in speech', pp. 1–32 in Scherer, K.R. and Giles, H. (eds), *Social Markers in Speech*, Cambridge University Press, Cambridge.

Leben, W. (1982) 'Metrical or autosegmental', pp. 177–90 in van der Hulst, H. and Smith, N. (eds), *The Structure of Phonological Representations* (2 Vols), Foris Publications, Dordrecht.

Liberman, A.M. (1984) 'On finding that speech is special', pp. 169–98 in Gazzaniga, M.S. (ed.), *Handbook of Cognitive Neuroscience*, Plenum Press, New York.

Liberman, M (1975) 'The intonational system of English', PhD dissertation, MIT, distributed by Indiana University Linguistics Club.

Liberman, M. and Prince, A. (1977) 'On stress and linguistic rhythm', *Linguistic Inquiry* 8, 249–336.

Lindblom, B. (1983) 'Economy of speech gestures', pp. 217–46 in MacNeilage, P.F. (ed.), *The Production of Speech*, Springer-Verlag, New York.

Linell, P. (1979) *Psychological Reality in Phonology*, Cambridge University Press, Cambridge.

Lyons, J. (1968) *Introduction to Theoretical Linguistics*, Cambridge University Press, Cambridge.

Lyons, J. (19770 *Semantics* (2 Vols), Cambridge University Press, Cambridge.

Maddieson, I. (1984) *Patterns of sounds*, Cambridge University Press, Cambridge.

Miller, G.A. and Gazzaniga, M.S. (1984) 'The cognitive sciences', pp. 3–14 in Gazzaniga, M.S. (ed.), *Handbook of Cognitive Neuroscience*, Plenum Press, New York.

Møller, A.R. (1983) *Auditory Physiology*, Academic Press, London and San Diego.

Moore, B.C.J. (1982) *An Introduction to the Psychology of Hearing* (2nd edition), Academic Press, London and San Diego.

Myers, T., Laver, J. and Anderson, J. (eds) (1981) *The Cognitive Representation of Speech*, North-Holland, Amsterdam.

Nolan, F. (1982) 'The role of Action Theory in the description of speech production', *Linguistics* 20, 287–308.

Nolan, F. (1983) *The Phonetic Bases of Speaker Recognition*, Cambridge University Press, Cambridge.

Oppenheim, A.V. and Schafer, R.W. (1975) *Digital Signal Processing*, Prentice-Hall, Englewood Cliffs, NJ.

Perkell, J.S. and Klatt, D.H. (eds) (1986) *Invariance and Variability in Speech Processes*, Lawrence Erlbaum Associates Inc., Hillsdale, NJ.

Pickles, J.O. (1982) *An Introduction to the Physiology of Hearing*, Academic Press, London and San Diego.

Pisoni, D., Nusbaum, H.C. and Greene, B. (1985) 'Perception of synthetic speech generated by rule', *Proceedings of the IEEE* 73, 1665–76.

Rabiner, L.R. and Schafer, R.W. (1978) *Digital Processing of Speech Signals*, Prentice-Hall, Englewood Cliffs, NJ.

Rumelhart, D.E., McClelland, J.L. and the PDP Research Group (eds) (1986) *Parallel Distributed Processing: Explorations in the Microstructure of Cognition*, Vol. 1: *Foundations*; Vol. 2: *Psychological and Biological Models*, MIT Press, Cambridge, Mass.

Scherer, K.R. (1982) 'Methods of research on vocal communication: Paradigms and parameters', pp. 136–98 in Scherer, K.R. and Ekman, P. (eds), *Handbook of Methods in Nonverbal Behavior Research*, Cambridge University Press, Cambridge; and Editions de la Maison des Sciences de l'Homme, Paris.

Scherer, K.R. and Giles, H. (eds) (1979) *Social Markers in Speech*, Cambridge University Press, Cambridge.

Schnelle, H. and Bernsen, N.-O. (eds) *Logic and Linguistics*, Lawrence Erlbaum Associates, Hillsdale, NJ.

Schroeder, M.R. (1975) 'Models of hearing', *Proceedings of the IEEE* 63, 1332–50.

Scott Kelso, J.A. and Tuller, B. (1984) 'A dynamic basis for action systems', pp. 319–56 in Gazzaniga, M.S. (ed.), *Handbook of Cognitive Neuroscience*, Plenum Press, New York.

Scott Kelso, J.A., Holt, K.G., Kugler, P.N. and Turvey, M.T. (1980) 'On the concept of co-ordinative structures as dissipative structures: II. Empirical lines of evidence', pp. 49–70 in Stelmach, G.E. and Requin, J. (eds), *Tutorials in Motor Behavior*, North-Holland, Amsterdam.

Scott Kelso, J.A., Tuller, B. and Harris, K.S. (1983) 'A dynamic pattern perspective on the control and co-ordination of movement', pp. 137–73 in MacNeilage, P.F. (ed.), *The Production of Speech*, Springer-Verlag, New York.

Selkirk, E. (1984) *Phonology and Syntax: The Relation Between Sound and Structure*, MIT Press, Cambridge, Mass.

Smolensky, P. (1986) 'Information processing in dynamical systems: Foundations of harmony theory', pp. 194–281 in Rumelhart, D.E., McClelland, J.L. and the PDP Research Group, *Parallel Distributed Processing: Explorations in the Microstructure of Cognition*, Vol. 1, *Foundations*, MIT Press, Cambridge, Mass.

Stevens, K.N. (1972) 'The quantal nature of speech: Evidence from articulatory-acoustic data', pp. 51–66 in David, E. and Denes, P.B. (eds), *Human Communication: A Unified View*, McGraw-Hill, New York.

Tuller, B., Harris, K.S. and Scott Kelso, J.A. (1982) 'Stress and rate: Differential transformations of articulation', *Journal of the Acoustical Society of America* 71, 1534–43.

Tuller, B., Scott Kelso, J.A. and Harris, K.S. (1982) 'Interarticulator phasing as an index of temporal regularity in speech', *Journal of Experimental Psychology: Human Perception and Performance* 8, 460–72.

Part II

The Description of Voice Quality

8 Language and Non-verbal Communication

Originally published as Laver, J. (1976) 'Language and Non-verbal Communication', in Carterette, E.C. and Friedman, M.P. (eds) *Language and Speech* (Vol. 7 of *Handbook of Perception*, Academic Press, New York), pp. 345–63

1. Introduction

It is a commonplace that the most frequent type of social interaction we experience is face-to-face communication in a conversational situation. 'Conversation' is often loosely taken to mean the exchange of factual, propositional 'semantic' information by verbal means, through the use of spoken language. In fact, conversation normally involves very much more than this. In addition to verbal communication of semantic information, many different types of information are conveyed by non-verbal means. For the purpose of this chapter, conversation will be interpreted as including both verbal and non-verbal communication.

The perceptual skills that allow us to participate successfully in face-to-face conversation are very complex. We are usually obliged to make a continuous stream of judgments, on the basis of the other participant's verbal and non-verbal behaviour, about a wide spectrum of information. We not only have to decode what he is saying, but also have to be able to draw conclusions about the speaker's personal characteristics, in terms of his physical, social, and psychological attributes and his momentary affective state, and shape our own behaviour into an appropriate relationship with him. Also, since conversation requires an intricate temporal meshing together of the performances of the participants, we need to be able to judge when a speaker is coming to the end of his current contribution to the conversation and is expecting a reciprocal contribution from us as the listener.

It would seem reasonable to suppose that language and non-verbal communication should have a degree of mutual relevance and that one might therefore look to linguistics for a major point of entry into the study of non-verbal communication. Unfortunately, the implicit pre-eminence given to 'language', over 'non-verbal communication' in the title of this chapter is an accurate reflection of the view taken by most scholars working in linguistics of the relative importance (and hence the mutual isolation) of the study of these two areas. The last sentence in what is arguably the most influential book in linguistics, de Saussure's *Course in General Linguistics* published in 1916, ends as follows: 'The true and unique object of linguistics is language studied in and for itself' (de Saussure, 1966: 232). As Lyons (1970: 8) points out, this principle of autonomy has had the result of promoting the study of language as a formal system, to the great benefit of the subject; the sophistication of modern linguistic theories owes much to the concentrating effect of obedience to this dictum. An inevitable and regrettable consequence, however, has been that the non-verbal aspects of communicative behaviour that accompany, support and complement language have, until recently, received little attention from most linguists. Most of the major contributions to the study of non-verbal communication have come from psychology, psychiatry, anthropology and sociology. Not surprisingly, research into conversational communication has not been the unified enterprise that it might have been in different historical circumstances; it has tended, rather, to be atomistic, with its focus normally on a single communicative channel.

Over the last decade or so, however, there seems to have been a swing toward a more broadly based attitude, promising a more productive union between linguistics and the other disciplines interested in social interaction (Argyle, 1969; 1973; Barnlund, 1968; Crystal, 1969; Duncan, 1969; Ekman and Friesen, 1969; Gumperz and Hymes, 1972; Hinde, 1972; Horton and Jenkins, 1971; Laver and Hutcheson, 1972; Moscovici, 1972; Sebeok, Hayes and Bateson, 1964; Siegman and Pope, 1972; Smith, 1966; Sommer, 1967; Sudnow, 1972). It is becoming more accepted that behaviour in face-to-face conversation can profitably be viewed as an interwoven complex of many different communicative strands and that these strands have an important degree of mutual relevance. Language is still seen as a principal strand, but nevertheless as only one among many strands contributing to the totality of the communication. The view is taken that the communicative function of language can be better understood in the context of the operation of the other strands than in isolation. All the means of communication capable of conventionally coded, short-term manipulation – language, tone of voice, gesture, posture, body-movements, spatial orientation, physical proximity, eye contact and facial expression can be thought of as being woven together to form the fabric of a conversation, and we can understand the communicative texture of an interaction best by seeing the relationship of the different strands (Laver and Hutcheson, 1972: 11).

2. Components of Non-verbal Communication

The behavioural features that make up non-verbal communication have often been called *paralinguistic*. They are paralinguistic in the sense that they share some of the criterial characteristics of linguistic features (see

Hockett, 1960; Crystal, 1969; Lyons, 1972) without sharing all of them – for example, they share with language the characteristic of being arbitrary, convention-governed codes, but they lack the 'duality of structure' intrinsic to language. They can be thought of as paralinguistic in another sense also, as being parasitic upon language, in the opinion at least of some writers, who see them as deriving relevance solely from their auxiliary relationship with linguistic communication.

There are almost as many interpretations of the term 'paralinguistic' as there are writers on the subject (Crystal, 1971). Some writers, such as Crystal himself (1969), Crystal and Quirk (1964) and Trager (1958), restrict the term to the vocal features that accompany spoken language; others, such as Hill (1958) and Abercrombie (1968), apply it to both vocal and non-vocal features. In this chapter, we shall follow Abercrombie's usage and distinguish between the audible, vocal features of non-verbal communication and the visible, non-vocal features.

A. Audible Paralinguistic Features

Abercrombie divides paralinguistic features into those that can function quite independently of verbal behaviour and those that have communicative function only when occurring simultaneously with verbal elements. He calls the former *independent* elements and the latter *dependent* elements. Independent audible paralinguistic features include interjections, such as the click of impatience, that have to occur sequentially separately from the performance of verbal elements. Dependent audible paralinguistic features are much more varied and include everything normally referred to as comprising *tone of voice*. Tone of voice, one of the most powerful vehicles for the expression of emotion (Crystal, 1969; Davitz and Davitz, 1959; Dusenbury and Knower, 1939; Fairbanks and Pronovost, 1939; Kramer, 1963; 1964; Thompson and Bradway, 1950), constitutes to some extent a ground against which the figures of the verbal elements of language have to be perceived. This is because the vocal parameters upon whose use the perception of tone of voice depend are not substantially different in principle from those that serve the perception of verbal elements. The difference lies rather in the time-scale involved. The vocal realisations of verbal elements are momentary, while those that act as evidence for tone of voice are rather longer-term. The phrase 'He spoke in an angry tone of voice' normally refers to a stretch of speech of at least one sentence and possibly many more. Because tone of voice relies on longer-term evidence than does verbal communication, one difference that does exist in the way that the vocal resources are exploited is that tone of voice is usually communicated by the perception of the range of a particular vocal parameter, while verbal identification is more a matter of the location of a speaker's momentary choice within that range. An example of this can be found in the control of loudness. In our culture, the attitude of anger is often paralinguistically communicated by boosting the overall range of loudness of speech production, compared with the lower range of loudness that characterises emotionally neutral speech. In either case, of anger or of neutral emotion, the speaker manipulates loudness on a momentary basis within the relevant range when using contrastive stress to signal such verbal differences as the one between *import* (noun) and *import* (verb).

A paralinguistic feature similar to loudness-range is pitch-range. Others include the tempo and continuity of speech and the long-term control of the auditory quality of speech production. Within the control of quality in this sense there are two separable areas: first, auditory quality that derives from the shape of the vocal tract and, second, auditory quality that derives from the fine detail of the mode of vibration of the vocal cords. Vocal tract quality, when the effect persists over a number of verbal elements in an utterance, can be exemplified by the persistent nasality of 'whining', the auditory colouring lent to a voice by the lips being held in a smiling position, or the tendency (mostly by female speakers) to keep the tongue raised toward the palate and the lips protruded and rounded when speaking to babies. Laryngeal quality, which derives from the mode of vibration of the vocal cords, when the effect persists over a number of verbal elements in the utterance (and where this is not a permanent characteristic of the speaker's voice production), can be exemplified by the so-called *breathy voice* in which confidential intimacies are often uttered or by the *harsh voice* associated with anger.

B. Visible Paralinguistic Features

1. PROXIMITY

Interpersonal distance is a paralinguistic feature that is surprisingly delicately controlled by participants in a conversation. Distances are chosen (sometimes to margins of accuracy of two inches or less in a standing face-to-face situation) that are appropriate not only to the status and intimacy relationship between the speakers but also to the particular phase (opening, medial, closing) of the interaction and to the physical and social locale in which the interaction takes place. The study of this feature has been given the name *proxemics* by Edward Hall, one of the major pioneers in its investigation. More research has been carried out on proxemics (Hall, 1959; 1963; 1964; 1966; Little, 1965; Sommer, 1959; 1969; Watson and Graves, 1966) than on any other visible paralinguistic feature, with the exception perhaps of the group of features that are discussed below under the heading *kinesics*. Proximity is also very strongly a culturally-relative code. A 'close' distance to an American is 'distant' to an Arab (Hall, 1963), and in inter-cultural encounters of this sort a continual readjustment of proximity takes place, with each participant seeking to reestablish his culturally comfortable distance each time it is disturbed by the other participant's movement.

2. SPATIAL ORIENTATION

It is obviously important for participants in face-to-face interaction to be able to see each other's faces, for facial expression and eye-contact purposes and, more generally, to be mutually available for visual inspection so that proximity, posture, body movements and gestures can be registered and appropriately controlled. In most situations, participants have a certain degree of choice as to exactly how to arrange themselves spatially to achieve this. The choice they make is informative about their view of the nature of the interaction between them. Sommer (1965) has shown, for example, that people choose different seating arrangements depending on the type of task they are engaged in. At an oblong table, people tend to choose adjacent positions (either side by side or across a corner) if they are involved in a cooperative task but choose seats opposite to each other if they are in competition. (See also Argyle and Kendon, 1967; Mehrabian, 1967; 1969.)

3. KINESIC FEATURES

a. POSTURE. The choice of posture is as much a limited code of systematic behaviour as any other paralinguistic feature. Scheflen estimates that for Americans there are less than thirty 'culturally standard postural configurations which are of shared communicative significance' (Scheflen, 1964: 316).

There are nevertheless levels of choice within the posture parameter. If we consider an interview between a high-ranking officer and an enlisted soldier, the posture of each participant, though almost certainly different, will reflect a number of levels of systematic control. First, their posture will be appropriate to an interview situation. Second, it will signal their assessment of the degree of formality that obtains in that particular interview. Third, it will reflect their view of their status relationship.

The ability of posture to signal people's view of their relationship with each other (Mehrabian, 1968) is also visible in small group interactions, in mechanisms closely related to those of spatial orientation. Scheflen (1964) draws attention to the way that members of small groups tend to delimit the group and protect it from invasion by outsiders. Group members, when standing, tend to form a circle; when seated in a row, the members at each end tend to 'turn inward and extend an arm or a leg across the open spaces as if to limit access in or out of the group' (Scheflen, 1964: 326). Scheflen calls this effect *bookending*. He also discusses how members of small groups covertly demonstrate sympathy with a particular fellow-member by choosing a similar, 'congruent' posture, or antipathy by choosing a non-congruent posture.

Further possibilities of choice exist that have to do not with interpersonal relationships but with the temporal segmentation of the interaction. Scheflen points out that, where an interaction has a structured progression (as in a psychiatric interview), each major stage in the progression is associated with a different posture. A substantial change in posture is thus likely to be linked to a substantial thematic change in the linguistic structure of the interaction.

b. BODY MOVEMENTS AND GESTURES. Body movements and gestures are the moment-to-moment variations superimposed on an overall posture and can involve minor movements of the whole body or movements of only a part of the body, as in arm, hand or head gestures. A major figure in the general study of bodily movement, to which he has given the widely accepted name *kinesics*, is the American anthropologist Ray Birdwhistell (1952; 1970).

In the terms introduced earlier, body movements and gestures as paralinguistic features have both independent and dependent aspects. Those conventional gestures that can stand for (or be replaced by) verbal elements (such as the head gestures of assent and dissent in our culture) are clearly independent. It is important to recognise, however, that there is no single independent gesture that has a meaning universally accepted by all cultures. Independent gestures are always part of a culturally relative arbitrary code (La Barre, 1947).

The dependent body movements and gestures, necessarily associated with speech, fall into two groups. The first group is used to regulate the exchange of speaker role, signalling either the incipient completion of a speech contribution or the incipient beginning of a contribution by the still silent listener. Kendon (1972) has called this a *regulative* function. Movements include the speaker raising his head to look directly at the listener at the end of his contribution, and also turning his head to look away from the listener, either when beginning to speak or during points of silence where he wants to keep possession of the role of speaker (Kendon, 1967).

The second group of body movements and gestures is more closely connected to the speech material itself, in a variety of ways. First, they are said to be used in a function of linguistic support, in serving to identify the grammatical class of the verbal units involved. Birdwhistell (1970: 121–6) has maintained that gestures that move away from the body (*distal* gestures), versus those that move toward the body (*proximal* gestures), are closely associated with verbal elements to do with distinctions of time and space and with various personal pronouns. Distal gestures accompany *he, she, it, those, they, that, then, there, any, some*, while proximal gestures accompany *I, me, us, we, this, here* and *now*. Past and future tenses are said to be linked to distal gestures, but with movement toward the rear and the front of the body, respectively. Birdwhistell goes on to suggest that characteristic gestures accompany plurality, such prepositions as *on, over, under, by, through, behind* and *in front of*, and such temporal adverbs as *slowly* and *swiftly*. He is supported in some of these findings by Kendon (1972).

Another function of body movements and gestures, noted by Bird-whistell, is to act as devices of emphasis, where the vocally most prominent verbal element in a stretch of speech tends to have a pattern of movement associated with it that stands in contrast to patterns of movement elsewhere. Body movements are also used to mark the semantic segmentation of a speaker's discourse, with each new development or new topic tending to be marked gesturally or with a slight body movement (Efron, 1942; Ekman and Friesen, 1969) or a small change in proximity (Erickson, 1975). This signalling of *thematic segmentation* is at a more delicate level than the grosser segmentation of topic signalled by large postural shifts mentioned earlier. Birdwhistell (1970) and Kendon (1972) would take this segmental signalling to an even more delicate level than thematic marking, however. They suggest that segmental units of speech, from groupings of phrases to individual phrases down even to the level of individual syllables, can be marked by distinct types of body movements and gestures. The marking by body movements of the rhythmic structure of speech at the level of the phrase is supported to some extent by Dittman and Llewellyn (1969) and by Dittman (1972).

If these findings about body movements and gestures being characteristically associated with both the grammatical identity and the syntactic structure of the speaker's linguistic performance are valid for the majority of speakers, then this provides the listener with a very important set of perceptual clues for decoding the verbal material of the conversation.

4. GAZE DIRECTION AND EYE CONTACT

Like proximity, with which it has an interactive relationship, gaze direction and eye contact is a paralinguistic parameter that participants in conversation control very delicately, and one to which they are very sensitive (Gibson and Pick, 1963; Kendon, 1967).

Eye contact seems to have three chief functions: monitoring the behaviour of the other participant, regulating the progress of the interaction, and controlling the expression of mutual affiliation (Kendon, 1967; Argyle and Dean, 1965).

There are two regulative aspects. The first is captured in the everyday saying 'to catch someone's eye'. To establish mutual eye contact is normally a necessary prerequisite to interaction and has the effect of signalling acknowledgement that channels of communication are open. The second aspect, mentioned above in connection with head movements, is in regulating the time-sharing of the interaction in negotiating moments of exchange of the speaker role. Eye contact on the part of the current speaker, when this is associated with appropriate intonation, body movement, and facial expression, offers the speaker role to the listener. A speaker's refusal to make eye contact signals resistance to giving up possession of the speaker role. Eye contact on the part of the listener, when an exchange of roles is offered by the current speaker, signals willingness to take over the speaker role, and a refusal to make eye contact declines the offered exchange. Characteristically, when a listener has accepted the offered speaker role by making eye contact, he then breaks eye contact as he begins to speak (Kendon, 1967).

During speech, the speaker looks intermittently at the listener, in order to monitor such details as whether or not the listener is attending to his messages and understanding them, whether or not the listener is making preliminary signals toward laying claim to the speaker role, and so forth. Correspondingly, the listener also makes intermittent eye contact, to offer appropriate signals of attention, comprehension, and agreement and, when relevant, to effect an exchange of speaker role. A participant becomes very uncomfortable when he can be seen by, but not himself see, the other participant (Argyle, Lalljee and Cook, 1968).

The amount of mutual gaze between participants in a conversation is an index of the degree of their affiliation. The greater the affiliation, the greater the amount of eye contact, and vice versa (Argyle and Dean, 1965; Exline, 1963; Exline and Winters, 1965; Kendon, 1967).

The degree of affiliation between the participants, though a powerful factor, is not the only one that affects the amount of mutual eye contact. Within the generalisation that eye contact lasts normally somewhere between 30 per cent to 65 per cent of the duration of the encounter, and that each glance lasts between three and ten seconds (Argyle and Dean, 1965), such factors as the topic of conversation and the sex and proximity of the speakers have all been shown to influence the amount of mutual gaze. Exline, Gray and Schuette (1965) have shown that eye contact is reduced when the topic becomes more personal. Women tend to engage in more eye contact than men, and same-sex pairs in more than opposite-sex pairs. When people are forced into greater proximity than is conventionally comfortable within the rules of the culture, the amount of eye contact decreases sharply to almost zero – as for example in a crowded elevator, where almost no eye contact is made during any conversation that might take place (Argyle and Dean, 1965).

5. FACIAL EXPRESSION

Together with tone of voice, facial expression must be one of the most powerful vehicles for the communication of emotion. Yet there is a surprising imbalance of research into facial expression as an independent paralinguistic parameter, compared with research into its use as a dependent parameter.

The major part of research has been directed toward facial expression as an independent parameter. The central controversy has been about whether communication of emotion by facial expression is universal or culturally relative. Birdwhistell (1970) is one worker who maintains that there is no single facial expression with a universally recognisable meaning, and that all facial expressions are culturally relative. His view is opposed by Tomkins (1962), Ekman and Friesen (1969), Ekman, Sorenson and Friesen (1969), Eibl-Eibesfeldt (1970; 1972) and Ekman (1972). There is a good commentary on the 'universalist' hypothesis in Dittmann (1972: 58–62), and two recent books on the subject are Izard (1971) and Ekman, Friesen and Ellsworth (1972).

There has been very much less research into facial expression as a dependent paralinguistic parameter. In this sense, facial expression can be considered dependent when used in support of verbal acts, such as interrogation, for example, with raised eyebrows. It would seem more profitable, however, to consider facial expression as being dependent not solely on verbal elements but, rather, on a combination of verbal elements and other non-verbal parameters, such as posture, gesture and eye control. This is to assert that, in its dependent aspect, facial expression is necessarily multi-valued and that a specific expression has communicative value only in conjunction with a constellation of particular values on both verbal and non-verbal parameters. This view can probably be extended to cover the dependent aspects of any non-verbal parameter, with dependency being to the total system of communication rather than merely to the linguistic component of the total system.

3. Interactional Synchrony

We have seen above that, while language conveys primarily semantic information, non-verbal communication conveys a wide range of different sorts of information. Non-verbal elements do sometimes convey semantic information, as in the case of independent vocal interjections and independent gestures. But much of the information conveyed by non-verbal means has the function of assisting the process of linguistic communication rather than substituting for it. The possibility of acts of linguistic communication taking place at all is facilitated by the regulative function of non-verbal behaviour. We saw that this function served to open the channels of communication, as it were, and to manage the necessary meshing of performances in negotiating exchanges of the role of speaker; it also indicated the progressions within the interaction from one major stage to the next. It is at this point, where the structure of the interaction is paralleled by the thematic semantic structure of the linguistic interchange, that the regulative function of non-verbal communication begins to blend with what we might call its *demarcative* function. Non-verbal communication was seen to convey perceptual clues to the listener about the demarcation of linguistic boundaries at different levels – semantic, grammatical and phonological.

In order for the regulative and the demarcative functions of non-verbal communication to succeed, various elements of non-verbal behaviour have to be in synchrony with aspects of the speaker's linguistic behaviour. This is particularly true of the visible paralinguistic features, all of which consist of very highly skilled muscular movements, as does speech itself. It is hardly surprising that there should be a high degree of temporal coordination of the different activities of vocal and non-vocal movement – to manage such an intricately skilled, multi-level performance on an asynchronous basis would be astonishing. So there is a synchronisation in the majority of bodily movements of a speaker, such that, comparing speech and body movement, the 'points of change in the flow of sound coincide with the points of change in body movement' (Kendon, 1970: 103).

What is perhaps more unexpected is that it has been found that self-synchrony of movements in the speaker is very often matched by an empathetic synchrony of movements by the listener, in what has been called *interactional synchrony*. The phenomenon was first described by Condon and Ogston (1966; 1967; 1971). It does not imply that the listener copies the movements of the speaker, merely that 'the boundaries of the movement waves of the listener coincide with boundaries of the movement waves in the speaker' (Kendon, 1970: 103). The actual movements of the listener may be quite different from those of the speaker and are probably on a much smaller scale. One plausible and economical perceptual explanation offered for interactional synchrony by Kendon (1970: 122–3) is that the linguistic output by the speaker is being decoded by the listener on an analysis-by-synthesis basis – that is, by intermittently sampling the speech output, setting up running hypotheses about future output and checking from time to time for correct prediction (Neisser, 1967) – and that the resultant interactional synchrony is a reflection of the listener's empathetic processes toward this end.

Kendon also advances an interesting social explanation for the phenomenon, to do with mechanisms for signalling involvement in interaction, rather similar to the 'bookending' phenomenon described by Scheflen (1964) and discussed earlier. Kendon (1970) writes:

> To *move* with another is to show that one is 'with' him in one's attentions and expectancies. Coordination of movement in interaction may thus be of great importance since it provides one of the ways in which two people signal that they are 'open' to one another, and not to others. (p. 124)

4. Interactional Equilibrium

The discovery of interactional synchrony highlights the fact that conversation is an intricately controlled act of collaboration between speaker and listener. We might expect that such collaboration would have other interesting aspects, and one of these is the phenomenon of interactional equilibrium.

We saw earlier that participants in an interaction adjust their mutual proximity until they reach their culturally comfortable distance for the type of encounter in which they are engaged. There will be momentary oscillations around this distance, but an equilibrium is maintained when the two participants come from the same cultural background. This is an example of collaboration in the maintenance of equilibrium on one interactional parameter. Argyle and Dean (1965) suggest that a more complex equilibrium process is managed by participants manipulating the interplay of a number of conversational parameters. They write:

> [A]n equilibrium develops for 'intimacy', where this is a joint function of eye contact, physical proximity, intimacy of topic, smiling, etc. This equilibrium would be at a certain degree of intimacy for any pair of people. . . . [I]f one of the components of intimacy is changed, one or more of the others will shift in the reverse direction in order to maintain the equilibrium.

Some of the evidence for this was mentioned above, where increased intimacy of topic and increased proximity were both said to have the effect of decreasing the amount of eye contact. A similar compensation between parameters is where interactants standing uncomfortably close in a face-to-face position change their spatial orientation to face each other at right angles, or stand side-to-side (Argyle and Dean, 1965). Similarly, seated interactants, too far apart, lean forward in their chairs, in a compensatory change of posture.

5. Indexical Information in Conversation

Explicit identification has been offered, so far in this chapter, of only three types of information communicated in conversation – semantic, demarcative and regulative. But there is a fourth type of informational exchange to which occasional allusion has been made, which is possibly the single most important aspect of conversation as a social act. This is the communication of information about aspects of the personal identity, attributes and attitudes of the participants. A prime function of conversation is to enable the interactants to manage their psychosocial relationship, and this relationship is subject to continuous negotiation throughout each interaction (Cicourel, 1972); it is on the basis of the conclusions the interactants draw about each other's personal characteristics that such negotiation is conducted. Abercrombie (1967: 6), borrowing one meaning of the term from the nineteenth-century American pragmaticist philosopher C.S. Peirce, has called this sort of information *indexical*, and writes of different types of *index*, classified in terms of the particular characteristic indicated. He distinguishes between indices that signal group membership (such as a particular regional accent), indices that individuate a speaker within his group (such as an idiosyncratic aspect of pronunciation or a speech defect), and affective indices that reveal changing states of the speaker's emotional condition (such as the loud, high-pitched, harsh voice of anger).

The examples of indices cited above all involve vocal evidence, but clearly indexical conclusions can also be drawn from non-vocal evidence. Gathering indexical information from a wide range of perceptual sources, we rapidly construct a profile of our fellow-participant in an interaction: first, about his physical characteristics of sex, age, size, physique, state of health, degree of fatigue and so forth; second, about his social identity, in terms of regional origin, social status and associated social values, and possibly occupation; and third, about psychological details of his personality and momentary mood. We will also come to conclusions about his assessment of our own individual characteristics and of his attitude to the current encounter, and we shape our behaviour accordingly, projecting the indexical persona (to the extent that it is within our control to do so) that we hope will achieve the effect we desire.

An account of indexical information in conversational interaction has to go beyond the verbal and non-verbal behaviour considered so far. We make indexical judgments about a person from wider evidence than this – for example, from visible aspects, such as person's style of dress and his habitual gait, and from audible aspects, such as the characteristic individual quality of his voice. So, indexical information is to be found not only in linguistic and paralinguistic phenomena but in extralinguistic factors as well.

We all make indexical judgments about other people every day, and these judgments influence our social relationships very powerfully. We seldom question the validity of the judgments we make, yet there is considerable evidence that, in subjective judgments of this sort, particularly on the basis of such extralinguistic vocal information as the quality of a man's voice, we operate with stereotypes (Cantril and Allport, 1935; Eisenberg and Zalowitz, 1938; Fay and Middleton, 1939; 1940a,b; Kramer, 1963; Laver, 1968; Starkweather, 1964). We tend to 'reach the same indexical conclusions from the same evidence, but the conclusions themselves may, on occasion, bear no reliable relation to the real characteristics of the speaker'. (Laver, 1968: 51).

The stereotypical nature of indexical perception compounds the possibility of making wrong indexical judgments when dealing with vocal phenomena that are ambivalent between paralinguistic non-verbal communication and extralinguistic voice quality. Consider the case of a participant in a conversation speaking in a *whispery voice*. The listener has to decide whether the speaker is using whispery voice as a paralinguistic feature, signalling secretive confidentiality, or whether whispery voice is part of the speaker's voice quality (either habitually or because of temporary laryngitis). Listeners often draw the wrong conclusion, and sufferers from laryngitis have often had the experience of people whispering back to them, mistaking the physical, medical index of laryngitis for a psychological, attitudinal index of conspiracy.

6. Conclusion

It has been argued in this chapter that language and non-verbal communication have an important degree of mutual relevance, if one views the communicative resources exploited in face-to-face interaction as a unified, total system, rather than in the more traditional atomistic way. The discovery of the phenomena of speaker synchrony, interactional synchrony and interactional equilibrium lends support to this position. It was also said that non-verbal communication accompanies, supports and complements language, and this was justified by appeal to the regulative and demarcative functions of non-verbal communication, in helping language to convey semantic information. The point was made, finally, that one of the most important functions of face-to-face interaction is to manage interpersonal relations, and that this is achieved largely by the communication of indexical information gathered from not only linguistic and paralinguistic but also extralinguistic aspects of behaviour.

References

Abercrombie, D. (1967) *Elements of General Phonetics*, Edinburgh University Press, Edinburgh.

Abercrombie, D. (1968) 'Paralanguage', *British Journal of Disorders of Communication* 3, 55–9.

Argyle, M. (1969) *Social Interaction*, Methuen, London.

Argyle, M. (1973) *Social Encounters*, Penguin, Harmondsworth.

Argyle, M. and Dean, J. (1965) 'Eye contact, distance and affiliation', *Sociometry* 28, 289–304.

Argyle, M. and Kendon, A. (1965) 'The experimental analysis of social performance', in Berkowitz, L. (ed.) *Advances in Experimental Social Psychology*, Academic Press, New York.

Argyle, M., Lalljee, M. and Cook, M. (1968) 'The effects of visibility on interaction in a dyad', *Human Relations* 28, 3–17.

Barnlund, D.C. (ed.) (1968) *Interpersonal Communication*, Houghton Mifflin, Boston.

Birdwhistell, R.L. (1952) *Introduction to Kinesics*, University of Louisville Press, Louisville, Kentucky.

Birdwhistell, R.L. (1970) *Kinesics and Context*, University of Pennsylvania Press, Philadelphia.

Cantril, H. and Allport, G.W. (1935) *The Psychology of Radio*, Harper, New York.

Carterette, E.C. and Friedman, M.P. (eds) (1976) *Language and Non-Verbal Communication*, Volume 7 of *Handbook of Perception*, Academic Press, New York.

Cicourel, A.V. (1972) 'Basic and normative rules in the negotiation of status and role', pp. 229–58 in Sudnow, D. (ed.), *Studies in Social Interaction*, Free Press, New York.

Condon, W.S. and Ogston, W.D. (1966) 'Sound film analysis of normal and pathological behavior patterns'. *Journal of Nervous and Mental Disease* 143, 338–47.

Condon, W.S. and Ogston, W.D. (1967) 'A segmentation of behavior'. *Journal of Psychiatric Research* 5, 221–35.

Condon, W.S. and Ogston, W.D. (1971) 'Speech and body motion synchrony of the speaker-hearer', pp. 150–73 in D.L. Horton and J.J. Jenkins (ed.), *The Perception of Language*, Merrill, Columbus, Ohio.

Crystal, D. (1969) *Prosodic Systems and Intonation in English*, Cambridge University Press, New York.

Crystal, D. (1971) 'Paralinguistics', in Sebeok, T.A. (ed.), *Current Trends in Linguistics*, Vol. 12, Mouton, The Hague.

Crystal, D. and Quirk, R. (1964) *Systems of Prosodic and Paralinguistic Features in English*, Mouton, The Hague.

Davitz, J.R. and Davitz, L.J. (1959) 'The communication of feelings by content-free speech', *Journal of Communication* 9, 6–13.

Dittman, A.T. (1972) *Interpersonal Messages of Emotion*, Springer, New York.

Dittman, A.T. and Llewellyn, L.G. (1969) 'Body movement and speech rhythm in social conversation', *Journal of Personality and Social Psychology* 11, 98–106.

Duncan, S. Jr. (1969) 'Nonverbal communication', *Psychological Bulletin* 72, 118–37.

Dusenbury, D. and Knower, F.H. (1939) 'Experimental studies of the symbolism of action and voice', *Quarterly Journal of Speech* 25, 65–75.

Efron, D. (1942) *Gesture and Environment*, Kings Crown Press, New York.

Eibl-Eibesfeldt, I. (1970) *Ethology: The Biology of Behavior*, Holt, New York.

Eibl-Eibesfeldt, I. (1972) 'Similarities and differences between cultures in expressive movements', in Hinde, R.A. (ed.), *Non-verbal Communication*, Cambridge University Press, New York, 297–311.

Eisenberg, P. and Zalowitz, E. (1938) 'Judgements of dominance feelings from phonograph records of the voice', *Journal of Applied Psychology* 22, 620–31.

Ekman, P. (1972) 'Universals and cultural differences in facial expressions of emotions', in Cole, J. (ed.), *Nebraska Symposium on Motivation*, University of Nebraska Press, Lincoln.

Ekman, P. and Friesen, W.V. (1969) 'The repertoire of nonverbal behavior: categories, origins, usage and coding', *Semiotica* 1, 49–98.

Ekman, P., Friesen, W.V. and Ellsworth, P. (1972) *Emotion in the Human Face*, Pergamon, New York.

Ekman, P., Sorenson, E.R. and Friesen, W.V. (1969) 'Pan-cultural elements in facial displays of emotion', *Science* 164, 86–8.

Erickson, F. (1975) 'An empirical investigation of one function of proxemic shifts in face to face interaction', *Proceedings of 9th International Congress of Anthropological and Ethnological Sciences, Conference on the Organization of Behavior in Face to Face Interaction, Chicago, 1973*, Mouton, The Hague.

Exline, R.V. (1963) 'Explorations in the process of person perception: Visual interaction in relation to competition, sex and the need for affiliation', *Journal of Personality* 31, 1–20.

Exline, R.V., Gray, D. and Schuette, D. (1965) 'Visual behavior in a dyad as affected by interview content and sex of respondent', *Journal of Personality and Social Psychology* 1, 201–9.

Exline, R.V. and Winters, L.C. (1965) 'Affective relations and mutual glances in dyads' pp. 319–50 in Tomkins, S.S. and Izard, C.E. (eds), *Affect, Cognition and Personality*, Springer, New York.

Fairbanks, G. and Pronovost, W. (1939) 'An experimental study of the pitch characteristics of the voice during the expression of emotion', *Search Monographs* 6, 87–104.

Fay, P.J. and Middleton, W.C. (1939) 'Judgment of Spranger personality types from the voice as transmitted over a public address system', *Character and Personality* 8, 141–55.

Fay, P.J. and Middleton, W.C. (1940) 'Judgment of Kretschmerian body types from the voice as transmitted over a public address system', *Journal of Social Psychology* 12, 151–62 (a).

Fay, P.J. and Middleton, W.C. (1940) 'Judgment of intelligence from the voice as transmitted over a public address system', *Sociometry* 3, 186–91. (b).

Gibson, J.J. and Pick, A.D. (1963) 'Perception of another person's looking behavior', *American Journal of Psychology* 76, 386–94.

Gumperz, J.J. and Hymes, D. (eds) (1972) *Directions in Sociolinguistics: The Ethnography of Communication*, Holt, New York.

Hall, E.T. (1959) *The Silent Language*, Doubleday, New York.

Hall, E.T. (1963) 'A system for the notation of proxemic behavior'. *American Anthropologist* 65, 1003–26.

Hall, E.T. (1964) 'Silent assumptions in social communication', in McK. Rioch, D. and Weinstein, E.A. (eds), *Disorders of Communication*, Association for Research in Nervous and Mental Diseases, Baltimore.

Hall, E.T. (1966) *The Hidden Dimension*, Doubleday, New York.

Hill, A.A. (1958) *Introduction to Linguistic Structures*, Harcourt, New York.

Hinde, R.A. (ed.) (1972) *Non-verbal Communication*, Cambridge University Press, New York.

Hockett, C.F. (1960) 'The origin of speech', *Scientific American* 203, 89–96.

Horton, D.L. and Jenkins, J.J. (eds) (1971) *The Perception of Language*, Charles E. Merrill, Columbus, Ohio.

Izard, C.E. (1971) *The Face of Emotion*, Appleton, New York.

Kendon, A. (1967) 'Some functions of gaze-direction in social interaction', *Acta Psychologica* 26, 22–63.

Kendon, A. (1970) 'Movement coordination in social interaction: Some examples described', *Acta Psychologica* 32, 100–25.

Kendon, A. (1972) 'Some relationships between body motion and speech', in Siegman, A.W. and Pope, B. (eds), *Studies in Dyadic Communication*, Pergamon, New York.

Kramer, E. (1963) 'Judgment of personal characteristics and emotions from non-verbal properties of speech', *Psychological Bulletin* 60, 408–20.

Kramer, E. (1964) 'Elimination of verbal cues in judgment of emotion from voice', *Journal of Abnormal and Social Psychology* 68, 390–6.

La Barre, W. (1947) 'The cultural basis of emotions and gestures', *Journal of Personality* 16, 49–68.

Laver, J. (1968) 'Voice quality and indexical information', *British Journal of Disorders of Communication* 3, 43–54.

Laver, J. and Hutcheson, S. (eds) (1972) *Communication in Face to Face Interaction*, Penguin, Harmondsworth.

Little, K.B. (1965) 'Personal space', *Journal of Experimental and Social Psychology* 1, 237–47.

Lyons, J. (ed.) (1970) *New Horizons in Linguistics*, Penguin, Harmondsworth.

Lyons, J. (1972) 'Human language' in Hinde, R.A. (ed.), *Non-verbal Communication*, Cambridge University Press, New York, 49–85.

Mehrabian, A. (1967) 'Orientation behaviors and non-verbal attitude communication', *Journal of Communication* 17, 324–32.

Mehrabian, A. (1968) 'Inference of attitudes from the posture, orientation and distance of a communicator', *Journal of Consulting and Clinical Psychology* 32, 296–308.

Mehrabian, A. (1969) 'Significance of posture and position in the communication of attitude and status relationships', *Psychological Bulletin* 71, 359–72.

Moscovici, S. (ed.) (1972) *The Psychosociology of Language*, Markham, Chicago.

Neisser, U. (1967) *Cognitive Psychology*, Appleton, New York.

de Saussure, F. (1966) *Course in General Linguistics*, Bally, C., Sechehaye, A. and Riedlinger, A. (eds), (trans. W. Baskin), McGraw-Hill, New York.

Scheflen, A.E. (1964) 'The significance of posture in communication systems', *Psychiatry* 27, 316–31.

Sebeok, T.A., Hayes, A.S. and Bateson, M.C. (eds) (1964) *Approaches to Semiotics*, Mouton, The Hague.

Siegman, A.W. and Pope, B. (eds) (1972) *Studies in Dyadic Communication*, Pergamon, New York.

Smith, A.G. (ed.) (1966) *Communication and Culture*, Holt, New York.Sommer, R. (1959) 'Studies in personal space', *Sociometry* 22, 247–60.

Sommer, R. (1965) 'Further studies of small group ecology', *Sociometry* 28, 337–48.

Sommer, R. (1967) 'Small group ecology', *Psychological Bulletin* 67, 145–52.

Sommer, R. (1969) *Personal space*, Prentice-Hall, Englewood Cliffs, New Jersey.

Starkweather, J A. (1964) 'Variations in vocal behavior', in Rioch, D. McK. and Weinstein, E.A. (eds), *Disorders of Communication*, Association for Research in Nervous and Mental Diseases, Baltimore.

Sudnow, D. (ed.) (1972) *Studies in Social Interaction*, Free Press, New York.

Thompson, C.W. and Bradway, K. (1950) 'The teaching of psychotherapy through content-free interview', *Journal of Consulting Psychology* 14, 321–3.

Tomkins, S.S. (1962) *Affect, Imagery, Consciousness*. Vol. 1. *The Positive Affects*, Springer, New York.

Trager, G.L. (1958) 'Paralanguage: A first approximation', *Studies in Linguistics* 13, 1–12.

Watson, O.M. and Graves, T.D. (1966) 'Quantitative research in proxemic behavior', *American Anthropologist* 68, 971–85.

9 Voice Quality and Indexical Information

Originally published as Laver, J. (1968) 'Voice quality and indexical information', *British Journal of Disorders of Communication* 3: 43–54

Introduction

As actors in a social world, we interact with other people by virtue of a constant interchange of information on many different levels. Perhaps the most explicit sort of information exchanged in social intercourse is language, and modern linguistic and phonetic theory has developed some elegant and effective concepts for the description of speech, the spoken medium of language. The description of the more narrowly linguistic aspects of speech does not, however, exhaust the possibilities of information carried in utterances. Any given utterance contains not only linguistic information, but also a great deal of information for the listener about the characteristics of the speaker himself. Abercrombie (1967) refers to the features in speech which convey this information as 'indexical' features. It is the purpose of this article to explore one major vehicle of such indexical information in speech, that of voice quality.

While the concepts available for linguistic description are well developed, it is only comparatively recently that phoneticians have begun to show more than a cursory interest in a descriptive theory of voice quality. For a long time other disciplines such as speech pathology, psychology and psychiatry have been more ready to acknowledge the relevance of the study of this topic. With the current expansion of research in the area, this may be an appropriate time to try to suggest the broad outline of an overall descriptive model of voice quality. One motive for attempting to set up such a descriptive model is to facilitate interdisciplinary discussion of the indexical function of voice quality; another is to incorporate the descriptive model into the wider theory of general phonetics. I hope to be able to show that general phonetics constitutes a legitimate framework for the study of this area, in that it offers an appropriate philosophy of analysis, and can make available an established and meaningful body of relevant descriptive concepts.

There has been a variety of usages in labelling voice qualities in the past.

With the exception of some phonetically sophisticated systems developed by speech pathology, the majority of previous systems have used single impressionistic labels for given voice qualities. Typical labels have been 'husky', 'plummy', 'thin', 'rich', 'velvety', 'reedy', et cetera. Such labels are often vague to the point of meaninglessness, except in a metaphorical sense, or as arbitrary imitation-labels. The great advantage of a general phonetic approach to the labelling problem is that, in its systems for describing the physiology of articulation, overall labelling is not attempted. The basic philosophy of phonetic analysis is that composite articulatory events are broken down into their component parts, and each independent physiological component is separately labelled. Thus, for example, the sound at the beginning of the English word 'fat' is described not as a 'sort of "f"-sound', but as a 'pulmonic, egressive, voiceless, labiodental fricative with velic closure', with each important physiological component analytically isolated.

It is the principal thesis of the descriptive model put forward here that voice quality is similarly susceptible of description in terms of components, and that general phonetic theory can supply the concepts necessary for a physiologically meaningful description of each of the components.[1]

Outline of a Descriptive Model of Voice Quality

Voice quality, the quasi-permanent quality of a speaker's voice (Abercrombie, 1967: 91), can be thought of as deriving from two main sources: firstly, the anatomical and physiological foundation of a speaker's vocal equipment; and secondly, the long-term muscular adjustments, or 'settings' (Honikman, 1964), once acquired idiosyncratically, or by social imitation, and now unconscious, of the speaker's larynx and supralaryngeal vocal tract.

The anatomy and physiology of a speaker determine the width of the potential range of operation for any voice quality feature, and the long-term habitual settings of the larynx and the vocal tract restrict this feature to a more limited range of operation. For example, a man's voice may be physically capable of spanning a wide pitch range; in normal speech, however, he habitually selects a more restricted range within the total possibilities. Basic anatomy and physiology thus determine the possible extremes, and voluntary muscular settings determine habitual ranges between those extremes.

While factors of basic anatomy and physiology are beyond the speaker's control, and the habitual settings are to a certain extent within his control, both these sources of voice quality can transmit indexical information, although of different sorts, as we shall see in a later section.

The anatomy and physiology of the vocal organs, and their habitual muscular settings, are all of legitimate professional interest to the phonetician, but for the moment the habitual muscular settings will be taken as the more direct focus of attention.

It is useful to divide the settings into two groups:

A. Settings of the larynx
B. Settings of the supralaryngeal vocal tract

A. Settings of the Larynx

Laryngeal settings fall into three sub-categories:

(a) phonation-types
(b) pitch-ranges
(c) loudness-ranges.

(a) Phonation-types

Phonation-types constitute an area which is still largely open to exploration. Certainly, some labels exist, and are used more or less widely in phonetics, but much research needs to be done before confident statements about the detailed physiology of a wide range of phonation-types can be made. The phonation-types relevant to this article about whose physiology something is known, besides 'normal voice', include 'breathy voice', 'whispery voice', 'creaky voice', 'falsetto voice', 'ventricular voice' and 'harsh voice'. One of the most valuable contributions to current phonetic knowledge about phonation-types has been that of Catford (1964), and he has done much to give both physiological and aerodynamic definitions to many of the above labels.

Some combinations of these phonation-types are possible, as in 'harsh, whispery voice', 'whispery, ventricular voice, 'creaky, falsetto voice', 'harsh, falsetto voice', 'harsh, whispery, falsetto voice', 'whispery, creaky voice', 'breathy, falsetto voice' and so forth. (See Catford, 1964.)

(b) Pitch-ranges

Pitch-ranges within the total possible range in any phonation-type can usefully be described on a five-point scale: 'very deep', 'deep', 'medium', 'high' and 'very high'.

Although the total pitch-possibilities for each phonation-type can be divided into the five suggested ranges, there seems to be a tendency for speakers using a given phonation-type to favour a particular pitch-range. This happens, for instance, in the case of falsetto voice, where speakers typically select a high pitch-range within the possibilities for falsetto voice, or in creaky voice, where the deeper ranges for creaky voice are often used. In acoustic terms, the absolute frequencies involved in deep falsetto voice and high creaky voice (which show less usual choices of pitch-range within the possibilities for the particular phonation-types) may overlap considerably. The 'normal voice' phonation-type does not show this tendency quite as much as the other phonation-types, and the pitch-ranges used are much more varied.

(c) *Loudness-ranges*

Loudness-ranges can also be described as selections from a five-point scale: 'very soft', 'soft', 'medium', 'loud' and 'very loud'.

The habitual settings of the laryngeal and associated musculature which result in characteristic pitch- and loudness-ranges are of a different order from the settings for characteristic phonation-types, in that while a person might be recognised solely by his phonation-type in the utterance of a single syllable, a much longer stretch of utterance would be necessary for a listener to be able to recognise the speaker by his characteristic pitch and loudness-ranges. However, partly because impressionistic labels for voice quality nearly always seem to contain an implicit reference to these features, and partly because of the quasi-permanent role of such features in characterising the speaker, pitch- and loudness-ranges are included in this outline model as features integrally associated with the overall quality of a speaker's voice. In a theoretically more rigorous analysis one would abstract such 'dynamic' features separately from features of 'quality' (Abercrombie, 1967: Ch. 6).

B. Settings of the Supralaryngeal Vocal Tract

Supralaryngeal settings of the vocal tract can be divided into four groups, referring to different sorts of modification of the shape and acoustic characteristics of the tract:

    (a) longitudinal modifications
    (b) latitudinal modifications
    (c) tension modifications
    (d) nasalisation.

(a) Longitudinal Modifications. Longitudinal modifications of the vocal tract can result from vertical displacements of the larynx upwards or downwards, from a neutral position, to give 'raised larynx voice' or 'lowered larynx voice'. Pouting-forwards of the lips also effects changes in the length of the longitudinal axis of the vocal tract, and has auditory and acoustic correlates in voice quality.

(b) Latitudinal Modifications. Latitudinal modifications of the vocal tract involve quasi-permanent changes in the cross-sectional area at a particular location of the tract, which result in local constrictive or expansive tendencies. These modifications include: different sorts of labialisation, with the space between the lips being narrowed either vertically or horizontally, or both; two types of pharyngealisation, involving muscular constrictions of the pharynx, or in narrowing of the pharynx by backward displacement of the tongue from its central position in the mouth; and thirdly, settings of the tongue that result in a constrictive or expansive tendency somewhere in the oral cavity.

The settings of the tongue in the oral and pharyngeal cavity are parallel to many of the 'secondary articulations' of traditional phonetic theory. One could speak of overall tendencies towards maintaining a particular 'secondary articulation', but of course such settings are in no sense 'secondary' as far as voice quality, as distinct from segmental features, is concerned (Abercrombie, 1967: 93). A less prejudicial conceptualisation of the general principle underlying these settings of the tongue, whether in the mouth or in the pharynx, is achieved if any local constrictive or expansive tendency is thought of as resulting from a shift, along one or both of the horizontal and vertical axes of the mouth, of the centre of gravity of the tongue away from the neutral position in which it would lie in an unmodified vocal tract. In this way, pharyngealisation can be said to result from backing in the mouth of the centre of gravity of the tongue; velarisation from backing and raising; palatalisation from raising; alveolarisation from fronting; and a quality which currently lacks a conventional phonetic term, but which is sometimes impressionistically called 'hot potato voice', as if the speaker literally had a hot object in his mouth, is the result of lowering, and perhaps backing, of the centre of gravity of the tongue.

For convenience in the labelling system, instead of the more cumbersome 'tongue-raised-and-backed voice', et cetera, the more usual phonetic labels such as 'velarised voice' can be retained, provided that it is remembered that no implications of secondary status enter their definition, which would be in terms of the relative position of the centre of gravity of the tongue.

It is probable, because the tongue is of a relatively fixed volume, that any constrictive tendency in the mouth has a corresponding compensatory expansive tendency in other parts of the mouth and pharynx. Similarly, some longitudinal modifications of the vocal tract probably involve a latitudinal component as well; raised larynx voice, for example, has a component of slight pharyngalisation. It is also probable that longitudinal modifications involving vertical displacements of the larynx and oral and pharyngeal latitudinal modifications of the vocal tract can affect the fine detail of the mode of vibration of the vocal cords within any phonation type, because of the interactions of the different muscle systems involved.

(c) Tension Modifications. In a detailed model of voice quality, account would have to be taken of the effect of variations in the degree of overall muscular tension of the vocal organs on the acoustic damping characteristics of the vocal tract, through factors of radiation and absorption of sound energy in the tract walls. Different degrees of muscular tension may contribute importantly, for example to the auditory differences between the qualities of the impressionistically-labelled 'metallic voice' and 'muf-fled voice'. More research is needed in this area, and factors of overall muscular tension will be omitted from further discussion in this article.

(d) Nasalisation. It is customary, in phonetic usage in this area, to distinguish only between 'nasalised voice' and 'denasalised voice'. In a more detailed model, it would perhaps be necessary to re-scrutinise these two categories and set up some finer sub-divisions. Speech pathology, for example, has shown that there are a number of auditorily distinguishable kinds of nasalisation arising from a variety of organic causes (Luchsinger and Arnold, 1965). Similarly, the term 'denasalised voice' seems to cover at least two different phenomena: firstly, a quality resulting from habitual velic closure, or, more accurately, from a complete lack of nasal reson-ance; secondly, the quality which is produced by a speaker with a severe cold in the head and nasal catarrh. The first can legitimately be called 'denasalised voice'; the second, speculatively, might be better thought of as a special case of 'nasalised voice', resulting from a partial or complete blockage of catarrhal mucus somewhere in the nasal cavity or nasopharyn-geal sphincter, which would allow the cavity to resonate, but in a highly damped manner. An auditory quality rather like that of velarisation seems also to be a component of such 'cold-in-the-head' voices, perhaps because of some feature of muscular adjustment in the vocal tract walls near the soft palate in this special condition.

In this exploratory article, such sub-divisions will be ignored, and the terms 'nasalised voice' and 'denasalised voice' will be used in the custom-ary phonetic sense mentioned above.

Features of habitual nasalisation may conceivably affect the setting of the vocal tract as a whole, and thereby the laryngeal settings also; this is because some of the depressor-relaxer muscles of the velum, *glosso-palatinus* and *pharyngopalatinus* (Kaplan, 1960: 188), which serve to open the velic valve, have their point of origin in the tongue and pharynx, and these muscles, to be effective, have to exert a pull, in contraction, against their points of origin.

The use of a quantitative scale is helpful when describing supralaryngeal modifications of the vocal tract. At least three degrees of modification can usually be auditorily distinguished – 'slight', 'moderate' and 'severe'. Thus one may choose to refer to 'slightly pharyngealised voice', 'severely nasalised voice', 'moderately raised larynx voice', and so on.

Labelling System for Voice Quality

We are now in a position to offer more specific comments on the suggested labelling system. Instead of single-term impressionistic labels such as 'beery', 'brassy', 'sepulchral', et cetera, we can use composite labels made up of a number of phonetic terms, each specifying a physiologically meaningful component of the voice quality in question. The labelling system concentrates, as a beginning to the problem, on the voluntary muscular settings rather than on the limitations imposed by the basic anatomy and physiology which underlie the settings.

As a convention, features of pitch-range and loudness-range are described first, then features of supralaryngeal modification, and lastly features of phonation-type. Typical labels might then be 'deep, loud, nasalised, harsh voice', 'high, soft, velarised, raised larynx, falsetto voice', 'very soft, nasalised, whispery, creaky voice', 'very high, pharyngealised, harsh, falsetto voice', 'deep, nasalised voice', and so forth.

Medium pitch, medium loudness, an unmodified vocal tract and the 'normal voice' phonation-type can be left to be assumed if no contrary specification is explicitly made. Scalar quantities of different degrees of vocal tract modification can be incorporated, as in 'high, loud, severely nasalised voice', or 'deep, soft, slightly velarised, whispery, creaky voice'. If the degree of vocal tract modification is left unspecified, it could be assumed that a moderate degree was applicable.

It becomes possible to communicate fairly reliably about voices, with a phonetically meaningful descriptive system of this sort. The translation of some impressionistic labels can be attempted, and some illustrative examples are suggested in the following list:

Equivalence of Labelling Systems

Impressionistic Label	*Phonetic Label*
Ginny voice	Deep, (harsh), whispery, creaky voice
Husky voice	Deep, soft, whispery voice
Golden voice	Deep, soft, slightly nasalised voice
Piping voice	High, falsetto voice
Bleating voice	High, loud, (severely) nasalised voice
Light blue voice	High, soft, raised larynx voice
Hoarse voice	Deep, (loud), harsh/ventricular, whispery voice
Gruff voice	Deep, harsh, whispery, creaky voice
Sepulchral voice	Very deep, pharyngealised, tongue-lowered, lowered larynx, (whispery), (creaky) voice
Adenoidal voice	Soft, denasalised, velarised voice

Because of the unreliability of reference of the impressionistic labels, not everyone might agree with the suggested translations, but at least the phonetic system, while not yet offering a complete specification, does allow positive statements to be made about assumed components. Communication in writing about voice qualities becomes much more feasible, because the phonetic labels in effect convey instructions for attempts at imitation of the voluntarily controllable components referred to.

Indexical Information in Voice Quality

The descriptive model of voice quality put forward here can now facilitate the discussion of the sources of indexical information in voice quality; the information falls broadly into three categories:

A. Biological information
B. Psychological information
C. Social formation.

A. Biological Information in Voice Quality

Biological information about the speaker, derived from the effects, outside his control, of his anatomy and physiology, itself falls into three sub-categories:

(a) size and physique
(b) sex and age
(c) medical state.

(a) Size and Physique – There seems to be a general correlation between a person's size and physique and the size of his larynx and vocal tract. If we hear a very deep, loud voice over the telephone, we confidently expect the speaker to turn out to be a large, strong male; and in general our expectations are fulfilled, within fairly wide margins of error (Moses, 1941; Fay and Middleton, 1940a). Exceptions to this rule are not uncommon, but they take one aback when they occur.

(b) Sex and Age – One usually forms fairly accurate impressions, from voice quality alone, of a speaker's sex and age (Mysak, 1959; Tarneaud, 1941; Zerffi, 1957). Deviations from 'normal' expectations about the correlation between a speaker's voice and his sex and age seem to have a powerful effect on impressions of personality.

(c) Medical State – Voice quality supplies a surprisingly varied amount of indexical information about the medical state of the speaker. It is useful to distinguish between permanent and slightly more ephemeral, although still relatively long-term, medical states. Information about permanent aspects can include details of general health, with crude correlations between, for instance, phonaesthenia, or soft, whispery/breathy voices, and poor health, and between so-called 'strong', 'resonant' or 'rich' voices, (deep, loud, (nasalised) voices), and good health. Permanent abnormalities of anatomy and physiology can be revealed by voice qualities associated with cleft palates, deafness and even exceptional singing voices which are sufficiently rare to be thought abnormal in this sense.

More ephemeral, but still quasi-permanent states of health can be signalled by voice quality when the speaker is suffering from conditions of local inflammation of his vocal organs, as in laryngitis, pharyngitis and tonsillitis, and from nasal catarrh, adenoids or a cold.

Other ephemeral factors in voice quality derive from changes in the hormonal state of the speaker, where, for example, these result in changes in the copiousness and consistency of the supply of lubricating mucus to the larynx, and in the characteristics of the mucous membrane covering the actual vocal cords. Such changes occur in the pregnant and pre-menstrual states in women (Perelló, 1962), and in conditions of sexual arousal in both men and women. These changes often seem to cause slight harshness and whispery or breathy voice.

Clues in voice quality to other more permanent, but occasionally reversible, hormonal states are sometimes found in the case of voice disorders resulting from diseases of the thyroid, adrenal and pituitary glands (Luchsinger and Arnold, 1965). Systematic research into the possible use of voice quality as a diagnostic index to these and other medical states would be extremely valuable; so far, the area has only sporadically attracted investigation (McCallum, 1954; Palmer, 1956; Punt, 1959; Sonninen, 1960; Canter, 1963).

Examples of temporary states which can become more permanent, and which can be detected in voice quality, are the effects of intoxicating agents like alcohol and tobacco smoke. In excess, these agents tend to damage the vocal cords. 'Whisky voice', 'ginny voice' and 'rummy voice' are popular labels for the deep, harsh, whispery voices that tend to signal one result of excessive habitual consumption of alcohol (Luchsinger and Arnold, 1965), and 'smoker's larynx' is a fairly frequently used medical label for the pathological effect of excessive tobacco smoke on the vocal cords (Myerson, 1950; Devine, 1960).

Lastly, information about temporary states such as fatigue can sometimes be found in voice quality.

B. Psychological Information in Voice Quality

We seem to be prepared as listeners, to draw quite far-reaching conclusions from voice quality about long-term psychological characteristics of a speaker, in assessments of personality. In Western culture, we are ready to believe, for example, that a harsh voice is correlated with more aggressive, dominant, authoritative characteristics, and a breathy voice with more self-effacing, submissive, meek personalities. The belief that personality characteristics, both normal and psychopathological, are correlated with voice quality has been tested experimentally by many writers, mainly in the medical and psychological fields (Allport and Cantril, 1934; Cohen, 1961; Diehl, White and Burle, 1959; Eisenberg and Zalowitz, 1938; Fay and Middleton, 1939b; 1940b; Froeschels, 1960; Goldfarb, Braunstein and Lorge, 1956; Mallory and Miller, 1958; Moore, 1939; Moses, 1954; Pear, 1957; Sapir, 1926–7; Starkweather, 1964; Taylor, 1934). Some controversy remains, but in general writers seem to agree that some such broad correlations do exist. Intuitively, one would agree with them, but one major obstacle in the way of reliable scientific statements has been the lack of any standard system of labelling the voice qualities concerned, and a related inability to attain more than a fairly crude quantification of the voice quality variables which act as the experimental stimuli.

If it is true that information about personality is conveyed by voice quality, then the information must be chiefly carried by aspects of the habitual muscular settings, rather than by the basically invariant anatomy and physiology of the speaker.

C. Social Information in Voice Quality

Social behaviour is largely learned behaviour. Because of this, clues in voice quality to social information must lie mainly in those features of voice quality which can be acquired by imitation. In this sense, a particular accent often has a special voice quality associated with it, and the voice quality can thereby act as a partial clue to any social characteristics that are typical of speakers of that accent. Thus voice quality may serve as an index to features of regional origin, social status, social values and attitudes, and profession or occupation, where these features characterise speakers of the particular accent in question. Nasalisation is a voice quality component very commonly associated with particular accents. It characterises most speakers of Received Pronunciation in England, and many accents of the United States and Australia. Velarisation is a regional marker in the speech of speakers from Liverpool and Birmingham (England) and some parts of New York.

Voice quality can also act as an index to membership of a group which is not necessarily an accent-group (Fay and Middleton, 1939a). For example, some British male stage actors used to seem consciously to strive to attain a voice quality like that of Sir Laurence Olivier; similarly, military drill sergeants typically have harsh voices, and these are not necessarily the result of habitual vocal abuse, but rather acquired by imitation, in the hope of projecting the characteristic persona of their profession.

Stereotyped Judgements in Voice Quality

We all act, as listeners, as if we were experts in using information in voice quality to reach conclusions about biological, psychological and social characteristics of speakers. Long experience of inferring such characteristics from voice quality, presumably often successfully confirmed by information from other levels, invests our implicit ideas about the correlations between voice quality and indexical information with an imagined infallibility. It is worth questioning the validity of this judgement process. We make judgements, and we act on them, but is the information we infer accurate, or is there a possibility that it is quite false? Since the correlations must be statistical in nature, and not always of a very high degree of statistical confidence, obviously listeners will sometimes be wrong in the conclusions they draw from particular voice qualities. There is a good deal of evidence that in such subjective judgements we operate with stereotypes (Cantril and Allport, 1935; Eisenberg and Zalowitz, 1938; Fay and Middleton, 1939b; 1940a; 1940b; Starkweather, 1964). Listeners, if they are from the same culture, tend to reach the same indexical conclusions from the same evidence, but the conclusions themselves may, on occasion, bear no reliable relation to the real characteristics of the speaker.

Of the three types of indexical information in voice quality, biological, psychological and social, it is the biological information which probably tends to lead to the most accurate conclusions, especially as to sex and age. Biological conclusions are possibly more reliable because of the fact that they derive principally from the involuntary, largely invariant aspects of a speaker's anatomy and physiology. Psychological and social conclusions are much more likely to be erroneous, because of their culturally relative nature and because they derive from a more variable strand of the speaker's voice quality, the habitual muscular settings of the larynx and vocal tract.

Experimental Investigation of Voice Quality

The descriptive model suggested in this article represents no more than an initial structuring of the area, and a good deal of work, both experimental and theoretical, will be necessary before the phonetic description of voice quality can approach adequacy. Happily, experimental phonetics is not lacking in appropriate techniques of investigation. Experimental research can follow two complementary lines of approach, in speech analysis and speech synthesis.

In the speech analysis approach to voice quality, data are needed on a number of different aspects. It would be valuable, for instance, to have anthropometric measurements of typical variations in anatomical dimensions, as well as acoustic and physiological information about long-term articulatory activity. Acoustic techniques currently available include a wide range of analytic devices, from spectrography for discovering the distribution in time and frequency of acoustic energy, to inverse filtering of the speech signal for recovery of the characteristics of the glottal waveform. Physiological techniques which might be utilised include cineradiography, stroboscopic cinelaminography (Hollien, 1964), electromanometry and electromyography (Cooper, 1965).

Speech synthesis is a useful avenue of research, in that hypotheses about physiological activities and their acoustic and auditory correlates can be easily tested. It is particularly valuable in that voice qualities of narrowly defined specifications can be fairly precisely simulated (Wendahl, 1963;

Laver, 1967), and psychophonetic perceptual tests and the training of judges in the phonetic labelling system can be correspondingly facilitated.

The Relevance of Voice Quality for the Disciplines
Concerned with Speech

I have maintained that while it is the business of general phonetics to suggest a descriptive model of voice quality, the study of this area has relevance for a number of disciplines.

Speech pathology has a direct interest in voice quality, and various systems of descriptive terminology are used by workers in this field. These systems, moreover, are not necessarily lacking in implications of phonetic specificity, as in the use of terms like 'hyperrhinolalia' and 'hyperrhino-phonia' as labels for 'severely nasalised voice', and 'dysphonia plicae ventricularis' for 'ventricular voice'. The limitation of such systems is in their emphasis on deviations, for whatever aetiological reasons, from socially acceptable norms of voice quality. This is not to disparage such systems; in many areas of speech pathology, attention is necessarily focused on abnormality. However, such systems are inherently too partial for general applicability to voice qualities of all kinds. The advantage of the more general type of system outlined in this article is in its being able to function without prejudice as to culturally-assessed factors of 'normality' or 'abnormality'. Both sorts of systems share the characteristic of analysing voice quality on a physiological, componential basis. Either system would be valuable, for instance, in the research area commented on earlier, that of the use of the voice as an indexical diagnostic clue to various pathological states.

Psychology and psychiatry have shown a frequent interest in voice quality research, because of the importance of the voice as an index to affective conditions and to personality. Psychological experimentation in this area might benefit considerably from the techniques of synthetic simulation of voice qualities mentioned earlier, in that the voice quality stimulus variable in experiments investigating the correlations between voice quality and personality, for example, might be brought under more delicate, reliable and quantified control in this way.

Finally, considerations of voice quality are crucial for some aspects of the specifically linguistic study of speech. The distinction between voice quality and 'phonetic quality' is one of the most fundamental distinctions in linguistic phonetics (Ladefoged, 1962), since phonetic quality is the basic datum of the subject, in its capacity as the vehicle for the meaningful distinctions of phonology. It is sometimes thought that phonetic quality and voice quality are independent aspects of the phonic continuum, and that therefore phonetic quality can be related directly, as a simple abstraction, to the 'real world' of 'phonic quality'. A case can nevertheless be made for considering that phonetic quality and voice quality are not completely independent, and that phonetic quality can in fact only be judged against the previously assessed background of the voice quality of the speaker producing the utterance. Phonetic quality in this view would thus be a more abstract concept than is perhaps often believed.

One of the difficulties facing phoneticians and linguists investigating the phonology of a particular language arises from the general fact that voice quality and phonetic quality can rely for their manifestation on many similar activities of the speech organs. Activities used on a quasi-permanent basis, in some of the habitual laryngeal and supralaryngeal settings, can potentially also be used, on a much shorter-term basis, in the contrastive articulations representing phonological units.

Thus many of the features discussed in this article in their role as contributors to voice quality, such as labialisation, palatalisation, velarisation, pharyngealisation, nasalisation, breathy voice and creaky voice, have also been found in various languages as signals used to differentiate the phonetic quality of the sounds representing phonological units in those languages.

It is because of the potential linguistic utilisation of such features that the phonetician or linguist conducting phonological research must take an early decision about the status of these features when they occur in the speech of his informant.

Conclusion

The study of speech attracts the research attention of a number of different disciplines, each with its own professional interests. For the majority of these disciplines speech is a partial interest, and the main focus of the discipline lies outside speech as such, as in the case of psychology and psychiatry. Speech therapy, on the other hand, takes speech as its principal data, but brings a specialised interest to bear on a restricted area within the wider field of speech as a whole. The one subject which takes as its professional domain the study of *all* aspects of speech is phonetics. As such, phonetics should be able to offer, to these other interested disciplines, comprehensive theoretical structures for the description of all aspects of speech. This article has outlined a general phonetic approach to the description of voice quality, as one particular aspect of speech, in the hope of facilitating interdisciplinary discussion about this aspect and about the indexical information conveyed by its different factors.

Acknowledgements

I gratefully acknowledge the helpful advice of Professor D. Abercrombie, Mrs S. Hutcheson, L.A. Iles, J.A. Kemp and W. Lawrence, who read preliminary drafts of this article. Final responsibility for the views expressed is entirely mine.

Notes

1. Abercrombie (1967), Garvin and Ladefoged (1963) and Fairbanks (1960) are among previous writers who have suggested a phonetic approach to voice quality. This article owes much, in particular, to Abercrombie's suggestions.

References

Abercrombie, D. (1967) *Elements of General Phonetics*, Edinburgh University Press.

Allport, G.W. and Cantril, H. (1934) 'Judging personality from voice', *J. soc. Psychol.* 5, 37–55.

Canter, G.J. (1963) 'Speech characteristics of patients with Parkinson's disease: I. Intensity, pitch and duration', *J. Speech Hear. Disorders* 221–9.

Canter, G.J. (1965) 'Speech characteristics of patients with Parkinson's disease: II. Physiological support for speech', *J. Speech Hear. Disorders* 30 44–9.

Cantril, H. and Allport, G.W. (1935) *The Psychology of Radio*, Harper, New York.

Catford, J.C. (1964) 'Phonation types: the classification of some laryngeal components of speech production', in D. Abercrombie et al. (eds), *In Honour of Daniel Jones*, Longmans, London.

Cohen, A. (1961) 'Estimating the degree of schizophrenic pathology from recorded interview samples', *J. clin. Psychol* 4, 403–6.

Cooper, F.S. (1965) 'Research techniques and instrumentation: EMG'. *ASHA Reports* 1, 153–68.

Devine, K.D. (1960) 'Pathologic effects of smoking in the larynx and oral cavity', *Proc. Staff Meet. Mayo Clin.* 35, 349–52.

Diehl, C.F., White, R. and Burle, K. (1959) 'Voice quality and anxiety', *J. Speech Hear. Res* 2, 282–5.

Eisenberg, P. and Zalowitz, E. (1938) 'Judgements of dominance feelings from phonograph records of the voice', *J. appl. Psychol.* 22, 620–31.

Fairbanks, G. (1960) *Voice and Articulation Drillbook* 2nd Ed. Harper and Row, New York.

Fay, P.J. and Middleton, W.C. (1939a) 'Judgement of occupation from the voice as transmitted over a public address system and over a radio', *J. appl. Psychol.* 23, 586–601.

Fay, P.J. and Middleton, W.C. (1939b) 'Judgement of Spranger personality types from the voice as transmitted over a public address system', *Character and Personality* 8, 144–55.

Fay, P.J. and Middleton, W.C. (1940a) 'Judgement of Kretschmerian body types from the voice as transmitted over a public address system', *J. soc. Psychol.* 12, 151–62.

Fay, P.J. and Middleton, W.C. (1940b) 'Judgement of intelligence from the voice as transmitted over a public address system', *Sociometry* 3, 186–91.

Froeschels, E. (1960) 'Remarks on some pathologic and physiologic conditions of the human voice', *A.M.A. Arch. Otolar* 71, 787–8.

Garvin, P. and Ladefoged, P. (1963) 'Speaker identification and message identification in speech recognition', *Phonetica* 9, 193–9.

Goldfarb, W., Braunstein, P. and Lorge, I. (1956) 'A study of speech patterns in a group of schizophrenic children', *Am. J. Orthopsychiat* 26, 544–55.

Hollien, H. (1964) 'Stroboscopic laminagraphy of the vocal folds', *Proc. 5th Int. Congr. Phonet. Sc.* Münster.

Honikman, B. (1964) 'Articulatory settings', in D. Abercrombie et al. (eds), *In Honour of Daniel Jones*, Longmans, London.

Kaplan, H.M. (1960) *Anatomy and Physiology of Speech*, McGraw-Hill, London.

Ladefoged, P. (1962) *The Nature of Vowel Quality*, Laboratorio de Fonetica Experimental, Coimbra.

Laver, J. (1967) 'The synthesis of components in voice quality', *Proc. 6th Int. Congr. Phonet. Sc.* Prague.

Luchsinger, R. and Arnold, G.E. (1965) *Voice-Speech-Language*, Constable, London.

Mallory, E.B. and Miller, V.B. (1958) 'A possible basis for the association of voice characteristics and personality traits', *Speech Monog.* 25, 255–60.

McCallum, J.R. (1954) 'Chronic laryngitis', *Speech* 18, 48–50.

Moore, W.E. (1939) 'Personality traits and voice quality deficiencies', *J. Speech Hear. Disorders* 4, 33–6.

Moses, P.J. (1941) 'Theories regarding the relation of constitution and character through the voice', *Psychol. Bull.* 38, 746(A).

Moses, P.J. (1954) *The Voice of Neurosis*, Grune and Stratton, New York.

Myerson, M.C. (1950) 'Smoker's larynx; – a clinical pathological entity?', *Ann. Otol. Rhinol. Lar.* 59, 541–6.

Mysak, E.D. (1959) 'Pitch and duration characteristics of older males', *J. Speech Hear. Res.* 2, 46–54.

Palmer, J.M. (1956) 'Hoarseness in laryngeal pathology: a review of the literature', *Laryngoscope* 66, 500–16.

Pear, T.H. (1957) *Personality Appearance and Speech*, Allen and Unwin, London.

Perelló, J. (1962) 'La disfonia premenstrual', *Acta ORL Ibero-Am.* 23, 561–3.

Punt, N.A. (1959) 'Alteration in the voice', *Med. Press* 235–8.

Sapir, E. (1926–27) 'Speech as a personality trait', *Am. J. Sociol.* 32, 892–905.

Sonninen, A. (1960) 'Laryngeal signs and symptoms of goitre', *Folia phoniat.* 12, 41–7.

Starkweather, J.A. (1964) 'Variations in vocal behaviour', in *Disorders of Communication*, Research Publications, Vol. XLII, A.R.N.M.D., U.S.A.

Tarneaud, J. (1941) *Traité pratique de phonologie et de phoniatrie*, Librairie Maloine, Paris.

Taylor, H.C. (1934) 'Social agreements on personality traits as judged from speech', *J. soc. Psychol.* 5, 244–8.

Wendahl, R.W. (1963) 'Laryngeal analog synthesis of harsh voice quality', *Folia phoniat.* 15, 241–50.

Zerffi, W. (1957) 'Male and female voices', *A.M.A. Arch. Otolar.* 65, 7–10.

10 The Semiotic Nature of Phonetic Data

Originally published as Laver, J. (1976) 'The semiotic nature of phonetic data', *York Papers in Linguistics* 6: 55–62

I would like to address myself to the question 'What is the nature of phonetic quality, and what assumptions underlie our claim to be able to abstract it from the phonic totality of any given utterance?'

The nature of phonetic quality, which as a phonetician I regard as the prime datum for the study of language, has only rarely been called into question (Jones, 1938; Ladefoged, 1967). Examining the concept from a semiotic point of view may help to clarify its nature, particularly with regard to the complex, mutually-defining relation that phonetic quality has, as the exponent of phonological and paraphonological elements, with the extralinguistic concept of speaker-identifying voice quality, or personal timbre.

I shall take the view that the phonic medium (Abercrombie, 1967) is used to signal three different sorts of information – phonological, para-phonological and extralinguistic information; and that all three sorts of information can depend, in different languages (or, within one language, in different accents, in different styles and registers and in different indivi-duals), on the use of identical vocal features. It then follows that, if the distinction between phonetic quality and voice quality is not always able to be drawn *a priori* by appeal to differences of phenomena, the ability to distinguish the particular semiotic function of any vocal feature in any given case is crucial to practical work in linguistics.

Looking downwards from phonology to its phonetic exponents, from a formal linguistic point of view for a moment, all that is necessary for the phonological elements of a language is that they should be able to be distinctively encoded by the speaker and distinctively identified by the listener. To achieve perceptual distinctiveness, phonological units as abstract entities have to be manifested by those aspects of the artefacts in a physical medium that can act as symbolic signals. This relationship between phonological units and the physical medium is clearly vital for linguistic theory, because it is through the successful analysis of the relationship, and *only* through it, that we can obtain any observational access to the phonological level and then to the referential complex of language.

A prerequisite in the linguistic phonetician's success in establishing the link between the relevant signal in the medium and the particular phonological unit is the ability to perceive the signal in the first place. This sounds self-evident. But the signal is not a simple percept. It is an abstraction of a particular pattern of phonetic quality (leaving aside the parallel phonetic factors of pitch, loudness and duration).

Phonetic quality is often treated in writings on linguistics as if it were 'raw data', as part of the 'real', 'directly observable', 'concrete' world. I would like to assert the view that this is emphatically not so. The phonetic level of analysis is a level of considerable abstraction from the phonic artefacts created by each act of speaking. The same is true of the abstract status of voice quality. Every analytic decision about phonetic quality entails a complementary decision about voice quality (and of course, vice versa); every decision about either is the product of a number of steps of analytic abstraction from the phonic artefacts of the medium.

It may be helpful here to trace, in Figure 10.1, the network of complementary typological distinctions that need to be drawn in an exhaustive analysis of the phonic medium. A basic premise is that the phonic totality of the vocal sound production of any speaker of any language during speech can be completely accounted for, with no uncategorised residue, by the typological distinctions put forward.

The first distinction is between the *intrinsic* vocal features and the *extrinsic* features. Intrinsic features are those which derive solely from the invariant, absolutely uncontrollable physical foundation of the speaker's voice apparatus. They contribute only to voice quality, and are the source of a great deal of indexical information[1] about physical aspects of the speaker – sex, age, physique, health, fatigue and so forth. The extrinsic features are made up of all aspects of vocal activity which are under the volitional control of the speaker, whether 'consciously' or not.

These extrinsic features are made up of two initial categories: firstly, *unique* events such as a momentary clearing of the throat to remove a build-up of mucus on the vocal folds. Such unique events are of no further interest, and are discarded from further consideration. Secondly, the *recurrent* features are those typically recurring vocal features which are in some sense under the control of the speaker. Without this notion of typical recurrence, there could be no concept of 'phonetic sameness'.

The recurrent features are the central focus of the whole analytic machinery of articulatory phonetics: the division proposed here of the recurrent features into exponent and concurrent aspects is intended to show, however, that they include not only a phonetic component supporting the linguistic code but also the learnable component of a speaker's voice quality.

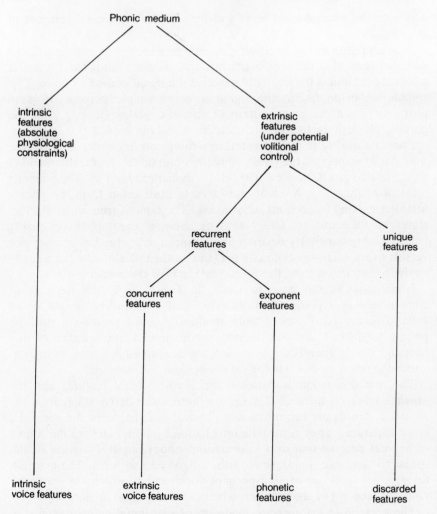

Figure 10.1 Summary diagram of the typological distinctions between features making up the phonic medium.

The *exponent* features are all and only those vocal features which serve as signals ('signs', 'manifestations', 'realisations') for phonological and paraphonological units. They are the familiar phonetic features.

It may be useful to emphasise at this point that no distinction between phonological and paraphonological features has been proposed in Figure 10.1 under any of the nodes dominated by the node labelled 'extrinsic features'. There are two reasons for this: firstly, it would be a confusion of levels of analysis. The classification in Figure 10.1 is of aspects of substance, not of form. The second reason is that in a general theory wider than that demanded by the scope of a given language, the phonetic features available for symbolising the units of phonology and paraphonology are very broadly one and the same set of features. There will perhaps be tendencies for paraphonology normally to exploit longer-term aspects of the phonetic features than the characteristically short-term aspects employed by phonology, but no necessary difference of principle exists between the phonetic parameters chosen. To take a very brief and obvious illustration from the use of labial activity in English, the paraphonological effect of lip-spreading in smiling is usually of longer duration than of lip-spreading for a particular vowel, but is not otherwise phonetically different in kind.

The *concurrent* features make up the extrinsic contribution to voice quality. They provide the background, quasi-permanent auditory colouring to the voices of speakers which together with the intrinsic features give them their characteristic overall voice quality. They are by definition learnable and imitable. Honikman (1964) called them 'articulatory settings', and Bishop Wilkins (1668) described them over three hundred years ago, though without giving them that name.

In Figure 10.2, the concurrent component of voice quality is shown as being divided into three major groupings of articulatory settings – settings of supralaryngeal adjustment, of laryngeal phonation types and of different degrees of overall muscular tension. Fuller accounts can be seen in Abercrombie (1967) and in Laver (1964; 1968; 1975). Briefly, typical supralaryngeal settings include quasi-permanent lip-protrusion, lip-rounding, velarisation, pharyngeal constriction, nasality, an 'open' jaw position, and so forth. Laryngeal settings include phonation types such as breathy voice, whispery voice, harsh voice, creaky voice, falsetto and combinations such as harsh whispery voice, as well as normal voice. Tension settings include, as well as neutral tension, tense voice and lax voice, often impressionistically labelled 'metallic voice' and 'muffled voice' respectively.

It is not accidental, in Figure 10.2, that the exponent phonetic features are shown, like the concurrent voice features, as being divided into supralaryngeal, laryngeal and tension aspects. All three are necessary to account for the phonetic manifestations of phonological and paraphonological units. Considering matters of quality alone, each of the three groups of exponent features has to be analytically sub-divided in much the same way as the corresponding group of concurrent features.

With rather few exceptions, any given vocal feature contributing to quality may be attributable in different circumstances to a different semiotic function. *A priori*, there is no way of telling (from quality alone) whether breathy voice, for example, is acting as a phonological signal (as in 'voiced aspiration' in Hindi and Gujarati), or as a paraphonological signal of confidential intimacy (as in English), or as a concurrent voice quality feature merely characterising the speaker. It is true that duration will

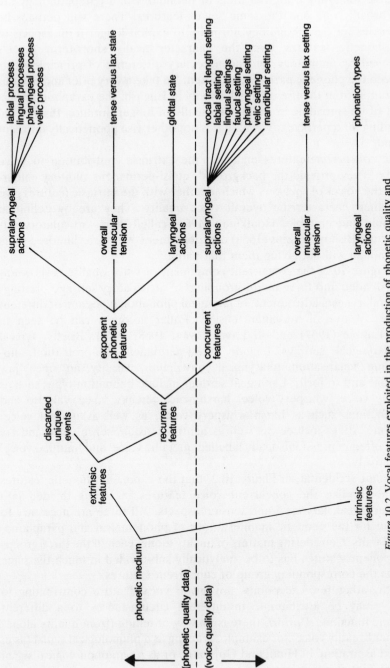

Figure 10.2 Vocal features exploited in the production of phonetic quality and voice quality.

normally be a very helpful clue, provided one's sample is extensive enough, with voice quality features being longest-term, phonetic features expounding paraphonological elements being medium-term and phonetic features expounding phonological elements being shortest-term. In any single case, the analysis of quality will thus be a complex perceptual problem, with several layers of figure-ground relations to be resolved. Firstly, the extrinsic features have to be seen as a figure against the ground of the intrinsic features. Then the exponent phonetic features are a figure against the ground of the concurrent voice features. Finally, those phonetic features exploited by phonology constitute a figure against the ground of the phonetic features used by paraphonology. If the operational decision about which particular features constitute the figure and which the ground in any given case cannot be taken according to purely phenomenal criteria alone, then the decision is eventually necessarily a semiotic decision about function rather than a descriptive decision about substance.

The difficulty of making an accurate decision about the semiotic functions involved is reflected in the not infrequent misallocation in everyday life of voice quality features as features of phonetic quality. In the situation where a speaker has whispery voice, say because of temporary laryngitis, it is not uncommon for listeners ignorant of the speaker's medical condition to reply using whispery voice themselves, misanalysing the whispery voice as a paraphonological signal of conspiratorial secrecy instead of the intrinsic index it is in reality to the speaker's state of health.

In linguistic fieldwork, operational decisions about the allocation of features to voice quality versus phonetic quality can be just as difficult. Key (1967: 19), cited by Crystal (1971: 191) reports that in Cayuvava, a language of Bolivia, nasalisation has an honorific stylistic function, in that 'an individual of lower social or economic status addresses one of higher rank with a prominence of nasalisation for all vowels of the utterance'. A linguist working on this language for the first time might well conclude, if faced with ubiquitous vowel nasality from an informant, that it was a feature of that speaker's voice quality, to be discarded from phonetic attention; whereas the alternative might simply be that the informant regarded the linguist as being of higher social or economic status. Such possibilities of misallocation arise partly from the fact that decisions about both voice quality features and paralinguistic phonetic features are often made tacitly, without explicit consideration. This situation is likely to persist as long as the linguist believes that his or her task is only to account for phonetic phenomena expounding phonological elements, and that the identification of those phonetic phenomena can be achieved without reference to the paralinguistic and voice quality features in which they are embedded. The profitability of the alternative view, where the linguist's task is seen rather as an attempt to account for all extrinsic signs used in spoken communication, is elegantly demonstrated by Trudgill (1973; 1974) in the field of sociological linguistics. In his study of the urban dialectology of social differentiation of Norwich English, he tried to develop a

> diasystem the aim of which is to produce all forms of Norwich English from a common underlying base. The diasystem comprises a single underlying systematic phonemic system, and [a number of different types of rules]. (Trudgill, 1974: 191)

One type of rule incorporated in his diasystem specified particular articulatory settings of the sort mentioned above. They are regarded as 'ancillary to the phonetic realisation rules' (ibid.), that is, to the rules for the realisation of phonological elements. Trudgill characterises the value of including concurrent extrinsic setting components of voice quality with the phonological specification of accents as follows:

> If we incorporate . . . rules of this type into the Norwich diasystem, . . . the statement of both the phonetic realisation and realisation level mutation rules can be much simplified. . . . Another advantage of setting rules is that they relate different types of Norwich English to each other in the diasystem in a much more generalised and significant way than a series of individual rules. Different social types of Norwich English may be characterised by the presence or absence, of, say (setting rule) 100, rather than by a whole series of rules. This is an important point, since it is clear that perhaps the single socially most significant feature of linguistic differentiation in Norwich is the type of voice quality produced by the particular type of setting employed by a speaker. It is in any case this feature which most clearly distinguishes [working-class] from [middle-class] speakers. This point, of course, did not emerge at all from our atomistic analysis of the covariation of linguistic and sociological phenomena.' (Trudgill, 1974: 190–1)

A further justification for linguistic interest in the participation of voice quality settings in considerations of phonetic quality lies in language change and in sociolinguistic aspects of multi-lingual societies.

Perceptually, the effect of a given setting is seen in terms of the consequent adjustments of articulatory position of susceptible segments. A setting of quasi-permanent velarisation, for example, will tend to affect not only various consonant segments, but also to retract and in some cases also or alternatively to raise the vowel segments. It is not inconceivable that historical vowel shifts in a language could arise from the adoption of a different voice quality setting, which would have the effect of adjusting the articulatory positions of the vowels in ways which depended on the individual vowels concerned and their relation to the setting.

In the multi-lingual situation, where the language of a particularly prestigious section of the community may influence the linguistic behaviour of other sections, it does not seem beyond the bounds of possibility that the prestigious behaviour chosen for imitation might include setting components of voice quality, or perhaps partial segmental reflections of a given setting.[2] A more traditional analysis would see such influence as being exercised on individual segmental performance alone, but to ignore its possible interpretation as an imitation of an aspect of voice quality is to lose a possibly valuable generality.

In conclusion, the attraction of looking at the problem of phonetic quality in semiotic terms is that it sets the analysis of phonetic data in a very wide framework. It allows the communicative substance of language to be seen as part of a more comprehensive communicative system, including not only the paralinguistic communication of mood, but also the indexical communication of the whole physical, psychological and social profile of the speaker, as portrayed in his or her voice quality. It is interesting that, in questioning the assumptions underlying the concept of phonetic quality, one is necessarily led to an examination of the complementary extralinguistic concept of voice quality, and thus, seeing the two together, to this view of phonetics set in the broader frame of semiotics. From this perspective, it is reassuring to be reminded that the concerns of phonetics as a discipline are *not* the construction of some elaborate but merely peripheral game of taxonomy, but the apprehension of a fundamental, central aspect of human communication. At the very least, a semiotic approach to phonetic theory may provide a stronger base, because it is a more explicit base, to the foundation of the rest of linguistic theory: at best, in a semiotic view of phonetics, we learn more about how we construct and sustain our identity as social, communicative beings.

Notes

1. The sense of C.S. Peirce's term 'index' adopted here is not the 'deictic' sense in current use by philosophers of language, but rather the 'evidential' sense, as used in Abercrombie (1967).
2. I am indebted to Professor R.B. Le Page for this observation.

References

Abercrombie, D. (1967) *Elements of General Phonetics*, Edinburgh University Press, Edinburgh.

Crystal, D. (1971) 'Prosodic and Paralinguistic Correlates of Social Categories', pp. 185–206 in Ardener, E. (ed.), *Social Anthropology and Language*, Tavistock, London.

Honikman, B. (1964) 'Articulatory Settings', in Abercrombie, D., Fry, D.B., MacCarthy, P.A.D., Scott, N.C. and Trim, J.L.M. (eds), *In Honour of Daniel Jones*, 73–84, Longman, London.

Jones, D. (1938) 'Concrete and abstract sounds', in *Proceedings of the Third International Congress of Phonetic Sciences*, Ghent.

Key, H. (1967) *Morphology of Cayuvava*, Series Practica 53, Mouton, The Hague.

Ladefoged, P. (1967) *Three Areas of Experimental Phonetics*, Oxford University Press, London.

Laver, J. (1964) 'The Synthesis of Voice Quality', PAT Report, University of Edinburgh.

Laver, J. (1968) 'Voice quality and indexical information', *British Journal of Disorders of Communication* 3, 43–54.

Laver, J. (1975) 'Individual Features of Voice Quality', PhD Dissertation, University of Edinburgh.

Trudgill, P. (1973) 'Phonological Rules and Sociolinguistic Variation in Norwich English', pp. 149–63 in Bailey, C.J. and Shuy R.W. (eds), *New Ways of Analysing Variation in English*, Georgetown University Press, Washington.

Trudgill, P. (1974) *The Social Differentiation of English in Norwich*, Cambridge University Press, Cambridge.

Wilkins, J. (1668) *An Essay towards a Real Character and Philosophical Language*, John Martyn, London.

11 Labels for Voices

Originally published as Laver, J. (1974) 'Labels for voices', *Journal of the International Phonetic Association* 4: 62–75

If semiotics is the general theory of communicative signs (Morris, 1938: 80), then phonetics constitutes part of that theory, in the sense that phonetics tries to model the means by which communication is achieved through the use of spoken signs. The technical vocabulary of phonetics is thus a sub-set of the metalanguage of semiotics, and one might reasonably expect that other terms and concepts from semiotic theory, such as that of INDEXICAL and ICONIC signs (Feibleman, 1946: 91), might be illuminating when applied to the subject-matter of phonetics.

The view of the domain and purpose of phonetics that will be used in this article[1] is that it is an attempt to develop an explicit descriptive model of the use of the speech apparatus, and to account unambiguously for all aspects of speech activity relevant to communication. Such a semiotically-oriented definition would include the study of speech activity not only in linguistic communication, but also in paralinguistic communication, and in the communication of indexical information about the speaker himself.

As laymen, we have an extremely wide and subtle vocabulary for talking about speech; but as phoneticians, we need to be able to make explicit scientific statements which can elucidate the vagueness and ambiguities which inherently characterise these lay comments. For example, we can be phonetically reasonably precise about what speech phenomena are being referred to by lay usages such as 'a London accent', or 'a lisp', or 'he speaks through his nose'. We have had slightly less success so far in being able to say exactly what might be meant by such phrases as 'he has a very broad accent', or 'he has very flat vowels'. One particular type of phrase in everyday lay usage which has so far largely evaded efforts towards phonetic specificity is the formula 'a . . . voice', where the adjective preceding 'voice' might be one of literally hundreds of labels on the pattern of 'dulcet, venomous, hollow, educated, foreign, British, metallic, angry, colourless, dark brown, sharp, brisk, soporific, pleasant, melodious, ingratiating, sepulchral', and so forth. Crystal (1969: 127–8) is the most recent phonetician to draw attention to the relative neglect of this area.

It would be a mammoth task to try to give an exhaustive specification of what the phonetic correlates of all such labels might be, and perhaps one which is in principle impossible, since in very many cases a particular label means different things to different users. But it should at least be possible to construct a semiotic typology of these labels, in which suggestions are offered as to the aspect of the semiotic process of speech to which the labels are making implicit reference. In some cases the reference will be to aspects of speech production, in others to imputed aspects of the speaker's identity, in others to the effect of the voice on the listener himself, and so on. The apparent unity of the formula 'a . . . voice' thus conceals a wide variety of different types of referent; and the purpose of this article is to try to identify, in a broad semiotic framework, the type of referent involved, in the hope of facilitating an explicitly phonetic approach to the analysis of those aspects of voices which will be seen as properly falling within the domain of phonetics. Specifically, I will address myself to the question 'On what principled basis can individual voices be labelled?' More broadly, I wish to explore the supplementary question 'What is the layman talking about, semiotically and phonetically, when he uses tokens of the phrase "a . . . voice"?'

The first and most fundamental semiotic distinction between different types of labels for voices concerns whether the label refers to the sounds produced by the speaker or to the characteristics of the speaker producing the sounds. It will be convenient to call the first sort of label a 'descriptive' label and the second an 'indexical' label.[2]

Descriptive labels themselves fall into two broad categories: 'impressionistic' labels and 'phonetic' labels. By impressionistic labels I mean labels which need an audible demonstration of the type of voice referred to before the listener or the reader can construct an accurate interpretation of the label. Pike has called such labels auditory 'imitation labels' (Pike, 1943: 16). Phonetic labels, on the other hand, are part of established phonetic vocabulary, and as such have exact and agreed definitions subscribed to by all trained phoneticians (in the ideal situation at least). One would hope that phonetic theory should eventually be able to offer translations of all descriptive impressionistic labels for voices into plausible descriptive phonetic labels.

One characteristic of most impressionistic labels is that they tend to use single adjectives for individual voices, and for these different single adjectives to have a very variable domain of reference. In trying to make the phonetic reference of impressionistic labels explicit, I shall follow Abercrombie in dividing the medium of speech into 'three strands, separable though closely woven together, all simultaneously and continuously present and together making up the totality of the medium' (Abercrombie, 1967: 89). These three strands are: segmental features, features of voice quality and features of voice dynamics (Abercrombie ibid.). Some impressionistic adjectives might refer implicitly to a single strand in the production of a particular voice (as in a 'sibilant voice', where one might conclude that reference is being made to features of segmental pronunciation). Others refer implicitly to two strands (as in a 'sepulchral voice', where reference to features both of voice dynamics and voice quality seems likely). Still others seem to refer to all three strands, segmental pronunciation, voice dynamics and voice quality together, in labels such as a 'twittering voice'. Most impressionistic labels seem to be of the more holistic sort, where multiple reference is implicit in a single label. Examples of this sort would be 'velvety, rich, golden, flat, thin, bird-like, thick'.

Phonetic labels used for voices share the same characteristics as the rest of the taxonomy for phonetic description: holistic description is avoided, and each controllable independent component is individually identified, giving a composite label rather than a single-word label. A standard anatomy and physiology is assumed, so that the labels can in effect act as instructions to the reader or listener about how to control his own vocal organs in such a way as to produce the same phonetic effect as the phenomenon under description. Inter-personal differences of anatomy are disregarded as irrelevant in this basic assumption of a universal phonetic theory – that the fundamental apparatus, and all parameters of vocal control, are standard to all human beings. So phonetic labels for voices, like phonetic labels for segments, are composite multi-term labels conveying componential articulatory instructions to the reader about how he himself can achieve the effect being described. Examples of phonetic labels for voices would be 'a slow, loud, ventricular, whispery voice', or 'a fast, soft, nasalised, labialised, lax, breathy, creaky voice'. It will be immediately obvious that many terms in the composite phonetic labels would be as much in need of prior audible demonstration for intelligibility as the holistic impressionistic labels, were an individual phonetician to meet a particular phonetic label for the first time in the form given above. In the last resort, all descriptive labels commonly used in phonetics have to have had a basis of audible demonstration during the training of the individual phonetician. There are two chief differences at this level, however, between the systems of impressionistic and phonetic labels. One is to do with the number of different labels available in each system, and the other is to do with the degree of shared interpretive conventions about the meaning of the labels in each system. With regard to the size of the labelling inventory, the number of individual phonetic terms which can be used to make up the available list of composite phonetic labels is fairly limited, but capable of producing a large number of such composite labels. This means that the phonetician has only to master (through training by audible demonstration in part) a small number of articulatory-auditory correspondences in order to be able to recognise and produce this large number of composite phonetic events. The list of impressionistic labels is perhaps larger, relying as it does to an important degree on the metaphorical resources of the language, but it is weaker than the phonetic system because of the second factor, to do with interpretive conventions. In the phonetic system, as mentioned above, the conventions for interpreting the reference of the small number of individual productive components are rigorous, explicit and universal amongst trained phoneticians, ideally at least. Communication in writing about any composite phonetic phenomena, between individuals trained in the system, is relatively simple and accurate, and there is no need for audible demonstrations of the composite events to which reference is being made. In the impressionistic system, each different holistic label needs an individual interpretive convention, and the users of the system have to rely therefore on the general conventions of the everyday language for effective communication with their readers or listeners. A number of inefficiencies arise from this, in the impressionistic system. Firstly, communication is less than adequate in cases where, in writing about voices, the writer is mistaken in his belief that the referent of a label he uses is accurately accessible to the reader through a culturally-disseminated convention. In cases of this sort, where the writer and the reader have different interpretations of the same label, both writer and reader are likely to be unaware that accurate communication is not being achieved. The difficulty arises because the convention specifying the meaning of the label is tacit, and not explicit as in the case of the phonetic system. The same difficulty underlies a similar breakdown of accurate written communication about voices when different writers attach different labels to the same referent. In all these ambiguous situations, the reader has at best only approximate information about the writer's communicative intentions, and at worst can be seriously misled.

I shall return to the existence of many impressionistic elements in supposedly scientific, precise phonetic description later.

Expanding on suggestions by Abercrombie (1967: 90), I shall try now to explore in some detail the types of correspondence between impressionistic labels for voices and the different phonetic strands in the production of speech. In this analysis, the reader may well find himself in disagreement about the phonetic correlates which I claim exist for a particular impressionistic label, for precisely the reasons of ambiguities of interpretation inherent in impressionistic labelling outlined above. However, my object is less to secure exact phonetic agreement about the correlates than to show the variety of implied reference to different aspects of sound production that impressionistic labels may have.

There seem to be very few impressionistic labels for voices which refer specifically to segmental pronunciation, or which include segmental pronunciation in the reference together with other features. Adjectives for voices which have some plausible reference to segmental pronunciation include not only 'sibilant', as mentioned above, but also 'bleary, blurred, distinct, lisping, orotund, precise, slurred, twittering', and perhaps terms like 'clipped' and 'thick'.

Impressionistic labels have frequent implications of reference to various voice-dynamic features. These include features of pitch-range, pitch movements, loudness-range, tempo, continuity and phonational register.

Adjectives with implications for pitch-range include 'bird-like, bleating, colourless, creaky, croaky, dark brown, deep, flat, fluting, grating, gravelly, gravy, graveyard, gruff, heavy, high, light, light blue, low, pale, pale pink, piping, rich, reedy, rumbling, sepulchral, shrill, silvery, sombre, sonorous, twittering, whining'.

Those with implications for particular types of pitch movements within a particular pitch-range include 'droning, melodious, monotonous, musical, quavery, querulous, sing-song, whining', and perhaps 'mellifluous'.

Reference to the feature of loudness-range seems to be implicit in impressionistic labels like 'big, booming, colourless, creaky, croaky, far-carrying, full, gravelly, gruff, husky, light blue, loud, low, orotund, pale, pale pink, piercing, querulous, raucous, resonant, rumbling, sharp, shrill, small, soft, sombre, sonorous, staccato, strident, strong, weak' and perhaps 'brazen' and 'rasping'.

Implications of tempo are contained in labels such as 'drawling, droning, fast, graveyard, quick, sepulchral, slow, sombre, staccato, twittering' and perhaps 'sharp'.

Continuity is referred to in labels like 'clipped, droning, jerky, staccato' and perhaps 'smooth, fluent' and 'fluid'.

Phonational register, as the mode of vibration of the vocal cords which the individual speaker can control on a moment-to-moment basis for linguistic and paralinguistic signals, seems to be implicitly referred to in many impressionistic labels, such as 'breathy, cracked, crackling, creaky, croaky, falsetto, grating, gravelly, gritty, gruff, harsh, hoarse, husky, rasping, rough, rumbling, shrill, sombre, thin, throaty, velvety, whispery', and perhaps 'thick', and possibly 'blurred'.

Reference to the voice quality strand in the production of speech falls into two groups: firstly, to the invariant anatomical and physiological foundation of the speaker's vocal equipment, and secondly, to the different types of muscular 'setting' the speaker habitually superimposes on this basic physical foundation (Laver, 1968).

Impressionistic labels for the first group, the physical foundation, are few in number and are the technical terms for different types of singing voices – 'tenor, baritone, bass, double-bass, soprano, contralto'.

Labels for the second group, the habitual long-term muscular settings, can be divided into a number of different sections, depending on the type of setting to which they refer. Impressionistic labels for settings which modify the basic length of the vocal tract, or 'longitudinal' settings, are more numerous for the modifications achieved by vertical adjustment of the larynx than by protrusion of the lips. One possible label for the latter may be 'a pursed-lips voice', but the type of lip activity being referred to in this label may not on occasion involve protrusion of the lips. Adjectives for the effect of vertical adjustment of the position of the larynx include 'clergyman's, dark brown, graveyard, hollow, light blue, pale pink, pulpit, preacher's, sepulchral'.

Long-term modifications of the cross-sectional area of the vocal tract at a particular location, or 'latitudinal settings', seem to be referred to by impressionistic labels for settings either in the pharynx, or involving the lips or the jaw, but not tongue settings in the oral cavity itself. Labels for latitudinal settings are 'clenched teeth, grinning, guttural, hot-potato, open-mouthed, orotund, plummy, slack-jawed, strangled'. There seems to be no impressionistic label corresponding to the phonetic label 'velarised voice', as a label for an aspect of speech production – though there are a number of indexical labels for the characteristics of the speaker that the listener thinks such a voice signals.

Velic settings in voice quality are included in the reference of labels such as 'droning, nasal, sonorous, whining' and perhaps 'plangent'.

Settings of overall muscular tension of the vocal tract (including the larynx as part of the tract) are referred to by labels like 'brassy, brazen, dull, hard, metallic, muffled, pig's whistle, plangent, rasping, raucous, resonant, soft, strident, tinny'.

Laryngeal settings, as the mode of vibration of the vocal cords which is quasi-permanent in the voice of the individual speaker, are included in the reference of quite a large number of impressionistic labels, most of which can also be used to refer to the shorter-term voice dynamic feature of phonational register, though not all. The labels include 'beery, bird-like, brandy, breathy, cracked, crackling, creaky, croaky, dark brown, dulcet, falsetto, fluting, fruity, ginny, grating, gravelly, gruff, harsh, hoarse, husky, light blue, mellifluous, mellow, melodious, metallic, muffled, musical, pale pink, pig's whistle, piping, rasping, rich, rough, rumbling, shrill, thick, thin, velvety, whisky, whispery'.

There are some impressionistic labels whose implied reference is extremely difficult to unravel. In most cases they seem more likely to be metaphorical comments on indexical aspects of the speaker, rather than descriptive comments on the sound of the voice itself. These are labels like 'oily, treacly, dry, cool, warm, brittle, sugary'.

Having tried to show the variety of implied reference to different aspects of sound production that impressionistic labels may have, I would like to go on now to a brief discussion, in semiotic terms, of how such reference is achieved by the labels.

If we take the literal meanings of the impressionistic labels, they fall into two groups: those that make direct reference to some aspect of the voice, and those that make metaphorical reference to some aspect. There are many labels with an obvious direct reference to auditory aspects of the voice, such as 'raucous, shrill, hoarse, strident'. In some cases there is additionally an iconic element of similarity of auditory impression between the sound of the word used as a label and the sound of the type of voice to which the label refers. (My claim that an iconic relationship between the two is applicable for each particular pair clearly depends on the acceptance of the conventions of phonetic symbolism by the reader.) Examples of auditorily iconic labels for voices would be 'booming, orotund, rumbling, staccato, tinkling, twittering'.

Some labels make direct reference to articulatory aspects of voice production, as for example 'breathy, nasal, throaty, whispery' and, slightly less directly, 'guttural' (and similarly but more misguidedly, 'pectoral'). Occasionally an iconic element enters the articulatory characteristics of the pronunciation of the word used to label the articulatory aspect of the voice in question, as in 'orotund', where one might think that the rounded, protruded lip posture necessary for the beginning of the word resembles the characteristic lip setting of the orator declaiming in an 'orotund' style.

Where the reference of impressionistic labels is metaphorical and not direct, there are many labels which exploit an implication of iconic similarity between the actual auditory impression of a particular voice and its impression in another sensory modality, in synaesthetic metaphors. Most of these labels concern a transference of impression from the auditory modality to the visual, as in 'bleary (?), blurred (?), colourless, dark brown, golden, light blue, liquid (?), pale, pale pink, rich (?), silvery, velvety'. The tactile sense is another perceptual modality involved in synaesthetic labels, such as brittle (?), hard, liquid, rough, silky, soft, velvety'.

As a final comment on impressionistic labelling of voices, I should like to return to the point made earlier about an impressionistic tinge that exists in many supposedly scientific phonetic labels for voices. A number of terms are used in phonetic labels whose reference could be interpreted by a trainee phonetician only in the same culturally-grounded way that he would interpret impressionistic labels: he could find no support from his familiarity with the basic taxonomy for articulatory description in other areas, such as the description of segmental pronunciation, for example. I have in mind the relative ease of interpretation of a label like 'nasalised voice', from experience of the technical reference of the term 'nasalised' in other technical phonetic contexts, compared with the vagueness of inter-pretation of a label like 'creaky voice' as a technical phonetic descriptive label new to the trainee phonetician (where he could not call on his previous phonetic experience for help with its interpretation, but would have to fall back on whatever direct or metaphorical reference he could make appeal to as a layman). Similarly impressionistically contaminated terms currently used in phonetic taxonomy are 'falsetto, head-register, chest-register, harsh, breathy'. One may concede that any of these terms can quite properly enter the technical vocabulary of phonetics, once a technical definition has been allocated to which all phonetician users then subscribe. But one may also question whether the prior descriptive resources of phonetic taxonomy could not handle the labelling problem more efficiently, by minimising the number of basic terms in the taxonomy and by revealing principles of vocal control of greater generality than would otherwise be evident. For example, following Catford (1964), the principle of labelling segmental articulation on the basis of the place and manner of stricture could be applied not only to segmental articulation, but also to the laryngeal components of very many types of voices. In such a system the voiced state of the glottis would be called 'a glottal trill'; 'whispery voice' would then be 'a glottal fricative trill'; 'breathy voice' (to the extent that it is different from 'whispery voice') could be a 'weakly fricative glottal trill'; 'harsh voice' would be an 'aperiodic glottal trill'; 'hoarse voice' (i.e. 'harsh whispery voice') would be an 'aperiodic fricative glottal trill' – and so on. The more impressionistic labels in this area, such as 'whispery falsetto voice', can usefully continue to stand for short-hand references to the more precise phonetic definitions, once those definitions can be scientifically justified. But until a precise phonetic explanation of the mechanisms that produce the voices in question *is* available, it is important to realise that this supposedly 'phonetic' part of our professional vocabulary is phonetic only in a limited sense, and has only a limited claim to scientific status. The terms are phonetic in the sense that they are what phoneticians use: as such, they at least serve to isolate auditorily separable components of composite phonetic events, and attach labels of agreed auditory reference to them. The terms will become fully phonetic, and more legitimately scientific, only when the articulatory and acoustic correlates of the currently auditorily identified components can be specified. Until that time, their strongly impressionistic foundation of auditory imitation should not be disregarded.

I would like to turn now to the second of the two most basic types of label for voices – indexical labels. These, it will be recalled, refer to the characteristics that the listener attributes to the speaker producing the voice, rather than directly to aspects of the sounds produced by the speaker. In a technical semiotic sense, the sounds produced by the speaker, in their different aspects, act as indices to his imputed characteristics. In discussing indexical labels, there are thus two factors to be taken into account – the type of vocal behaviour involved, and the type of speaker-characteristic for which it is taken to be an index. In this section, I shall try to show that speaker-characteristics can be divided into a number of groups, and shall make some suggestions about the aspects of vocal behaviour that indicate particular characteristics. That the reader may well occasionally disagree about the claimed correlation between a particular type of characteristic and a given vocal index emphasises the need for research in this area: once again, however, my object is not so much to secure exact phonetic agreement about the correlates, but rather to make some plausible suggestions about the typology of the correlations.

I should like to draw an initial basic distinction between 'intrinsic' and 'extrinsic' features of the human voice. Intrinsic features lie outside the normal control of the individual, are universal rather than culturally specific, and are not normally learnable. These intrinsic features are the reflection of the basic physical foundation of a speaker's vocal equipment: they serve as indices only to physical characteristics of the speaker, such as his sex, age and health. A speaker's intrinsic physical limitations set the range of potential performance from which he must learn to make his culturally and idiosyncratically specific choices of vocal behaviour. All such choices of vocal activity, over which he can exercise volitional control, constitute the extrinsic features of his voice. Such extrinsic features will include not only the segmental choices of pronunci- ation, but also all the choices of manipulation of the voice-dynamic strand of voice production, and all the controllable habitual muscular settings which characterise the manipulable component of his voice quality. Extrinsic features of a person's voice serve as indices to all learnable aspects of his persona, and are thus almost all social and psychological indices.

There are rather few indexical labels for voices which could be called intrinsic indexical labels. Making reference only to sex, age and health, they would include such labels as 'a man's voice, a young voice, a senile voice, a robust voice' and possibly 'a weak voice', and the phonetic correlates of such labels are confined almost entirely to features of voice dynamics such as pitch-range and loudness-range, with occasional implicit reference to uncontrollable aspects of voice quality production such as the fine detail of mode of vibration of the vocal cords. The one type of intrinsic indexical label with very specific voice quality correlates is the type that labels transient states of health such as 'a cold-in-the-head voice' and 'an adenoidal voice'.

There are, on the other hand, very many extrinsic indexical labels for voices: they can be descriptively divided into two major classes, referring to social aspects of the speaker's identity (both permanent and transient), and to psychological aspects (also both permanent and transient).

As a preliminary comment, it should be said that many extrinsic indexical labels make implicit reference to levels of spoken language higher than that of phonology alone. Thus 'an upper-class voice' may be indexically signalled not only by phonetic correlates of phonology and paraphonology, but also by details of syntactic, morphological and lexical choices – that is to say, not only by phonetic features of accent, but also by linguistic features of dialect (Abercrombie, 1956: 43). I shall leave such considerations of levels of linguistic behaviour higher than phonology and paraphonology out of account, and consider only directly-phonetic features in their role as indices to extrinsic characteristics of the speaker's identity.

Finally, it may be helpful to point out that in the previous section on descriptive labels, the discussion concentrated on the plausible identification of which of the three strands of voice production was implicitly referred to in the label: segmental pronunciation, voice dynamics, or voice quality. In this section on extrinsic indexical labels, there is less possibility of such phonetic specificity, and I should like to move to a level which is slightly more abstract, but still I hope illuminating. My main concern here, apart from drawing relevant distinctions between different types of indexical characteristics, will be to identify phonological versus paraphonological aspects of vocal behaviour, and try to show something of the typology of their correlation with the indexical characteristics identified by the labels for the voices. I take it that phonology and paraphonology, within the speech of a single speaker, are partly mutually defining. I am assuming that 'paraphonology depends for its exponents on departures from the neutral point or norm in any appropriate parameter' (Laver, 1964: 34). Phonology is the set of phonetic norms in the emotionally neutral speech of the individual from which his affective paraphonology takes its phonetic deviations for its exponents. Norm and deviation, in this sense, are complementarily defined. I also take it that a speaker's accent is made up of the phonetic correlates of his phonology and his paraphonology. This is not a definition often put forward, most definitions of accent being restricted to normal phonology and ignoring paraphonology; but that is surely the result merely of the historical accident that phonetics has not yet come properly to grips with the task of coping with paraphonological description. I would like to stretch the definition of an individual speaker's accent slightly further yet, and say that it includes all the phonetic correlates not only of phonology and paraphonology, but also of all the controllable habitual muscular settings in voice quality. Put simply, a speaker's accent consists of all the extrinsic features of his vocal behaviour; and the ideal objective of phonetics in my own view would be the capability of offering a description of the auditory, articulatory and acoustic correlates of those extrinsic features.

I shall make the assumption in the following discussion of extrinsic indexical labels that the vocal behaviour which is acting as an index to any given labelled characteristic is some composite part of the speaker's accent, as defined above. I shall only occasionally make specific phonetic comment about one of the isolable components of the accent.

The first social characteristic of speakers for which extrinsic features of the voice can act as an index is that of regional origin. There are very many labels such as 'an English voice', where 'English' could be replaced by 'American, countryman's, foreign, Liverpool, Yorkshire' and so on. The one comment I would like to offer here, in support of my earlier definition of accent, is that a phrase such as 'a Liverpool voice' has implications, phonetically, as much for velarised, denasalised aspects of voice quality as it has for the other phonetic features more normally associated with 'accent', such as segmental pronunciation and voice-dynamic features of phonology and paraphonology.

Social status is often the direct referent of indexical labels, and the vocal correlate is usually the whole amalgam of the speaker's accent. Indexical adjectives of this sort include 'upper-class, middle-class, working-class' and possibly such terms as 'superior'. Educational status labels often seem to carry an implication of social class, when people speak of 'an educated voice' or 'an illiterate voice'; and there is the further possibility here that the aspect of vocal behaviour to which implicit reference is being made may well be aspects of dialectal choices as well as of accent.

Indexical labels for the speaker's profession, particularly the apparent imputation of profession implies a derogatory comment on the sound of the speaker's voice, seem often to limit themselves to vocal indices to do with voice dynamics and voice quality. Examples are: 'a lecturer's, a politician's, a schoolteacher's, a sergeant-major's' or 'a newsreader's voice'.

There are areas where social and psychological indexical labels tend to fall together, when comment is implied about the nature of the psycho-social interaction in which the speaker is participating. The first group concerns what one might call the interactional status of the speaker, in his relationship to the listener. Adjectives for voices in this circumstance would include such items as 'condescending, flattering, grovelling, patron-ising, smarmy' and perhaps 'superior'. A second category concerns the type of interaction involved between speaker and listener, but still with the emphasis on the speaker, in labels such as 'his telephone voice'. The third group shifts the emphasis to the effect of the voice on the listener himself. Of course all indexical labels imply a conclusion being drawn by the listener about the characteristic of the speaker, so in that sense all indexical labels imply 'an effect on the listener', but I have in mind an effect on the listener by means of vocal behaviour that Austin (1962: 101) has called a 'perlocutionary' effect. Labels for such voices would be 'annoying, boring, calming, frightening, interesting, irritating, persuasive, soothing, soporific' and so forth. The first two categories here, indices of 'interactional status' and 'type of interaction', would involve features of paraphonology; the last category, 'perlocutionary' indices, is much more difficult to pin down, and may perhaps be the result of a more holistic effect of the total accent of the speaker. It seems to constitute a category of index that is closer to a psychological index than a social one, being more akin to judgements about overall personality than the speaker's mood in single interactions alone.

Indexical labels for psychological characteristics of a speaker themselves fall into two chief grouping – those that concern relatively short-term aspects of psychological states, in the communication of mood, or attitude, by paraphonological means, and those that concern long-term aspects of personality. The vocal indices of personality are a highly controversial field (Kramer, 1963), but it seems likely that they involve not only paraphonological behaviour, but also all other features of accent, together with some of the intrinsic features of speech production as well. In other words, a speaker's personality may be judged by listeners not only on the basis of the choices of behaviour he makes, but also possibly to some extent on physical features over which he has no possibility of volitional control at all. In our culture, a man with a long vocal tract and large vocal cords, with a correspondingly deep-pitched bass voice with low formants, may well have attributed to him personality characteristics of mature authority that have rather little in common with the actuality of his psychological make-up – purely because of our cultural stereotypes of 'authoritative' voices.

Labels for indicating the speaker's mood constitute a long list of terms such as 'amused, angry, bored, cold, dry, excited, irritated, remote, sarcastic, sardonic' and so on. Labels for indicating personality include often rather similar terms, such as 'assured, dominating, effeminate, excitable, irritable, neurotic, nervous, virile'.

A final group of indexical labels which certainly falls within the extrinsic category involving culturally-specific learned behaviour, but which is difficult to classify as psychological indices solely, rather than partly as indices of physical characteristics also, are labels like 'mannish, womanish, childish'. In these cases, the label implies a discrepancy between the normal indexical value of the vocal behaviour involved and the visibly establishable truth about the physical identity of the speaker. That such a discrepancy exists then has psychological implications for conclusions drawn by the listener about the personality of the speaker.

Finally, as is usually the case in Procrustean typologies such as the one I have been suggesting, the analysis is not exhaustive, nor is it completely decisive, even between the major divisions suggested. Occasionally, labels for voices just do not fit as easily as I have been suggesting into the particular categories. For example a 'sepulchral voice' (if this is meaningful to writer and reader as members of the same culture) does have some implications for the sound of the voice involved. But it also has implications for the perlocutionary effect of the voice on the listener, and possibly for the indexical impression of the mood and personality of the speaker. However, I hope that I have been able to show that the large majority of labels for voices can be typologically classified in the way suggested, and that some plausible phonetic relevance can be given to the wide variety of lay usages for labelling voices, provided that the major semiotic distinction between labels for the sound of the voice versus labels for the imputed characteristic of the speaker is maintained. In this way, we can begin to advance in our professional capability in this area for elucidating the vagueness and ambiguities which characterise lay comments about speech, offering descriptive phonetic translations for descriptive impressionistic labels, and identifying specific phonetic phenomena which act as indices to the personal characteristics of speakers.

Notes

1. A preliminary version of this article was given as a paper to the Colloquium of British Academic Phoneticians in April 1973.
2. The concept of an 'indexical sign' was first put forward, in a variety of definitions, by C.S. Peirce, the nineteenth century pragmaticist philosopher. One interpretation that has been taken up by modern philosophers is the use of 'index' to mean a deictic device (Lyons, 1968: 275). This sense of 'index' will not be adopted here. Instead, I shall use the term in the sense advocated by Abercrombie (1967: 6), where he specifies it, following one of Peirce's other interpretations, as a sign which 'reveals personal characteristics of the . . . speaker'.

References

Abercrombie, D. (1956) *Problems and Principles*, Longmans, London.
Abercrombie, D. (1967) *Elements of General Phonetics*, Edinburgh University Press, Edinburgh.
Austin, J.L. (1962) *How to Do Things with Words*, Oxford University Press, Oxford.
Catford, J.C. (1964) 'Phonation types', pp. 26–37 in Abercrombie, D. et al. (eds), *In Honour of Daniel Jones*, Longmans, London.
Crystal, D. (1969) *Prosodic Systems and Intonation in English*, Cambridge University Press, London.
Feibleman, J.K. (1946) *An Introduction to the Philosophy of Charles S. Peirce*, New York.
Kramer, E. (1963) 'Judgement of personal characteristics and emotions from non-verbal properties of speech', *Psychological Bulletin*, 408–20.
Laver, J. (1964) 'The synthesis of voice quality', *Edinburgh University Department of Phonetics PAT Report*.
Laver, J. (1968) 'Voice quality and indexical information', *British Journal of Disorders of Communication*, 43–54.
Lyons, J. (1968) *An Introduction to Theoretical Linguistics*, Cambridge University Press, London.
Morris, C. (1938) 'Foundations of the theory of signs', pp. 77–138 in Neurath, O., Carnap, R. and Morris, C. (eds), *Foundations of the Unity of Science*, Vol. I, University of Chicago Press, Chicago.
Pike, K.L. (1943) *Phonetics*, The University of Michigan Press, Ann Arbor.

12 The Description of Voice Quality in General Phonetic Theory

Originally published as Laver, J. (1979) 'The description of voice quality in general phonetic theory', *Edinburgh University Department of Linguistics Work in Progress* 12: 30–52

The business of phonetics is to describe speech. There are of course many different ways of approaching such a task, given the many-stranded nature of speech. It is striking, however, that nearly all general phonetic theories give major prominence to segmenting the continuum of speech into short stretches representing the basic linguistic units of consonants and vowels. It is easy to understand why phonetic theory should concentrate on the correlation of phonetic segments with consonants and vowels. One reason is that phonetics is preoccupied with linguistic uses of the vocal apparatus, and a second reason is that the intellectual roots of modern phonetics are embedded in a culture whose alphabetic influence is very pervasive.

The time-domain of phonetic segments of this sort is typically very short, and there is considerable variety in the articulatory activities involved. Because phonetic description finally has a linguistic motivation, it is the differences between segments that tend to be emphasised, rather than the similarities.

There is an alternative, wider approach to the task of articulatory description, that concerns itself with both differences and similarities in vocal performance in speech and sees individual segments as momentary actions superimposed on a longer-term *setting* of the vocal apparatus. The settings account for the similarities and the segments for the differences, as it were. A setting gives a background, auditory colouring to sequences of short-term segmental articulations. A phonetic theory that accounts for underlying settings as well as for superimposed segments is a richer theory, with a wider application, than one that merely describes segmental behaviour in terms of differences between segments.

Being by definition non-segmental, a setting must be a property of a stretch greater than a single segment, but there is no upper bound to its extent. A setting can thus be used for phonological purposes, on a relatively short-term basis, in signalling affective information through tone of voice; or for extralinguistic purposes, on a quasi-permanent basis, identifying the individual speaker, as a phonetic component of this voice quality.

For example, nasality can be exploited phonologically both as a segment and as a setting. As a segmental quality in vowels, it is used for contrastive lexical identification in many languages, including French, Portuguese and Yoruba. As a setting, nasality is used phonologically in Sundanese, a language of Java, as a marker of verb forms. Once initiated by a nasal consonant in any position in the syllable, nasality in Sundanese runs forward through all syllable boundaries until checked by a word boundary or by a supraglottal consonant (Robins, 1953; 1957). Nasality is also manipulated for paraphonological purposes. Crystal cites Key (1967) as reporting that in Cayuvava, a language of Bolivia, nasality is used stylistically, with an honorific function: 'an individual of lower social or economic status addresses one of higher rank with a prominence of nasalisation for all vowels of the utterance; and similarly with a woman being polite to her husband, or a man asking a favour' (Crystal, 1971: 191). Finally, nasality is a very common component of voice quality, either idiosyncratically or as an indicator of membership of particular sociolinguistic groups. It characterises most speakers of Received Pronunciation in England, and many accents of the United States and Australia.

One fundamental principle emerges from these illustrations: if duration is excluded, auditory quality alone does not predict the communicative function of a given vocal phenomenon on any *a priori* basis. It follows that a descriptive model set up to account for settings exploited in any one of the three communicative areas mentioned, phonology, paraphonology or voice quality, will be capable of describing a great deal that is potentially relevant to the study of the other areas.

This article gives a descriptive outline of the phonetic settings found in voice quality.[1] But it is worth emphasising that the descriptive scheme is equally applicable to phonological and paraphonological phenomena.

Many linguists have explicitly rejected voice quality as a valid area of interest to linguistics, but, commenting on this attitude, Henderson (1977) suggests that

> Inconvenient as it may still be, it is now a matter of some urgency that we should include in our study of language at least such 'voice quality modulations' as have been found to be exploited for lexical and grammatical purposes, and I would guess that once we have managed to incorporate them in a coherent phonetic theory, the spin-off for other fields such as historical and comparative linguistics will be immense.

I find Henderson's view very attractive, and I shall try to demonstrate that the incorporation of a descriptive model for voice quality into general phonetic theory is indeed feasible. Throughout the discussion that follows, voice quality is conceived as the overall auditory colouring of an individual speaker's voice to which both laryngeal and supralaryngeal features contribute, and not (as used by Henderson, for example) just as the quality deriving solely from the activities of the speaker's larynx. Perceptually, voice quality in this broad interpretation is a cumulative abstraction over a period of time of a speaker-characterising quality gathered from the momentary, spasmodic fluctuations of the shorter-term articulations used by the speaker for phonological and paraphonological communication.

Before embarking on the outline of the descriptive model, let me comment briefly on the essential characteristics of a *phonetic* model. First, it must rest on some scientific base, and not rely on impressionistic description (Laver, 1974). Second, the descriptive analysis of a given voice must be communicable in writing, without requiring an audible demonstration of the qualities to which particular labels refer. Part of this requirement is a usable transcription system. Third, the model must be such that judges can be trained in its use and can make consistent judgements. Last, as an ideal requirement, the model should integrate work from the same areas as segmental analysis – auditory and articulatory analysis, acoustics and physiology.

In these terms, the descriptive system for voice quality about to be discussed is a general phonetic one, applicable to the vocal performance of all human beings of normal anatomy and physiology.

The descriptive system rests on an auditory foundation. The auditorily-identified components all have articulatory, physiological and acoustic correlates capable of instrumental verification. This article is limited to articulatory analysis, largely, but for the detailed acoustic specifications and the physiological hypotheses see Laver (1975; 1980). Demonstrations of the auditory qualities concerned can be heard on a tape-recording available with Laver (1980). A classified research bibliography on voice quality is offered in Laver (1979).

The basic approach is one of componential analysis rather than holistic identification. Each given voice is analysed into some fifty independently controllable elements whose composite effect characterises the overall voice, and which enable us to describe a very large number of different composite voice qualities. In a holistic approach, one would have to have an individual identification for each of this very large number of different voices, giving an impossibly cumbersome system.

For the system to be learnable, the user must be able to discriminate and identify the different auditory elements. This condition seems likely to be able to be satisfied given that the qualities concerned can all be imitated by anatomically and physiologically normal speakers. This is because voice quality derives from two separate factors in vocal performance, the first of these being such physical features as the dimensions, geometry and mass of the vocal organs. Thus, *organic* features (Ladefoged, 1960) such as the length of the vocal tract, the size of the tongue, velum and pharynx, the shape of the laryngeal structures and the volume of the nasal cavity, will all affect the overall quality of the speaker's voice.

The second factor is the use to which the vocal apparatus is put. Each speaker tends to use particular long-term muscular adjustments (Abercrombie, 1967), or settings, of his vocal apparatus, as part of his habitual style of speaking. The descriptive system offered here treats the organic features merely as a ground against which an individual setting is perceptible and is concerned primarily with the second, *phonetic* type of feature. Since these phonetic setting features are all controlled by the muscular apparatus for speech, all normal speakers should be able to learn to imitate the articulatory basis of the settings and to recognise their auditory correlates. The descriptive model therefore refers to settings superimposed on an idealised vocal apparatus, and ignores inter-speaker differences of vocal anatomy. Figure 12.1 shows the relationship between the different aspects of vocal quality perceptible in a given piece of speech. The overall quality, yet to be differentiated, we can call *phonic* quality. Within phonic quality, one aspect of the overall auditory texture is voice quality, which has both an organic component and a setting component. The other aspect is phonetic quality, part of the subject matter of general phonetic theory. In the definitions used here, phonetic quality has both a segmental component and a setting component. Settings are therefore regarded as the common ground between voice quality and phonetic quality, and the notion of a setting is basic in the description of controllable, learnable aspects of voice quality.

A second basic concept here is the principle of segmental susceptibility to the articulatory and auditory effect of a setting. No setting normally applies to every single segment a speaker utters. For instance, as a redundancy condition, a setting has no effect on segmental performance in the case of a velar stop in speech characterised by velarisation, or a nasal stop in speech with a nasal voice quality. Equally, the phonological requirements of an oral stop to show orality pre-empt (at least in normal, non-pathological speakers) the setting effects of nasality. It is thus useful to distinguish segments which are susceptible to the influence of a given setting, and those which are non-susceptible, because of their redundant or pre-emptive articulatory and acoustic requirements (Laver, 1978). This general notion could certainly be developed further, with susceptibility being made a scalar concept. Parallels with notions of phonological strength, in comparative and historical linguistics, and in sociolinguistics, immediately suggest themselves.

The final basic concept that needs to be discussed is the notion of a neutral setting. It would be difficult to describe each of the settings in the abstract; a simple solution is to describe them by reference to a common baseline, the *neutral* setting. This neutral setting (in no way to be confused with any idea of some putative 'normal' setting) is defined as the constellation of settings where:

  – the supralaryngeal vocal tract is most nearly in equal cross-section
    along its full length
  – the larynx is neither raised nor lowered
  – the lips are not protruded
  – front oral articulations are performed by the blade of the tongue
  – the tongue-root is neither advanced nor retracted
  – the faucal pillars do not constrict the vocal tract
  – the jaw is neither closed nor unduly open
  – the use of the velopharyngeal system causes audible nasality only
    where necessary for linguistic purposes
  – the vibration of the true vocal folds is regularly periodic, efficient,
    and without audible friction
  – overall muscular tension throughout the vocal system is neither high
    nor low.

Each setting to be described can then be contrasted with at least one of
these requirements. Each of the requirements of the neutral setting has a

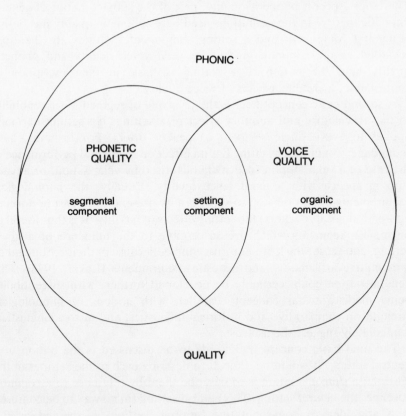

Figure 12.1 Relationship between phonic quality, voice quality and phonetic
quality.

specifiable acoustic correlate: for example, when the supralaryngeal vocal tract is most nearly in equal cross-section along its full length, then all higher formant frequencies will be odd multiples of that of the first formant. In this configuration, therefore, when the average frequency of the first formant is 500 Hz, which it would be for a vocal tract of 17.5 cm length, then that of the second formant would be 1500 Hz, the third 2500 Hz, and so on.

The settings will be discussed in three groupings:
1. supralaryngeal settings
2. laryngeal settings
3. overall muscular tension settings.

These are represented by the symbols in Figure 12.2, which are intended to preface conventional segmental transcriptions. A major assumption incorporated here is that the segmental behaviour of two speakers may be judged identical, if the articulatory differences between them are attributable exclusively to a difference of articulatory setting. This raises interesting questions about segmental analysis. For example, does placing two vowels from two different speakers in exactly the same place on a phonetic vowel chart mean that the speakers are judged to have performed directly equivalent articulatory gestures (equivalent in the sense of producing identical auditory phonetic qualities)? Or is it possible that the gestures may have been tangibly different, and that the vowels were judged to be equivalent only after the tacit discounting of the articulatory and auditory effect of a voice quality setting such as velarised voice in one of the speakers?

1. Supralaryngeal Settings

The neutral reference setting of the supralaryngeal vocal tract can be modified by three different groups of settings: firstly, settings of the longitudinal axis of the vocal tract; secondly, settings of the latitudinal axis of the tract; and thirdly, velopharyngeal settings.

(i) Longitudinal Settings

The longitudinal axis of the vocal tract can be modified by upwards or downwards displacements of the larynx and its muscular framework, giving *raised larynx voice* and *lowered larynx voice*, or by protrusion forwards of the lips, giving voices with *labial protrusion*. An early account of these and other vocal tract settings is given in Laver (1968).

(a) RAISED LARYNX AND LOWERED LARYNX VOICE

The muscle systems above and below the larynx can keep it raised or lowered throughout speech, with momentary positional fluctuations caused by the movements of the muscles directly involved in, or passively affected by, the production of segmental articulation. One might also speculate

uvularised voice	Ṿ̲	tense voice	T+
pharyngalised voice	Ɏ̲	lax voice	T-
laryngopharyngalised voice	Ɏ̲	raised larynx voice	Lˆ
close jaw	Jˆ	lowered larynx voice	Lˇ
open jaw	Jˇ	open rounding	Vʷ
nasal voice	Ṽ	close rounding	Vʷʷ
denasal voice	V̐	spread lips	V<>
modal voice	V	labiodentalised voice	Vᵥ
falsetto	F	tip articulation	Vˆ
creak	C	blade articulation	Vˇ
whisper	W	retroflex articulation	V̢
creaky voice	V̰	dentalised voice	V̱
whispery voice	Ṿ	alveolarised voice	V++
breathy voice	V̤	palatoalveolarised voice	V+
harsh voice	V!	palatalised voice	V̡
ventricular voice	V!!	velarised voice	Ṿ

Figure 12.2 A notational system for voice quality.

that, because of muscular interconnections between the larynx and other parts of the vocal tract, the articulatory activities of the tongue, the pharynx and the jaw might be affected in their turn. Sundberg and Nordström (1976) have shown, however, that in vertical shifts of larynx position of up to 1.5 cm, the main resonatory effect can be explained by the resulting change in the length of the pharynx. Associated changes of cross-sectional area contribute little, apparently, to the overall acoustic effect.

Laryngeal elevation tends be accompanied by a rise in the fundamental frequency, and most voices produced with a raised larynx seem comparatively higher-pitched. This, however, is not mechanically inevitable, and can be compensated by adjustments of the laryngeal pitch-control mechanism. Since the laryngeal mechanism for achieving higher pitch has as one of its contributors a raising of the larynx, then to raise the larynx and leave the pitch undisturbed will necessarily require a compensatory adjustment of some sort.

Conversely, it is possible to compensate for a naturally low pitch-range by raising the larynx as a continuously-held setting. In this way, many would-be tenor singers who have an optimum natural pitch-range slightly lower than that appropriate for a tenor voice manage nevertheless to achieve a tenor-like pitch-range. Auditorily, and with an implication of an emphathetically-sensed physiological state, raised larynx voice often sounds rather strained.

In lowered larynx voice, the fundamental frequency tends to be lower. Although this can be compensated for by muscular adjustment of the laryngeal pitch control mechanism, pitch compensation seems uncommon in this setting, and low pitch is an almost ubiquitous accompaniment of lowered larynx voice.

Speakers who use lowered larynx voice often seem to 'tuck in' their chin and rotate their head slightly downwards. Reducing the angle between neck and the under-surface of the chin, this prevents uncomfortable stretching of the musculature above the larynx and makes it easier to lower the larynx. It also facilitates the lower pitch-range by not opposing the pitch-lowering effect of contraction of the muscles below the larynx on the cricothyroid pitch-control system of the larynx.

Lowered larynx voice seems very often to be produced with a marked relaxation of muscular effort at the laryngeal level, which frequently produces breathy voice as the mode of laryngeal vibration.

(b) LABIAL PROTRUSION

Protruding the lips adds a short section to the longitudinal axis of the vocal tract, which lowers all formant frequencies, with the higher formants more affected. This is similar to the effect of elongation of the longitudinal axis of the tract by lowering the larynx. The two settings can be differentiated, however, by their effect on segmental activities, since labial protrusion constrains the articulatory onset and offset of segmental labial actions in a way which is unlike the corresponding effects of lowered larynx voice.

Anything more than slight labial protrusion usually involves a certain amount of horizontal constriction of the space between the lips, though this latitudinal action is not inevitable, since it is physiologically possible to have substantial protrusion without any such horizontal compression. However, protrusion without lip-rounding of this sort seems rare.

Protrusion of the lips is occasionally asymmetrical, in either the vertical or horizontal plane, or both, but the discussion of idiosyncratic factors such as these is beyond the scope of this article.

(ii) *Latitudinal Settings*

Latitudinal settings of the supralaryngeal vocal tract tend to constrict or expand the cross-sectional area at some given location along the length of the tract. The constriction and expansion are caused by the action of a number of vocal organs, and the different settings will be discussed in five groups, according to the organ chiefly responsible. The five groups relate to the activities of the lips, tongue, the faucal pillars, the pharynx and the jaw.

(a) LABIAL SETTINGS

These settings tend to constrict or expand the interlabial space, in two dimensions of the coronal plane of the lips. Although it is not quite true, it is assumed for descriptive convenience that these two dimensions lie on the same plane.

Leaving aside scalar variations within a parameter, there are eight labial settings which involve expansion or constriction of the maximum horizontal and vertical dimensions of the interlabial space. Figure 12.3 gives a schematic diagram of these settings.

If labial protrusion is combined with all these different latitudinal settings, and with the neutral latitudinal setting, then the scheme yields eighteen different settings of the lips. All are physiologically possible but some seem to be used much more frequently than others. Labial settings have a mutually-enabling interaction with settings of the jaw.

(b) LINGUAL SETTINGS

Of the five different groups of lingual settings, four concern constraints on articulation in the sagittal plane. Three of these involve the body of the tongue, the tip and blade of the tongue, and the tongue root, while the fourth involves limitation on the movements of the tongue radially away from its neutral position. The fifth setting involves a more minor aspect: it is concerned with the degree of lateral curvature of the tongue surface in the side-to-side plane. These last two types of settings relate to overall muscular tension and will be discussed in the section on tension settings.

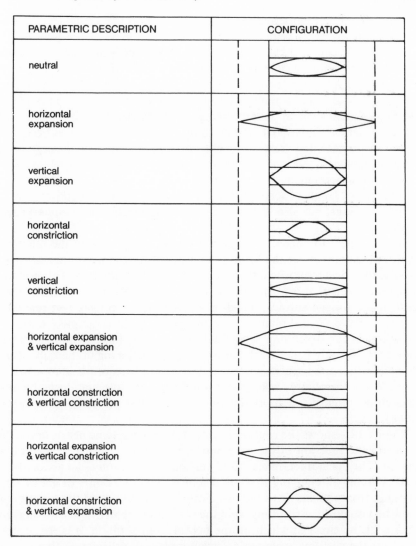

PARAMETRIC DESCRIPTION	CONFIGURATION
neutral	
horizontal expansion	
vertical expansion	
horizontal constriction	
vertical constriction	
horizontal expansion & vertical expansion	
horizontal constriction & vertical constriction	
horizontal expansion & vertical constriction	
horizontal constriction & vertical expansion	

Figure 12.3 Schematic diagram of the front view of labial settings (all with protrusion and non-protrusion).

The sagittal settings of the body, tip and blade of the tongue all tend to maintain the relevant part of the tongue displaced from its neutral position in the vocal tract, thereby constricting or expanding the oral cavity or the pharynx. Pike describes the effect of lingual adjustments of this sort on vowels, in terms of 'moving the vowel triangle AS A WHOLE frontwards, backwards, upwards and downwards in the mouth during connective speech. The auditory effects are startling, and easy to achieve' (Pike, 1967: 224). How is this lingual displacement to be described in articulatory terms? Phonetic theory already has, in the notion of 'secondary articulation', a means of describing secondary displacements of the bulk of the tongue which colour the auditory quality of types of segmental articulation of a greater primary degree of stricture. We can thus call a long-term tendency to keep the body of the tongue slightly raised and retracted 'velarised voice', and a tendency to keep it simply retracted 'pharyngealised voice', and so forth. Abercrombie (1967: 93) discusses this application of 'secondary articulation' to the description of voice quality; it is necessary here only to note that velarisation etc. are secondary only on the segmental level of analysis, and not on the level of voice quality analysis as such, where quasi-permanent velarisation is in no sense analytically 'secondary'.

The use of labels of secondary articulation can be extended not only to lingual settings, but also to labial, faucal, pharyngeal and velopharyngeal settings.

With respect to lingual settings, both in the mouth and in the pharynx, we think chiefly about the location and degree of the maximum constriction of the vocal tract when describing segmental articulation. This point of maximum constriction is then taken to characterise the configuration of the rest of the tongue surface, which is assumed to be convex and regularly curved, in the sagittal plane. Using this point as the descriptive datum is economical for describing segmental articulation. In describing settings, however, we state general tendencies for the positioning of the bulk of the tongue rather than specify relatively fine distinctions of place of articulation. We can profitably take as our reference point the long-term average speech position of the approximate centre of mass of the tongue (Laver, 1968).

Figure 12.4 shows the centre of mass of the tongue lying nearly vertically beneath the junction of the hard and soft palates, in the neutral configuration. The vocal tract, in a stylised version, can be seen as an arc of about 270°, curving at relatively constant distance round the centre of mass of the tongue, from the larynx to the lips. Settings of the body of the tongue can now be visualised as resulting from the shift of the centre of mass along any radius of the circle of which, in the neutral configuration, it is the centre.

Using the customary phonetic labels for place of articulation (but cf: the remarks above on 'secondariness'), we can describe the effects of the following radial movements of the location of the centre of mass of the tongue: upwards towards the hard palate and slightly forwards, to give *palatalised voice*; forward and upwards for *palato-alveolarised voice*; backwards and upwards for *velarised voice*; backwards and slightly upwards for *uvularised voice*; and backwards for *pharyngealised voice* (where the pharyngeal part of the vocal tract is constricted by retraction of the body of the tongue into the pharynx, rather than by the sphincteric action of the muscles of the pharynx bringing the back wall of the pharynx forward as well).

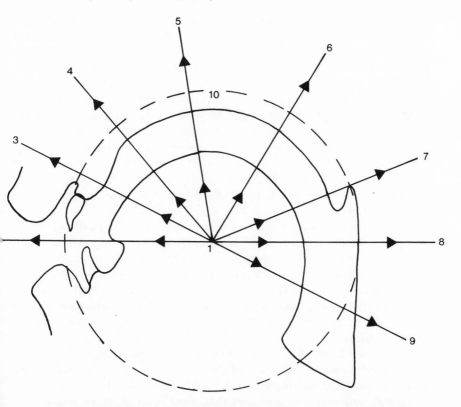

Figure 12.4 Stylised diagram of the sagittal section of the vocal tract in the neutral configuration, showing radial directions of movement of the centre of mass of the tongue in extrinsic settings of the body of the tongue.

1. Centre of mass of the tongue
2. Dentalisation
3. Alveolarisation
4. Palato-alveolarisation
5. Palatalisation
6. Velarisation
7. Uvularisation
8. Pharyngealisation
9. Laryngo-pharyngealisation
10. Junction of the hard and soft palates

Finer sub-divisions, such as 'pre-velarised voice', 'alveolo-palatalised voice' and 'post-alveolarised voice' are probably not possible when one is gathering the necessary diagnostic information over quite a long stretch of speech. Indeed, it may be more practical for most purposes to distinguish only settings with a fronting component, in *tongue-fronted voice*, with a retracting component, in *tongue-retracted voice*, and with the tongue raised, in *tongue-raised voice*.

On the other hand, the lingual settings for pharyngealisation could be sub-divided into *pharyngealised voice*, for constriction chiefly of the middle pharynx, and *laryngo-pharyngealised voice*, for constriction of the lower pharynx and upper larynx, with the centre of mass of the tongue moving backwards and slightly downwards. One difficulty in drawing this auditory distinction is that the constriction of the pharynx usually involves other phenomena, such as a vertical shift of larynx position downwards, giving a lowered larynx component (and a somewhat breathy phonatory setting), and a tendency to pull the velum downwards (velum and tongue being connected by the palatoglossus muscle), giving some nasalisation. All of which makes pharyngealised voice into a perceptual complex in which the specific contribution of the pharyngealisation is particularly hard to isolate.

The tongue being a relatively fixed volume, unless there are strong, compensating tensions any lingual constrictive setting tends to cause expansion in one or more other parts of the vocal tract; pharyngealisation, for example, enlarges the front part of the oral cavity, as does velarisation, to a smaller extent.

There is a small group of settings where the centre of mass of the tongue is displaced from the neutral position merely as an enabling factor. This is the group of settings of the tip and blade of the tongue. For example, the tip of the tongue can be the principal active articulator in the front of the mouth instead of the blade, and vice versa. Honikman (1964) describes differences of shape and posture characteristically distinguishing the settings of the tip and blade of the tongue in English, French, Iranian, Russian and Turkish.

At least two types of retroflex articulation must be distinguished. In the most extreme one the underside of the tip and blade are presented to the front of the hard palate. Catford (1977: 153) calls these 'sublamino-prepalatal' articulations, and says that Tamil and other Dravidian languages are often of this type. Ladefoged (1971: 40) suggests that other languages from South Asia use a less extreme articulation with the tip of the tongue articulating against or near the back of the alveolar ridge: Ladefoged calls these articulations 'apical post-alveolars' (1971: 39), and Catford (1977: 152) calls them 'apico-post-alveolar'. Retroflex vowels, as in the accents of south-west England, typically involve 'apical' and not 'sub-laminal' retroflexion. The same seems to be true of retroflexion used as a voice quality setting.

For all these tongue tip and blade settings, the body of the tongue has to be set so that the tip/blade can move appropriately. This is particularly necessary with the retroflex setting, especially the sub-laminal type, where to allow the tongue tip to curl up, the body of the tongue is probably set slightly lower and possibly slightly backed. The tongue body is assisted in this 'enabling' function by the jaw. In tip settings, the body of the tongue is slightly retracted, and in the blade setting, it is in a neutral position. It therefore seems reasonable to maintain that the tip/blade system is only relatively independent, depending to some extent on the major tongue-body system, which is in turn partly dependent on the jaw.

This relative independence is reflected in the fact that while the tongue body setting can usually be heard underlying nearly every segment in continuous speech, the tip/blade settings (except in the case of retroflexion) are perceptible only when the tip or blade is the active articulator, and even then they compete with the tongue-body setting on which they are superimposed.

(c) FAUCAL SETTINGS

The faucal pillars, which are made up of the two paired muscles *palatoglossus* and *palatopharyngeus* which pull down the velum in nasalisation, can constrict the pharynx and the back oral cavity by moving laterally inwards, if the velum is braced to resist their downwards pull. This gives *faucalised voice*, sometimes heard in deaf speakers. Pike (1943: 123–4) tentatively associates faucalisation with a more general tension throughout the lower end of the vocal tract, involving 'lower pharyngeal constriction, glottal tension, and usually a raising of the larynx'.

(d) PHARYNGEAL SETTINGS

We have seen that the shape of the pharynx can be modified by the action of the body of the tongue, in pharyngealised voice, by the root of the tongue, in advanced and retracted tongue-root articulations, and by the faucal pillars, in faucalised voice. The pharynx can also be constricted by the pharyngeal constrictor muscle, to give another version of *pharyngealised voice*, though it is not yet known whether this can be distinguished auditorily from other types of pharyngealisation.

(e) MANDIBULAR SETTINGS

Settings of the jaw have an interactive, mutually enabling relationship with all other types of latitudinal settings. Leaving aside laterally asymmetric settings of the jaw, it is possible to distinguish the effects of *close jaw position* from that of *open jaw position* and *protruded jaw position*.

Honikman (1964: 80) points out that languages differ with respect to jaw settings, the greater part of English articulation taking place behind (loosely) closed jaws but the jaw setting for the languages of India and Pakistan being very different, with the jaws held inert and loosely apart. This makes the aperture between upper and lower teeth relatively wide and the oral cavity relatively large, which enables retroflex consonants to be produced more comfortably. This setting also explains the lack of pressure in bilabial stops and the characteristic timbre of Indian languages.

(iii) Velopharyngeal Settings

Nasality is seen here as essentially an auditory phenomenon. A vital factor in inducing resonance in the nasal cavity is the ratio of the latitudinal cross-sections of the relatively horizontal opening from the pharynx into the nasal cavity and the relatively vertical opening from the pharynx into the mouth. Only when this ratio exceeds a critical level is audible resonance induced. If we abandon the over-simplistic articulatory notion of necessary velopharyngeal closure for non-nasal segments, it is clear that the actual position of the velum will be highly variable during speech, in response jointly to the type of segments being produced and to the need to maintain the ratio of the oral and nasal port areas below the critical level for inducing nasal resonance.

Condax et al. (1976) showed that the velum has five distinct positions during speech, depending on the type of segment being articulated. Extending this finding, and drawing on published experimental work on nasality using endoscopic, fibre-optic, cineradiographic, electro-myographic and aerodynamic techniques, Cagliari (1978: 159–6) proposes a very useful 'neutral velic scale', on an articulatory basis. Velic height, he notes, varies from maximally high in blowing to maximally low in respiratory position. Within these limits, different types of speech segments correlate with different velic heights on this scale, in the following progression from highest to lowest: voiceless stops; voiced stops; voiceless fricatives; voiced fricatives; all close vowels; all open vowels; nasalised close vowels; nasalised open vowels; nasal segments. The neutral velopharyngeal setting was described earlier as one where the use of the velopharyngeal system causes audible nasality only where necessary for linguistic purposes. This would involve an absence of nasality except on phonologically nasal or contextually-nasalised segments. For the velopharyngeal setting to change from neutral to nasal, Cagliari suggests that at least some segments in the speech of the speaker concerned must show a drop in velic height, compared with the values of the neutral scale. Conversely, a denasal quality involves a rise in velic height, compared with the neutral scale. The neutral velic scale for segmental performance will be taken to underlie the position that the nasal settings of the velopharyngeal system include any setting of the velum which produces more audible nasality than is appropriate for the neutral setting. Similarly, denasal settings of the velopharyngeal system can be taken to include any setting of the velum which produces less audible nasality than is appropriate for the neutral setting.

2. Laryngeal Settings

Each of the major laryngeal settings will be discussed individually, but there are two criteria by which they can be grouped into categories, and the grouping reveals some useful generalities. The two criteria are: 'can the phonation-type occur alone as a *simple* type?' and 'can the phonation-type occur in combination with other phonation-types, as a *compound* type, and if so, with which?'.

On this basis, there are three different categories involved. The first category is made up of *modal voice* and *falsetto*, which can occur alone, as simple types, or combine with members of other groups, as compound types, but not with the other (Laver, 1975).

The second category consists of *whisper* and *creak*. These can occur alone, as simple types, and together as a compound type, to give *whispery creak*. They can also occur as compound types with either member of the first group, giving *whispery voice* and *whispery falsetto*, and *creaky voice* and *creaky falsetto*; and they can occur as compound types with members of the first group and with each other, giving *whispery creaky voice* and *whispery creaky falsetto*.

The third category is formed by modificatory settings which can only occur in compound types of phonation, and never by themselves as simple types. These are *harshness* and *breathiness*.

Harshness can combine with modal voice and with falsetto, to produce *harsh voice* and *harsh falsetto*. Breathiness can only combine with modal voice, to give *breathy voice*. Harshness and breathiness cannot combine with whisper and creak and whispery creak unless either modal voice or falsetto is present. Because breathiness and falsetto are incompatible, the only multiple compound products of this third category of settings are thus *harsh whispery voice, harsh creaky voice, harsh creaky falsetto, harsh whispery creaky voice* and *harsh whispery creaky falsetto*.

The lack of combinations such as breathy falsetto is explained either by redundant or conflicting acoustic requirements or by conflicting physiological requirements. A tentative explanation can be based on mutually exclusive specification of the phonatory settings involved in one or more of three muscular parameters concerned in adjustment of the vocal folds, mainly longitudinal tension, adductive tension and medial compression. Although tentative, this explanation is supported by the wide range of laryngeal research available and is attractive in that the compatibility or incompatibility of the various different phonatory settings in compound phonations is given a physiological basis. But the hypothesis must be tested by physiological research before being accepted as a reliable explanation.

Adductive tension is the tension of the interarytenoid and lateral cricoarytenoid muscles and tends to bring the arytenoid cartilages together, closing the cartilaginous glottis and hence also the ligamental glottis. *Medial compression* is the adductive pressure on the vocal processes of the arytenoid cartilages achieved by tension of the lateral cricoarytenoid muscles. This closes the ligamental glottis, but whether the cartilaginous glottis also closes depends on the analytically separate interarytenoid component of adductive tension. Medial compression would also be aided by contraction of the lateral parts of the thyroarytenoid muscles. *Longitudinal tension*, straightforwardly, is achieved by the vocalis and/or cricothyroid muscles. Each different phonatory setting has different specifications in terms of these three physiological parameters.

The descriptive model of phonation types offered here is broadly similar to that of Catford (1964), from which it takes its point of departure, and to that of Ladefoged (1971), as well as to Catford's later development of his system in Catford (1977). But there are a number of differences of definition and terminology, explained in detail in Laver (1980).

(*i*) *Modal Voice*

The laryngeal characteristics of the neutral mode of phonation are reasonably well agreed. The full glottis is involved, with both the ligamental and the cartilaginous sections functioning as a single unit. The vibration of the true vocal folds is regularly periodic, efficient in producing vibration, and without audible friction brought on by any incomplete closure of the glottis. This is the type of phonation to which Hollien (1974: 126) has given the name *modal* register. Modal voice is the type of vocal fold vibration which phonetic theory assumes takes place in ordinary voicing, when no specific feature is explicitly changed or added. The production of modal voice is carried out with only moderate adductive tension and moderate medial compression, with moderate longitudinal tension when the fundamental frequency is in the lower part of the range used in ordinary conversation. Other phonatory settings can now be contrasted with modal voice.

(*ii*) *Falsetto*

Hollien (1971: 329) suggests that modal voice and falsetto are completely different laryngeal operations. While modal voice has moderate adductive tension, moderate medial compression and moderate longitudinal tension, falsetto is different in all three respects. Van den Berg (1968: 298) states that adductive tension of the interarytenoid muscles is high, medial compression of the glottis is large, and longitudinal passive tension of the vocal ligaments is also high (though there is little active longitudinal tension in the vocalis muscles).

The consensus of the literature on phonation describes the production of falsetto as follows. The arytenoid cartilages adduct the vocal folds, by contraction of the interarytenoid and the lateral cricoarytenoid muscles. The vocalis muscles along the glottal edge of each vocal fold remain relaxed, but the mass of each vocal fold is made stiff and immobile by contraction of the thyroarytenoid muscles, which make up the outer bulk of the folds. The vocal ligaments along the glottal edge of the vocal fold are put under strong tension by the contraction of the cricothyroid muscle. This results in the vertical cross-section of the edges of the vocal fold becoming thin. The glottis often remains slightly apart, and the characteristic sub-glottal air pressure is lower than for modal voice (Kunze, 1964).

The average pitch range for male falsetto was found by Hollien and Michel (1968: 602) to be from 275 to 634 Hz as against the average range for modal voice, which was from 94 to 287 Hz. The 'thin' auditory quality which is characteristic of falsetto derives from the interaction of high fundamental frequency and the mode of vibration of the vocal folds, which vibrate and come into contact only at the free borders, the remainder of the folds remaining relatively fixed (cf. Zemlin, 1964: 155).

(iii) Whisper

The physiology of the whisper setting of the phonatory mechanism is not controversial. Nearly all writers agree that the chief physiological characteristic of whisper is a triangular opening of the cartilaginous glottis, comprising about one third of the full length of the glottis. The shape of the glottis in whispering is often referred to as an inverted letter 'Y'. In weak whisper, the triangular opening can be fairly long, including part of the ligamental as well as the cartilaginous glottis. With increasing intensity, the glottis is increasingly constricted until only the cartilaginous section remains just open. Taken together, these factors suggest low adductive tension and moderately high medial compression.

The triangular opening of the glottis is achieved by the following factors: the lateral cricoarytenoid muscles contract, toeing in the vocal processes of the arytenoid cartilages. The interarytenoid muscles which normally approximate the bodies of the arytenoid cartilages remain relaxed. This facilitates the toeing in of the arytenoids as they pivot on the cricoid. As the air flows past the edges of the open cartilaginous glottis, the characteristic 'whisper' sound quality is produced by 'eddies generated by friction of the air in and above the larynx' (van den Berg, 1968: 295).

When whisper is involved in a compound phonation such as whispery voice, there are two possibilities for the production of the whisper component. The first is that the cartilaginous part of the glottis remains open in a triangular shape with the ligamental part of the glottis being responsible for the regular oscillation of the vocal folds giving voicing. The second is that the full glottis is involved in regular oscillation but that the vocal folds do not completely meet in the mid-line, leaving a space through which there is continuous transglottal air flow.

(iv) Creak

Creak is also called vocal fry or glottal fry in the phonetic literature, particularly by American researchers. The low fundamental frequency of this creak type of phonation is one factor which distinguishes it from harsh voice, which is otherwise somewhat similar. While the mean fundamental frequency for creak has been found to be 34.6 Hz, in an average range for male speakers of 24–52 Hz, the mean fundamental frequency for harsh voice is said to be 122.1 Hz, with a range similar to that of modal voice, whose average range is said above to be 94–287 Hz. Michel (1968) also reports that harsh voices seem to have fundamental frequencies consistently above 100 Hz, and vocal fry (i.e. creak) consistently below 100 Hz.

The specification of fundamental frequency characteristics is not, of course, enough. Comment on laryngeal factors contributing to auditory quality is also needed. These factors are described by Hollien et al. (1966: 247) as follows:

(1) The vocal folds when adducted are relatively thick and apparently compressed,

(2) The ventricular folds are somewhat adducted also, and

(3) The inferior surfaces of the false folds actually come in contact with superior surfaces of the true vocal folds. Thus, an unusually thick, compact (but not necessarily tense) structure is created prior to the initiation of phonation.

The picture suggested by Hollien and his co-workers is of phonation with strong adductive tension and medial compression, but little longitudinal tension, and with vigorous ventricular involvement. More recent work by Hollien et al. (1969) supports this picture, in their finding that the control of fundamental frequency in vocal fry is not achieved by the same mechanism as in modal voice; while vocal fold length in modal voice increases with fundamental frequency, and vocal fold thickness is inversely related to the frequency, in vocal fry neither the length nor the thickness of the vocal folds seems to vary with the changes in pitch. This suggests that the control of fundamental frequency is managed by the aerodynamic component of the aerodynamic-myoelastic phonatory action, rather than by the myoelastic component, and the sub-glottal air pressure should reflect this.

The effect of continual, separate taps in rapid sequence is an essential part of the characteristic auditory quality of creak. The acoustic correlate of this effect is a train of discrete laryngeal pulses. In order for the individual pulses to be heard as discrete, the vocal tract has to be nearly completely damped in between the occurrence of successive wave fronts. Coleman (1963) specifies that vocal fry is perceived whenever the vocal tract wave is allowed to decay by 42–44 db of its maximum amplitude for a single pulse, and when the wave is allowed to decay for only 30 db between the excitation pulses, vocal fry is not perceived.

The creak component in the compound phonation of *creaky voice*, which combines creak with modal voice, may well differ from speaker to speaker. One suggestion is that the creak is made at the arytenoid end, but in the case of *whispery creaky voice* it seems more likely that the creak component would be produced at the thyroid end of the glottis, leaving the cartilaginous glottis free for the production of the whisper and voice components – but this remains a speculation for the present.

(v) Harshness

It will be recalled that 'harshness' is a quality taken on by a number of other phonation types. It will be discussed here as a modification of modal voice, for convenience of exposition. Applied to modal voice, harshness should be thought of not as contributing substantially new parameters to the mode of phonation, but rather as boosting the values of some of the parameters already operating.

The acoustic characteristics of harsh voice derive mainly from the regularity of the glottal wave form and spectral noise. Wave form irregularity concerns cycle-to-cycle variations both of fundamental frequency and of amplitude. Irregularity of this sort gives a characteristic 'rough' auditory quality to a voice. One physiological correlate of harshness is widely agreed. It is laryngeal hyper-tension, which results in excessive approximation of the vocal folds. It was stated earlier that harshness showed fundamental frequencies consistently (but not markedly) above 100 Hz. This strongly suggests that the laryngeal tension in harshness does not result primarily from longitudinal tension but from extreme adductive tension and extreme medial compression, brought about by over-contraction of the muscle systems responsible for these two parameters in modal voice.

(vi) Breathiness

Breathiness is a quality which is quite often heard as a modification of modal voice, giving *breathy voice*. By comparison with modal voice, the mode of vibration of the vocal folds is inefficient, and is accompanied by slight audible friction. Muscular effort is low, with the result that the glottis is kept somewhat open along most of its length, and the folds never meet on the mid-line. Because each closing movement of the folds tends to be abortive, the lessened glottal resistance leads to a higher rate of air-flow than in modal voice.

The muscle tension adjustments necessary for breathy voice can be seen as involving minimal adductive tension and weak medial compression, just sufficient to allow aerodynamic forces in the comparatively large volume of trans-glottal air-flow to superimpose on the outflowing air a very inefficient vibration of the vocal folds, with the folds not meeting at the centre line. The one laryngeal tension factor that is controlled more finely is longitudinal tension, in the production of appropriate fundamental frequency for the purposes of intonation. We can assume that the degree of longitudinal tension is rather low, generally. High-pitched breathy voices seem rare.

Breathiness can combine with only one other type of phonation in the system for describing voice quality offered here – that is, modal voice. This is because, while modal voice requires only moderate medial compression, all the others, falsetto, whisper, creak and harshness need a greater amount than is compatible with breathiness.

Many writers have used the label 'breathy' to describe components in given voice qualities that should rather have been called 'whispery'. In the descriptive scheme used here it would not be possible, for example, to accept a label which combined 'breathiness' and 'harshness', such as *harsh breathy voice*, for the voice quality often described as 'husky' or 'hoarse', because of the mutually-exclusive prerequisites *breathiness* as here defined and *harshness*. Such a quality would instead be labelled *harsh whispery voice*.

However, it is reasonable to acknowledge that there is a close auditory relationship between breathy voice and whispery voice, as these two compound types of phonation are understood in this descriptive scheme. Both involve the presence of audible friction: to the extent that such friction is concerned, the transition from breathiness to whisperiness is part of an auditory continuum, and the placing of the borderline between the two categories is merely an operational decision. The physiological relationship between the two is a good deal more distant, however, when their specification in terms of the muscular parameter of medial compression is considered, as indicated immediately above. Breathy voice has extremely weak medial compression, with little tendency on the part of the lateral cricoarytenoid muscles to swivel the vocal processes of the arytenoids in towards each other. The whisper component of whispery voice requires moderate to high medial compression, so that the whisper-producing channel is relatively confined to the cartilaginous glottis.

From an auditory point of view, it is practical to use the label 'breathy voice' for the range of qualities produced with a low degree of laryngeal effort, and where only a slight amount of glottal friction is audible. If one thinks of the friction component and the modal voice component as being audibly co-present but able to be heard individually, then the balance between the two components in breathy voice is one where the modal voice element is markedly dominant. 'Whispery voice' can then be used for phonations produced with a greater degree of laryngeal effort, and where a more substantial amount of glottal friction, from a more constricted glottis, is audible. The audible balance between the friction component and the periodic component is different from that in breathy voice; the friction component is more prominent than in breathy voice, and may on occasion even equal the periodic component (and sometimes dominate it strongly, as in 'extremely whispery voice'). In the interpretation offered here, the friction component of whispery voice can thus be sub-divided into a larger number of audible increments than can the friction component of breathy voice.

3. Overall Muscular Tension Settings

Tension settings could alternatively be described as constellations of co-occurring local settings. However, because their production is explainable in terms of a single underlying tendency to boost or drop muscular tension throughout the vocal apparatus, it seems preferable to label these 'overall' settings more globally. An overall increase in muscular tension is therefore called *tense voice*, and an overall decrease, compared to the neutral setting, is called *lax voice*.

The local components of tense voice will tend to have the following characteristics: ligamental, harsh or ventricular phonation, which will sound comparatively louder and higher-pitched; higher sub-glottal air pressure; slightly raised larynx; constriction of the upper larynx and lower pharynx; a tensed velum; vigorous and extensive radial movements of the convex-surfaced tongue in consonant and vowel articulation; vigorous labial activity; and a more mobile jaw. Contrastively, lax voice has the opposite characteristics: breathy or whispery phonation, which will sound comparatively softer and lower-pitched; lower sub-air pressure; a slightly lowered larynx; an unconstricted pharynx; moderate nasality; inhibited minimised radial movements of the relaxed, relatively flat-surfaced tongue in consonant and vowel articulations; minimised labial activity; and a less mobile jaw.

4. Indication of Scalar Degrees of Settings

Most of the settings can be classed as 'slight', 'moderate' or 'extreme'. Where the degree is not explicitly mentioned, it can be assumed that a given setting is moderate. Composite componential labels form the vocabulary of the descriptive system. A given voice might thus be described as 'a labialised, slightly velarised, extremely nasal, slightly harsh, whispery voice'. Where labels for any major category of setting are omitted, it can be assumed that in that respect the speaker is using a neutral setting. Thus 'a breathy voice' means that the degree of breathiness is moderate, and that all other factors are as prescribed for the neutral setting. Where no explicit mention of a phonation type is made, beyond the term 'voice', it can be assumed that modal voice is implied. Thus 'a labialised voice' means 'modal voice with labialisation'.

5. Applications of the Descriptive System

Phonetic variations in voice quality are of potential interest to a wide range of different disciplines. In speech therapy, for example, voice quality can be a useful indicator of rehabilitative progress in therapy. In musicology and ethnomusicology, there is a complex problem of analysis and notation involved in the specification of different types of vocal effects. The ability to describe phonetic components in voice quality which this descriptive system offers may be useful here. The descriptive model could also be useful to researchers interested in the complexities of non-verbal interaction in face-to-face communication, including psychologists, psychiatrists and ethnologists. In addition, since voice quality can signal membership of many types of social and regional groupings, sociologists, social anthropologists, social psychologists and sociolinguists may find something interesting (cf. Trudgill, 1974: 186–7; Laver and Trudgill, 1979; Esling, 1978).

Spoken communication between humans and computers is almost certain to be a widespread social reality in the not-too-distant future. There are very many intelligible speech synthesisers. Speech recognition systems are becoming increasingly sophisticated and successful. Many speaker-recognition systems already exist, in voice security applications, for example. In all these areas, voice quality is an important consideration.

Finally, because linguistic settings and voice quality settings differ more in the time-scale involved than in their phonetic form, a number of the setting features described in this article are of direct relevance to linguistic phonetics. Register in South-East Asian languages is perhaps the clearest example of what Henderson was referring to, in the quotation mentioned earlier, when she wrote of 'such "voice quality modulations" as have been found to be exploited for lexical and grammatical purposes' (Henderson, 1977).

Note

1. This article is based on two lectures on voice quality given to the Northern Ireland Speech and Language Forum on November 15, 1978, and on a seminar given to the University of Cambridge Linguistic Society on April 26, 1979.

References

Abercrombie, D., Fry, D.B., MacCarthy, P.A.D., Scott N.C. and Trim, J.L.M. (eds) (1964) *In Honour of Daniel Jones*, Longman, London.

Abercrombie, D. (1967) *Elements of General Phonetics*, Edinburgh University Press, Edinburgh.

Ardener, E. (ed.) (1970) *Social Anthropology and Language*, ASA Monograph No. 10, Tavistock Press, London.

Berg, J. van den (1968) 'Mechanism of the larynx and the laryngeal vibrations', pp. 278–308 in Malmberg, B. (ed.).

Cagliari, L.C. (1978) 'An experimental study of nasality with particular reference to Brazilian Portuguese'. PhD Dissertation, University of Edinburgh.

Carterette, E.C. and Friedman, M.P. (eds) (1976) *Handbook of Perception Vol. 7, Language and Speech*, Academic Press, New York.

Catford, J.C. (1964) 'Phonation types: the classification of some laryngeal components of speech production', pp. 26–37 in Abercrombie, D. et al. (eds).

Catford, J.C. (1977) *Fundamental Problems in Phonetics*, Edinburgh University Press, Edinburgh.

Coleman, R.F. (1963) 'Decay characteristics of vocal fry', *Folia Phoniatrica* 15, 256–63.

Condax, I.D., Acson, V., Miki, C.C. and Sakoda, K.K. (1976) 'A technique for monitoring velic action by means of a photo-electric nasal probe: application to French', *Journal of Phonetics* 4, 173–81.

Crystal, D. (1970) 'Prosodic and paralinguistic correlates of social categories', pp. 185–206 in Ardener, E. (ed.).

Esling, J.H. (1978) 'Voice quality in Edinburgh: a sociolinguistic and phonetic study', PhD Dissertation, University of Edinburgh.

Fant, G. and Scully, C. (eds) (1977) 'The Larynx and Language', *Phonetica* 34 (Special Issue).

Henderson, E.J.A. (1977) 'The larynx and language: a missing dimension?', pp. 256–63 in Fant, G. and Scully, C. (eds).

Hockett, C.F. (1958) *A Course in Modern Linguistics*, Macmillan, New York.

Hollien, H. (1971) 'Three major vocal registers: a proposal', pp. 320–1 in Montreal, Rigault, A. and Charbonneau, R. (eds), *Proceedings of the 7th International Congress of Phonetic Sciences*, Mouton, The Hague.

Hollien, H. (1974) 'On vocal registers', *Journal of Phonetics* 2, 125–43.

Hollien, H., Damsté, H. and Murry, T. (1969) 'Vocal fold length during vocal fry phonation', *Folia Phoniatrica* 21, 257–65.

Hollien, H., Moore, P., Wendhal, R.W. and Michel, J.P. (1966) 'On the nature of vocal fry', *Journal of Speech and Hearing Research* 9, 245–7.

Hollien, H. and Michel, J.F. (1968) 'Vocal fry as a phonational register', *Journal of Speech and Hearing Research* 11, 600–4.

Honikman, B. (1964) 'Articulatory settings', pp. 73–84 in Abercrombie, D. et al. (eds).

Key, H. (1967) *Morphology of Cayuvava*, Mouton, The Hague.

Kunze, L.H. (1964) 'Evaluation of methods of estimating sub-glottal air pressure', *Journal of Speech and Hearing Research* 7, 151–64.

Ladefoged, P. (1960) 'The nature of vowel quality', *Revista do Laboratorio de Fonetica Experimental da Faculdade de Letras da Universidade de Coimbra* 5, 73–162.

Ladefoged, P. (1971) *Preliminaries to Linguistic Phonetics*, University of Chicago Press, Chicago.

Laver, J. (1968) 'Voice quality and indexical information', *British Journal of Disorders of Communication* 3, 43–54.

Laver, J. (1974) 'Labels for voices', *Journal of the International Phonetic Association* 4, 62–75.

Laver, J. (1975) 'Individual features in voice quality'. PhD Dissertation, University of Edinburgh.

Laver, J. (1976) 'Language and non-verbal communication', pp. 345–62 in Carterette, E.C. and Friedman, M.P. (eds).

Laver, J. (1978) 'The concept of articulatory settings: an historical survey', *Historiographia Linguistica* 5, 1–14.

Laver, J. (1979) *Voice Quality: A Classified Research Bibliography*. John Benjamins, Amsterdam.

Laver, J. (1980) *The Phonetic Description of Voice Quality*, Cambridge University Press, Cambridge.

Laver, J. and Trudgill, P. (1979) 'Phonetic and linguistic markers in speech', in Scherer, K.R. and Giles, H. (eds).

Malmberg, B. (ed.) (1968) *Manual of Phonetics*, North-Holland, London.

Michel, J.F. (1968) 'Fundamental frequency investigation of vocal fry and harshness', *Journal of Speech and Hearing Research* 1, 439–43.

Pike, K.L. (1943) *Phonetics*, University of Michigan Press, Ann Arbor.

Pike, K.L. (1967) 'Tongue-root position in practical phonetics', *Phonetica* 17, 129–40.

Robins, R.H. (1953) 'The phonology of the nasalised verbal forms in Sundanese', *Bulletin of the School of Oriental and African Studies* 15, 138–45.

Robins, R.H. (1957) 'Vowel nasality in Sundanese', pp. 87–103 in *Studies in Linguistic Analysis*, special volume of the Philological Society.

Sapir, E. (1921) *Language*, Harcourt, Brace and World, New York.

Scherer, K.R. and Giles, H. (1979) *Social Markers in Speech*, Cambridge

University Press, Cambridge and Editions de la Maison des Sciences de l'Homme, Paris.

Sundberg, J. and Nordström, P.E. (1976) 'Raised and lowered larynx – the effect on vowel formant frequencies', *Quarterly Progress and Status Report* 2–3, 35–9, Speech Transmission Laboratory, Royal Institute of Technology, Stockholm.

Trudgill, P. (1974) *The Social Differentiation of English in Norwich*, Cambridge University Press, Cambridge.

Zemlin, W.R. (1964) *Speech and Hearing Science*, Stipes, Champaign, Illinois.

13 Describing the Normal Voice

Originally published as Laver, J. and Hanson, R.J. (1981) 'Describing the Normal Voice', in Darby, J.K. (ed.) (1981) *Speech Evaluation in Psychiatry*, Grune and Stratton, New York (pp. 57–78)

Listeners infer a vast amount of information about the characteristics of the speaker. This process of attribution often includes conclusions about physical aspects of the speaker's identity such as his or her sex, age, height, weight, physique and state of health, psychological aspects such as his or her personality and mood, and social aspects such as his or her regional origin and social status (Laver, 1968; Laver and Trudgill, 1979). The capacity of speech to signal identity characteristics of the speaker is a vital part of communication in everyday spoken interaction. Furthermore, in medicine and psychiatry, this capacity can become vital in a more directly literal sense, when the voice is taken to furnish evidence of pathological conditions in the speaker. Both in everyday life and in the professional domains of medicine and psychiatry, the experienced ear helps us to make remarkably skilful subjective evaluations of speakers from the speech they produce.

One of the difficulties inhibiting our scientific understanding of the objective basis of this skilled attributional process, however, is that we lack a comprehensive system for describing the vocal phenomena, both normal and abnormal, which act as imputed evidence for the attributions. A comprehensive system of this sort, in which the description of the normal and the abnormal voice is unified, can be regarded as an ideal eventual goal; attainment of this goal is some way in the future, at least as far as incorporation of the description of the abnormal voice into a unified theory is concerned. This is partly because any adequate attempt to define the nature and range of vocal abnormality necessarily presupposes an understanding of the nature and range of the normal voice. It is one of the multidisciplinary tasks of phonetic and allied sciences to provide an explicit descriptive theory of the normal voice, and it has to be said that this task is some way from completion. It is true that very substantial progress has been made towards this objective over the last fifteen years, especially in research on the normal mode of laryngeal vibration in the work, for example, of Baer (1975), Crystal (1966), Hirano (1975; 1977), Ishizaka and

Flanagan (1972), Matsushita (1969; 1975), Titze (1973; 1974) and Titze and
Strong (1975). But there are some major gaps in the theory. There are two
areas in particular where more research is needed before we can hope for a
properly adequate understanding of the resources of the normal voice. The
first is the range of auditory qualities potentially available to the normal
voice as a consequence of long-term muscular adjustments by the speaker.
The second is the contribution that individual anatomy makes to a
speaker's voice. The purpose of this chapter, which should be read in
conjunction with those by Ohala (1981), Darby (1981), Scherer (1981a,
1981b), and Scherer and Scherer (1981), is to offer some comments on the
nature and range of the normal voice (particularly in the two areas just
mentioned) and to explore some of the problems inherent in the attempt to
provide an adequately comprehensive descriptive system for the normal
voice.

Preliminary Analytic Concepts

It will be helpful to preface the discussion of the normal voice with a brief
commentary on some initial analytic concepts.

We can consider first the notion of a time-base, as it affects different
types of vocal features. Speech is often divided into three types of features
– linguistic features, paralinguistic features of *tone of voice*, and extralinguistic features that make up the speaker's habitual *voice* (Laver and
Trudgill, 1979: 6). These three aspects of vocal performance can be
thought of as being organised on three broadly different types of time-
base. Linguistic aspects of vocal performance characteristically exploit
muscular activities on a relatively short time-base, with segmental and
syllabic actions making up rapidly changing states of the larynx and the
supralaryngeal vocal tract. Paralinguistic aspects of vocal performance,
which are conventional signals of affective states such as anger, amusement, contempt and confidentiality, typically involve activities on a more
medium-term time-base, where the muscular actions can be seen as
exercising a constraint, or bias, on the shorter-term muscular realisations
of the linguistic elements.

Paralinguistic constraints of this sort usually colour a whole utterance in
everyday conversation. An example would be the raising of a speaker's
pitch-range throughout an entire utterance as a paralinguistic signal of
anger. Finally, there are those extralinguistic, long-term aspects of vocal
performance which, being neither linguistic nor paralinguistic, serve only
to individuate the speaker. They constitute the speaker's *voice*, as reflected
in phrases like *voice recognition*.

It is the voice features that are the focus of this chapter. Acoustically, the
voice features emerge as the long-term aspects cumulating through the
more momentary and sporadic linguistic and paralinguistic acoustic events
of vocal performance. Two different facets of linguistic and paralinguistic

performance are reflected in the long-term voice features: firstly, the acoustic nature of each of the realisations of the different elements in the linguistic and paralinguistic systems in the speaker's accent; and secondly, the frequency of occurrence of each of these items in the habitual patterns of his speech. From an auditory point of view, the voice features can be envisaged as a background against which the linguistic and paralinguistic actions gain their perceptual clarity. If the voice features are the *carrier* for the rest of speech, they set the base-line values from which linguistic and paralinguistic realisations achieve their characterising deviation.

By definition, voice features are the least variable of all the factors in a speaker's vocal performance. It is precisely for this reason that the voice features, as the long-term laryngeal and supralaryngeal output, constitute a suitable candidate for speaker-characterisation, either auditorily or by machine analysis.

There is a practical problem of determining the minimum sample duration that will allow the long-term aspects to emerge from the shorter-term perturbations of the linguistic and paralinguistic events. If the speech sample is free from a biasing paralinguistic tone of voice, as in unemotional reading, then text-independence seems to be reached fairly successfully between 45 seconds (Frøkjaer-Jensen and Prytz, 1976: 6) and 70 seconds (Markel, Oshika and Gray, 1977: 330). With a sample of this length, the characteristics of the voice as a carrier for the rest of speech are available for assessment.

The second analytic concept to be considered is the distinction between *organic* and *phonetic* factors in a speaker's voice (Laver, 1980: 9). Organic factors are derived from the nature of the speaker's individual apparatus, and the phonetic factors from the use to which he or she habitually puts the apparatus. Organic factors are the aspects of the voice that reflect the dimensions and geometry of a speaker's vocal organs, including the nasal and oral structures, the pharynx, larynx and respiratory system. Phonetic factors, whose description will make up the major part of the remainder of this chapter, reflect the habitual, long-term muscular biases that the individual speaker imposes on his vocal performance of linguistic and paralinguistic elements. Examples would be habitual tendency to maintain the lips in a protruded position throughout speech or the quasi-permanent use of a breathy mode of phonation or the characteristic adoption of a nasal quality of voice. Muscularly constraining biases of this sort have been called *settings* (Honikman, 1964), and this term will be adopted here.

In a machine analogy, organic aspects of the vocal apparatus relate to the notion of an *effector* component of a mechanical system, and the phonetic aspects to the *control* component. Phonetic theory has tradition-ally concerned itself primarily with control considerations, idealising the effector component. Inter-speaker differences of anatomy within the normal distribution have been largely ignored. While this might be adequate when the focus of analytic attention is on linguistic performance, it becomes less helpful when voice features are being considered. To highlight the relevance of incorporating both control and effector components in a descriptive model of vocal performance, we can examine the analysis of pitch in a situation where a listener is hearing a particular speaker for the first time. The absolute values of fundamental frequency that the listener hears will be the product in the speaker of a number of factors, some relevant to the analysis of voice and some to the analysis of speech as a linguistic and paralinguistic medium. From the point of view of the speaker, his or her choice of the actual fundamental frequency will be constrained by two voice factors, one organic (effector) and one phonetic (control). In organic terms, the geometry, size and mass of his or her laryngeal structures will set the outer limits to the maximum range of fundamental frequency of which the speaker is physically capable. Within that maximum range set by effector limits, the speaker will have developed, as part of his or her phonetic control, a habitual span, or setting, of fundamental frequency within which he or she feels comfortable. On any given occasion, a speaker will normally choose a yet more limited range of fundamental frequency as appropriate for the paralinguistic communication of the particular mood of the moment – anger, amusement, sarcasm or whatever. Finally, within the appropriate paralinguistic range of fundamental frequency, the speaker will select the actual contours which contribute to linguistic aspects of intonation. Now, it is clear that of all these factors which determine the details of fundamental frequency used by the speaker, only the first factor – the organic, effector limitations of the larynx – results in a constraint on the absolute values of fundamental frequency. All the other factors concern relative values and derive from a hierarchical set of control decisions, all of them perhaps outside conscious awareness on the part of the speaker. In order to evaluate the communicative status of any one of these factors, the listener has to be able to perceive the pitch details correlated with that factor as a figure against the perceptual ground of the pitch details correlated with the other factors. Thus, in order to be able to decide whether a particular intonation level is to count as a high pitch or a low pitch, the listener has to know something about the voice factors. For example, do organic factors constrain the speaker's voice to a naturally high range of pitch? Similarly, within the organic limits of his voice, does the speaker habitually opt for a low pitch-setting? The listener also needs, in order to interpret the linguistic value of a particular intonation level, to know something about the paralinguistic context of the utterance. Within the organic and voice-setting limits, is the speaker currently using a raised paralinguistic pitch-range, as in anger, or a low one, as in consolation?

The final analytic concept that needs briefly to be mentioned in this preliminary section is a distinction between some different acoustic aspects of the speech signal. One distinction (discussed by Ohala) is that between the laryngeal *source* of sound energy and the vocal tract *filter* system. The distinction to which appeal is made in this chapter cross-cuts the source-filter distinction; it is the distinction between spectral aspects of acoustic quality and the dynamic features of fundamental frequency and amplitude. It will be convenient to use the terms *voice quality* and *voice dynamics*. Voice quality will be used to refer to the spectral correlates of the organic and phonetic setting features, and voice dynamics to their fundamental frequency and amplitude correlates. There exist other long-term vocal features that characterise speakers, such as rate or tempo, continuity, rhythmicality and breath support, but these can be considered to be features of temporal organisation on a rather different principle.

Within voice quality and voice dynamics as defined, Markel, Oshika and Gray (1977: 337) have shown that, at least within their data, spectral parameters are the most successful in discriminating between speakers, then fundamental frequency parameters, and then amplitude parameters. Most of the commentary below will be devoted to a discussion of voice quality. But before embarking on that discussion, it is necessary to say a little about problems of terminology and its standardisation.

Problems in the Standardisation of Voice Terminology

The question of an appropriate terminology for the description of voice features, both in the normal and the abnormal areas, is inherently problematic. The ideal solution would be one in which a given single label were taken universally to refer to a given vocal phenomenon. This is certainly not the present situation. As an example, we will use two current British otolaryngological textbooks. One book, Ballantine and Groves (1971), uses the terms *slight hoarseness* and *persistent huskiness* to discuss contact ulcers of the vocal fold, while the other, Hall and Coleman (1971), uses the terms *hoarse* and *rough* to discuss vocal fold lesions. In the absence of objective, acoustically based measures, it is not possible to be sure whether the term 'hoarse' in these two textbooks refers to the same perceptual quality or not. In addition, it is not clear whether *hoarse* and *rough*, as used by Hall and Coleman, are intended as synonyms for the same quality or as descriptors of different perceptual components in the overall quality to which reference is being made. In short, the situation that exists is one where a single label has multiple potential referents, and a single phenomenon has multiple potential labels. The only practicable way of escaping from such vicious ambiguity, short of arranging for an audible demonstration every time reference was made to a given quality, would be to adopt a standardised terminology. Given that this is not easily achieved over a short period, perhaps the best that we can hope for is an awareness of the communicative problems involved in labelling vocal features, while working slowly towards progressive standardisation.

The problem is compounded by the fact that labels for voices are of two different semiotic types (Laver, 1974). The first type of label, which we can call a *descriptive* label, refers to the sound-quality produced by the speaker. The second type of label, which can be called an *indexical* label, is one which is taken to indicate a characteristic of the speaker producing the voice. *A husky voice* would thus be an example of a descriptive label, and an *authoritative voice* an example of an indexical label. The majority of descriptive labels used in everyday life are subjective and impressionistic, relying for effective communication on our everyday understanding of metaphorical association. *A sepulchral voice*, for example, can only have metaphorical validity. Descriptive labels become scientific only to the extent that they have an objective basis, where the physical characteristics of the sound-quality being labelled are capable of being verified by techniques of physical measurement.

It seems a basic argument that descriptive labels should be used in any account of normal voice quality and voice dynamics. They should also be used for symptomatic description in discussion of the abnormal voice, provided that standardised terminology is available. But indexical labels have a crucial part to play in discussion of the abnormal voice, in the diagnosis of the causes underlying particular vocal effects. Present practice in speech pathology often combines description of symptoms with an indication of their aetiology within a single label. Examples would be *myopathic dysphonia*, in which the symptom of dysphonia is attributed to a myopathic cause, and *hysterical falsetto*, in which a psychogenic cause is suggested for the vocal symptom of falsetto. Terminology of this sort furnishes a very convenient shorthand, as it were, for post-diagnosis discussion, but the danger in using such a vocabulary for the initial description of symptoms is that it amalgamates prejudicial, indexical aspects of aetiological diagnosis with the symptomatic description.

With the range of possible descriptive labels for voices, many subjective and objective systems are conceivable. Some objective, scientific system is clearly preferable to an impressionistic, subjective method. But whatever objective system is preferred, it will be necessary to have a set of established auditory correlates for routine professional use. This chapter presents the outline of one such system, based on articulatory and acoustic criteria, which is described in greater detail in Laver (1980). The auditory correlates of the system, which attempts to describe only the phonetic possibilities of the normal voice, are illustrated on a tape-recording accompanying that book. Readers who are interested in descriptive and indexical aspects of research on voice quality and voice dynamics are referred to Laver (1979), which is a bibliography of some 1300 items classified into 100 topics.

The Description of Phonetic Settings in Voice Quality

This section offers a summary account of a phonetic model for the description of the long-term muscular adjustments, or settings, that can form part of the production of the normal voice. The model is couched in phonetic, articulatory terms and specifies correlations with auditory, acoustic and muscular characteristics. The discussion presented here will concern chiefly the articulatory and acoustic levels of description: the other levels are discussed more fully in Laver (1980).

The contribution of individual anatomy to the overall quality of a voice can often be very marked, but for convenience of exposition the assumption will be made that all the settings to be described are performed on a standard vocal apparatus. This assumption, however, is merely conve-nient, since it preserves the generality of the descriptive model; but the inadequacy of the assumption will be further explored after the presentation of the model.

The analysis of each type of setting will be described in isolation. Once again this is a convenient approach only, because the vocal apparatus, though treated descriptively as if it were a chain of relatively independent muscle systems, is in fact a complex of interlinked, synergistically interdependent systems that are so highly interactive that virtually no activity can take place anywhere in the apparatus without repercussions of varying degrees elsewhere. This is also true to some extent at the acoustic level. Not all settings, however, can co-occur in a given voice. Certain settings have conflicting muscular or perceptual requirements. There is thus a *compatibility* principle, based upon muscular and acoustic criteria, that governs the potential combinability of settings.

A second important principle, which derives from the compatibility principle, is that of segmental *susceptibility* to the biasing effect of a given setting. Depending on their articulatory and acoustic characteristics, individual consonant and vowel segments will vary in their susceptibility (Laver, 1978). When a speaker uses a velarising setting, which tends to keep the body of the tongue in a raised position towards the back of the mouth, as in a Brooklyn accent, vowels which are normally performed close to that area will be less affected than those performed furthest away. Similarly, when a speaker habitually maintains his lips in a rounded posture, vowels and consonants whose necessary linguistic performance requires lip-rounding will be less affected than those with linguistically unspecified lip-position. Conversely, in some cases segments override the effect of a given setting, as in the case of nasal consonants in the speech of a speaker who uses a nasality setting as part of his habitual voice quality. The most obvious example of differential susceptibility is that any phonatory setting of the internal laryngeal musculature will affect only voiced segments, with voiceless segments being largely unaffected.

The most convenient way to describe the individual settings is to compare them with a standard, *neutral* setting of the vocal apparatus. This neutral setting is acoustically defined and has the status only of a reference point. There are no implications of *normality*, nor is any suggestion of a *representative rest-position* of the vocal organs intended.

The neutral setting of the vocal apparatus can be defined as the one which, if we take a vocal tract representative of an average, adult male speaker, will produce the following long-term-average acoustic characteristics:

● The frequencies of the higher formants are odd multiples of that of the first formant. When the formant frequencies are in this ratio of 1 : 3 : 5 . . . the average configuration of the vocal tract will be the one in which it is most nearly in equal cross-section along its full length (Stevens and House, 1961). In the case of a 17 cm vocal tract, F_1 will be 500 Hz, F_2 1500 Hz and F_3 2500 Hz.

● The frequency-ranges for the first three formants are F_1 150–850 Hz, F_2 500–2500 Hz and F_3 1700–3500 Hz (Fant, 1956)

● The bandwidths of the first three formants are 100 Hz (Stevens and House, 1961).

● There is no acoustic coupling of the nasal tract to the rest of the vocal tract, except when necessary for nasal segments as linguistically required.

● The range of fundamental frequency is from 60–240 Hz (Fant, 1956).

● The larynx pulse shape is approximately triangular, regular in amplitude and frequency, with maximum excitation of the resonatory system of the supralaryngeal vocal tract occurring during the closing phase of the glottal cycle (Miller, 1959).

● The closing phase lasts for approximately 33 per cent of the glottal cycle (Monsen and Engebretson, 1977).

● Phonation is at moderate effort and in this condition the spectral slope of the glottal waveform is −12dB per octave above 250 Hz and closer to −10dB per octave at frequencies below 250 Hz (Flanagan, 1958; Stevens and House, 1961).

● The larynx pulse has only a limited range of frequency jitter and amplitude shimmer. The distribution of these perturbations is normal, with the standard deviation 2 per cent or less of the mean (Hanson, 1978). There is no aperiodic noise in the glottal waveform.

To achieve this constellation of acoustic characteristics, the vocal apparatus has to conform on a long-term-average articulatory basis to the following requirements:

● The longitudinal axis of the vocal tract must be undistorted, in that the lips must not be protruded, and the larynx must be neither raised nor lowered.

- The latitudinal axis of the vocal tract must be undistorted, in that no local constrictions by the lips, tongue, jaw, faucal pillars or pharynx must disturb the long-term tendency of the tract to equality of cross-section along its length.
- Front oral articulations must be performed by the blade of the tongue.
  - The velopharyngeal system must cause audible nasality only where necessary for linguistic purposes.
- The vibration of the true vocal folds must be 'regularly periodic, efficient in air use, without audible friction, with the folds in full glottal vibration under moderate longitudinal tension, moderate adductive tension and moderate medial compression' (Laver, 1980: 14).
- Muscle tension through the vocal apparatus must be neither unduly high nor unduly low.

Each of the individual settings can be described as departing from at least one of these acoustic and articulatory requirements of the neutral setting. The settings will be discussed in five groups, corresponding to settings of the longitudinal axis of the vocal tract, those of the latitudinal axis, velopharyngeal settings, phonatory settings and overall muscle-tension settings.

Longitudinal Settings of the Vocal Tract

The longitudinal axis of the vocal tract can be distorted by muscular adjustments at either end. A short section can be added to the length of the tract at the lips by the action of protruding them forwards. *Labial protrusion* of this sort is usually a concomitant of a lip-rounded setting, and in this condition has the acoustic effect of lowering all formant frequencies, relative to the values for the neutral setting. In absolute terms, the higher formants are more affected (Lindblom and Sundberg, 1971: 1176).

The vocal tract can also be elongated by lowering the larynx from its neutral position, by contraction of the infrahyoid musculature. The acoustic effect of this setting is broadly similar to that of labial protrusion, in that all formant values are lowered, but in this case the lower formants are more affected (Fant, 1960: 64). Lindblom and Sundberg (1971) suggest that for most vowel segments F_1 is reduced by approximately 5 per cent, F_2 lowers by 8 per cent for close front vowels but less for others, and F_3 is relatively insensitive.

The longitudinal axis of the vocal tract can be shortened in two ways: firstly, by adopting a *labiodentalised* setting, where the lower lip is drawn inwards and upwards, and held close to the upper front teeth and, secondly, by raising the larynx. The acoustic effect of habitual labiodentalisation is not unlike that of labial protrusion in that the higher formant frequencies are lowered.

These three settings: labial protrusion (with rounding), labiodentalisation and a *lowered larynx* position have acoustic correlates which all rely broadly on lowering formant frequencies. But we have seen that a lowered larynx position can be distinguished from the two labial settings by the fact that the former affects the lower formants more markedly, while the latter affects chiefly the higher formants. The audible distinction between the lowered larynx setting and the labial settings is also clear when the effect of the settings on individual susceptible segments is considered. The labial settings will constrain the detailed articulatory performance of labial segments, particularly in their onset and offset, in ways which are quite unlike the corresponding effects in lowered larynx voice. The performance of individual susceptible segments also distinguishes the audible character-istics of each of the labial settings. Both labial settings alter the apparent pitch of front oral fricatives. Both lower the pitch of alveolar fricatives, as in the consonant beginning the word *sin*, but to different degrees. But while labial protrusion with rounding also lowers the pitch of dental fricatives, as at the beginning of the word *thin*, labiodentalisation raises it. This example of the way in which the audible clues to the identity of settings have to be gathered from the characteristics of ephemeral and intermittently occurring susceptible segments serves as a paradigm for the perception of phonetic aspects of voice quality.

Shortening the vocal tract by raising the larynx using the suprahyoid musculature has an acoustic effect which is quite different from that of all the settings so far mentioned. With this setting, all formant frequencies rise. Sundberg and Nordström (1976: 38–9) show that F_3 rises as the larynx rises and that F_2 rises substantially for close front vowels but without a comparable rise in F_1, while F_1 and F_2 both rise in open vowels.

Because of the interactive nature of the muscle systems involved, adjustments of vertical larynx position are very often associated with dynamic changes in the frequency of vibration of the vocal folds. *Raised larynx voice* is often accompanied by a raised range of fundamental frequency, and lowered larynx voice by a lowered range. The mode of vibration of the vocal folds is also usually affected and raised larynx voice normally sounds rather tense, as in the voice of a would-be tenor singer who has to strain to achieve the necessary high pitch-range. In the case of lowered larynx voice, the mode of phonation is often rather lax and breathy in quality.

It is not that the adjustments of fundamental frequency which tend to accompany vertical changes of larynx position are mechanically inevitable. Appropriate muscular compensations can readjust the frequency-range. But it is a reflection of the interactive nature of the vocal apparatus that such compensations have to be specifically adopted. The interactivity of muscle systems thus results in the observable tendency for certain voice quality settings to co-occur in constellations.

Latitudinal Settings of the Vocal Tract

Latitudinal settings result in a long-term tendency to constrict (or to expand) the cross-sectional area of the supralaryngeal vocal tract at some point along its length. This can be achieved by the action of the lips, the tongue or the jaw. Additional possibilities such as settings of the faucal pillars, the pharynx and the root of the tongue will not be discussed here.

Latitudinal labial settings manipulate the interlabial space in the vertical and transverse dimensions of the coronal plane of the lips. If analysis is restricted merely to expansion and constriction of these two dimensions compared with the neutral values, then eight different, non-neutral, latitudinal settings of the lips can be distinguished. For most practical purposes, however, it is probably sufficient to limit the non-neutral categories to just three. These are, firstly, the (goldfish-like) position of *open rounding*, which consists of vertical expansion of the interlabial space with lateral constriction, normally with labial protrusion. Secondly, *close rounding*, which is sometimes given the lay description of a *pursed-lips* position and which is made by vertical and lateral constriction of the interlabial space, normally with slight protrusion. Thirdly, *lip-spreading*, as in smiling, which is produced by lateral expansion of the interlabial space, normally without either vertical adjustment or protrusion.

Rounding has the acoustic effect noted above of lowering the formants with a greater influence on the higher formants, while lip-spreading results in a raising of formant frequencies (Fant 1957: 19). Labial settings have a mutually enabling interaction with mandibular settings, as do lingual settings.

The muscle systems of the tongue have such a complex interplay that many different types of settings could potentially be described. Discussion here will be limited to settings of the body of the tongue and of the tip and blade of the tongue.

The tip and blade of the tongue can be regarded as an articulatory system which is only partially independent of the actions of the body of the tongue. Just as the movements of the body of the tongue have to be facilitated by appropriate adjustments of the jaw, so also are articulatory activities of the tip and blade of the tongue enabled by accommodation of the tongue-body. The neutral setting of the tip/blade system is one where front oral lingual articulations, as in the consonants in *sun, dot, lose* and *rush*, are performed by the blade rather than by the tip. This can be achieved with the tongue-body in a variety of positions. But when the tip/ blade system is in a *retroflex* setting, with the tip (or in more extreme cases the underside of the tip) being presented to the palato-alveolar region of the front of the hard palate, then there is more constraint on the range of settings open to the body of the tongue. A raised tongue-body setting, for example, would be incompatible with a retroflex setting of the tip/blade system.

It would be possible to distinguish many different categories of tongue-body settings. Once again, however, it is probably sufficient for practical purposes to limit the delicacy of description to a small number of settings, and we can consider these as long-term adjustments of the gross positioning of the tongue in the mouth in two dimensions of the sagittal plane, vertical and horizontal. Distinctions can be drawn between a *raised* versus a *lowered* position, relative to the neutral setting, and between a *fronted* versus a *retracted* position. A retracted, lowered setting, for instance, would be one where the long-term-average posture of the tongue was low and back in the mouth, constricting the lower part of the pharynx and expanding the front oral cavity. As a consequence of this setting, front oral articulations of the tip/blade would be correspondingly retracted.

In contrast, a raised, fronted tongue-body would constrict the front oral cavity and expand the pharynx. Raising and fronting of the tongue-body are the articulatory basis for our imitations of *little girl* voices in Western culture. Such adjustments in effect copy the smaller vocal tract whose auditory quality they are imitating and are not infrequently exploited for the projection of infantile or vulnerable personality traits. Marilyn Monroe, for example, used this setting.

Finer analysis could resort to traditional phonetic labels of place of articulation and could use such terms as *laryngopharyngalised voice* (for lowering and retraction), *pharyngealised voice* (retraction), *velarised voice* (retraction and raising), *palatalised voice* (raising), *palato-alveolarised voice* (raising and fronting) and *dentalised voice* (for fronting).

Acoustically, there is an interaction between the results of fronting and raising the body of the tongue, such that in palatalisation (raising only) F_2 is very high, is close to F_3 (Fant, 1962: 14), and drops progressively as the tongue moves through palato-alveolarisation (raising and fronting) to dentalisation (fronting only). F_3 remains relatively high throughout. In settings with a backing component, there is an F_1–F_2 proximity, with F_1 higher and F_2 lower than in the neutral setting.

It is more difficult to specify acoustic characteristics of tip/blade settings, because of the acoustic contamination by the enabling tongue-body setting. But the retroflex setting has an accessible acoustic profile, in that in slight retroflexion F_4 lowers towards F_3, and in extreme retroflexion F_3 lowers to close to F_2 (Fant, 1962: 14). The film actor James Stewart characteristically uses a retroflex setting.

Mandibular contributions to speech tend to be overlooked in most phonetic discussion. Yet the lower jaw has a very important influence on articulatory performance in general in that it constrains the operational baseline for the activities of all the other supralaryngeal structures. To the extent that the mandible is the carrier of the lower lip, it necessarily participates as a working partner in the achievement of all labial settings (Sussman, MacNeilage and Hanson, 1973). The mandible coexists in an even more intimate working relationship with the tongue. Every lingual setting has to be performed within the mechanical context set by the jaw. Furthermore, since the tongue is muscularly linked to the velopharyngeal system by the paired palatoglossus muscle and to the pharyngeal system by the pharyngeal constrictors, the mandible can be seen as exercising an indirect influence even on the articulatory operation of these systems.

The articulatory versatility of the jaw, even though this is best reflected in long-term settings rather than short-term movements, arises from its four dimensions of movement – vertical, horizontal, lateral and rotational. All four are exploited in voice quality settings, but the laterally offset and asymmetrically rotated settings seem much rarer than the vertical settings of an *open* or a *close jaw position*, which are the most frequent, and the horizontally *protruded* or *retracted* position which one sees from time to time. The extremes of vertical settings are the slack-jawed, open position and the clenched-teeth position. A retracted jaw setting is sometimes seen as a concomitant of habitual labiodentalisation.

In acoustic terms, all formants rise as the jaw opening becomes larger. Lindblom and Sundberg (1971: 1174) have shown that when all other articulatory parameters are held stable, movement of the jaw alone causes considerable changes in F_1. Higher formants are less sensitive. In a close jaw position, not only does the value of F_1 decrease, but its range is diminished (Lindblom and Sundberg, 1969).

Velopharyngeal Settings

'Nasality' is a cover term for a very wide range of phenomena. It will be treated here as essentially an auditory concept, correlated with particular articulatory characteristics and with side-branch resonance induced by acoustic coupling of the nasal cavity to the rest of the vocal tract by velic opening. This is not to say that velic opening as such is a sufficient condition for nasality in speech. A crucial factor in inducing side-branch resonance in the nasal cavity is the ratio of two cross-sectional areas – the area of the oral entry from the pharynx to the mouth, and the area of the nasal port at the pharyngeal entry to the nasal cavity. This ratio has to surpass a critical level before audible nasal resonance is produced. This means that velic openings of sub-critical proportions can exist in speech without audible nasality.

The velum is in constant movement during speech, and so of course is the tongue. The position of the velum will tend to be correlated with the type of segment being performed (Condax, Acson, Miki and Sakoda, 1976), and this can be used to reach a definition of nasality. Cagliari (1978: 159–66), drawing together findings on nasality from endoscopic, fibre-optic, cineradiographic, electromyographic and aerodynamic techniques, proposes a *neutral velic scale* based on the covariation of velic height with segment type. Within a scale from highest in blowing to lowest in the respiratory position, velic height drops progressively in the following hierarchy of segment type: voiceless then voiced stops; voiceless then voiced fricatives; close then open oral vowels; close then open nasalised vowels; and nasal consonants. Earlier in this chapter, the neutral velo-pharyngeal setting was described as one where the velopharyngeal system produced audible nasality only as linguistically required. For the voice quality to change from neutral to *nasal*, Cagliari specifies that at least some segments must show a drop in velic height from their neutral value. Conversely, a *denasal* quality will derive from a rise in velic height for some segments relative to the neutral scale (Laver, 1980: 87–8). A nasal setting thus produces more nasality than can be accounted for by the neutral setting and a denasal setting produces less.

The acoustic characteristics of nasality are multiple and are summarised in Laver (1980: 91–2). Briefly, nasal formants and anti-resonances are introduced into the spectrum. The most prominent nasal formant in average male speakers is between 200 and 300 Hz, with a bandwidth of approximately 300 Hz: higher-frequency nasal formants have bandwidths that increase in width with frequency, reaching 1000 Hz for frequencies near 2500 Hz (House, 1957). The introduction of anti-resonances results in an overall attentuation of power (Dickson, 1962), particularly in the higher frequencies. All formant bandwidths are broadened and spectral peaks flattened.

The acoustic characteristics of a denasal setting consist of the minimis-ation of these features on susceptible segments.

Phonatory Settings of the Larynx

The theory of vocal fold vibration that is assumed in this account of modes of phonation is the standard aerodynamic-myoelastic theory as proposed by Müller (1837), Smith (1954), Faaborg-Andersen (1957), van den Berg (1958) and others.

It was suggested earlier that in the neutral mode of phonation, the vibration of the true vocal folds was 'regularly periodic, efficient in air use, without audible friction, with the folds in full glottal vibration under moderate longitudinal tension, moderate adductive tension and moderate medial compression' (Laver, 1980: 14). This is the mode of phonation that Hollien (1974) calls the *modal register*, because of its overwhelmingly wide distribution. *Modal voice* in the definition offered contrasts with five other major phonatory settings, some of which can co-occur while others cannot. Their combinability is in part tentatively explained in terms of the different specifications of the phonatory settings on the three muscular parameters of longitudinal tension, adductive tension and medial compression. These are parameters suggested by van den Berg (1968) and, in a slightly modified form, can be described as follows. *Longitudinal tension* is muscular tension in the vocalis and/or the cricothyroid muscles, and is a major determinant of fundamental frequency; *adductive tension* is the muscular tension of the interarytenoid muscles. In contraction, these approximate the arytenoid cartilages, thus closing the cartilaginous and the ligamental glottis. *Medial compression* is the force exercised on the vocal processes of the arytenoid cartilages by the lateral cricoarytenoid muscles, in collaboration with tension in the lateral parts of the thyroarytenoid muscles. Medial compression closes the ligamental glottis, but whether the cartilaginous glottis also closes will depend on the adductive tension exerted by the interarytenoid musculature.

Specification of the six phonation-types in terms of these three myo-elastic parameters is advanced as an explanatory hypothesis based on a wide range of published work on the larynx. But it should be emphasised that further research is necessary to test the hypothesis.

The five phonatory settings to be compared with the neutral, modal setting are *falsetto, whisper, creak, harshness* and *breathiness*.

The laryngeal mechanisms for falsetto are fairly well understood. In contrast with the moderate values in modal voice of the three laryngeal parameters, falsetto has high values. The cross-section of the vocal folds is thin and triangular. Sub-glottal pressure is low (Kunze, 1964) and air-use frugal (Van Riper and Irwin, 1958). The range of fundamental frequency is raised but still overlaps that of modal voice (Hollien and Michel, 1968). The control of fundamental frequency is different from that of modal voice, in that in falsetto the vocalis muscles remain relaxed and the characteristic high longitudinal tension is the product of vigorous contraction of the cricothyroid system, putting the vocal ligaments under strong tension (van den Berg, 1968). Contraction of the lateral parts of the thyroarytenoid muscles keeps the mass of each vocal fold stiff and relatively immobile, limiting vibratory movement chiefly to the thin glottal edges of the folds.

Because of the high fundamental frequency, harmonics are more widely spaced in the spectrum, and falsetto has in consequence a somewhat thin auditory quality. The spectral slope of the laryngeal waveform, falling at about −20 dB per octave (Monsen and Engebretson, 1977), is steeper than in modal voice, whose spectral slope falls at approximately −12 dB per octave.

The physiology of the whisper setting is also comparatively well understood. In strong whisper, the ligamental glottis is closed and the cartilaginous glottis open. Flowing copiously through this narrow constriction in a high-velocity jet into the pharynx at flow-rates of up to 500 cl/sec, the trans-glottal airflow becomes turbulent (Catford, 1964), the eddies generated by this friction give rise to the characteristic auditory quality of whisper (van den Berg, 1968). The Y shape of the glottis is achieved by weak adductive and longitudinal tension, but moderate to high medial compression caused by the action of the lateral cricoarytenoid muscles pivoting the vocal processes of the arytenoid cartilages together (Zemlin, 1964).

Creak, which in American terminology is more often called *vocal fry* or *glottal fry*, is less well understood. The auditory effect is familiar, however, resembling a rapid series of taps, like a stick being run along a railing' (Catford, 1964: 32). Fundamental frequency is very low, with a range in adult males of 24–52 Hz (Michel and Hollien, 1968), with both trans-glottal airflow (Murry, 1969) and sub-glottal pressure (Murry and Brown, 1971) less than for modal voice. Neither length nor thickness of the thick, slack vocal folds vary with fundamental frequency (Hollien and Michel, 1968), suggesting that the control of pitch is managed by aerodynamic means. Fundamental frequency is also irregular on a cycle-to-cycle basis (Monsen and Engebretson, 1977).

Wendahl, Moore and Hollien (1963) suggest that the auditory effect of discrete, low-frequency taps in creak is criterial, and that this effect is due to an unusually high degree of damping of the vocal tract. Coleman (1963) established that creak is perceived when the sound-wave decays by approximately 43 dB between excitation pulses. Damping of laryngeal pulses may also be produced mechanically by the tendency, observed by Hollien, Moore, Wendahl and Michel (1966), of the ventricular folds to compress the laryngeal ventricle, and, coming into contact with the upper surfaces of the true vocal folds, to vibrate together as damped, composite structures.

Ladefoged (1971: 14–15) suggests that in creak the 'arytenoid cartilages are pressed inward so that the posterior portions of the vocal cords are held together and only the (ligamental) portions are able to vibrate'. This would indicate that creak is made with strong adductive tension and strong or moderate medial compression, but with only weak longitudinal tension.

Harshness is not a voice quality that can exist by itself; it can only modify other types of phonation. It will be described here as a modification applied to modal voice, giving *harsh voice*. It is characterised by irregular perturbations of fundamental frequency (jitter) and of intensity (shimmer), together with spectral noise. The mean fundamental frequency is similar to that of modal voice. Muscularly, harshness is the product of laryngeal hyper-tension, and in extreme harshness the ventricular folds also participate in vibration (Aronson, Peterson and Litin, 1964). *Ventricular voice* of this sort, according to Plotkin (1964), 'once heard is never forgotten', and the 'characteristic deep, hoarse voice, alike in male and female, causes an almost sympathetic tightening of the listener's throat'. It may be that such extreme tension produces a quality that speech pathology would class as dysphonic. The point being made here is that it is capable of being produced by the normal vocal apparatus, and therefore offers a useful indication of the very wide-ranging potential repertoire of the organically non-pathological voice.

The muscular hyper-tension in harsh voice is thus likely to be extreme medial compression and extreme adductive tension, but with longitudinal tension remaining moderate.

Breathiness is also a quality that can only modulate other types of phonation. It is the inverse of harshness, in that it is the result of extreme relaxation of muscle tension in the larynx. In combination with modal voice, when giving *breathy voice*, adductive tension is low and medial compression and longitudinal tension are weak. In consequence, the vocal folds vibrate inefficiently, not always meeting at the mid-line. Airflow rates are high (Catford, 1977), giving a *sighing* quality to the voice, and intensity is low (Fairbanks, 1960), with flattened spectral peaks and broad bandwidths.

In the analysis offered here, breathiness in fact combines only with modal voice. In all other cases, the requisite values of at least one of the three laryngeal parameters are mandatorily higher than permissible for a breathy quality.

Compound Phonatory Settings

In suggesting that harshness and breathiness are unlike other phonation types in that they cannot stand alone, appeal is being made to a distinction between simple and compound types of phonation (Laver, 1980: 111). Simple phonation-types can occur alone and compound types are made up of combinations of phonatory settings. Modal voice, falsetto, whisper and creak are all examples of simple phonation-types, but they fall into two categories as far as their behaviour in compound phonations is concerned. In the first category, modal voice and falsetto can each occur alone and can combine with whisper and creak in compound phonations, giving *whispery voice, whispery falsetto, creaky voice* and *creaky falsetto*. Modal voice and falsetto, because they compete for use of the same laryngeal apparatus in mutually pre-emptive ways, cannot combine in a compound phonation with each other.

In the second category, whisper and creak can not only occur alone as simple types and as compound types with modal voice and falsetto, but, because they do not compete for the same laryngeal apparatus, can occur together in the compound phonation *whispery creak*. They also form triple compound phonations with modal voice and falsetto, giving *whispery creaky voice* and *whispery creaky falsetto*.

Lastly, as a third category, harshness and breathiness can only participate in compound phonations. As mentioned, breathiness is restricted to combination with modal voice in breathy voice. Harshness, however, has wider latitude. It combines with modal voice and falsetto to give *harsh voice* and *harsh falsetto*, and it figures in triple compounds such as *harsh whispery voice, harsh creaky voice, harsh whispery falsetto* and *harsh creaky falsetto*. Finally, harshness participates in quadruple compound phonation types: in *harsh whispery creaky voice* and *harsh whispery creaky falsetto*.

Harsh whisper and harsh creak are missing from these listings, not for reasons of physiological incompatibility, but because their components are acoustically mutually redundant. Harshness shares a necessary irregularity with both whisper and creak.

Settings of Overall Muscular Tension

There is one final category of types of phonetic setting to discuss. Some voices differ in the overall level of muscular tension exerted throughout the vocal system. Such adjustments will find their manifestation at many different locations in the vocal apparatus, and tension settings could alternatively be described as constellations of co-occurring local settings. However, because their production is explainable in terms of a single underlying tendency to boost or drop muscular tension levels throughout the vocal apparatus, it seems preferable to categorise these *overall* settings more globally. An overall increase in muscular tension, compared to that of the neutral setting, is therefore called *tense voice*, and an overall decrease is called *lax voice*.

The local components of tense voice will tend to include the following characteristics: loud, high-pitched, tense or harsh phonation with higher sub-glottal air pressure and slightly raised larynx; constriction of the upper larynx and lower pharynx (and possibly of the faucal pillars); a tensed velum; vigorous and extensive radial movements of the convex-surfaced tongue in segmental articulation; and vigorous labial and mandibular activity (Laver, 1980: 154–5).

A lax voice will tend to involve contrasting characteristics: soft, low-pitched, lax, breathy phonation with lower sub-glottal air pressure and slightly lowered larynx; a relaxed pharynx; moderate nasality; inhibited, minimised radial movements of the flat-surfaced tongue in segmental articulation; and minimal labial and mandibular activity (Laver, 1980: 155).

A summary list of all the settings included in the descriptive system outlined above is given in Figure 13.1.

The Relation Between Phonetic Description and Organic Factors

In order to reach a proper understanding of the normal voice, future research will have to establish the theoretical and empirical basis for the union of phonetic and organic factors in the voice of the individual speaker. This applies even more strongly to the abnormal voice.

By exploiting the convenient assumption of a standard vocal apparatus, a largely phonetic model of the normal voice has a certain demonstrable measure of descriptive success. Inter-personal organic differences can to some extent be minimised by taking relative rather than absolute mea-

SUPRALARYNGEAL SETTINGS	LARYNGEAL SETTINGS
longitudinal axis settings	*simple phonation types*

labial   labial protrusion
          labiodentalization
laryngeal   raised larynx
          lowered larynx
	modal voice
	falsetto
	whisper
	creak

latitudinal axis settings	*compound phonation types*

labial   close rounding
          open rounding
          lip-spreading
	whispery voice
	whispery falsetto
	creaky voice

lingual tip/ tip articulation blade blade articulation retroflex articulation	creaky falsetto whispery creak whispery creaky voice whispery creaky falsetto

tongue-body   dentalized
          palato-alveolarized
          palatalized
          velarized
          pharyngealized
          laryngopharyngealized
	breathy voice
	harsh voice
	harsh falsetto
	harsh whispery voice
	harsh whispery falsetto
	harsh creaky voice

mandibular   close jaw position
          open jaw position
          protruded jaw position
          retracted jaw position
	harsh creaky falsetto
	harsh whispery creaky voice
	harsh whispery creaky falsetto

	OVERALL MUSCULAR TENSION SETTINGS
velopharyngeal settings	tense voice lax voice
nasal denasal	

Figure 13.1 Listing of labels for phonetic settings in normal voice quality.

sures. Thus Nolan (1980) was able to show in an acoustic comparison of two phoneticians' performance of the same nine phonetic settings on readings of a standard passage that a good match between the two sets of performances was found provided that the ratios of formant frequencies were used rather than absolute frequency values. Another technique for normalising the effects of inter-personal differences in vocal tract length has been proposed by Wakita (1977). In this study, he transformed actual formant frequency values obtained from the vowel productions of fourteen male and twelve female speakers to values for the same articulatory configuration in a vocal tract of reference length. The resulting normalised formant frequency values had much more compact distributions than the measured values, indicating that differences in vocal tract length can account for a substantial portion of the inter-speaker variability. Other techniques for defining relative measurements, based on aspects of inter-personal organic differences other than vocal tract length, are also important and are the object of current research.

A relative measurement approach allows comparative statements about the phonetic performance of speakers to be made; but these statements are strictly only reliable when the speakers are taken from an organically reasonably homogeneous group, and where organic proportions are comparable. The problem is that the human population forms at least two different groups, in terms of proportional organic dimensions. One group is made up of adult male speakers, of whom the acoustic specifications offered in this chapter are representative. The other group consists of adult female speakers and of children of both sexes, of whom the acoustic assumptions are not necessarily representative. One major difference between the two groups is that the ratio of mouth cavity length to pharynx length is different. Adult male vocal tracts are thus not merely larger-scale versions of adult female and child tracts. A consequence of this is that male-female comparisons have normally to be calculated on a different basis for different articulatory zones of segmental performance (Fant, 1966: 22).

Even within comparisons of speakers from one of these groups, there are problems of phonetic interpretation that arise from organic factors. A given acoustic output reflects a given configuration of the vocal tract, within certain limits. But there are two ways in which a given configuration can occur. The first is by phonetic adjustment. The second is by the accident of individual anatomy. For example, labiodentalisation as a long-term articulatory tendency can be the result either of phonetic control or of a naturally undershot jaw. Similarly, palatalisation can be the consequence of phonetic action or of a large tongue and a small palate. Another example of long-term articulatory compensation for anatomical abnormalities can be found in speakers with cleft lip and palate. In a study of two speakers, Hanson and D'Antonio (1979) found that the immobility of the upper lip was compensated by unusually large and rapid movements of the normal lower lip. A more general example would be the difficulty of deciding whether a particular speaker is a natural tenor with a short vocal tract and a comparatively small larynx, or a larger speaker with a raised larynx setting and a raised range of fundamental frequency.

Abercrombie, whose phonetic description of voice quality furnished the point of departure for the model offered here, expresses the range of this problem succinctly:

> The relative importance of the learnt and the unlearnt in voice quality is difficult to assess . . . It is . . . possible to neutralise, by means of muscular adjustments, the components in voice quality which are anatomically derived – at least to some extent, and perhaps even,

given enough skill, entirely. There are many professional mimics on stage, radio and television who are able to give convincing imitations of their fellow actors and of public figures, imitations in which the performer's own voice-quality characteristics are effectively submerged . . . The extreme of virtuosity, probably, was reached by a certain music-hall performer, a large, middle-aged man, who had learnt to produce, completely convincingly, the voice quality of a seven-year-old girl, showing that it is possible to compensate, by muscular adjustments, for extreme anatomical differences. (Abercrombie, 1967: 94)

There is a wide range of organic research on vocal anatomy that needs to be done on a correlational basis, linking vocal anatomy to other general anatomical characteristics. When we hear a low-pitched voice on the telephone, with low formant ranges, we confidently expect the speaker to be a tall, adult male. But we do not yet know, on an objective basis, the detailed correlation between vocal tract length and a speaker's height. Objective data of this sort would be useful, to take one application, in the investigation of correlations between genetic disorders and a speaker's voice-type. In genetic disorders with an influence on general anatomy, it is not unreasonable to expect this to be reflected in characteristic vocal anatomy as well. Thus the tendency to greater-than-average height in speakers of, say, an xxy genotype (Slater and Cowie, 1971: 301), or the tendency to short stature in xo genotype speakers with Turner's syndrome (Slater and Cowie, 1971: 303), might be found to correlate with bigger-than-average vocal tracts and larynges versus smaller-than-average vocal tracts and larynges respectively, with consequent acoustic effects. More subtly, in the case of xxy genotype, the voice of speakers with Klinefelter's syndrome may reflect this, to the extent that the syndrome is marked by the tendency towards anatomically or hormonally female characteristics. There is usually a close resemblance between the phenotypes of patients with a given chromosomal aberration (Pashayan, 1975: 154). It would be interesting to establish whether this resemblance extends to include voice features. In this application, the interest would lie not so much in the diagnostic role of such characterising voice-types, since diagnosis is essentially carried out on quite different criteria, but rather in completing the symptomatic mosaic of the disorders concerned.

Conclusion

The description of the normal voice is far from being a finished task. One important area of improvement would be the comprehensive statement of the susceptibility relation between all types of segmental articulations and individual settings. Another would be the development of more detailed acoustic statements about each of the settings and the implementation of automatic computer-based voice-analysis programs which could factor out the acoustic contributions of the settings. Most important of all for the overall development of a descriptive theory for the normal voice are the two areas mentioned at the beginning of this chapter: firstly, establishing the range of auditory qualities potentially available to the normal voice on a phonetic basis; and secondly, incorporating an adequate organic component to take account of inter-speaker differences of anatomy and their acoustic correlates.

Underlying the discussion in this chapter has been the attitude that it should be possible to aim towards a unified model for the description of the normal and the abnormal voice. The two areas will probably never entirely overlap, because of the different assumptions that have to come into play when the nature of the speech apparatus itself changes in pathological conditions. But there are many areas of the abnormal voice, particularly in the control aspects of functional disorders, and possibly in the control aspects of organic pathology, where it would be thoroughly profitable to explore commonalities between the normal and the abnormal. If it becomes possible to develop an adequately powerful descriptive theory for the range of variations potentially found in the normal voice, then it is at least plausible that some aspects of abnormal vocal performance could usefully be seen as extensions of some of the dimensionalities of normal performance, as explored, for example, in Davis (1976). The benefit of establishing continuities between the normal and the abnormal is that such an approach facilitates both measures of distance between the two for diagnostic use and measures of progress towards the normal in rehabilitative therapy.

The exploration of such continuities cannot be properly achieved by any single discipline: it should be the focus of multidisciplinary effort by the range of professions represented in the source volume of this chapter.

Note
Preparation of this chapter was funded by a Medical Research Council project on 'Vocal Profiles of Speech Disorders' (Grant # G987/1192/N), in the Phonetics Laboratory of the University of Edinburgh. Robert Hanson is a Visiting Senior Scientist on the project, and we are grateful to Sheila Wirz, Janet Mackenzie and John Fisher, our project colleagues, for advice and comment.

References
Abercrombie, D. (1967) *Elements of General Phonetics*, Edinburgh University Press, Edinburgh, Scotland.

Aronson, A.E., Peterson, H.W. and Litin, E.M. (1964) 'Voice symptomatology in functional dysphonia and aphonia', *Journal of Speech and Hearing Disorders* 29, 367–80.

Baer, T. (1975) 'Investigation of phonation using excised larynxes', unpublished PhD dissertation, Massachusetts Institute of Technology.

Ballantine, J. and Groves, J. (1971) *Diseases of the Ear, Nose and Throat* (Vol. 4): *The Throat*, Butterworth, London.

Berg, J. van den. (1958) 'Myoelastic-aerodynamic theory of voice production', *Journal of Speech and Hearing Research* 1, 227–44.

Berg, J. van den. (1968) 'Mechanisms of the larynx and the laryngeal vibrations', pp. 278–308 in Malmberg, B., (ed.), *Manual of Phonetics*, North-Holland, London.

Cagliari, L.C. (1978) 'An experimental study of nasality with particular reference to Brazilian Portuguese', PhD dissertation, University of Edinburgh, Edinburgh, Scotland.

Catford, J.C. (1964) 'Phonation types: The Classification of some laryngeal components of speech production', in Abercrombie, D., Fry, D.B., MacCarthy, P.A.D., et al. (eds), in *In Honour of Daniel Jones*, Longmans, London.

Catford, J.C. (1977) *Fundamental Problems in Phonetics*, Edinburgh University Press, Edinburgh, Scotland.

Coleman, R.F. (1963) 'Decay characteristics of vocal fry', *Folia Phoniatrica* 15, 256–63.

Condax, I.D., Acson, V., Miki, C.C. et al. (1976) 'A technique for monitoring velic action by means of a photo-electric nasal probe: Application to French', *Journal of Phonetics* 4, 173–81.

Crystal, T.H. (1966) 'A model of laryngeal activity during phonation', unpublished PhD dissertation, Massachusetts Institute of Technology.

Darby, J.K. (1981) 'Speech and voice studies in psychiatric populations', pp. 253–84 in Darby (ed.).

Darby, J.K. (ed.) (1981) *Speech Evaluation in Psychiatry*, Grune and Stratton, New York.

Davis, S.B. (1976) *Computer evaluation of laryngeal pathology based on inverse filtering of speech* (monograph no. 13), Speech Communication Research Laboratory, Santa Barbara, CA.

Dickson, D.R. (1962) 'An acoustic study of nasality', *Journal of Speech and Hearing Research* 5, 103–11.

Faaborg-Andersen, K. (1957) 'Electromyographic investigation of intrinsic laryngeal muscles in humans', *Acta Physiologica Scandinavica* Supplement No. 140, 1–149.

Fairbanks, G. (1960) *Voice and Articulation Drill-book* (ed. 2), Harper and Row, New York.

Fant, G. (1956) 'On the predictability of formant levels and spectrum envelopes from formant frequencies, pp. 109–20 in Halle, M., Lunt, H. and MacLean, H. (eds), *For Roman Jakobson*. Mouton, The Hague.

Fant, G. (1957) 'Modern instruments and methods for acoustic studies of speech', pp. 282–388 *Proceedings of the 8th International Congress of Linguists*, Oslo. Also (1958) in *Acta Polytechnica Scandinavica* 1, 1–81.

Fant, G. (1960) *Acoustic Theory of Speech Production*, Mouton, The Hague.

Fant, G. (1962) 'Descriptive analysis of the acoustic aspects of speech', *Logos* 5, 3–17.

Fant, G. (1966) 'A note on vocal tract size factors and non-uniform f-pattern scalings', *Quarterly Progress and Status Report*, Speech Transmission Laboratory, Royal Institute of Technology, Stockholm, 4, 22–30.

Flanagan, J.L. (1958) 'Some properties of the glottal sound source', *Journal of Speech and Hearing Research* 1, 99–116.

Frøjaer-Jensen, B. and Prytz, S. (1976) 'Registration of voice quality', *Bruel and Kjaer Technical Review*, 3, 3–17.

Hall, I.S. and Coleman, B.H. (1975) *Diseases of the Nose, Throat and Ear*, Livingstone, Edinburgh, Scotland.

Hanson, R.J. (1978) 'A two-state model of F_0 control', *Journal of the Acoustical Society of America* 64:1, 543–544.

Hanson, R.J. and D'Antonio, L.L. (1979) 'Long-term compensation for upper-lip immobility', *Journal of the Acoustical Society of America* 65:1, 526. Also in Wolf, J.J. and Klatt, D.H. (eds) (1979) *Speech Communication Papers Presented at the 97th Meeting of the Acoustical Society of America*, Acoustical Society of America.

Hirano, M. (1975) 'Phonosurgery: Basic and clinical investigations', *Otologia* (Fukuoka), 21: 239–440 [in Japanese].

Hirano, M. (1977) 'Structure and vibratory behavior of the vocal folds', pp.13–27 in Sawashima, M. and Cooper, F.S. (eds), *Dynamic Aspects of Speech Production*, University of Tokyo Press, Tokyo.

Hollien, H. (1974) 'On vocal registers'. *Journal of Phonetics* 2, 125–43.

Hollien, H. and Michel, J.F. (1968) 'Vocal fry as a phonational register', *Journal of Speech and Hearing Research* 11, 600–4.

Hollien, H., Moore, P., Wendahl, R.W., et al. (1966) 'On the nature of vocal fry', *Journal of Speech and Hearing Research* 9, 245–7.

Honikman, B. (1964) 'Articulatory settings', pp. 73–84 in Abercrombie, D., Fry, D.B., MacCarthy, P.A.D. et al. (eds) *In Honour of Daniel Jones*, Longmans, London.

House, A.S. (1957) 'Analog studies of nasal consonants', *Journal of Speech and Hearing Disorders* 22, 190–204.

Ishizaka, K. and Flanagan, J.L. (1972) 'Synthesis of voiced sounds from a two-mass model of the vocal cords', *Bell System Technical Journal* 51, 1233–68.

Kunze, L.H. (1964) 'Evaluation of methods of estimating subglottal air pressure', *Journal of Speech and Hearing Research* 7, 151–64.

Ladefoged, P. (1971) *Preliminaries to Linguistic Phonetics*, University of Chicago Press, Chicago.

Laver, J. (1968) 'Voice quality and indexical information', *British Journal of Disorders of Communication* 3, 43–54.

Laver, J. (1974) 'Labels for voices', *Journal of the International Phonetic Association*, 4, 62–75.

Laver, J. (1978) 'The concept of articulatory settings: An historical survey', *Historiographia Linguistica* 5, 1–14.

Laver, J. (1979) *Voice Quality: A Classified Bibliography*. John Benjamins, Amsterdam.

Laver, J.(1980) *The Phonetic Description of Voice Quality*, Cambridge University Press, Cambridge, England.

Laver, J. and Trudgill, P. (1979) 'Phonetic and linguistic markers in speech', pp. 1–32 in Scherer, K.R. and Giles, H. (eds) *Social Markers in Speech*, Cambridge University Press, Cambridge, England.

Lindblom, B. and Sundberg, J. (1969) 'A quantitative model of vowel production and the distinctive features of Swedish vowels', *Quarterly Progress and Status Report*, Speech Transmission Laboratory, Royal Institute of Technology, Stockholm, 1, 14–32.

Lindblom, B.E.F. and Sundberg, J. (1971) 'Acoustical consequencies of lip, tongue, jaw, and larynx movement', *Journal of the Acoustical Society of America* 50, 1166–79.

Markel, J.D., Oshika, B.T. and Gray, A.H. (1979) 'Long-term feature-averaging for speaker-recognition', *IEEE Transactions on Acoustics, Speech, and Signal Processing* ASSP-25, No. 4, 330–7.

Matsushita, H. (1969) 'Vocal cord vibration of excised larynges: A study with ultra-high-speed cinematography', *Otologia* (Fukuoka), 15, No. 2, 127–42 [in Japanese].

Matsushita, H. (1975) 'The vibratory mode of the vocal folds in the excised larynx', *Folia Phoniatrica* 27, 7–18.

Michel, J.F. and Hollien, H. (1968) 'Perceptual differentiation in vocal fry and harshness', *Journal of Speech and Hearing Research* 11, 439–43.

Miller, R.L. (1959) 'Nature of the vocal cord wave', *Journal of the Acoustical Society of America* 31, 667–77.

Monsen, R.B. and Engebretson, A.M. (1977) 'Study of variations in the male and female glottal wave', *Journal of the Acoustical Society of America* 62, 981–93.

Müller, J. (1837) *Handbuch der Physiologie des Menschen*, Vol. 2. Holscher, Coblenz.

Murry, T. (1969) 'Subglottal pressure measures during vocal fry phonation', PhD dissertation, University of Florida.

Murry, T. and Brown, W.S. 'Subglottal air pressure during two types of vocal activity: Vocal fry and modal phonation', *Folia Phoniatrica* 23, 440–9.

Nolan, F. (1980) 'The phonetic bases of speaker recognition', PhD dissertation, University of Cambridge.

Ohala, J.J. (1981) 'The non-linguistic components of speech', pp. 39–50 in Darby (ed.).

Pashayan, H.M. (1975) 'The basic concepts of medical genetics', *Journal of Speech and Hearing Disorders* 40, 147–63.

Plotkin, W.H. (1964) 'Ventricular phonation: A clinical discussion of etiology, symptoms and therapy', *American Speech and Hearing Association Convention Abstracts* 6, 409.

Scherer, K.R. (1981a) 'Vocal indicators of stress', pp. 171–88 in Darby, (ed.).

Scherer, K.R. (1981b) 'Speech and emotional states', pp. 189–220 in Darby (ed.).

Scherer, K.R. and Giles, H. (eds). (1979) *Social Markers in Speech*, Cambridge University Press, Cambridge, England.

Scherer, K.R. and Scherer, U. (1981) 'Speech behaviour and personality', pp. 115–36 in Darby (ed.).

Slater, E. and Cowie, V. (1971) *The Genetics of Mental Disorders*. Oxford University Press, London.

Smith, S. (1954) 'Remarks on the physiology of the vibrations of the vocal cord', *Folia Phoniatrica* 6, 166–78.

Stevens, K.N. and House, A.S. (1961) 'An acoustical theory of vowel production and some of its implications', *Journal of Speech and Hearing Research* 4: 303–20.

Sundberg, J. and Nordström, P.E. (1976) 'Raised and lowered larynx: The effect on vowel formant frequencies', *Quarterly Progress and Status Report*, Speech Transmission Laboratory, Royal Institute of Technology, Stockholm, 2–3: 35–39.

Sussman, H.M., MacNeilage, P.F. and Hanson, R.J. (1973) 'Labial and mandibular dynamics during the production of bilabial consonants: Preliminary observations', *Journal of Speech and Hearing Research* 16, 397–420.

Titze, I.R. (1973) 'The human vocal cords: A mathematical model' (Part I), *Phonetica*, 28, 129–70.

Titze, I.R. (1974) 'The human vocal cords: A mathematical model' (Part II), *Phonetica*, 29, 1–21.

Titze, I.R. and Strong, W.J. (1975) 'Normal modes in vocal cord tissues', *Journal of the Acoustical Society of America* 57, 736–44.

Trojan, F. (1952) 'Experimentelle Untersuchunger uber den Zusammenhang zwischen dem Ausdruck der Sprechstimme und dem vegetativen Nervensystem', *Folia Phoniatrica* 4, 65–92.

Van Riper, C. and Irwin, J.W. (1958) *Voice and Articulation*, Prentice-Hall, Englewood Cliffs.

Wakita, H. (1977) 'Normalization of vowels by vocal-track length and its application 18 vowel identification', *IEEE Transactions on Acoustics, Speech, and Signal Processing* ASSP-25: 2, 183–92.

Wakita, H. (1977) 'Normalization of vowels by vocal-tract length and its application to vowel identification', *IEEE Transactions on Acoustics, Speech, and Signal Processing* ASSP-25: 2, 183–92.

Wendahl, R.W., Moore, P. and Hollien, H. (1963) 'Comments on vocal fry', *Folia Phoniatrica* 15, 251–5.

Wolf, J.J. and Klatt, D.H. (eds). (1979) *Speech Communication Papers Presented at the 97th Meeting of the Acoustical Society of America*, Acoustical Society of America.

Zemlin, W.R. (1964) *Speech and hearing science*, Stipes, Champaign, Illinois.

14 Phonetic and Linguistic Markers in Speech

Originally published as Laver, J. and Trudgill, P. (1979) 'Phonetic and Linguistic Markers in Speech', in Scherer, K.R. and Giles, H. (eds) *Social Markers in Speech*, Cambridge University Press, Cambridge, and Editions de la Maison des Sciences de l'Homme, Paris (pp. 1–32)

Many disciplines are professionally interested in the analysis of markers of identity in speech, and in the nature of the listener's performance in attributing particular characteristics to the speaker on the basis of such markers. A necessary prerequisite for the development of research in this area, from the standpoint of any discipline, is the provision of an adequate phonetic and linguistic account of the marking phenomena themselves. The aim of this chapter is to indicate some ways in which concepts already available in phonetic and linguistic theory can help to refine the analysis of markers in speech.

The structure of the chapter begins with a brief discussion of the semiotic basis of how speech can serve a marking function as well as fulfilling its role as a vehicle for linguistic communication. Then the phonetic nature of markers in speech is discussed, in terms of voice features, features of tone of voice and features of linguistic articulations. This is followed by an account of the way in which phonological differences between accents can mark social aspects of speakers' identities. Syntactic markers are then considered. Recent work in the study of discourse and conversational interaction is touched on, and some aspects of lexical markers are examined. The chapter concludes with some tentative hypotheses about the listener's process of attribution which emerge from the phonetic and linguistic discussion.

1. The Semiotic Basis of Marking

Given that the concept of marking deals essentially with the production and perception of communicative and informative signs, it forms part of a general theory of semiotics (cf. Giles, Scherer and Taylor, 1979). In recent years, there has been a surge of interest in semiotic theory (cf. Eco, 1976), but the history of semiotics as a discipline can be traced back to Greek medicine. Morris (1946: 285–7) says that it was first used to refer to the theory of medical symptoms used as signs in the diagnosis and prognosis of disease. The Stoic philosophers then used 'semiotic' to mean the general theory of signs. Morris traces the history of semiotics into medieval Europe, through the works of Augustine and Boethius. There, the subject (known as 'scientia sermocinalis') developed in the work of figures such as Petrus Hispanus, Abelard, Roger Bacon, Thomas of Erfurt, Sigur of Courtrai and William of Occam. From them, two divergent traditions developed: one led to the work of the British empiricist philosophers like Francis Bacon, Hobbes, Locke, Berkeley, Hume and Bentham; the other, through the work of Leibniz, led to that of modern symbolic logicians such as Boole, Frege, Peano, Russell, Whitehead, Carnap and Tarski. The philosophical basis of an interest in the notion of marking stands on a very long-established foundation, therefore, and there is much of value to be gained from these earlier writings on the subject.

One of the most accessible of the semiotic philosophers, and probably the most relevant for the purposes of this volume, is Charles Saunders Peirce, the American pragmaticist philosopher of the late nineteenth century. Six volumes of his collected papers have been edited by Hartshorne and Weiss (1931–5), and Feibleman (1946) provides a useful condensed version of his writings.

Peirce's definition of 'semiotic' was 'the formal doctrine of signs (where) a sign is something which stands to somebody for something in some respect or capacity' (Hartshorne and Weiss, 1931–5: Vol. 2, 227–8). Peirce divided the different sorts of signs into three mutually intersecting trichotomies. The second trichotomy is the most relevant here. Feibleman (1946: 90) gives a compressed quotation of this as follows:

> The second trichotomy of signs consists of the *icon*, a sign which refers to an object by virtue of characters of its own which it possesses whether the object exists or not (2. 247); the *index*, a sign which refers to the object that it denotes by virtue of being really affected by that object (2. 248); and the *symbol*, a sign which refers to the object that it denotes by virtue of a law, usually an association of general ideas, which operates to cause the symbol to be interpreted as referring to that object (2. 249).

This concept of a symbolic relationship holding between a sign and its referent, where the relationship is conventional and arbitrary, lies at the heart of the linguistic code. But it is Peirce's notion of an index that is the most interesting in any consideration of how speech identifies the speaker. He used the term in a number of rather different senses, but the one most useful for marking purposes is his evidential sense illustrated by the quotation above, where an index was said to refer to its object 'by virtue of being really affected by that object'. The orientation of a weathercock would in this usage be evidence for, or an index of, wind-direction; the height of a column of mercury in a thermometer would be an index of heat.

'Index' can thus be equated with 'marker', and terms derived from 'index', such as 'to indicate', 'indicative' and 'indication', can be used as technical terms in association with 'to mark' and 'marking'. One modification to Peirce's basic concept needs to be accepted, however. For Peirce, the connection between an index and its object was non-arbitrary; we shall find it useful, nevertheless, to allow an arbitrary connection between some markers in speech and the personal characteristics indicated by them, or taken by the listener to be so indicated.

One writer in particular who has developed a quite explicit typology of markers of identity in speech, based partly on some of Peirce's ideas, is Abercrombie (1967). He used Peirce's term 'index', and describes three classes of indices in speech that reveal personal characteristics of the speaker:

(a) those that indicate membership of a group (e.g. a regional or a social group);
(b) those that characterise the individual;
(c) those that reveal changing states of the speaker (e.g. changing affective states (Abercrombie. 1967: 7–9).

We shall refer to these three types of indices as *group markers, individuating markers* and *affective markers* respectively. The typology that Abercrombie suggests will be adopted here, in conjunction with a cross-cutting classification of markers into three other categories:

(a) those that mark social characteristics, such as regional affiliation, social status, educational status, occupation and social role;
(b) those that mark physical characteristics, such as age, sex, phys- ique and state of health;
(c) those that mark psychological characteristics of personality and affective state.

We shall call these three types of markers *social markers, physical markers* and *psychological markers* respectively. The two typologies differ chiefly in the way that psychological attributes are handled.

Another linguist who has taken an explicit interest in indexical infor- mation in speech is Lyons. His position on the distinction between 'communicative' and 'informative' signs (which is a not uncontroversial distinction) will be followed in this chapter. Lyons suggests that:

a signal is communicative if it is intended by the sender to make the receiver aware of something of which he was not previously aware. Whether a signal is communicative or not rests, then, upon the possibility of choice, or selection, on the part of the sender. If the sender cannot but behave in a certain way (i.e. if he cannot choose between alternative kinds of behaviour), then he obviously cannot communicate anything by behaving in that way . . . 'Communicative' means 'meaningful for the sender'. (Lyon 1977: 33)

This is contrasted with 'informative' in the sense that:

a signal is informative if (regardless of the intentions of the sender) it makes the receiver aware of something of which he was not previously aware. 'Informative' therefore means 'meaningful to the receiver'. (Lyons, 1977: 33)

What a speaker says is thus communicative, but his accent, unless he has the possibility of speaking with more than one accent, is informative.

Lyons adopts Abercrombie's classification of indices, but proposes one further category, based on Abercrombie's third type: 'those that reveal changing states of the speaker'. Lyons calls this proposed category a 'symptom', recalling the diagnostic use of signs in medicine, but widens the scope of a symptom beyond the indication of affective information:

any information in a . . . signal which indicates to the receiver that the sender is in a particular state, whether this be an emotional state (fear, anger, sexual arousal or readiness, etc.), a state of health (suffering from laryngitis, etc.), a state of intoxication, or whatever, [can be] described as symptomatic of that state. (Lyons, 1977: 108)

2. Phonetic and Phonological Markers

In order to be able to discuss details of the phonetic and phonological phenomena that act as markers in speech, it will be helpful briefly to consider the physical and auditory variables involved in speech production and perception. Many good introductions to general phonetic theory are available (e.g. Pike, 1943; Abercrombie, 1967; Ladefoged, 1971; 1976; O'Connor, 1973). Ladefoged (1962) offers a lucid, short introduction to the acoustic basis of speech, and Hardcastle (1976) gives a schematic, readable account of the anatomy and physiology of speech. The reader is referred to these sources for a more detailed exposition, and the comments on speech production and perception that are offered here are intended only as an orientation.

We can initially consider speech production from the point of view of the different muscle systems which make up all the vocal apparatus. The muscle systems exploited in speaking are almost all anatomically interconnected (Laver, 1975), so that no muscular action takes place without affecting the activity of many other parts of the vocal apparatus. Each muscular action has to be cooperatively facilitated by all the muscle systems that could potentially counteract the desired effect of its execution. Speaking thus requires the most complex and skilful collaboration between the different muscle systems, whose cooperative actions all have to be precisely and intricately coordinated in time. It is not at all surprising, therefore, that in learning to control such a complex apparatus sufficiently to be able to produce auditorily acceptable imitations of speech patterns heard in one's social environment, speakers should nevertheless develop idiosyncrasies of pronunciation that serve to individuate them within their own social group.

The notion of an isolable muscle system is itself something of a fiction. But if we accept the fiction as analytically convenient, then there are seven basic muscle systems whose contributions to speech can be distinguished. These are: the *respiratory system*, which supplies the driving force that pushes air out of the lungs, up to the larynx and the rest of the vocal tract, for speech purposes; the *phonatory system*, which controls the actions of the vocal folds in producing phonation; the *pharyngeal system*, which controls articulatory activity at the bottom end of the vocal tract; the *velopharyngeal system*, which controls the production of nasality; the *lingual system*, which is responsible for the oral articulations underlying most consonant and vowel segments; the *labial system*, which controls the actions of the lip structures; and the *mandibular system*, which controls movements of the jaw.

From an articulatory and aerodynamic point of view, speech is the joint product of the collaborative interaction of all these muscle systems, as reflected in the continually changing configurations of the vocal tract and larynx, and the pattern of airflow from the lungs to the outside air. These articulatory and aerodynamic changes give rise to associated acoustic changes, which can be described in terms of a number of acoustic parameters. The acoustic parameters in turn have a statable relationship to perceptual, auditory parameters. The auditory variables in speech are basically of two sorts: quality features and dynamic features.

The acoustic correlates of features of auditory quality are essentially spectral in nature, and include such aspects as formant frequencies and amplitudes, and the frequency and amplitude of aperiodic noise in the spectrum. The acoustic correlates of dynamic auditory features include fundamental frequency as the correlate of *pitch*, intensity as the correlate of *loudness* and duration as the correlate of *length*. It should be noted, however, that the allocation of fundamental frequency and intensity to the acoustic realisation of dynamic auditory features is not always completely valid: pitch 'jitter' and loudness 'shimmer' (that is, aperiodic cycle-to-cycle variability of fundamental frequency or intensity around the mean value) are both heard as contributing to auditory quality, giving a 'rough', 'harsh' auditory texture.

Auditorily, all speech is made up of sounds describable in terms of quality, pitch, loudness and length. All markers in speech thus depend on these variables for their phonetic realisation, and the discussion that follows is an attempt to explain the phonetic basis of different types of speaker-characteristics.

There are three different facets of vocal performance to be considered. Each of these facets is subject to a different time-perspective. Firstly, there is the facet of vocal performance that represents the speaker's permanent or quasi-permanent *voice*, by which he is recognisable even when his consonants and vowels are unintelligible, for example, when heard speaking on the other side of a closed door. The other two facets are *tone of voice* and the *phonetic realisations of linguistic units*. The time-perspective of tone of voice is usually medium-term, and that of linguistic articulations is very short-term.

Because voice features are by definition long-term, they lie quite outside any possibility of signalling linguistic meaning, so it is appropriate to refer to such voice features as *extralinguistic*. Since they are not normally consciously manipulated by the speaker, voice features are informative but not communicative. The medium-term features that make up tone of voice, and which have the function of signalling affective information, have a rather closer resemblance in some ways to the short-term use of the vocal apparatus for signalling linguistic meaning, and such features are therefore often referred to as *paralinguistic*. They are 'para'linguistic in the sense that they form a communicative code subject to cultural convention for its interpretation; paralinguistic features are not fully linguistic in the sense that they lack the possibility of signalling meaning through sequential arrangement into structures, which is a criterial property of linguistic communication.

Neither extralinguistic nor paralinguistic features are irrelevant to directly linguistic interests, since they constitute a background against which the linguistic articulations can achieve their perceptual prominence. Strictly, each of the three types of vocal feature, extralinguistic, para-linguistic and linguistic, acts as a perceptual ground for the figures of the other two types of figure.

Each of these categories of vocal behaviour will now be discussed in more phonetic detail. A summary of the relationship between these vocal variables and their marking functions is given in Figure 14.1.

2.1 Extralinguistic Voice Features

Long-term speaker-characterising voice features are of two different sorts. One type of voice feature arises from anatomical differences between speakers. The second type is the product of the way in which the individual speaker habitually 'sets' his vocal apparatus for speaking. Unlike this second type, which will be discussed in a moment, the first type of feature is by definition outside any possibility of control by the speaker. It includes anatomical influences on aspects of voice quality and of voice dynamics.

Anatomical influences on voice quality are due to factors such as basic vocal tract length, dimensions of lips, tongue, nasal cavity, pharynx and jaw, dental characteristics and geometry of laryngeal structures (Aber-crombie, 1967: 92). These anatomical factors impose limits on the range of spectral effects (in terms of formant frequency and amplitude-ranges, and on the distribution of aperiodic noise through the spectrum) that the speaker can potentially control acoustically.

Anatomical influences on voice dynamics are due to factors such as the

	informative		informative and communicative	
Signalling function				
Relation to language	extralinguistic voice characteristics		paralinguistic 'tone of voice'	phonetic realisations of linguistic units
Temporal perspective	permanent	quasi-permanent	medium-term	short-term
Vocal variables	vocal features deriving from anatomical differences between individuals influencing both quality and dynamic aspects	voice settings, i.e. habitual muscular adjustments of the vocal apparatus, including voice quality settings and voice dynamic settings	'tone of voice' achieved by temporary use of voice settings, including paralinguistic quality settings and paralinguistic dynamic settings	momentary articulatory realisations of phonological units, including short-term manipulations of phonetic quality features and short-term manipulations of phonetic dynamic features
Marking function	physical markers	social and psychological markers		
Potential controllability	uncontrollable, therefore unlearnable	under potential muscular control, therefore learnable and imitable		

Figure 14.1 The relationship between vocal variables and their marking functions.

dimensions and mass of the vocal folds, and respiratory volume. These influence pitch- and loudness-ranges, by imposing limits on the ranges of fundamental frequency and amplitude that the speaker can produce.

Listeners' judgements of physical attributes, based on the product of such anatomically derived features, are amongst the most accurate conclusions drawn. This is precisely because they are based on invariant, involuntary aspects of a speaker's vocal performance. Physique, age and sex are all judged with a fair accuracy, and interesting information about a speaker's medical condition is also sometimes accurately inferred.

Physique and height are probably judged accurately because of the good correlation that seems to exist between these factors and the dimensions of the speaker's vocal apparatus. A tall, well-built man will tend to have a long vocal tract and large vocal folds. His voice quality will reflect the length of his vocal tract by having correspondingly low ranges of formant frequencies, and his voice-dynamic features will indicate the dimensions and mass of his vocal folds by a correspondingly low range of fundamental frequency. His large respiratory volume will be reflected in a powerful loudness range. If we then hear such a voice over the telephone, we normally have a confident expectation that the speaker will turn out to be a large, strong male. In general, our expectations are fulfilled, within a reasonable margin of error. Bonaventura (1935) gave subjects pictures and voices to match, and found that fair accuracy was achieved: in terms of Kretschmerian body-types (Kretschmer, 1925), judgments of *pyknic* types were most accurate, while accuracy was less for *leptosome* types and least for *athletic* types. Moses (1940; 1941) gives general support to this, and Fay and Middleton (1940a) report a more detailed finding: they found that in judging body-types from voices transmitted over a public address system, the results were 22 per cent above chance for pyknic types, 20 per cent for leptosomes, but only 1 per cent above chance for athletic types. Lass, Beverly, Nicosia and Simpson (1978) report that listeners typically judge weight to within three or four pounds (though overestimating the weight of males and underestimating that of females), and that they judge height to within 1.5 inches (though underestimating the height of both males and females). There is one class of voices where the general correlation does not apply, but where listeners nevertheless seem to be able to reach successful conclusions about the physical attributes. That is where the formant ranges of the voice are radically discrepant with the fundamental frequency, as in particular types of dwarfism (Vuorenkoski, Tjernlund and Perheentupa, 1972; Weinberg and Zlatin, 1970). In these cases, the dimensions of the vocal folds are smaller than their general correlation with vocal tract length would lead one to expect.

Exceptions to the general rule of our ability as listeners to attach a particular size and physique to a given voice are sufficiently rare to take us aback when they occur.

Age is judged accurately (Dordain, Chevrie-Muller and Grémy, 1967; Hollien and Shipp, 1972; Mysak, 1959; Ptacek, Sander, Maloney and Roe Jackson, 1966; Shipp and Hollien, 1969). Voice quality features probably play their part in marking this characteristic, but voice-dynamic features are likely to be the more primary cues. Age is marked by pitch in both males and females: Hollien and Shipp (1972) show a progressive lowering of mean pitch with age for males from 20 up to 40, then a rise from age 60 through the 80s. Mysak (1959) also showed this rise in mean pitch from the 50s upwards. Dordain et al. (1967) report a drop in mean pitch for older women, but a rise with extreme age. Ptacek et al. (1966) also report a reduced pitch-range with extreme age.

Features of auditory quality can signal aspects of the age of a speaker. These include the quality associated with the 'breaking' voice of puberty and the quality of extreme old age. Vocal indications of puberty, referred to in clinical literature as 'vocal mutation', often include whispery voice. Luchsinger and Arnold (1965: 132) write that 'In addition to the lowering of the average speaking pitch, the voice is frequently husky during mutation, or it may sound weak'. The senescent voice of extreme old age derives from a complex of endocrinal, anatomical and physiological changes. The mucal fluid supply often becomes disturbed, either greatly increasing or decreasing, tissues become increasingly less elastic, and cartilages become calcified and ossified (Fyfe and Naylor, 1958; Luchsinger and Arnold, 1965; Meader and Muyskens, 1962; Terracol and Azémar, 1949). Meader and Muyskens (1962: 77) comment that 'Since the rigidity of tissue is one determination of its resonating qualities, the gradual deposition of lime in . . . cartilages (replacing them by bone) helps to explain the shrill voice and thin voice (deficient in harmonics) of age'. Because muscles atrophy, the glottis of old speakers often has a bowed appearance (Luchsinger and Arnold, 1965: 136; Tarneaud, 1941); this means that, to achieve phonation, greater effort has to be exerted to bring the vocal folds together, and a rather harsh voice is often the result. When this is combined with inefficient phonation because of an excess of mucus, the type of voice that results is a harsh, whispery voice, as suggested by the following comment from Luchsinger and Arnold (1965: 136): 'Tracheal and laryngeal mucous secretions are increased, sometimes on an allergic basis. Together with a tendency to chronic bronchitis, this over-secretion of mucus produces the hacking, coughing, throat-clearing or "moist" hoarseness of the old man'. In old age, fatty tissue can build up in the ventricles in the sides of the upper larynx (Ferreri, 1959), and the ventricular folds above the ventricles can shrink towards the sides of the larynx, giving a wider entrance to the ventricles (Luchsinger and Arnold, 1965: 136). All these factors can contribute significantly to the fine detail of the auditory quality of the phonation being produced. Luchsinger and Arnold also mention work by Braus (1924), who 'pointed out that the larynx and the entire respiratory and digestive tract are in a lowered position with senility' (1965: 137), because of the loss of elasticity of the muscular and ligamental structures from which these organs are suspended. Any such elongation of the vocal tract tends to lower the ranges of the formant frequencies. A more extensive discussion of age markers in speech can be found in Helfrich (1979).

One usually forms fairly accurate impressions of a speaker's sex from vocal clues. The clearest indicator is probably pitch-range. Hollien, Dew and Philips (1971) measured the mean minimum and maximum fundamental frequency for a group of 332 adult males and 202 young adult females. The male range was 78–698 Hz, and the female range 139–1108 Hz. Differences of pitch-range are directly attributable to different laryngeal dimensions. Kaplan (1960: 144) reports typical dimensions for glottal length in adult males as 23 mm, and in adult females as 17 mm. Differences of spectral quality also contribute to signalling the sex of the speaker, because female vocal tracts are shorter than male tracts, on average, as reflected in higher formant frequency ranges. Fant (1960) gives a list of acoustic values for average male subjects, and compares them with those for females and children. He writes that:

> The natural range of variation of the voice fundamental frequencies for non-nasal voiced sounds uttered by average male subjects is as follows:
>
> > F0: 60–240 Hz
> > F1: 150–850 Hz
> > F2: 500–2500 Hz
> > F3: 1500–3500 Hz
> > F4: 2500–4500 Hz
>
> Females have on average one octave higher fundamental pitch but only 17% higher formant frequencies: see Peterson and Barney (1952); Fant (1953). Children about 10 years of age have still higher formants, on the average 25% higher than adult males, and their fundamental pitch averages 300 Hz. The individual spread is large. (Fant, 1960: 242)

In an article in 1966, Fant amended this position slightly, when he said that:

> The common concept of physiologically induced differences in formant patterns comparing males and females is that the average female F-frequencies are related to those of the male by a simple scale factor inversely proportional to the overall vocal tract length (i.e. female F-pattern about 20% higher than male). This simple scale factor rule has important limitations. (Fant, 1966: 22)

He points out that the deviations from the rule are obscured if an average is taken over all vowels, and says that female-male relations are

> typically different in (1) rounded back vowels, (2) very open

unrounded vowels, (3)closed front vowels . . . The main physiological determinants of the specific deviations from the average rule are that the ratio of pharynx length to mouth cavity length is greater for males than for females, and that the laryngeal cavities are more developed in males. (Fant, 1966: 22)

The scale factor relating average female formant frequencies to those of men is a function of the particular class of vowels . . . The female-to-male scale factor is of the order of 18% averaged over the whole vowel system . . . The scaling of children's data from female data comes closer to a simple factor independent of vowel class. (Fant, 1966: 29)

A further discussion of sex markers in speech can be found in Smith (1979).

The discussion immediately above concerned universal parameters on which all speakers can be placed. We now turn briefly to consider the case of some physical attributes which can be indicated by voice features which normally apply to smaller sections of the population, in considerations of a speaker's medical state. This covers such aspects as abnormalities of anatomy or physiology, the physical effects of trauma or disease, the noxious effects of alcohol, drugs or smoking, transient effects of endocrinal changes and signs of fatigue.

Voice features indicate a surprisingly wide range of information about a speaker's medical state (Laver, 1968: 49), in both what might be considered 'normal' and 'abnormal' conditions. Abnormalities of anatomy can be revealed by voice features associated with such conditions as unusual patterns of dentition (Lawson and Bond, 1968), the use of dentures (Lawson and Bond, 1969) and unusual conformations of the jaw. A number of abnormal congenital conditions can also be indicated: vocal fold sulcus (a furrow along the glottal edge of the vocal fold, which gives rise to so-called *diplophonic voice*, a mode of phonation with two different simultaneous fundamental frequencies (Kiml, 1962)); some types of cleft palate (Jaffe and de Blanc, 1970; Lowry, 1970); subglottal bars of tissue in the lower larynx (Howie, Ladefoged and Stark, 1961); and anatomical similarities in the voices of monozygotic twins (Alpert and Kurtzberg, 1963). More generally, to the extent that any given genetically transmitted condition influences vocal anatomy, then the voice quality and voice-dynamic features of the particular speaker will act as markers of his genetic make-up. One might therefore expect that genetic disorders such as sex-chromosome anomalies and autosomal anomalies like Down's Syndrome (mongolism) would be characterised by symptomatic voices, although this is a research area which has not yet been developed.

Abnormal physiological conditions due to pathology and laryngeal paralysis can be indicated by voice features (Luchsinger and Arnold, 1965: 218–62). Parkinson's disease, for example, is marked by tremulous pitch

(Canter, 1963), and chronic laryngitis by a whispery voice (McCallum, 1954).

Clues in voice quality to endocrinal abnormalities are found in cases of voice disorders resulting from diseases of the thyroid, adrenal and pituitary glands (Luchsinger and Arnold, 1965: 188–217). Laver (1968) suggests that systematic research into the possible use of the voice as a diagnostic marker of these and similar medical states would be extremely valuable. So far, the area has only sporadically attracted investigation (McCallum, 1954; Palmer, 1956; Punt, 1959; Sonninen, 1960; Canter, 1963).

More transient medical states, which while not permanent are outside the speaker's control, can be indicated by voice features when the speaker is suffering from conditions of local inflammation of his vocal organs, as in laryngitis, pharyngitis and tonsillitis, and from nasal catarrh, adenoids or a cold (Abercrombie, 1967: 92; Laver, 1968: 49).

Other transient factors in voice quality derive from changes in the copiousness and consistency of the supply of lubricating mucus in the larynx, and in the characteristics of the mucal lining covering the vocal folds, affecting the efficiency of their vibration. One such state is the voice of sexual arousal in both men and women, which is often rather whispery, and in which fine control of pitch becomes more difficult. A similar endocrinal effect is found in the voices of women in the pregnant or pre-menstrual state, according to Tarneaud (1941) and Perelló (1962). Greene (1964: 80) cites Hildernisse (1956) as reminding us that 'singers often have a clause in their contracts to exempt them from singing during the menstrual period'. See also Amado (1953).

Voice features sometimes reveal aspects of a speaker's medical state as a result of the abusing of his vocal apparatus. The hoarse voice of the chronic smoker (Devine, 1960; Myerson, 1950) and of the chronic drinker (Luchsinger and Arnold, 1965) is a familiar experience.

Lastly, information about more transient states such as fatigue can sometimes be marked by voice features. In extreme fatigue, the mode of phonation can become inefficient, resulting in whispery voice or in weak, breathy voice. It should be noted, however, that in less extreme cases of fatigue, Fay and Middleton (1940b) showed that the ability of listeners to judge a speaker's rested or tired condition from his voice alone appears to be based on stereotypes, in that judges agree with each other in their judgments but are much less often accurate.

Attributions of psychological characteristics of a speaker are sometimes made on the basis of markers which are in fact the product solely of physical characteristics. Listeners are often ready to believe that a speaker with a loud, low-pitched voice that is due to a large, robust physique is also thereby endowed with an authoritative personality (cf. Scherer, 1979b). Misattributions of this sort, where anatomically derived information is used as the evidence for erroneous psychological conclusions, will be discussed in the final section.

It was said earlier that extralinguistic voice features fall into two major divisions. The second division was described as the product of the way in which the speaker 'sets' his muscular vocal apparatus for speaking. *Voice settings* of this sort are habitual tendencies towards maintaining particular muscular adjustments (Abercrombie, 1967: 92; Honikman, 1964). Settings in this category include *voice quality settings* and *voice-dynamic settings*. The acoustic parameters that characterise voice quality and voice-dynamic settings are the same as those that reflect anatomically derived features of the voice, although voice settings necessarily exploit a more limited range of values on those parameters.

Voice quality settings include habitual adjustments of the vocal tract and of the larynx. Settings of the vocal tract involve habitual tendencies towards constricting (or expanding) the tract at some particular point along its length. Examples would be the tendency to keep the tongue raised towards the soft palate, in 'velarised voice'. Another would be the tendency to maintain the lips in a rounded posture throughout speech, in 'labialised voice'. Another would be a tendency to keep the soft palate lowered throughout speech, giving 'nasal voice'. Habitual laryngeal settings involve adjusting the phonatory muscle system in such a way that the vocal folds tend to vibrate in an auditorily characteristic mode. Examples would be 'whispery voice', 'harsh voice', 'harsh whispery voice', 'creaky voice', etc. Laver (1975) gives an extended account of all such voice quality settings and their acoustic correlates.

Voice-dynamic settings include pitch settings and loudness settings, as habitual choices of a comfortable range within the anatomically limited extremes. Discussion of voice quality settings and voice-dynamic settings will be limited here to a consideration of their marking function.

Because voice settings are under potential muscular control, they are learnable and imitable. The adoption of a particular voice setting often acts as an individuating marker, when its use is idiosyncratic to a particular speaker. But voice settings often form part of the typical vocal performance of particular regional accents, and can thus also act as social markers.

Habitual nasality is a frequent component of many accents: it characterises speakers of Received Pronunciation (RP) in Britain, and many accents of the United States and Australia (Laver, 1968: 50). Velarised voice marks the speech of speakers from some areas of New York, from Liverpool and from Birmingham, England (Laver, 1968: 50). Trudgill (1974) has shown, in a sociolinguistic study of speech in Norwich, that the speech of working-class speakers, compared with that of middle-class speakers, is marked by the habitual use of a number of settings: a 'creaky' phonation, a high pitch-range, a loud loudness-range, a fronted, lowered tongue position, a raised larynx position, a particular type of nasality and a relatively high overall degree of muscular tension throughout the vocal tract (Trudgill, 1974: 186–7). Esling (1978: 176) has shown, in a sociolinguistic study of speech in Edinburgh, that social class correlates with laryngeal settings, in that greater social status corresponds to a greater incidence of 'creaky' phonation and lower social status to a greater incidence of whisperiness and harshness.

The notion of voice settings has been developed in phonetic theory mainly to account for general articulatory tendencies distinguishing the pronunciation of different languages (Laver, 1978). In this application, voice settings are usually called 'basis of articulation', or 'articulatory setting'. Heffner (1950: 99), for example, describes French as being spoken 'from a high and tense forward basis of articulation', and English 'from a comparatively low and relaxed basis of articulation'. Honikman (1964: 73–84) describes the voice settings of many languages, including English, French, German, Russian, Arabic, Italian, Polish, Danish and Spanish. She points out, for example, that in many of the languages of India and Pakistan the jaws are held 'rather inert and loosely apart', which she says gives them a distinctive quality which 'is very noticeable in the English spoken by Indians' (Honikman, 1964: 80). Settings of this sort can thus act as markers of linguistic group membership.

2.2 Paralinguistic Features of Tone of Voice

Extralinguistic voice features involve relatively permanent vocal effects. We move now to vocal effects with a medium-term temporal relevance, to consider the paralinguistic communication of affect by manipulations of 'tone of voice'. Many of the same vocal phenomena are concerned, in that a more temporary use is often made of settings. Anger in English is frequently conventionally conveyed, for example, by a harsh phonatory setting, with a raised pitch-span and an increased loudness-span ('span' is a useful term taken from Brown (1977), to distinguish between the range of a quasi-permanent voice-dynamic setting and the more temporary use of a particular span of the same parameter for paralinguistic uses). Other paralinguistic dynamic features are those of *rate* and *continuity*. Rate, sometimes called *tempo*, is self-explanatory; continuity refers to 'the incidence of pauses in the stream of speech – where they come, how frequent they are, and how long they are' (Abercrombie, 1967: 96).

Affect in English, and probably in all languages, is signalled not only by paralinguistic settings, but also by various shorter-term segmental effects. Unfortunately, the field of affective markers in speech is still very much in the early stages of exploration. We still lack an adequate account of the paralinguistic conventions governing affective communication in spoken English – or in any other language. A number of scholars have made a start on this theoretically and methodologically very difficult area. One of the most comprehensive surveys is by Crystal (1969), who gives detailed coverage of paralinguistic dynamic settings involving pitch, loudness and rate. Others include Abercrombie (1968), Brown (1977), Crystal and Quirk (1964), Key (1975) and Scherer (1979). A satisfactory theory of paralinguistic communication is not likely to be available for some years, because of the complexity of the problem.

The experimental research that has been done in the area of paralinguistic communication has tended to focus less on the communication of affect and more on markers of personality, particularly as conveyed by dynamic features. For example, Markel, Phillis, Vargas and Howard (1972) conducted an experiment where 104 male college students were rated both for personality factors and for loudness and rate of speaking. They identified four groups on the basis of these dynamic factors: 'loud-fast', 'loud-slow', 'soft-fast' and 'soft-slow'. In an analysis of variance, they showed a significant difference between the four groups in personality traits. In experiments using synthetic speech, Brown, Strong and Rencher (1974) and Smith, Brown, Strong and Rencher (1975) showed that the attribution of 'competence' and 'benevolence' as personality factors was directly affected by manipulation of rate. Increased rate led to increased ratings of competence and decreased ratings of benevolence. Brown et al. (1974) also showed that ratings of competence and benevolence decreased with both decreased variance of pitch and increased mean pitch.

When attributions of personality are made on the basis of vocal settings, an interesting interaction is suggested between the personality feature concerned and the more ephemeral affective equivalent normally signalled by the use of that same setting in the paralinguistic code governing tone of voice. Since a harsh phonatory setting conventionally signals anger in the paralinguistic code of English, the habitual use of harshness can prompt listeners to conclude, linking anger and aggressiveness, that the speaker has an aggressive personality. A similar example would be the habitual use of a 'smiling' lip setting leading to judgments of a 'cheerful' personality. Further examples of personality markers in speech can be found in Scherer (1979b).

2.3 Features of Phonetic Realisations of Linguistic Units

We come now to the last entry in Figure 14.1, the short-term manipulation of vocal features for the signalling of linguistic units such as consonants and vowels, intonation, tone, rhythm, stress and length. The articulatory realisations of these units make up the phonetic basis of the speaker's accent. Accent is perhaps the outstanding example of a social marker in speech. It serves to indicate regional affiliation, and often social class as well. A number of linguistic concepts are available which can be directly helpful in the analysis of social markers in this area. The following comments on differences between accents are based partly on two very useful articles, by Wells (1970) and Abercrombie (1977). Discussion will be limited to a consideration of accent differences involving consonant and vowel phonemes.

There are four major ways in which the accents of two speakers may be different. The first two concern differences of phonological resources. The two accents can differ either in having different phonemic sound-systems, or in allowing different structural types of phonemic sequences. We can call the first type of difference a *systemic* difference, after Wells (1970: 232) and Abercrombie (1977: 22), and the second type a *structural* difference, after Abercrombie (1977: 21). A systemic difference between two accents is a matter of the number of word-differentiating distinctions that can be made by speakers of the two accents. One account might have a vowel system made up of ten different vowel phonemes, capable therefore of signalling ten word-differentiating distinctions by means of vowel quality alone. Another accent of the same language might have a vowel system made up of eleven different vowel phonemes, and speakers of that accent would thus be capable of making one more word-differentiating distinction by vowel quality alone than speakers of the first accent. A good example of systemic differences of this sort is offered by the accents of England and Scotland, where many differences exist between the vowel systems concerned. Scots accents often differ from English accents in allowing a smaller number of word-differentiating distinctions to be made. An example would be in the following situation: an English speaker of RP will differentiate *Sam* and *psalm* by using different vowel phonemes; many Scots speakers make no distinction between the two words, using the same vowel phoneme in both. Similarly, *tot* and *taut* are differentiated in RP but are indistinguishable in most Scots accents. *Pull* and *pool* would be another example. Conversely, the Scots consonant system allows more lexical distinctions to be made than that of RP. *Lock* and *loch* are pronounced identically in RP, with a final /k/, but in Scots accents, while *lock* is pronounced with a /k/, *loch* is pronounced with a final voiceless velar fricative consonant /x/.

A structural difference between two accents is a matter of the different rules governing the phonemic make-up of word shapes, in terms of the permissible sequences of phonemes. In some accents, /r/ is never pronounced before another consonant. In other accents, it is always pronounced in this position. The pronunciation of a word like *card* would have a different sequential structure in these accents. There are many examples of structural differences between accents involving /r/. All accents of Scotland, and all of the mid-west and west of the United States, have the structural possibility of pronouncing an /r/ before a consonant or a pause; the accents of Australia, South Africa, many accents of England (including RP) and many accents of the east and south of the United States do not have this possibility (Abercrombie, 1977: 22). Whether or not an accent is '*r*-pronouncing' in this way thus marks regional affiliation, in a rather broad way.

There are other examples of structural differences between accents, involving other sounds than /r/, but generally structural differences are less varied than systemic differences. They are none the less perceptually striking when they do occur. Both systemic and structural differences are powerful markers of regional affiliation.

The third major type of difference between accents concerns the way in which otherwise systemically and structurally identical phonological resources are lexically distributed, by choosing different phonemes for the pronunciation of a given word. J.D. O'Connor has suggested the term *selectional* as a name for this kind of difference (Wells, 1970: 244). Abercrombie gives the following example of a selectional difference (which, after Trubetzkoy, he calls a 'distributional' difference): 'two accents might have different vowel phonemes in *pat* and *past*, but one might have *photograph* with the *pat* vowel in the last syllable, while the other has the *past* vowel in the last syllable' (Abercrombie, 1977: 22). A selectional difference involving the choice of different consonant phonemes is where two speakers both include /s/ and /z/ in their consonant systems, but where one pronounces the first *s* in *diagnosis* as /s/ (as speakers from England usually do) and the other pronounces it as /z/ (as speakers from Scotland often do).

The fourth major type of difference between accents is a phonetic matter, of how particular phonemes are actually pronounced. Both Wells (1970: 245) and Abercrombie (1977: 23) call this type a *realisational* difference. Thus two speakers may share the same vowel and consonant systems, have the same structural possibilities, choose the same lexical selection of phonemes, and yet have slightly different accents. The fine detail of how a given speaker pronounces his sounds can act as a marker of group membership, but it can also function as an individuating marker, distinguishing him from fellow members of his sociolinguistic group as we noted earlier. Realisational details can also be very influential as social markers allowing the attribution of gradations of particular social characteristics. As Wells states, 'Accent is still significantly linked to social class in England, and often constitutes an important index of class affiliation' (1970: 248). Because vowel quality is a continuum, small differences of vowel quality can be used, in England at least, as markers of small gradations of social class (cf. Giles, Scherer and Taylor, 1979).

These comments about accent differences between speakers make the assumption that a speaker's accent is fixed and unchanging. It seldom is, of course, and a further area where linguistic concepts can help us to refine our analysis of social markers in speech concerns certain aspects of the notion of *linguistic variability*.

Work in the field of sociolinguistics has shown that social groups may differ not simply in terms of their phonological systems or what pronunciations they use but in *how often* they use certain pronunciations. In the pioneering work in this field, Labov (1966a) demonstrated that in New York City speech the pronunciation of /r/ in words such as *farm* (where the *r* occurs before another consonant) and *far* (where it occurs word-finally) is a *linguistic variable*. While very few New York City speakers actually pronounce the /r/ in these positions on every occasion, most pronounce it on some occasions. (In many other parts of the United States, of course, as mentioned earlier, the /r/ in *farm* is always pronounced, while in British RP it is never pronounced. In these varieties, then, /r/ is not a linguistic variable.) In New York City the frequency with which /r/ in *far, farm*, etc. is pronounced correlates very clearly with the age and social class of the speaker, and with the social context in which he is speaking. The methodology employed in this and other subsequent studies involved carrying out tape-recorded interviews with a random sample of informants and subjecting these recordings to analysis. In the New York City study, counts of how many /r/s were actually pronounced, and of how many could have been but were not, showed that middle-class speakers, on average, pronounced a higher percentage of /r/s than working-class speakers, that younger speakers had a higher percentage than older speakers, and that formal styles of speech produced more /r/s than informal styles. Interestingly enough, studies of English towns where /r/ is also a variable, such as Reading, show exactly the reverse pattern (see Trudgill, 1975) – a good illustration of the arbitrary nature of linguistic markers of social categories.

This sort of technique can be applied to a large number of variable features of pronunciation in very many linguistic varieties. Obvious examples from British English would include the percentages of /h/s that are 'dropped', i.e. not present in words such as *hammer, house* for different groups of speakers; and the percentage of *t*s in words such as *butter, better* that are pronounced as glottal stops. Figure 14.2 gives figures (from Trudgill, 1974) for the percentage of *-ing* suffixes in words like *jumping, running* which were in fact pronounced as *-in'*, from tape-recordings of sixty speakers in Norwich. The correlation with social class and formality is clear.

It is important to note that in all such cases correlations of this type apply to *averaged* scores for *groups* of speakers, and do not of course mean that any given individual will necessarily score at the same sort of level as those who have objectively the same social status characteristics. Indeed, it is clear that many other factors such as social mobility (Labov, 1966b) and strength of social ambition (Douglas-Cowie, 1978) can lead to differential behaviour. However, it is equally clear that individual speakers are not 'sociolinguistic automata' (Giles, 1977), and there is much room for idiosyncratic and random variation. The correlations, nevertheless, are

	Formal speech	Casual speech
Middle class	3	28
Lower middle class	15	42
Upper working class	74	87
Middle working class	88	95
Lower working class	98	100

Figure 14.2 -in' suffixes (%) in Norwich (after Trudgill, 1974).

sufficiently strong that, other things being equal, speakers who use a high percentage of -*ing* (rather than -*in'*) suffixes will be perceived as middle-class unless or until there is stronger evidence to the contrary, and that '*h*-dropping' and glottal stop realisations of *t*s are stereotyped as working-class characteristics. It is also interesting to note that, while speakers and groups of speakers often differ merely in terms of percentages and proportions, and we are thus in many cases presented with linguistic continua, it is often the case, it seems, that listeners *perceive* differences dichotomously (cf. Giles, Scherer and Taylor, 1979). It may well be the case that there are thresholds such that speakers are heard as 'dropping their *h*s' only if they drop x per cent (rather than x−1 per cent) of all possible *h*s.

A relatively more recent and more refined type of analysis – and one that is more interesting to the theoretical linguist – has shown that the probability of occurrence of particular variants of a variable (e.g. /r/ or zero; [*t*] or glottal stop) may also be determined by *linguistic* context. For example, the occurrence of /r/, in those accents where it constitutes a linguistic variable, may be more likely after some vowels than after others. In the English of Reading, for example, /r/ is more likely in *bird, fur* than in *beard, beer*, and more likely here than in *far, farm*.

This finding is of relevance here, because it appears that the influence of different linguistic contexts may be relatively more or less important for different social groups. For instance, in most varieties of English, conso-nant clusters of the type /pt/, /kt/, /st/, as in *apt, act, mast*, are simplified, in certain circumstances, by the omission of the *t*. Most people, for example, will normally say *mos' people* rather than *most people*. The linguistic context in which the *t* appears, however, is very important in determining the probability of its omission. In some varieties of American Black English, where consonant cluster simplification of this type is more frequent than in many other English varieties, it has been demonstrated that, on average, simplification is (a) more likely before a following consonant, as in *past five, passed five*, than before a following vowel, as in *past eleven, passed eleven*, and (b) more likely where the *t* is not a marker of the past tense – *past five, past eleven* – than where it is – *passed five, passed eleven* (*-ed* is of course pronounced as [t] in these cases). However, closer examination of the relative importance of the two factors shows that, while for adults the grammatical constraint (past tense vs non-past tense) is the stronger of the two, for adolescents it is the phonological constraint (following vowel or consonant) which is the more powerful. This is illustrated in Figure 14.3. This also raises the interesting question, however, as to how far these social differences in language can legitimately be described as social markers. As we have seen, linguists were until recently not aware of these differences, and awareness came only as the result of detailed analyses. Speakers and hearers are certainly not consciously aware of them, and if, therefore, they do function in some way as social markers, it must be at a very low level of consciousness.

3. Grammatical Aspects of Markers

Linguistic variability is not confined to phonological phenomena. Grammatical features are also variable in many varieties, and can be subject to the same kind of analysis as phonological variability. In most areas of the English-speaking world, for example, use of multiple negation (*I don't want none* vs *I don't want any*) correlates very closely with social class background, as does use of most other non-standard grammatical forms. Again, moreover, we most often find that we are dealing with a social dialect continuum, with groups of speakers differing in terms of proportions of forms used rather than absolutely. However, unlike phonological variables, for which speakers most often are ranged along the continuum in such a way that more speakers are found in central ranges rather than at the ends, grammatical variables tend to stratify speakers more sharply with most speakers appearing at the 'top' or 'bottom'. Grammatical variables are also more difficult to investigate in that they occur less frequently than phonological variables in any given stretch of speech. They are also, like phonological variables, liable to be subject to linguistic constraints which may vary from social group to social group. In the non-standard English of the town of Reading, for instance, present-tense verb forms variably add *-s* in persons other than the third-person singular, and the percentage of non-standard *s*s that occur again correlates clearly with social-class membership and social context. For adolescent speakers, however, there is a constraint such that this non-standard *-s* may not occur on the main verb if there is a following complement clause containing a finite verb (Cheshire, 1978). That is, we find *I likes it* and *I wants to do it*, but not *I knows that it's true*. Older speakers do not have this particular constraint.

Sociolinguistic research on linguistic variation thus encourages us to be more sophisticated in a number of ways in our analysis of social markers in speech. It suggests, first of all, that linguistic differences are very often a matter of probabilities and tendencies: high percentages of *r* pronounced in New York City do not mean that a speaker is upper middle class but that

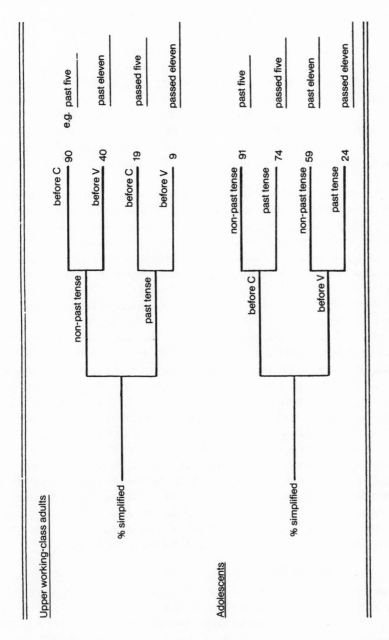

Figure 14.3 Consonant cluster simplification in New York City Black English (after Labov, 1972).

he probably is. This also means that we have to be reasonably careful in our usage of labels for linguistic varieties. We can refer to 'Cockney' as if this label referred to a discrete linguistic variety, but we must be aware that this is not the case. We can also use terms such as 'Bristol accent', but here again we must be aware that it is a term which permits degrees of more or less (and linguistic analysis can of course help us to quantify exactly how 'Bristol' a particular variety is and give us some insights into what features of a Bristol accent listeners may and may not be reacting to in evaluating speakers in real life or experimental situations). Sociolinguistic research also indicates, as mentioned above, that while linguistic variation is often continuous, perception of it is often dichotomous: listeners may thus not be sufficiently consciously aware of linguistic differences to be able to report on them.

The differential realisation of grammatical categories (e.g. /s/ vs zero for present tense) may, we have seen, correlate with social categories. It has also been suggested, however, that social groups and individuals may also differ in their *usage* of different grammatical categories and constructions. Some workers have counted different parts of speech in texts and indicated that some speakers use a 'nominal style' (high proportion of nouns) while others use a 'verbal style' (high proportion of verbs) (cf. Brown and Fraser, 1979). Bernstein's early work, too, produced counts of features such as adverbs, pronouns, passive verbs and subordinate clauses, and showed that use varied with social class membership (see Bernstein, 1971; Robinson, 1979). It is possible, although not certain, that more refined grammatical analyses than these would throw up more detailed grammatical markers of social features. It is possible that it is differential use of certain types of verb form, clause structures and so on that may lead listeners to characterise certain types of speech style as 'impressive', 'boring', 'tentative', 'blunt', etc. It might therefore be profitable to construct 'syntactic profiles' for speakers approximately after the manner in which language pathologists construct profiles for subjects who suffer from some form of syntactic disability. Crystal, Fletcher and Garman (1976) developed a methodology for carrying out work of this type involving the enumeration and measurement of sentence length, clause structures, etc., including details down to the level, for example, of how many phrases had the structure Determiner + Noun, Adjective + Noun, and so on.

4. Markers in Discourse and Conversational Interaction

Work in the study of discourse and conversation also leads to a possibility similar to the one discussed immediately above. A project currently being led by Bent Preisler of the English Department of the University of Aarhus in Denmark seeks to investigate the linguistic correlates of Bales' (1970) communicative act categories by exploring the relationship between the role adopted by a speaker in a conversation and the characteristics of his

Speakers	Male	Female
% sentence type		
Interrogative	14.8	25.0
Statement	77.8	75.0
Imperative	3.7	0.0

Figure 14.4 Grammatical forms of speech acts 'Gives Suggestion' (after Preisler).

speech in that conversation. For example, if a speaker taking part in a conversation makes relatively few suggestions, are those suggestions expressed differently from (for example, more 'carefully' than) those made by a speaker who makes many suggestions? And what exactly are the linguistic correlates of 'carefully'? Preliminary work has already produced some interesting results. Analyses of English conversations among groups of four people have shown that those speech acts which are categorisable, after Bales, as 'Gives Suggestion' constitute 8.1 per cent of the total number of speech acts for the male speakers but 2.8 per cent of the total for women. Even more interesting is the linguistic breakdown of the way in which these speech acts were performed. Figure 14.4 shows that, when 'giving suggestions', men do so by means of imperative constructions more often and by means of interrogatives less often than women. The percentage of statements made is similar for the two groups, but further analysis indicates that 33.3 per cent of all statements functioning as 'giving suggestions' were accompanied by tag-questions in the case of the women, whereas this was true of only 3.7 per cent of cases for the men. These, it must be stressed, are preliminary findings only and can be no more than suggestive. They do suggest, however, that if there are sex-linked differences of this type in linguistic behaviour, then role is probably the primary factor at work here and that sex differences appear only because sex and role selection appear to be linked (cf. Smith, 1979).

Other work in conversational analysis (for a survey, see Coulthard, 1977) demonstrates that conversation is a structured and rule-governed activity. There are norms and conventions for features of conversation such as turn-taking, silences, interruptions, speaker-selection and topic-changing. It has also been shown that these norms and conventions may vary from culture to culture (see Bauman and Sherzer, 1975). (In some cultures, for example, it is apparently possible for more than one speaker to speak at once for extended periods.) This opens up the possibility that variation may also occur from community to community and group to group, and that there may be reasonably rigorous methods for studying this. Since rules of this type are clearly also less firm, in some ways, than, say, syntactic rules, there is also the likelihood that they may be broken, and that the frequency and manner of their being broken may be socially significant.

5. Lexical Aspects of Markers

Finally, we can note that one of the most obvious areas where speech can act as a social marker is in the area of vocabulary. This, however, is probably one of the hardest and least profitable to study, and one where linguistic concepts and techniques have relatively little to offer. The difficulty is that particular lexical items occur, generally speaking, relatively infrequently, and that they are also liable to conscious suppression on the part of the speaker. Their function as social markers, nevertheless, is undeniable. The bulk of the vocabulary of any language is shared by all its speakers, but there are also usually certain sets of lexical items which are restricted to, or more probable in, the speech of certain groups. This may be a reflection of the qualifications, interests, experience or occupation of speakers: technical vocabulary, for instance, will normally be confined to groups who specialise in the topic concerned. Very often, though, group-typical vocabulary is social rather than, or as well as, technical in function. Minority groups such as homosexuals, drug addicts and criminals are well-known to have developed specialised vocabularies which both reflect their particular interests and reinforce group solidarity, as well as excluding outsiders who are not familiar with the words involved (cf. Brown and Fraser, 1979). And that area of colloquial – and often fashionable and temporary – vocabulary known as slang is also a very powerful social marker – particularly, it seems, of age. Many speakers appear to keep abreast of changing patterns in slang vocabulary for so long and then stop, so that usage of 'outdated' slang words labels them as of a certain age. Stereotypes are also significant in vocabulary use. Certain words, for example, are felt to be more common in the speech of women than in the speech of men: *divine, sweet, adorable, maddening* might qualify for this category. We have, however, no empirical evidence to confirm that this is in fact the case, and it is clear that if they are typical of women's speech, then they are typical only of certain sorts of women. Probably more reliable are claims that women in many societies use taboo words and swear generally less than men (see Thorne and Henley, 1975; Smith, 1979).

6. Markers and the Attribution Process

A number of interesting questions arise from the discussion above of phonetic and linguistic markers in speech, about the listener's process of attribution.

It is possible to draw a distinction between *actual markers* and *apparent markers*. Actual markers accurately indicate a true characteristic of the speaker. Apparent markers fall into two classes: *misleading markers*, which are deliberately projected by a speaker in order to lay claim to characteristics of identity which are not actually his; and *misinterpreted markers*, which are mistakenly interpreted by the listener as signalling a particular characteristic of the speaker when in fact the speaker is not actually thus characterisable.

An example of a misleading marker would be the consciously manipulated accent of a socially aspiring speaker. Using the terms 'informative' and 'communicative' as defined at the beginning of this chapter, we can say that the speaker in this situation manages to mislead the listener, if he is successful in his deception, by taking over communicative control of a factor normally understood by the listener to be of informative value only.

An example of a misinterpreted marker is illustrated by the following situation: a speaker with acute laryngitis has an extremely whispery voice; whispery voice is a type of phonation used paralinguistically in English as a conventional signal of a conspiratorially confidential interaction; the listener, in answering the speaker, himself adopts what he takes to be a situationally appropriate whispery voice, joining in the confidentiality which he mistakenly believes the speaker initiated. Here the listener misinterprets the actual, symptomatic marker of the speaker's medical state as an apparent marker of the speaker's affective state. An actual physical marker has been misinterpreted as a psychological marker. In this case, the listener has mistakenly interpreted information that was in fact solely informative as if it were deliberately communicative.

The topic of misleading markers would be an interesting field of research. The concept of misinterpreted markers, or of misattribution, brings us closer to the heart of the attribution process, however. Two general research strategies are possible, in examining misattribution. One could explore the relations between the types of markers involved in cases of mistaken attribution. Or one could investigate discrepancies between listeners, which would give insight into the individual's process of attribution.

Beginning with the first possibility, we can ask whether mistaken attribution characteristically involves a mistake between major categories of markers, or more typically a mistake of degree within a marking category.

Certainly some categorial mistakes are made in the attribution process, as in the laryngitis example. It would be interesting to explore the question of whether inter-category mistakes between any two categories, say psychological and physical, or psychological and social, are equally common in both directions, or whether misattribution is usually biased in favour of a particular category. As a hypothesis, we might suggest that categorial mistakes tend to lead to psychological conclusions being drawn from physical and social evidence, more often than vice versa. For example, the fact that a given speaker has a long vocal tract, and that he speaks with a prestigious accent, might persuade a listener to attribute to him an authority that was in fact quite spurious. Such a hypothesis would imply that listeners sometimes use wider ranges of evidence to support conclusions about personality than is strictly legitimate.

It may be, more probably, that misattribution more often involves a misinterpretation of degree within a marking category. We saw earlier, in the case of linguistic variability, where percentage of use of a given linguistic form constituted a social marker, that listeners' perception of a continuum of this sort tended to be dichotomous. Such a phenomenon is one basis for the stereotyping process in attribution.

In considering the second avenue of research into misattribution, that of discrepancies between individual listeners, one obvious research area is the extent to which the judge's own personal physical, psychological or social characteristics lead him to minimise or maximise attributions on the particular marking parameter concerned.

Being a listener to speech is not unlike being a detective. The listener not only has to establish what it was that was said, but also has to construct, from an assortment of clues, the affective state of the speaker and a profile of his identity. Fortunately, the listener's task is made a little easier by the fact that the vocal clues marking the individual physical, psychological and social characteristics of the speaker are numerous. This chapter has attempted to show how phonetic and linguistic theory can help us to refine the analysis of markers of these characteristics in speech, by providing descriptions of the extralinguistic, paralinguistic and linguistic factors concerned.

References

Abercrombie, D. (1967) *Elements of General Phonetics*, Edinburgh.

Abercrombie, D. (1968) 'Paralanguage', *British Journal of Disorders of Communication* 3, 55–9.

Abercrombie, D. (1977) 'The accents of Standard English in Scotland', *University of Edinburgh Department of Linguistics Work in Progress* 10, 21–32.

Alpert, M. and Kurtzberg, R.L. (1963) 'Comparison of the spectra of the voices of twins', *Paper B9, 66th Meeting of Acoustical Society of America*.

Amado, J.M. (1953) 'Tableau général des problèmes posés pour l'action des hormones sur le développement du larynx, le classement d'une voix, la génèse des activités rythmogènes encéphaliques et l'excitabilité du sphincter laryngien', *Annales d'Otolaryngologie* (Paris), 70, 117–37.

Bales, B.F. (1970) *Personality and Interpersonal Behaviour*, London.

Bauman, R. and Sherzer, J. (1975) *Explorations in the Ethnography of Speaking*, Cambridge.

Bernstein, B. (1971) *Class, Codes and Control*, vol. I. London.

Bonaventura, M. (1935) 'Ausdruck der Persönlichkeit in der Sprechstimme und in Photogramm', *Archiv für die gesamte Psychologie* 94, 501–70.

Braus, H. (1924) *Anatomie des Menschen*, Berlin.

Brown, B.L., Strong, W.J. and Rencher, A.C. (1974) 'Fifty-four voices from two: the effects of simultaneous manipulations of rate, mean fundamental frequency and variance of fundamental frequency on ratings of personality from speech', *Journal of the Acoustical Society of America* 55, 313–18.

Brown, G. (1977) *Listening to Spoken English*, London.

Brown, P. and Fraser, C. (1979) 'Speech as a marker of situation', pp. 33–62 in Scherer and Giles (eds).

Canter, G.J. (1963) 'Speech characteristics of patients with Parkinson's disease 1. Intensity, pitch and duration', *Journal of Speech and Hearing Disorders* 28, 221–9.

Cheshire, J. (1978) 'Present tense verbs in Reading English', in Trudgill, P. (ed.) *Sociolinguistic Patterns in British English*, London.

Coulthard, M. (1977) *An Introduction to Discourse Analysis*, London.

Crystal, D. (1969) *Prosodic Systems and Intonation in English*, Cambridge.

Crystal, D. and Fletcher, P. (in press) Profile analysis of language disability, in Fillmore, C. and Wang, W. (eds) *Individual Differences in Language Ability*, London.

Crystal, D. and Quirk, R. (1964) *Systems of Prosodic and Paralinguistic Features in English*, The Hague.

Crystal, D., Fletcher, P. and Garman, M. (1976) *The Grammatical Analysis of Linguistic Disability*, London.

Devine, K.D. (1960) 'Pathologic effects of smoking in the larynx and oral cavity', *Proceedings of Staff Meetings of the Mayo Clinic* 35, 349–52.

Dordain, M., Chevrie-Muller, C. and Grémy, F. (1967) 'Etude clinique et instrumentale de la voix et de la parole des femmes agées', *Revue française de gerontologie* 13, 163–70.

Douglas-Cowie, E. (1978) 'Linguistic code-switching in a Northern Irish village: social interaction and social ambition', in Trudgill, P. (ed.) *Sociolinguistic Patterns in British English*, London.

Eco, U. (1976) *A Theory of Semiotics*, Bloomington, Ind.

Esling, J.K. (1978) 'Voice quality in Edinburgh: a sociolinguistic and phonetic study', PhD dissertation, University of Edinburgh.

Fant, G. (1953) 'Discussion of paper read by G.E. Peterson at the 1952 Symposium on the Application of Communication Theory', in W. Jackson (ed.) *Communication Theory*. London.

Fant, G. (1960) *Acoustic Theory of Speech Production*, The Hague.

Fant, G. (1966) 'A note on vocal tract size factors and non-uniform F-pattern scalings', *STL-QPSR* 4, 22–30, Royal Institute of Technology, Stockholm.

Fay, P.J. and Middleton, W.C. (1940a) 'Judgement of Kretschmerian body types from the voice as transmitted over a public address system', *Journal of Social Psychology* 12, 151–62.

Fay, P.J. and Middleton, W.C. (1940b) 'The ability to judge the rested or tired condition of a speaker from his voice as transmitted over a public address system', *Journal of General Psychology* 24, 211–15.

Feibleman, J.K. (1946) *An Introduction to Peirce's Philosophy*, New York.

Ferreri, G. (1959) 'Senescence of the larynx', *Ital. Gen. Rev. Oto-rhinolaryng.* 1, 640–709.

Fyfe, F.W. and Naylor, E. (1958) 'Calcification and ossification in the cricoid cartilage of the larynx with annotation on the mechanism of change of pitch', *Proceedings of the Canadian Otolaryngological Society*, pp. 67–9.

Giles, H. (1977) 'Social psychology and applied linguistics: towards an integrative approach', *ITL: Review of Applied Linguistics* 33, 27–42.

Giles, H., Scherer, K.R. and Taylor, D.M. (1979) 'Speech markers in social interaction', pp. 343–82 in Scherer and Giles (eds) (1979).

Greene, M.C.L. (1964) *The Voice and its Disorders*, London.

Hardcastle, W. (1976) *Physiology of Speech Production*, New York.

Hartshorne, C. and Weiss, P. (1931–5) *C. S. Peirce: collected papers*, Cambridge, Mass.

Heffner, R.-M.S. (1950) *General Phonetics*, Madison.

Helfrich, H. (1979) 'Age markers in speech', pp. 63–108 in Scherer and Giles (eds) (1979).

Hildernisse, L.W. (1956) 'Voice diagnosis', *Acta Physiologia et Pharmacologica Neerlandica* 5, 73ff.

Hollien, H. and Shipp, F.T. (1972) 'Speaking fundamental frequency and chronological age in males', *Journal of Speech and Hearing Research* 15, 155–9.

Hollien, H., Dew, D. and Philips. P. (1971) 'Phonational frequency ranges of adults', *Journal of Speech and Hearing Research* 14, 755–60.

Honikman, B. (1964) 'Articulatory settings', in D. Abercrombie et al. (eds) *In Honour of Daniel Jones*, London.

Howie, T.O., Ladefoged, P. and Stark, R.E. (1961) 'Congenital sub-glottic bars found in 3 generations of one family', *Folia Phoniatrica* 13, 56–61.

Jaffe, B.F. and de Blanc, G.B. (1970) 'Cleft palate, cleft lip, and cleft uvula in Navaho Indians: incidence and otorhinolaryngologic problems', *Cleft Palate Journal* 7, 300–5.

Kaplan, H.M. (1960) *Anatomy and Physiology of Speech*, New York.

Key, M.R. (1975) *Paralanguage and Kinesics*, Metuchen, NJ.

Kiml, J. (1962) 'Trouble de la voix dans le sillon des cordes vocales', *Folia Phoniatrica* 14, 272–9.

Kretschmer, E. (1925) *Physique and Character*, New York.

Labov, W. (1966a) *The Social Stratification of English in New York City*, Washington, DC.

Labov, W. (1966b) 'The effect of social mobility on linguistic behaviour', in S. Lieberson (ed.) *Explorations in Sociolinguistics*, The Hague.

Labov, W. (1972) *Sociolinguistic Patterns*, Oxford.

Ladefoged, P. (1962) *Elements of Acoustic Phonetics*, Chicago.

Ladefoged, P. (1971) *Preliminaries to Linguistic Phonetics*, Chicago.

Ladefoged, P. (1976) *A Course in Phonetics*, New York.

Lass, N.J., Beverly, A.S., Nicosia, D.K. and Simpson, L.A. (1978) 'An investigation of speaker height and weight identification by means of direct estimation', *Journal of Phonetics* 6, 69–76.

Laver, J. (1968) 'Voice quality and indexical information', *British Journal of Disorders of Communication* 3, 43–54.

Laver, J. (1975) 'Individual Features in Voice Quality', PhD dissertation, University of Edinburgh.

Laver, J. (1978) 'The concept of articulatory settings: an historical survey', *Historiographia Linguistica* 5, 1–14.

Lawson, W.A. and Bond, E.K. (1968) 'Speech and its relation to dentistry II. The influence of oral structures on speech', *The Dental Practitioner* 19, 113–18.

Lawson, W.A. and Bond, E.K. (1969) 'Speech and its relation to dentistry III. The effects on speech of variations in the designs of dentures', *The Dental Practitioner* 19, 150–6.

Lowry, R.B. (1970) 'Sex-linked cleft palate in British Columbia Indian family', *Pediatrics* 46, 123–8.

Luchsinger, R. and Arnold, G E. (1965) *Voice–Speech–Language*, London.

Lyons, J. (1977) *Semantics*, 2 vols. Cambridge.
Markel, N.N., Phillis, J.A., Vargas, R. and Howard, K. (1972) 'Personality traits associated with voice types', *Journal of Psycholinguistic Research* 1, 249–55.
McCallum, J.R. (1954) 'Chronic laryngitis', *Speech* 18, 48–50.
Meader, C.L. and Muyskens, J.H. (1962) *Handbook of Biolinguistics*, Toledo, Ohio.
Morris, C.W. (1946) *Signs, Language and Behavior*, New York.
Moses, P.J. (1940) 'Is medical phonetics an essential part of otorhinolaryngology?' *Archives of Otolaryngology* (Chicago), 31, 444–551.
Moses, P.J. (1941) 'Theories regarding the relation of constitution and character through the voice', *Psychological Bulletin* 38, 746.
Myerson, M.C. (1950) 'Smoker's Larynx – a clinical pathological entity?', *Annals of Otology, Rhinology and Laryngology* 59, 541–6.
Mysak, E.D. (1959) 'Pitch and duration characteristics of older males', *Journal of Speech and Hearing Research* 2, 46–54.
O'Connor, J.D. (1973) *Phonetics*, Harmondsworth, Middx.
Palmer, J.M. (1956) 'Hoarseness in laryngeal pathology: a review of the literature', *Laryngoscope* 66, 500–16.
Perelló, J. (1962) 'La disfonia premenstrual', *Acta Oto-Rino-Laryngologica Ibero-Americana* 23, 561–3.
Peterson, G.E. and Barney, H.L. (1952) 'Control methods used in a study of vowels', *Journal of the Acoustical Society of America* 24, 175–84.
Pike, K.L. (1943) *Phonetics*, Ann Arbor, Mich.
Ptacek, P.H., Sander, E.K., Maloney, W.H. and Roe Jackson, C.C. (1966) 'Phonatory and related changes with advanced age', *Journal of Speech and Hearing Research* 9, 353–60.
Punt, N.A. (1959) 'Alteration in the voice', *The Medical Press*, 18 March, pp. 235–8.
Robinson, W.P. (1979) 'Speech markers and social class', pp. 211–50 in Scherer and Giles (eds) (1979).
Scherer, K.R. (1979a) 'Non-linguistic vocal indicators of emotion and psychopathology', in Izard, C.E. (ed.) *Emotions in Personality and Psychopathology*, New York.
Scherer, K.R. (1979b) 'Personality markers in speech', pp. 147–210 in Scherer and Giles (eds) (1979).
Scherer, K.R. and Giles, H. (eds) (1979) *Social Markers in Speech*, Cambridge University Press, Cambridge, and Editions de la Maison des Sciences de l'Homme, Paris.
Shipp, F.T. and Hollien, H. (1969). 'Perception of the aging male voice', *Journal of Speech and Hearing Research* 12, 703–10.
Smith, B.L., Brown, B.L., Strong, W.J. and Rencher, A.C. (1975) 'Effects of speech rate on personality perception', *Language and Speech* 18, 145–52.
Smith, P.M. (1979) 'Sex markers in speech', pp. 109–46 in Scherer and Giles (eds) (1979).
Sonninen, A. (1960) 'Laryngeal signs and symptoms of goitre', *Folia Phoniatrica* 12, 41–7.
Tarneaud, J. (1941) *Traité pratique de phonologie et de phoniatrie, la voix – la parole – le chant*, Paris.
Terracol, J. and Azémar, R. (1949) *La senescence de la voix*, Paris.
Thorne, B. and Henley, N. (eds) (1975) *Language and Sex: difference and dominance*, Rowley, Mass.

Trudgill, P. (1974) *The Social Differentiation of English in Norwich*, Cambridge.

Trudgill, P. (1975) 'Sex, covert prestige and linguistic change in the urban British English of Norwich', in Thorne, B. and Henley, N. (eds) *Language and Sex: Difference and Dominance*, Rowley, Mass.

Trudgill, P. (ed.) (1978) *Sociolinguistic Patterns in British English*, London.

Vuorenkoski, V., Tjernlund, P. and Perheentupa, J. (1972) 'Auditory perception of voice quallties and speaking fundamental frequency in Mulibreynanism and in some other children with growth failure', *STL-QPSR* 2–3, 64–74, Royal Institute of Technology, Stockholm.

Weinberg, B. and Zlatin, M. (1970) 'Speaking fundamental frequency characteristics of five- and six-year-old children with mongolism', *Journal of Speech and Hearing Research* 13, 418–25.

Wells, J.C. (1970) 'Local accents in England and Wales', *Journal of Linguistics* 6, 231–52.

15 A Perceptual Protocol for the Analysis of Vocal Profiles

Originally published as Laver, J., Wirz, S., Mackenzie, J. and Hiller, S.M. (1981) 'A perceptual protocol for the analysis of vocal profiles', *Edinburgh University Department of Linguistics Work in Progress* 14: 139–55

Introduction

A vocal profile will be taken here to consist of a statement of the speaker-characterising, long-term features of a person's overall vocal performance. It includes comment on laryngeal and supralaryngeal aspects of voice quality, on means, ranges and variability of prosodic aspects such as pitch and loudness, and on factors of temporal organisation such as rate and continuity. In lay terms, a vocal profile summarises the phonetic features of a speaker's habitual 'voice'.

It is reasonable to describe a statement of these features as a 'profile', rather than merely as a listing, to the extent that a theoretical relationship exists between the items within the profile. A descriptive model, set in the framework of general phonetic theory, has recently been put forward which analyses a speaker's voice as the product of perceptually distinguishable components, each specified in terms of acoustic, articulatory and physiological correlates (Laver, 1968; 1974; 1975; 1979; 1980; Laver and Hanson, 1981; Laver and Trudgill, 1979). The basic unit of this scheme is an auditory component correlated with an articulatory 'setting' (Honikman, 1964), which is a long-term muscular bias on articulation. Examples are habitual tendencies to lip-rounding, to nasality or to a whispery mode of phonation. Each such setting or component is defined in terms of its deviation from an acoustically and articulatorily specified *neutral* reference configuration of the vocal apparatus (Laver, 1980: 14; Laver and Hanson, 1981: 59). There are certain constraints of mutual compatibility between individual settings, on both physiological and acoustic grounds, and it is this necessary theoretical relationship between the elements of the descriptive model that justifies the use of the term 'profile'. The perceptual product of constellations of such settings in the speech of a given speaker makes up his or her vocal profile.

The analytic model in the references listed above is (largely) confined to a description of phonetic aspects of the normal voice. A three-year research project[1] which started in 1979, employing two speech therapists, two speech scientists and a clerical assistant, is currently extending the descriptive technique beyond normal voices to include abnormal voices found in speech disorders. A major objective of the project is to test the medical applicability of the descriptive system, and to make it available as a standard descriptive tool in speech therapy and speech pathology clinics.

A working hypothesis of the project is that particular speech disorders have characteristic vocal profiles associated with them. To create a database on which this hypothesis can be tested, tape-recordings are being made of not less than thirty young male and female adult speakers, mostly from Scottish hospitals, day-centres and clinics,[2] for each of eight types of disorder. The task of making the recordings is nearly complete, and to date some 200 recordings have been made.

The eight types of disorder, some containing sub-types, are:
1. Profound hearing loss[3]
2. Cerebral palsy[4]
3. Down's Syndrome[5]
4. Sex-chromosome anomalies[6]
5. Parkinson's Disease[7]
6. Thyroid disorders[8]
7. Dysphonia[9]
8. Cleft palate[10]

It will be noted that the above list contains abnormalities both of anatomy and of neurological control. An important conclusion of the research will concern the extent to which such abnormalities constrain any attempt to unify the description of normal and pathological vocal performance.

The primary analytic task of the project has been to construct perceptual and acoustic profiles of the voice of each subject in the above groups. The purpose of this report is to give an account of the work to date on the development of a protocol form for the analysis of the perceptual profiles of the subjects. The construction of corresponding acoustic profiles, derived from computer analysis of the recordings, largely using linear predictive coding signal-processing techniques, is the subject of further research.

Development of the Vocal Protocol

Given the objective of clinical applicability, it was decided from the outset of the project that the protocol form would be designed in collaboration with experienced speech therapists, during sessions of training in the use of the descriptive system. The present version, shown in Figure 15.1, is the tenth generation of the protocol. The content and rationale of the protocol have been the product of collaborative experience with four successive training panels, two from Lothian Region, one from Glasgow, and one from Newcastle, comprising over fifty individual therapists. Two further panels have been arranged for the immediate future, one in Nottingham and one in London, and further minor evolution of the protocol is not ruled out, though development seems now to have reached a relatively stable plateau.

Using the Vocal Profile Analysis Protocol

It may be helpful from the outset to distinguish sharply between the terms 'profile' and 'protocol'. The VPA protocol is the form shown in Figure 15.1; the profile is represented by the data entered on the protocol. A therapist uses a protocol to record a patient's vocal profile; changes in a patient's vocal profile during a course of remedial therapy can be quantified by noting changes in the data entered on the corresponding VPA protocols; and the completed protocol constitutes a permanent, written record that can be stored in a patient's case-notes and interpreted by anyone trained in the descriptive system (and readily explained to untrained medical personnel).

The ultimate goal of the project is to link the perceptual and the acoustic analysis approaches. However, important though it is for automatic acoustic analysis to be made available for clinical use, the major value of the scheme for clinicians is likely to lie initially in the perceptual technique. The immediate accessibility of perceptual judgments allows a therapist to make direct assessments of vocal factors independently of complex, expensive and often physically remote technology; and provided that the perceptual system has a demonstrable correlation with objective acoustic measurement, then the main function of the acoustic technology will for some time to come, until powerful computers become standard equipment in speech clinics, be a back-up, confirmatory function.

1. The Speech Sample

Normally, the perceptual analysis is performed on tape-recordings. Ideally, this should be supplemented by visual observation of the patient. This is not essential, but as in segmental analysis, visual clues may be valuable in confirming auditory judgments. Labial and mandibular settings are obviously associated with visible factors, but this is also true, to a smaller extent, of lingual and larynx position settings.

Good-quality audio-recording is advisable for the accurate analysis of vocal features, as some setting components are extremely prone to distortion by poor recording. Attenuation of high-frequency energy, for example, mimics the acoustic damping correlated with nasality, and so tends to bias perceptual judgments towards higher ratings on the nasal setting. Tape hiss interferes with the assessment of the fricative qualities attributable to whisperiness, breathiness or audible nasal escape.

The speech sample must be long enough to allow long-term-average setting effects to be perceptually abstracted from the shorter-term segmental performance. The time needed for accurate assessment varies from setting to setting, and depends in part on the proportion of segments which

Vocal Profile Analysis Protocol

Judge: . . . . **Tape:** . . . . **Sex:** . . . .
Date of Analysis: . . . . **Speaker:** . . . . **Age:** . . . .

I. VOCAL QUALITY FEATURES

CATEGORY	FIRST PASS			SECOND PASS						
	Neutral	Non-neutral		SETTING	Scalar Degrees					
		Normal	Abnormal		Normal			Abnormal		
					1	2	3	4	5	6
A. Supralaryngeal Features										
1. Labial				Lip Rounding/Protrusion						
				Lip Spreading						
				Labiodentalisation						
				Extensive Range						
				Minimised Range						
2. Mandibular				Close Jaw						
				Open Jaw						
				Protruded Jaw						
				Extensive Range						
				Minimised Range						
3. Lingual Tip/Blade				Advanced						
				Retracted						
4. Lingual Body				Fronted Body						
				Backed Body						
				Raised Body						
				Lowered Body						
				Extensive Range						
				Minimised Range						
5. Velopharyngeal				Nasal						
				Audible Nasal Escape						
				Denasal						
6. Pharyngeal				Pharyngeal Constriction						
7. Supralaryngeal Tension				Tense						
				Lax						
B. Laryngeal Features										
8. Laryngeal Tension				Tense						
				Law						
9. Larynx Position				Raised						
				Lowered						
10. Phonation Type				Harshness						
				Whisper(y)						
				Breathiness						
				Creak(y)						
				Falsetto						
				Modal Voice						

Figure 15.1 (above and on facing page)

are susceptible to the influence of each setting. Phonation type, audible in all phonetically voiced segments, can be judged over samples of only a few syllables, but settings which exert their influence on a more limited number of susceptible segments, such as advanced or retracted articulation of the tip/blade of the tongue, will require much longer samples. Laver and Hanson (1981: 53) review evidence suggesting that 45–70 seconds of speech are necessary for the automatic abstraction of long-term features by computer, but human judges may need a sample of a longer duration.

Vocal Profile Analysis Protocol

II. PROSODIC FEATURES

CATEGORY	FIRST PASS			SECOND PASS							
	Neutral	Non-neutral		SETTING	Scalar Degrees						
		Normal	Abnormal		Normal			Abnormal			
					1	2	3	4	5	6	
1. Pitch				High Mean							
				Low Mean							
				Wide Range							
				Narrow Range							
				High Variability							
				Low Variability							
2. Consistency				Tremor							
3. Loudness				High Mean							
				Low Mean							
				Wide Range							
				Narrow Range							
				High Variability							
				Low Variability							

III. TEMPORAL ORGANISATION FEATURES

CATEGORY	FIRST PASS		SECOND PASS			
	Adequate	Inadequate	Scalar Degrees			
			Inadequate			
			1	2	3	
1. Continuity						Interrupted
2. Rate						Fast
						Slow

IV. COMMENTS

	Adequate	Inadequate	1	2	3			Present	Absent
Breath Support						Diplophonia			
Rhythmicality									

'Vocal Profiles of Speech Disorders' Research Project. (MRC Grant No. G978/1192) Phonetics Laboratory, Department of Linguistics, University of Edinburgh. © June 1981.

2. Completing the VPA Protocol

The protocol shown in Figure 15.1 is made up of four sections: vocal quality features, prosodic features, temporal organisation features and comments. The procedure to be followed when completing the VPA protocol will be described as it applies to the vocal quality section, as a model for the other sections.

On the left-hand side of the vocal quality section are listed the major categories within which adjustments away from neutral may occur: labial, mandibular, lingual tip/blade, lingual body, velopharyngeal, pharyngeal, supralaryngeal tension, laryngeal tension, larynx position and phonation-type. (See Chapters 12 and 13 in this volume for a fuller explanation of 'neutral').

Supralaryngeal and laryngeal features are separated on the form, but this is to some extent a pragmatic division. The interdependence of supralaryngeal and laryngeal settings is very close, both at the level of perceptual analysis, and at the level of the underlying muscular systems. Laryngeal settings may mask or enhance the perception of supralaryngeal settings quite markedly, and vice versa. Velopharyngeal factors, for example, seem to be prone to masking by the presence of whisper as a component of phonation-type. At the muscular level, the interactivity of muscle groups responsible for the production of different categories of setting leads to the common co-occurrence of particular constellations of laryngeal and supralaryngeal settings. Raised larynx and pharyngeal constriction are good examples of this, showing a closely overlapping distribution. There is, however, a traditional tendency to treat laryngeal output rather differently from articulatory modifications of the supralaryngeal vocal tract. Laryngeal output (and often nasality also) has generally been considered as a long-term feature, while supralaryngeal adjustments have more commonly been analysed at a shorter-term, segmental level. The division also accommodates itself readily to a source-filter type of acoustic model.

A major factor in preferring to distinguish laryngeal from supralaryngeal settings is the fact that in some clinical populations, such as speakers with dysphonia or certain groups of speakers with articulation disorders, there is an obvious tendency for severe deviations from neutral to occur solely in either the laryngeal or the supralaryngeal section. There are, of course, many other types of speech disorder where severe deviations occur throughout the vocal apparatus.

The balance of these arguments has been to favour the separation of laryngeal and supralaryngeal factors on the protocol, but the close relationship between them is important enough that its implications should be stressed.

The layout of the protocol allows a two-stage process of evaluation of different levels of decision-taking. There is a vertical division into two sections headed 'First Pass' and 'Second Pass'.

(i) FIRST PASS:

On the first pass, which might correspond to the first listening to the speech sample, the judge is required to make only a rather broad decision regarding each category of setting, by marking each as neutral or non-neutral. If the voice is thought to be non-neutral with respect to any category, the judge can then decide whether it falls within the normal or the abnormal range.

The inclusion of a 'First Pass' is a response to the experience that it is often a much easier perceptual task to judge that a given voice deviates from neutral within some category than it is to specify the exact direction of that deviation. It seems to be true, for example, that people learning the scheme find it relatively easy to discern an adjustment of larynx position away from neutral, but find it considerably more difficult to differentiate between the qualities associated with raising and lowering of the larynx. This is in spite of the clearly differentiable acoustic correlates of raised and lowered larynx. The first pass, then, allows the judge to comment on a deviation away from neutral without specifying the polarity of the deviation, and it also leaves the judge free to ignore all neutral categories when making a second pass through the material.

It deserves emphasis that, in nearly all circumstances, it is important to fill in the whole protocol, even when interest might be thought to focus on sub-sections of the form. It has been a repeated experience of the therapists in the project that the settings relevant to decisions about treatment have been grouped in constellations, rather than as single settings.

(ii) SECOND PASS:

Under 'Second Pass' are listed all the settings within each category, and the judge is here required to specify not only the precise direction of any deviation away from neutral, but also the scalar degree of deviation.

There are six scalar degrees for each setting,[11] with three exceptions. Falsetto and modal voice are scored simply for presence or absence, and audible nasal escape has only three scalar degrees, in the abnormal range. For all other settings, the scale from 1 to 3 is considered to be normal, and the scale from 4 to 6 is considered to be abnormal.

Taking the lingual body category as an illustration, a judge who had decided on the First Pass that there was a normal but non-neutral setting of both fronting-backing and raising-lowering components of tongue body, and an abnormal disturbance of range of lingual movement, might be able on a second listening to fill in the detail of the settings to show that there was, say, grade 2 fronting, grade 3 raising, and grade 5 minimised range of tongue body movement.

The completion of the 'Second Pass' thus provides a detailed graphic representation of the speaker's vocal profile. In other words, it specifies the complex of long-term components which characterise the speaker's voice.

(iii) NORMAL/ABNORMAL:

The normal/abnormal division is somewhat problematic. There is insufficient information about the distribution of vocal settings in the population for the term 'normal' to have a rigorous statistical sense, and it is difficult to formulate strict criteria for placing a given setting judgment on either side of the dividing line. A rough rule of thumb might be that settings judged as being in the abnormal range are those which require treatment. The suggestion does not stand up well to examination, however. The decision about treatment will obviously never be based on the protocol in isolation. Even when the vocal profile is taken into account alongside other factors – such as diagnosis of pathology, and the patient's own assessment of voice – it is seldom single settings, but rather, as mentioned above, constellations of settings which cause the vocal profile as a whole to indicate the need for treatment. It is also the case that particular speakers may have profiles for which their protocols show no single setting as abnormal, but that nevertheless they are judged as in need of treatment because of unusual combinations of settings all within the normal range.

It does seem that speech therapists trained in the scheme agree about the 3/4 boundary rather more closely than they agree about other scalar degree boundaries, and it is tempting to assert that the normal/abnormal boundary must therefore be, in some as yet ill-defined way, a valid one. Given that the training programme presents this boundary as being important, and concentrates discussion upon it, the argument becomes very circular. It might be interesting to see if non-clinical phoneticians showed different tendencies.

In spite of the inherent theoretical problems, the normal/abnormal distinction does seem to be helpful, and serves as an anchor for perceptual judgments by emphasising an approximate mid-point in the scale.

A further danger in the normal/abnormal area is that the protocol implies a continuum from grade 1 (normal) to grade 6 (abnormal). At a perceptual level this is acceptable, but it is necessary to differentiate quite clearly between a continuum of auditory quality and a continuum of underlying physiology. The auditory qualities we are concerned with can all be produced by anyone with a normal vocal apparatus, and most have relatively well-defined physiological correlates. The relationship between auditory quality and physiology is not yet completely understood, however, even in anatomically and physiologically normal speakers. Perceptually equivalent qualities may be produced by physiologically different mechanisms, and in pathological speech the auditory quality–physiology relationship may become very unclear. The continuum implicit in the form is therefore an auditory one only, and the evidence regarding the extent to which there is an underlying physiological continuum is not yet available.

A prerequisite of any clinical assessment is that the time expended in making the assessment should be in sensible proportion to the information gathered. On first exposure, the task of completing a protocol form may seem somewhat formidable, and one which is out of proportion to the information gained. In practice, trained judges take between only five and fifteen minutes to evaluate each voice. Given the substantial amount of information contained in a completed protocol, this does not appear an excessive expenditure of time.

Other methods of transcription might have been chosen, but the graphic 'profile' approach has the two clear advantages of ease of completion and ease of assimilation. Long-hand verbal labels, following the tradition of the three-part labels used in segmental phonetics, would be very cumbersome with a scheme of this complexity, as the need would be for twenty (or more) part labels. Not only would transcription be laborious, but also reading and interpretation would be tedious. Phonetic symbols (available in Laver (1980: 163) and in Chapter 12 of this volume) are slightly faster to write, but both transcription and interpretation require considerable familiarity with the symbols.

Complex systems are generally most easily assimilated if presented in graphic form, and the additional ability of a semi-diagrammatic form to structure the process of auditory evaluation favours the use of the protocol for most purposes.

Nature and Effectiveness of Training in the Use of the Perceptual System

An early assumption in the project had been that the perceptual system would be learnable from a package of audio-taped material, with support from a manual. It soon became clear that a small amount of face-to-face training was desirable. A standard pattern of training has now emerged which seems economical and effective: the training programme starts with a preliminary half-day of theoretical presentation, with practical demonstrations. The members of the panel are then asked to read Laver (1980) and Laver and Hanson (1981), and to listen to the cassette provided with Laver (1980). In addition, they are given a sixty-minute cassette (the 'Graded Reference Tape'), which contains patients' voices exemplifying nearly all the scalar degrees for all the setting categories, in ascending order of scalar degree. Some weeks later, a two-day course is held, of intensive practical training in small groups, on both perception and production of all the settings. The ability to manipulate one's own vocal apparatus to produce a given setting is not essential, but it serves pedagogically as a useful focusing device, economically demonstrating the trainee's successful perception, and of course the ability is a potential asset in remedial work with patients. A tape of six test voices is then judged by the panel, and a final follow-up session is held some weeks later, both to communicate the statistical results of the tape-test and to discuss the experiences of members of the panel in using the protocols in their own clinics.

The descriptive statistics on the most recent panel we have trained show that the two-and-a-half-day pattern is broadly satisfactory. Our method of assessment was as follows: three fully-trained judges in the MRC project team listened to the six voices on the test tape and determined the notionally 'correct' perceptual judgments for each voice. The performance of each panel-member was then quantified in terms of errors relative to the 'correct' protocols.

The 'correct' results were reached by each of the MRC judges listening independently and then agreeing a consensus. This was reached under the following criteria: where three judgments occupied two adjacent scalar degrees, the majority judgment was taken as 'correct'; where three judgments occupied three adjacent scalar degrees, the middle judgment was taken as 'correct'; if the 3/4 boundary was involved in either of these cases, relistening was carried out until consensus was reached; in all other cases, the voices were relistened to until consensus was agreed under the above criteria. In determining these 'correct' results, 'neutral' was included as a scalar degree; some settings had a scalar range of seven degrees, therefore; and some, where polarity allowed a plausible continuum, as in the tension factors, had a scalar range of thirteen degrees. Modal voice and falsetto had ranges of only two degrees each, and audible nasal escape a range of four degrees. On this basis, considering only the vocal quality features, the average initial disagreement between any two MRC judges was 16.33 errors per voice – i.e. a discrepancy of slightly less than one scalar degree for each of the twenty-nine parameters.

Before discussing the panel results, it is perhaps necessary to state what, under acceptably severe criteria, would constitute adequate performance on the part of the panel of trainees. Three 'classes' of performance were decided. The first (Class 1) would be where a judge scored an average, over the six test voices, of not more than one error on a given setting. This would be a standard broadly comparable to that of the experienced judges of the MRC group, and would therefore show a need for no further training on that setting.

Class 2 would represent a performance scoring an average error on a given setting of between one and two. This would constitute the minimum acceptable performance allowing the descriptive system to be used practically in clinics. To maximise the usefulness of the setting involved, a slight amount of further work with taped material would be necessary.

Class 3 would represent an unacceptable performance on a given setting, where the average error score over the six test voices was two or more. Substantial further training would be necessary before that judge could reliably use that setting in clinical situations.

The overall results for the ten panel judges were that the average number of errors per voice over the twenty-one settings on the protocol ranged from 18.67 (comparable to the standard of the MRC judges) to 25.67 (still very competent). The acceptability of the performance of the whole panel, averaging the error scores across all judges and listing the averages per setting, is shown in Figure 15.2. It will be noted that eighteen settings out of twenty-one were scored at Class 2 or less. It should be said that none of the test voices had non-neutral values of labiodentalisation, breathiness or falsetto. Good scores on these settings are somewhat misleading, therefore. But a positive judgment of 'neutral' is still necessary in such cases to score a correct result, so their relative success should not be entirely discounted.

Figure 15.3 shows a comparable set of results for ten judges trained over

Vocal Quality Setting	Average Error	Acceptability Class
Breathiness	.03	1
Labiodentalisation	.05	1
Modal Voice	.07	1
Falsetto	.12	1
Retroflexion	.17	1
Audible Nasal Escape	.20	1
Tongue Body Range	.48	1
Tip Articulation	.53	1
Nasality–Denasality	.78	1
Whisperiness	.85	1
Creakiness	.93	1
Mandibular Range	1.15	2
Open–Close Jaw	1.30	2
Harshness	1.37	2
Lip Rounding–Spreading	1.37	2
Labial Range	1.72	2
Laryngeal Tension	1.77	2
Supralaryngeal Tension	1.90	2
Larynx Position	2.23	3
Fronted–Backed Tongue Body	2.35	3
Raised–Lowered Tongue Body	2.43	3

Figure 15.2 Acceptability of average error scores per vocal parameter for ten judges trained on a two-and-a-half-day programme (Class 1 = 'good performance'; Class 2 = 'acceptable'; Class 3 = 'needs substantial further training').

Vocal Quality Setting	Average Error	Acceptability Class
Falsetto	0.03	1
Labiodentalisation	0.13	1
Audible Nasal Escape	0.17	1
Modal Voice	0.48	1
Tongue Body Range	0.58	1
Breathiness	0.85	1
Creakiness	0.92	1
Mandibular Range	1.05	2
Harshness	1.30	2
Whisperiness	1.58	2
Labial Range	1.60	2
Laryngeal Tension	1.60	2
Open–Close Jaw	1.63	2
Rounded–Spread Lips	1.70	2
Nasal–Denasal	1.75	2
Larynx Position	2.20	3
Supralaryngeal Tension	2.20	3
Fronted–Backed Tongue Body	2.25	3
Raised–Lowered Tongue Body	2.35	3

Figure 15.3 Acceptability of average error scores per vocal parameter for ten judges trained on an eight-week, one-and-a-half-hour programme (Class 1 = 'good performance'; Class 2 = 'acceptable'; Class 3 = 'needs substantial further training').

a period of eight weeks, at eight ninety-minute sessions. (Tip/blade factors were not tested.) The differences in the scores are virtually negligible.

Using non-parametric statistics, it is possible to penetrate the performance shown by the judges in Figure 15.2 a little more deeply. Taking the average error for a given setting-category, we can ask the question 'Does this degree of agreement with the MRC group's result reliably indicate that the panel judges were using a standard criterion of judgment in listening to this setting in the six voices, or could their judgments have arisen by chance?' Taking two results, Harshness (Average Error 1.37) in Class 2, and Tongue Body Raising-Lowering (Average Error 2.43) in Class 3, Kendall's Coefficient of Concordance (W) (Siegel, 1956: 229) was computed.[12] In the case of Harshness, where $W = 0.45$ and $s = 647.5$, we can reject the hypothesis that the panel reached their judgments by chance, at a level of significance greater than 0.01. In the case of Tongue Body Raising-Lowering, the association between W (0.182) and s (171.5) is not significant at the 0.05 level, so we cannot confidently reject the hypothesis that the error score was due merely to chance.

The results of the two panels illustrated suggest that the Class 3 performances need considerable further work – either conceptually in the descriptive system or in the training of the panel judges, but that the remaining Class 2 and Class 1 performances, on the very large majority of settings, reflect the acceptable effectiveness of a two-and-a-half-day training method, and the basic fact that experienced speech therapists can be reliably trained in the use of the descriptive system.

Applications of the Descriptive System

The descriptive system can readily find applications in any discipline where a quantified, written record of long-term vocal features is of interest. Some of these applications, in phonology, sociolinguistics, paralinguistics, anthropology, ethnomusicology, social psychology, psychiatry and communications engineering, are discussed in Laver (1980: 10–11). In the immediate context of this project, the most central applications are those in speech therapy and speech pathology. Within the project, use of the VPA protocol on the eight groups of disorders is showing interesting early results. Figure 15.4 is a 'summated' protocol, amalgamating the protocols for the first fourteen of the Down's Syndrome subjects. The numbers in the cells represent numbers of individual subjects judged as showing the scalar degree of the setting concerned. The group protocol was prepared from a computer printout: all the individual protocols are being stored on computer disks, using interactive programs written by Steven Hiller for the Phonetics Laboratory DEC 11/40 computer, and this store can be explored in a variety of ways. PROSUM is the program which amalgamates specified protocols, and is proving an extremely convenient way of showing group trends. As Figure 15.4 demonstrates, our working hypothesis (that particular speech disorders have characteristic vocal profiles associated with them) is only a little too strong. Very clear trends are visible in the Down's

Vocal Profile Analysis Protocol

I. VOCAL QUALITY FEATURES

CATEGORY	Neutral	Normal	Abnormal	SETTING	1	2	3	4	5	6
A. Supralaryngeal Features										
1. Labial	8	6	0	Lip Rounding/Protrusion	1	2				
				Lip Spreading	1	2				
				Labiodentalisation						
	3	10	1	Extensive Range						
				Minimised Range	1	3	6	1		
2. Mandibular	2	12	0	Close Jaw						
				Open Jaw	4	2	1			
				Protruded Jaw	5	6	1			
	3	10	1	Extensive Range		1				
				Minimised Range		6	4	1		
3. Lingual Tip/Blade	2	11	1	Advanced	3	1	3	1		
				Retracted	1	3				
4. Lingual Body	0	10	3	Fronted Body		5	3	3		
				Backed Body		1	1			
	0	10	0	Raised Body	1	6	3			
				Lowered Body						
	0	9	5	Extensive Range						
				Minimised Range		3	6	5		
5. Velopharyngeal	0	7	6	Nasal			7	7		
				Audible Nasal Escape				1		
				Denasal						
6. Pharyngeal	9	5	0	Pharyngeal Constriction	4	1				
7. Supralaryngeal Tension	3	11	0	Tense	1	2	1			
				Lax	3	3	1			
B. Laryngeal Features										
8. Laryngeal Tension	0	14	0	Tense	1	7	4			
				Law		1	1			
9. Larynx Position	6	8	0	Raised						
				Lowered	4	3	1			
10. Phonation Type	0	11	2	Harshness		7	4	1	1	
		6	8	Whisper(y)		1	5	7	1	
				Breathiness						
		7	0	Creak(y)	3	1	3			
		0		Falsetto	0					
		14		Modal Voice	14					

Figure 15.4 (above and on facing page) Summated protocol for fourteen Down's Syndrome subjects.

Syndrome group towards characterisation by a constellation of central features, with some other features of the profile playing a weaker role.

Collaborative applications of the vpa protocol system with members of the speech therapy panels, using the protocols in their own clinics, have focused on use in three functions: as an instrument to record a quantified judgment of a vocal profile on one occasion; as an aid in planning strategies and goals of remedial therapy; and as a device for measuring the detail and scale of progress under rehabilitative treatment.

Vocal Profile Analysis Protocol

II. PROSODIC FEATURES

CATEGORY	FIRST PASS			SECOND PASS						
	Neutral	Non-neutral		SETTING	Scalar Degrees					
		Normal	Abnormal		Normal			Abnormal		
					1	2	3	4	5	6
1. Pitch	3	10	1	High Mean	2					
				Low Mean	2	4	2	1		
	1	13	0	Wide Range						
				Narrow Range	5	5	3			
	10	4	0	High Variability						
				Low Variability	1	1	2			
2. Consistency	13	1	0	Tremor		1				
3. Loudness	1	12	1	High Mean	5	2	1			
				Low Mean	1		3	1		
	7	7	0	Wide Range						
				Narrow Range	2	3	2			
	10	4	0	High Variability						
				Low Variability		2	2			

'Vocal Profiles of Speech Disorders' Research Project. (MRC Grant No. G978/1192) Phonetics Laboratory, Department of Linguistics, University of Edinburgh. © June 1981.

Notes

1. The project is funded by the Medical Research Council (Grant No. G978/1192, 'Vocal Profiles of Speech Disorders') and is under the direction of John Laver and Sheila Wirz.
2. We are very grateful to our two project consultants, Dr W.I. Fraser, MD, DPM, FRCPsych, consultant psychiatrist at the Royal Edinburgh and Gogarburn Hospitals, and Senior Lecturer in Psychiatry and Rehabilitation Studies, University of Edinburgh, until recently Physician Superintendent at Lynebank Hospital, Fife, and Dr Shirley Ratcliffe, MB, BS, FRCP, consultant pædiatrician in the MRC Clinical Population and Cytogenetics Unit at the Western General Hospital in Edinburgh, for their advice and help in arranging access to many of our patient subjects. We are also very grateful to our cooperative subjects.
3. From the National Technical Institute for the Deaf, Rochester, New York, through the kind assistance of Professor Joan Subtelney.
4. From the Scottish Council for Spastics, through the collaboration of Mrs Alison McDonald, the Council's Chief Therapist.
5. Mostly from Gogarburn and Lynebank Hospitals, through Dr Fraser. Each subject had already been included in a prior MRC genetic survey, so that cases of Trisomy-21 were distinguishable from mosaic cases.
6. This group was made up mostly of patients with Klinefelter's Syndrome, with access through Dr Ratcliffe and her colleagues, notably Dr W.H. Price, BSc, MB, BCh, FRCPE, in the MRC Clinical Population and Cytogenetics Unit.

   The rationale for including both Down's Syndrome (as an example of an autosomal defect) and Klinefelter's Syndrome (as a sex-chromosome defect) is that 'Patients with chromosomal aberrations usually have characteristic phenotypes, closely resembling those of other patients with the same abnormality' (Pashayan, 1975: 154). We hypothesise an extension of this organic resemblance to include vocal features.

7. This group of recordings was kindly made available by Professor F.I. Caird, MA, DM, FRCP, of the Department of Geriatric Medicine, Southern General Hospital, University of Glasgow, and is being analysed collaboratively with Ms Sheila Scott, the speech therapist on Professor Caird's project on Parkinson's Disease.
8. The thyroid group was made up of two sub-groups: an edamatous hypothyroid group on chemotherapy, and a hyperthyroid group undergoing chemotherapy or surgery. Access was kindly arranged by Dr A.D. Toft, BSc, MD, MRCP, consultant endocrinologist in the Department of Medicine, Royal Infirmary, University of Edinburgh.
9. Dysphonic patients' recordings were provided by a number of collaborating therapists. The large majority came from Mrs Marion Mackintosh, in charge of the Voice Clinic, Royal Infirmary, Edinburgh.
10. The recordings of cleft-palate speakers were kindly provided by the members of a Scottish Home and Health Department research project on cleft palate, Dr A.C.H. Watson, MB, CHB, FRSCE, of the Department of Clinical Surgery, University of Edinburgh, Mr. J.K. Anthony, CEng, MIEE, of this Department, and Ms R. Razzell of the Speech Therapy Department, Royal Hospital for Sick Children, Edinburgh. The material is being analysed collaboratively with Ms Razzell.
11. The therapists in the training panels (to all of whom we express our cordial thanks) seemed comfortable with six scalar degrees, usually. It may be, however, that for particular applications, a smaller number might be more suitable (or in special circumstances, say in the judgment of nasality in cleft palate speech, a larger number of degrees for the velopharyngeal settings might be desirable). Six degrees seems a practical number, to allow the assessment of progress in therapy and to facilitate training in the system.
12. We are grateful to Mrs Anne Anderson of the Department of Linguistics of the University of Edinburgh for statistical advice in this connection.

References

Honikman. B. (1964) 'Articulatory settings', pp. 73–84 in Abercrombie, D. et al. (eds) *In Honour of Daniel Jones*, Longman, London.

Laver, J. (1968) 'Voice quality and indexical information', *British Journal of Disorders and Communication* 3, 43–54.

Laver, J. (1974) 'Labels for voices', *Journal of the International Phonetics Association* 4, 62–75.

Laver, J. (1975) *Individual features in voice quality*, PhD Dissertation, University of Edinburgh.

Laver, J. (1979) *Voice Quality: A Classified Bibliography*, John Benjamins, Amsterdam.

Laver, J. (1980) *The Phonetic Description of Voice Quality*, Cambridge University Press, Cambridge.

Laver, J. and Hanson, R. (1981) 'Describing the normal voice', pp. 51–78 in Darby, J. (ed.) *Speech Evaluation in Psychiatry*, Grune and Stratton, New York.

Laver, J. and Trudgill, P. (1979) 'Phonetic and linguistic markers in speech', pp. 1–32 in Scherer, K.R. and Giles, H. (eds) *Social Markers in Speech*, Cambridge University Press, Cambridge.

Pashayan, H.M. (1975) 'The basic concepts of medical genetics', *Journal of Speech and Hearing Disorders* 40, 147–63.

Siegel, S. (1956) *Non-parametric Statistics*, McGraw-Hill Book Company, New York.

16 Structural Pathologies of the Vocal Folds and Phonation

Originally published as Mackenzie, J., Laver, J. and Hiller, S.M. (1983) 'Structural pathologies of the vocal folds and phonation', *Edinburgh University Department of Linguistics Work in Progress* 16: 80–116

The project ('Acoustic Analysis of Voice Features', funded by the Medical Research Council, Grant No. 8207136N, 1982–5) described in this chapter is designed to explore the feasibility of developing an automatic acoustic method for characterising pathological voices. It has three broad objectives. These are, in order:

1. the development of an automatic acoustic system for screening voices for potential laryngeal pathology
2. the acoustic differentiation of various pathologies of the larynx
3. the acoustic evaluation of the degree of progressive deterioration of a laryngeal pathology, or of the degree of rehabilitative progress being made.

The project brings together two strands of research. One is research into acoustics and computing. A progress report on this work is available in Hiller, Laver and Mackenzie (1983). The other strand, which is the topic of the present article, concerns normal and pathological aspects of laryngeal anatomy and physiology.

The plan of this article will be to consider first the concept of the true vocal fold as a multi-layered structure made up of a body (the vocalis muscle) and a cover (the epithelium and the underlying lamina propria). Then there is a discussion of the mechanical properties of the tissue-types in each of these layers. The effect of disruptions of inter-layer relationships is then examined, and a typology of structural pathologies of the vocal folds is suggested, based on the type of disruption and changes in mechanical properties. Hypotheses are framed about the possible consequences of different types of pathology for the detailed mode of laryngeal vibration. Finally, summary descriptions of each major vocal pathology are given in an Appendix.

The preoccupation of the project is the potential for acoustic measurement of vocal disorders. To be susceptible of acoustic registration, a vocal disorder must show either a structural or a functional change from the characteristics of the healthy normal larynx. This article will concentrate on 'structural' pathologies only, where the disorder involves a structural alteration of the vocal fold. Further, we shall survey only the more commonly encountered structural pathologies of the vocal fold. Phonatory problems that arise in the absence of any structural alteration will not be considered in any detail. These include neuromuscular disorders, such as paralyses of the vocal folds, as well as a range of psychogenically induced voice disorders where there is no organic change.

An examination of the literature on vocal fold pathology reveals that classification of disorders usually uses criteria related either to the underlying pathology, or to the presumed aetiology. The term 'pathology' is used here to describe processes acting within the tissues in the development of a disorder, such as inflammation or neoplastic change ('neoplastic' refers to altered patterns of tissue growth in tumour formation). The term 'aetiology' can then be reserved for factors which arise externally to the tissues, as in infection, or mechanical abuse of the tissues.

The overriding concern of the medical profession, properly, is to identify the pathological processes involved in a given disorder, since these play a large part in determining the most appropriate treatment. The medical literature is therefore typified by classifications based on the underlying pathology (e.g. Hall and Colman, 1975; Ballantyne and Groves, 1977; Birrell, 1977), such as that shown below:

1. Inflammatory conditions
   i. acute
   ii. chronic
2. Neoplasms (tumours)
   i. benign
   ii. malignant
3. Congenital malformations
4. Traumatic injury

There are some demarcation difficulties with this approach, in that there is no clear agreement about the borderline between chronic inflammatory conditions and some benign tumours. Vocal polyps, for example, are considered by some authors to be inflammatory in origin (New and Erich, 1938; Arnold, 1962; Aronson, 1977; Friedman and Osborn, 1978), and by others to be instances of benign tumours (Birrell, 1977).

The speech therapy literature is understandably more concerned with the extent to which poor phonatory habits may be involved in the aetiology of a vocal fold disorder. Hence a distinction is often drawn between those disorders which arise apparently independently of any vocal misuse, versus those which are considered to be the sequel of faulty habitual phonation. The latter type are often called 'functional' or 'psychogenic' disorders (Luchsinger and Arnold, 1965; Greene, 1972; Aronson, 1977; Perkins, 1977), in contrast to the former group of 'organic' disorders.

This approach also has a demarcation problem. There seems to be general agreement that vocal nodules, for example, are 'functional' in that they arise most often in speakers who habitually misuse their vocal folds. They may therefore be classed with disorders like conversion aphonia (hysterical loss of voice) or spastic dysphonia (extreme adductive compression of the vocal folds), which exhibit no structural abnormality. Vocal nodules are, however, clearly 'organic', in the sense that there is a structural abnormality of the vocal folds. When fully developed, they may even be indistinguishable, both macroscopically and histologically, from certain types of tumour (Shaw, 1979). It is also very difficult to disentangle the relative contributions of 'organic' predisposition and 'functional' misuse in the causation of a disorder. Arnold (1962) considers the role of various predisposing factors in vocal nodule formation, and even in this most 'functional' of vocal fold lesions it seems likely that factors such as general bodily health and infection may play an important part.

The focus of this project is the potential effect of vocal fold disorders on vibratory patterns of the folds, and hence on the acoustic signal. Alterations in aerodynamic and mechanical properties of the larynx thus become of no less importance than pathological and aetiological factors. This paper aims to draw together some of the available information on structural disorders of the vocal fold, in such a way that it may be possible to develop preliminary hypotheses about their differential effects on phonatory output.

Normal Vocal Fold Structure

It is not possible to predict the mechanical consequences of alterations in vocal fold structure without having some acquaintance with the structure and mechanical properties of the normal vocal fold.

The anatomy of the cartilages, muscles and other tissues which make up the larynx has been extensively described elsewhere (Kaplan, 1960; Saunders, 1964; Hardcastle, 1976; Romanes, 1978; Laver, 1980). We shall concentrate only upon the tissues of the vocal folds themselves, and the cartilages with which they are intimately associated. This is not meant to imply that structural alterations elsewhere in the larynx are expected to have no phonatory consequences, since this is clearly not the case. Growths in the areas above and below the glottal zone may indeed have quite dramatic effects on phonation if they physically impede vocal fold movement or cause significant airway obstruction. More subtle effects can also be expected from any structural anomaly that disturbs the rate or direction of airflow through the glottis itself. These can be thought of as external constraints on vocal fold vibration, however, and as such they will not be considered in this article.

The anatomical focus of attention will be the region bordered anteriorly and laterally by the thyroid cartilage, and extending as far back as the

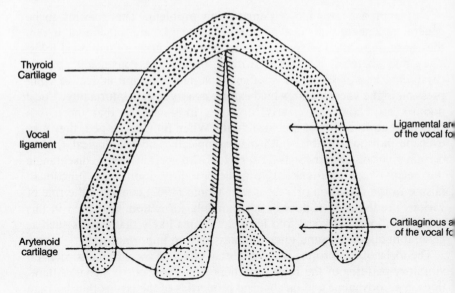

Figure 16.1 A schematic view of the vocal folds, seen from above.

posterior edges of the arytenoid cartilages. In the vertical dimension, the
region includes only the true vocal folds, and so the inferior border can be
drawn at the level of the upper edge of the cricoid cartilage.

A convenient distinction can be made between the anterior two thirds of
each vocal fold, which is bordered at the glottal edge by the vocal ligament,
and the posterior one third, where the inner edge of the arytenoid
cartilage, from the vocal process to the inner 'heel' of the cartilage, forms
the glottal border. We can then refer to the 'ligamental' part of the fold and
the 'cartilaginous' part. This follows the convention initiated by Morris
(1953) of distinguishing between the intermembraneous (or ligamental)
glottis and the cartilaginous glottis.

A schematic plan of the vocal fold region is shown in Figure 16.1. The
following account offers a brief description of the tissues which make up
the vocal folds, together with some comment on the mechanical properties
of each tissue type. Implications for pathological alterations within the
folds are then discussed.

The Ligamental Area of the Vocal Fold

The ligamental area of the vocal fold is the one most freely involved in
vibration during phonation, and it has therefore attracted the most
attention from researchers concerned with vocal fold mechanics. Hirano
and his associates have recently built up a considerable body of information about the histological structure of the vocal fold, and their work
necessarily forms a base for the account that follows (Hirano et al., 1980;

Hirano, 1981; Hirano et al., 1982). Background sources also include standard texts on anatomy and histology (Davies and Davies, 1962; Freeman and Bracegirdle, 1967; Romanes, 1978).

Tissue Types

The vocal fold is a layered structure, which in the ligamental area consists of the vocalis muscle and a covering of mucous membrane. The importance of these two layers in determining the fine detail of phonation has long been accepted (Smith, 1961; Perelló, 1962; Baer, 1973) but Hirano's work focuses attention on yet further tissue distinctions within the mucous membrane. This is divisible into four layers: an outer layer of epithelium and three layers of underlying connective tissue. These inner three layers together make up the lamina propria (see Figures 16.2 and 16.3).

EPITHELIUM

Epithelium is the generic name for all the tissues which line the internal and external surfaces of the body. It occurs in various forms, but all are characterised by a pattern of closely packed cells, cemented together by a minimal amount of inter-cellular matrix. The epithelial covering of the free border of the vocal fold is of a type known as non-keratinising stratified squamous epithelium (see Figure 16.2). These three descriptive labels relate simply to the detailed structure of this area. It is non-keratinising because it does not produce keratin. Keratin is the substance which forms the horny layer in the skin covering the external surface of the body. The term 'stratified' describes the arrangement of the cells, which are here arranged in orderly layers, with the deepest layer resting on a basement membrane. The basement membrane is a zone where substances similar to those found between the cells and fibres of the underlying lamina propria are highly condensed, to form a thin sheet dividing the two tissue types.

Epithelium undergoes constant regeneration by replication of the basal cell layer (i.e. the layer of cells lying closest to the basement membrane), and in normal tissue this process is sufficiently organised to give a clearly stratified structure. The most mature cells are those on the surface of the fold. The number of cell layers in the epithelium probably varies considerably, but in a large post-mortem study of 942 adult male larynges, Auerbach et al. (1970) found most samples of vocal fold epithelium to be between five and ten cells thick. Hirano et al. (1982: 278) report that there is no systematic relationship between epithelial thickness and age.

The term 'squamous' refers to the shape of the cells, which are commonly likened to paving stones. In surface view they are usually polygonal, but cross-sections show flattening, especially in the surface layers.

On the upper and lower surfaces of the vocal fold there is a transition to ciliated columnar epithelium (see Figure 16.3). The cells here are taller

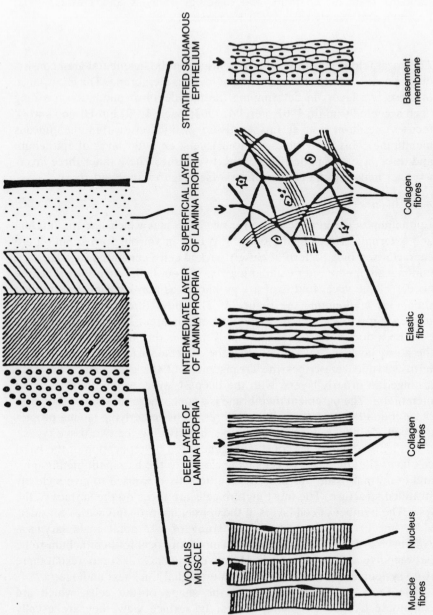

Figure 16.2 A diagrammatic representation of the tissue layers of the vocal

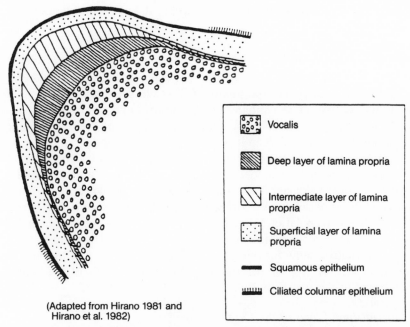

Vocalis

Deep layer of lamina propria

Intermediate layer of lamina propria

Superficial layer of lamina propria

Squamous epithelium

Ciliated columnar epithelium

(Adapted from Hirano 1981 and Hirano et al. 1982)

Figure 16.3 A schematic representation of the ligament portion of the vocal fold, seen in cross-section.

than the squamous cells, and carry cilia (microscopic hair-like projections) protruding from their surfaces.

The epithelium of the canine vocal folds, which appears histologically to be very similar to that in humans, has been tested mechanically by Hirano and his colleagues (Hirano et al., 1982), and it seems to be a relatively stiff, non-elastic tissue. In other words, compared with the underlying lamina propria, it requires greater stress to stretch it by a given amount. It is assumed, because the cells do not show any directionality in their arrangement, that the tissue will be isotropic. That is, it will be equally easy (or difficult) to stretch it in longitudinal or transverse directions.

LAMINA PROPRIA

The lamina propria consists of three layers of connective tissue. Some types of connective tissue (bone, cartilage) form the skeletal framework of the body, whilst others act as structural coordinators, binding organs, muscles and nerves to each other and to the skeleton. The nature of any given connective tissue is determined less by the cells than by the non-cellular matrix within which they are contained. This matrix may contain fibres of various kinds which can also be important in determining the mechanical properties of the tissues.

The vocal ligament derives from a thickening of the intermediate and deep layers of the lamina propria, but it will be discussed in more detail in a later section.

Superficial Layer of the Lamina Propria

The layer of the lamina propria lying immediately below the epithelium consists of areolar tissue (see Figure 16.2). Cells are embedded in a soft, semi-fluid matrix, which contains a loose network of haphazardly arranged elastic and collagen fibres. These fibres will be discussed further in relation to the intermediate and deep layers of the lamina propria.

Hirano (1981: 5) likens this layer to soft gelatin, and it is probably the most pliable of the vocal fold tissues. Titze (1973) in his mathematical model of vocal fold vibrations assumes that it acts like a fluid. Unfortunately, the experiments by Hirano et al. (1982) on canine lamina propria do not allow extrapolation to the human tissue, because the lamina propria of the dog does not exhibit a comparable three-layered structure.

An alternative name for this layer, Reinke's Space, signals that this is a potential site for loss of the normally tight attachment of the mucous membrane to the vocalis muscle.

Intermediate Layer of the Lamina Propria

The next layer of connective tissue has a much higher fibre content. These are mostly elastic fibres, formed from a protein called elastin, and they are arranged in an orderly fashion running parallel to the free border of the vocal fold (i.e. anterior to posterior). Elastic fibres are quite fine, and they form branches and cross-links with adjacent fibres (see Figure 16.2). Hirano's (1981: 5) analogy between elastic fibres and rubber bands highlights, as does the name, their marked elastic properties. Freeman and Bracegirdle (1967: 20) describe them as having 'considerable' elasticity, and Fields and Dunn (1973) report that they are three times easier to stretch than collagen fibres (see next section). Freeman and Bracegirdle (ibid.) also state that they have 'little tensile strength'. The parallel arrangement of the fibres in the tissue is assumed to cause considerable anisotropy. That is, elasticity, as judged by the stress required to stretch the tissue by a given amount, will be different when the stress is applied in a direction parallel to the fibres from that measured with the stress at right angles to the course of the fibres. The tissue is further assumed to be incompressible (Titze, 1973).

Deep Layer of the Lamina Propria

The deep layer of the lamina propria is similar in structure to the intermediate layer, in that it is rich in fibres which are arranged parallel to the edge of the vocal fold. In this layer, however, the fibres are mostly formed from the protein collagen. This forms rather coarser fibres than elastin, and collagen fibres are unbranched. Hirano's analogy here is with cotton thread, emphasising the relative non-elasticity of collagen when compared with elastin (Freeman and Bracegirdle, 1967; Fields and Dunn, 1973). Like the intermediate layer, the deep layer is assumed to be anisotropic and incompressible.

THE VOCALIS MUSCLE

The body of the vocal fold is composed of part of the thyroarytenoid muscle, the vocalis, which is voluntary striated muscle tissue (ordinary skeletal muscle). In spite of controversial suggestions by Goerttler (1950) that the vocalis muscle fibres run at an angle to the edge of the vocal fold, it is now generally accepted that they in fact run parallel to the edge of the fold.

The mechanical properties of muscle vary dramatically, depending on its state of contraction. Hill (1970), cited by Hirano et al. (1982), suggests as much as a tenfold difference in elasticity between resting and contracted muscle. Resting muscle from the canine vocal fold is easier to stretch than either the lamina propria or the epithelium, but like them it is assumed to be incompressible. Anisotropy is also expected, because of the parallel fibre arrangement.

The Vocal Ligament

Figure 16.3, which represents a cross-section of the vocal fold at the mid-point of the ligamental area, shows the uneven distribution of three tissue layers. Over the upper and lower surfaces of the vocal fold the intermediate and deep layers of the lamina propria are very thin, but at the glottal edge they become greatly thickened, and constitute the part known as the vocal ligament.

The relative thicknesses of the layers of the lamina propria vary along the length of the vocal ligament. The superficial layer is thinner at the ends than in the middle, whilst the intermediate, elastic layer is thicker at the ends (Hirano, 1981: 7; Hirano et al., 1982: 276). Figure 16.4a shows our calculations for longitudinal variations in tissue thickness from data presented by Hirano et al. (1982: 275) for five females and five males. This represents a rather small sample, but the figures can probably be accepted as being illustrative of general tendencies.

Figure 16.5 shows that the intermediate layer of the lamina propria is greatly thickened in a small area at each end of the vocal ligament. These thickened areas, the anterior and posterior maculae flavae, act as cushions of elastic material, and probably afford some protection against impact during vocal fold vibration. The reduced depth of elastic and collagen fibres at the centre of the ligamental portion increases pliability in this area.

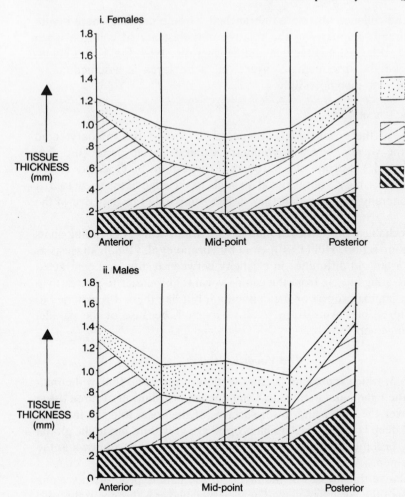

Figure 16.4a A graphic representation of tissue thickness variation along the glottal edge of the ligament portion of the vocal fold; subjects of 20–29 years (using data given in Hirano et al., 1982: 274).

Age-related Changes in Tissue Thickness

The measurements used in Figure 16.4a reflect the state of the laryngeal tissues in young adults, and cannot be taken as representative of all age groups. Young children seem to exhibit only a rudimentary vocal ligament, and the adult tissue layer relationships are not seen until after puberty. After histological examination of forty-eight male vocal folds of subjects between 0 and 70 years of age, Hirano, Kurita and Nakashima (1981: 39) wrote:

In a newborn, no vocal ligament is observed. The entire lamina

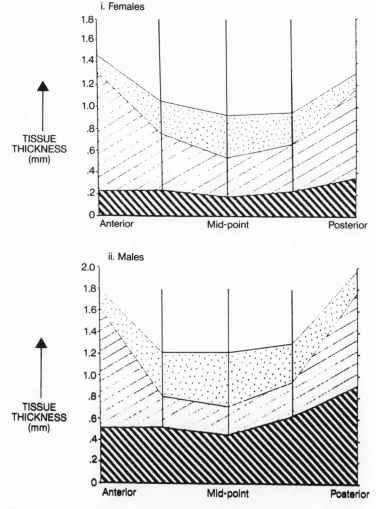

Figure 16.4b A graphic representation of tissue thickness variation along the glottal edge of the ligament portion of the vocal fold; subjects of 50–59 years (using data given in Hirano et al., 1982: 274).

propria looks rather uniform and pliable in structure. The fibrous components are slightly dense only at the ends of the vocal fold. In a four-year-old child, a thin and immature vocal ligament is observed. The vocal ligament is still immature at the ages of 12 and 16. It is only after puberty that a mature layer structure forms.

After reaching maturity, too, there may be continuing changes in tissue thickness, and these are indicated in Figure 16.4b which represents measurements of larynges from subjects in their 50s. A comparison between Figures 16.4a and 16.4b suggests that in the older larynx there is an increase in the thickness of the cover relative to the intermediate and deep layers of the lamina propria. Hirano et al. (1982: 278) found no systematic age-related changes in epithelial thickness, so the increased depth of the cover is attributed to changes in the superficial layer of the lamina propria. A decrease in fibre density in this layer is also reported. It would be interesting to know if this trend could be confirmed by examination of a larger sample of larynges, because this pattern of generalised thickening of the cover corresponds very closely to clinical descriptions of Reinke's Oedema (see Appendix). If Figure 16.4 reflects a widespread trend, then it may be that some degree of Reinke's Oedema is a not uncommon feature of ageing, especially in males.

A Summary of the Mechanical Properties of Vocal Fold Tissue

Given the preceding description of vocal fold structure, it is now possible to summarise the mechanical properties of each tissue type, and to consider how they might interact during vibration.

Figure 16.6 summarises the tissue properties which have already been discussed. 'Tensile stiffness' is used in this context as an indication of elasticity – i.e. tensile stiffness means the stress required to stretch a tissue sample of given cross-section by a given amount. All tissues are assumed to be incompressible.

Independence of Tissue Layers

The picture so far is of a structure with clearly defined layers, separated from each other by well-marked boundaries, but this is something of an oversimplification. The extent to which tissue layers are actually differentiated and kept separate from one another has important implications of two kinds. Firstly it is relevant to the mechanical independence of each layer. Secondly it is relevant to the ease of spread of pathological change from one layer to another.

MECHANICAL IMPLICATIONS

It is a reasonable assumption that two tissue layers are more likely to behave independently of one another during vocal fold vibration if they fulfill two basic criteria:

    a. They should exhibit clearly different mechanical properties.
    b. There should be a rapid transition of mechanical properties at the border between the two tissues.

The mechanical properties of each tissue have already been outlined, and it can be seen that each of the five tissue layers differs from its neighbours in at least one mechanical parameter. The question of transitions between the tissue types now needs to be addressed.

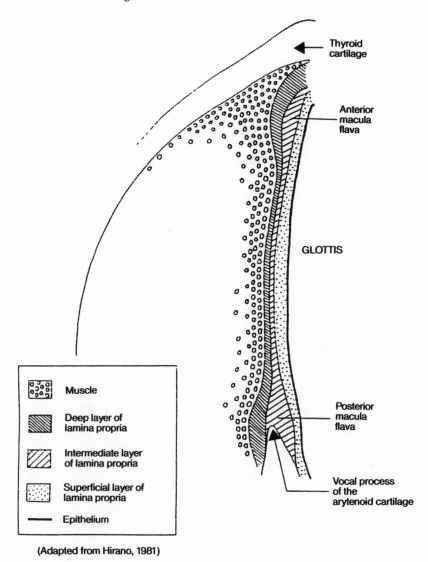

Figure 16.5 A diagram of the vocal fold in horizontal section, to show the maculae flavae.

Epithelium/lamina Propria

The basement membrane of the epithelium forms a well defined boundary between the tightly packed cells of the epithelium and the gelatinous superficial layer of the lamina propria, so that both the suggested criteria for mechanical independence are fulfilled. The fluid nature of this layer of the lamina propria has already been mentioned. Titze (1973) suggests that,

TISSUE LAYER		ANISOTROPY		TENSILE STIFFNESS	
		Canine	Human	Canine	Human
EPITHELIUM		−	−	high*	high
LAMINA PROPRIA	SUPERFICIAL				(fluid)
	INTERMEDIATE	+*	+	moderate*	low
	DEEP		+		high
VOCALIS MUSCLE		+*	+	LOW* (relaxed) → HIGH	LOW (relaxed) → HIGH

Figure 16.6 A summary of the mechanical properties of vocal fold tissue.

* Indicates an entry based on experimental evidence from canine tissue. Remaining entries are based on information about histological structure of the tissues, or on reports of tissue behaviour during vocal fold vibration.

because the epithelium is relatively thin, these two layers do in fact act in concert, with the epithelium mimicking the effect of a high surface tension.

Superficial/intermediate Layers of the Lamina Propria

Hirano et al. (1982: 274) report that there is generally a clearly marked and rapid transition between these two layers. There is a very dramatic difference in mechanical properties between the fluid or semi-fluid areolar tissue of the superficial layer and the much denser, anisotropic elastic tissue of the intermediate layer. A fairly high degree of independence may therefore be expected.

Intermediate/deep Layers of the Lamina Propria

In the same study, Hirano et al. found that the transition from elastic to collagen tissue is not so well defined. There is a gradual transition, with an intervening area where collagen and elastic fibres occur in equal numbers. In spite of their very different mechanical properties these two layers are not, therefore, likely to act truly independently.

Deep Layer of the Lamina Propria/vocalis Muscle

Skeletal muscles are typically contained within connective tissue sheaths (epimysia) (Freeman and Bracegirdle, 1967), and the muscle tissue is thus clearly delimited and separated from the lamina propria. The degree of disparity in mechanical properties of collagen and muscle tissue depends on the contractile state of the muscle. The mechanical properties of the collagen tissue are relatively invariable, but the tensile stiffness of the muscle may vary as much as tenfold. It is probable that under at least some conditions of muscular contraction these two tissue layers are sufficiently different to act with a degree of independence.

Many researchers have noted that a travelling wave can be observed on the surface of the vibrating vocal fold (Farnsworth, 1940; Smith, 1956; van den Berg, Vennard, Berger and Shervanian, 1960; Perelló, 1962; Hiroto, 1966; Matsushita, 1969; Baer, 1973; Hirano, 1975; Titze and Strong, 1975; Broad, 1977). This ripple-like mucosal wave can be taken as illustration of the fact that at least the outer two layers of the vocal fold (the fluid-like superficial layer of the lamina propria and the epithelium) are acting relatively independently of the deeper tissues.

It may be useful to examine some approaches to mathematical modelling of vocal fold vibration in the light of the above comments on tissue mechanics. Workers in this field have been conscious for some time of the need to consider at least two semi-independent masses when modelling cross-sectional movement of the fold (Ishizaka and Flanagan, 1972; Titze, 1973; 1974). Ishizaka and Flanagan (1972: 1235) comment that 'a two-mass approximation can account for most of the relevant glottal detail, including

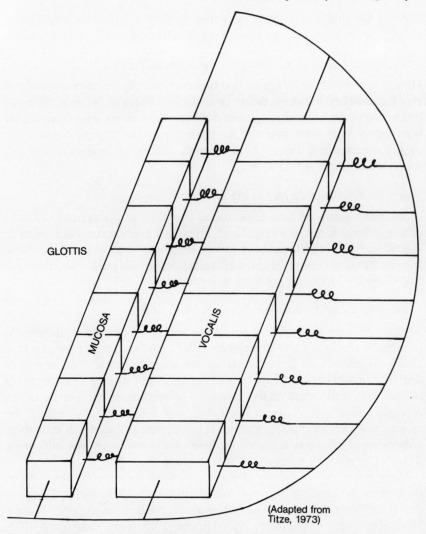

GLOTTIS

MUCOSA

VOCALIS

(Adapted from
Titze, 1973)

Figure 16.7 A diagram of Titze's (1973; 1974) sixteen-mass model of vocal fold
vibration.

phase differences of upper and lower edges'. Titze's model further
subdivides the mass of each vocal fold into eight individual sections (see
Figure 16.7). One of the suggested virtues of the sixteen-mass model is that
it allows simulation of longitudinal variations in mass and stiffness, and so
can simulate some of the effects of vocal fold pathologies. The shortcoming
of both the Ishizaka and Flanagan and the Titze models is that they are not
capable of separating abnormalities arising in different layers of the
mucosa, because all the different mucosal tissue layers are represented

within a single mass. In a later paper, Titze and Strong (1975) do, indeed conclude that a more accurate model would require at least three masses in cross-section.

This conclusion is supported by Hirano and his associates (Hirano, 1980; Hirano et al., 1981; 1982). While they do not offer a comparable mathematical model, they do stress the need to discriminate between three mechanically different tissue layers. The five tissue layers which have been described earlier are regrouped as follows:

Epithelium
Superficial layer of the lamina propria   = COVER

Intermediate layer of the lamina propria
Deep layer of the lamina propria   = TRANSITION LAYER

Vocalis muscle   = BODY

This grouping relates well to the expectations of mechanical independence discussed above, and the three-layered system offers a framework for classification of vocal fold pathologies which will be used in a later section.

PATHOLOGICAL IMPLICATIONS

The spread of disease or pathological change depends on the presence of biological barriers, which need not necessarily coincide with mechanical transitions. In the case of the vocal fold, the only effective biological barrier is the basement membrane of the epithelium. This is of considerable medical importance, because the great majority of potentially malignant disorders originate in the epithelium. As long as the basement membrane is intact, the disorder is contained within the epithelium, but if the basement membrane disintegrates, invasion may be limited only by the surrounding cartilages. No comparable barriers exist between the layers of the lamina propria, where the intercellular matrix is continuous throughout all three layers. For this reason it is often not possible to specify which layer is predominantly involved in any pathology. The barrier between the lamina propria and the vocalis muscle is also not complete, because thin extensions of connective tissue do penetrate the muscle. These have no great mechanical significance, but may in some circumstances allow the spread of disease into the body of the fold.

The Cartilaginous Area of the Vocal Fold

Much of what has been said about the ligamental area of the vocal fold applies equally to the cartilaginous area of the fold, which is also built up from a series of tissue layers. The body in this area, however, includes the arytenoid cartilage, and is therefore much more rigid. The mucous membrane covering is roughly similar to that covering the ligamental area, with one major difference. Because the cartilage lends rigidity to the edge of the vocal fold, taking the place of the vocal ligament, there is no modification and thickening of the intermediate and deep layers of the lamina propria.

This area of the vocal fold is much less freely involved in vibration than the ligamental area, so that disorders in this region may have minimal consequences for vibration. Much more important in terms of acoustic output will be the inhibition of approximation by any mass protruding into the glottis.

Structural Factors Likely to be Important in Predicting Vibratory and Acoustic Effects of Pathologies

Given the structural framework outlined above, we can begin to suggest factors that are likely to be influential in determining the effect of structural change on vibration. We shall look first at the different types of change of tissue consistency and distribution that can occur within a tissue layer, and then at changes of tissue geometry that affect the spatial relationships between different tissue layers. We shall then discuss changes in the physical parameters of rigidity/flexibility, tensile stiffness/elasticity, mass and symmetry, and their consequence for acoustic parameters.

Changes of Tissue Consistency and Internal Distribution Within a Layer

The consistency of a tissue layer can change in a number of ways. One particular instance is inflammation. This is described in more detail in the Appendix, but, in brief, inflammation can involve capillary dilation, an infusion of white blood cells, collection of oedematous fluid in the intercellular space, a proliferation of collagen fibres and granulation tissue, and the deposition of hyaline. Another instance is keratinisation (described above and in the Appendix), where, in the skin-forming process, the epithelium becomes stiffened by the deposition of keratin.

Changes in the distribution of cells within a tissue layer include processes such as hyperplasia (see Appendix), where a multiplication of cell numbers results in a thickening of the layer, often with a folding, buckling consequence for the overall layer. The density of cell distribution can also change, in that oedematous fluid collection in the intercellular space can cause an effective decrease in both cell and fibre density. Fibre density can also increase, in fibrosis.

Changes of the Geometrical Relationship Between Tissue Layers

Three kinds of disruption of the geometrical relationship between two tissue layers can be described. The first is one involving the intrusion of one layer into another, where invasion is achieved by displacement. This is characteristic of disorders such as verrucous carcinoma and sessile polyps (see Appendix for further descriptions of these). The second involves invasion by infiltration, where cells of the first tissue intermingle with those of the second. This happens in squamous cell carcinoma (see Appendix). The third is a disruption of the geometrical relationship between the two layers by material from one layer penetrating the frontier of the other to form a narrow-necked extrusion. This is found in disorders such as papilloma and pedunculated polyps (see Appendix).

Changes in Physical Parameters, and Their Acoustic Consequences

A survey of various models of vocal fold vibration (Ishizaka and Flanagan, 1972; Titze, 1973; 1974; Hirano et al., 1982) suggest various factors which should be considered. These are:

  i) Rigidity/flexibility
 ii) Tensile stiffness/elasticity
iii) Mass
 iv) Symmetry

Rigidity (i.e. resistance to bending) and tensile stiffness (i.e. resistance to stretching) can both for convenience be included under the general concept of 'stiffness'. This seems to follow Hirano's (1981: 52) undefined usage of the term 'stiffness', when referring to visual examination of the vocal folds.

A further factor which can influence the acoustic output is the degree of approximation of the vocal folds, since under certain conditions of airflow inadequate approximation may induce turbulence. This will be seen in the acoustic signal as interharmonic energy (Laver, 1980: 121).

Boone (1977: 47) organises voice disorders according to mass/size changes and approximation changes, but these two factors alone allow only a rather vague prediction of phonatory quality. We will try to expand this approach to classifying organic vocal fold pathologies by taking the following criteria into account:

  i) In which tissue layers are there structural alterations?
 ii) Do these alterations involve a significant change in mass?
iii) Do they involve a significant change in stiffness?
 iv) Is there a protrusion of any mass into the glottal space, so as to interfere with vocal fold approximation, or to cause turbulent airflow?
  v) Is the structural alteration symmetrical, affecting both folds equally?
 vi) Are the normal geometric relationships between the different tissue layers maintained?

Structural changes of the above sort will have a number of consequences for phonatory parameters. Hirano (1981: 52–3) mentions some of these in his comments on the interpretation of strobolaryngoscopic examination. His guidelines can be briefly summarised:

a. Increased mass tends to decrease fundamental frequency and amplitude.

   b. Increased stiffness tends to increase fundamental frequency,
      decrease amplitude and prevent full approximation of the vocal
      folds. It also inhibits the action of the mucosal wave.
   c. Localised protrusion of any mass into the glottal space will
      interfere with approximation of the vocal folds.
   d. Asymmetry of mass, configuration or consistency will cause dys-
      periodic vibration, as will any localised mass or stiffness change.
The rationale underlying these guidelines deserves some consideration.

MASS

An increase in mass adds inertial force to the vocal fold, which will tend to
decrease the speed of oscillation. It may be expected to exert its effect most
strongly at the onset of phonation, when the vocal fold is accelerating from
a relatively stationary position. The influence of mass on amplitude of
vibration is less straightforward, and it should be noted that Hirano,
Gould, Lambiase and Kakita (1981) contradict the above guideline, where
they suggest that a larger mass should increase amplitude and speed of
vocal fold excursion. Oedematous increases in mass, as associated for
example with chronic laryngeal inflammation, should actually be expected
to result in a lower fundamental frequency. Fritzell et al. (1982) demonstrate that this is in fact the case.

The detailed location of any increase in mass needs also to be taken into
account. A local increase in mass will have the greatest inertial contribution to vocal displacement when it is close to the point of maximum
excursion, i.e. close to the longitudinal mid-point and near the surface of
the fold.

STIFFNESS

It is reasonable to expect that increasing the stiffness of a vibrating body
should inhibit the vibratory movement, causing a decrease in amplitude of
excursion. The mucosal wave, which is visible during normal vocal fold
vibration, is a travelling wave in the mucosal layer. This presumably
depends on having a semi-fluid superficial layer of the lamina propria
behaving relatively independently of the deeper tissues. Increased stiffness
of this layer, or of the epithelial layer (as in keratosis), should therefore
limit the mucosal wave. Changes in stiffness of the underlying tissues
would not necessarily have the same effect.

PROTRUSION

Protrusion of a mass into the glottal space will only interfere with vocal fold
approximation if it is relatively localised. A uniform swelling along the full
length of a vocal fold may actually improve approximation, as seems to be
the case in some speakers with mild inflammation of the vocal folds during
upper respiratory tract infections. A distinction must therefore be drawn

between localised and non-localised protrusions. An example of localised protrusion is a vocal polyp, which may become wedged between the vocal folds, thus preventing the folds from meeting.

In considering localised protrusions, the site and attachment of the protruding body need also to be taken into account. Pedunculated polyps and papillomata, because of their flexible, stalk-like attachments, may be displaced by the trans-glottal airflow, causing only intermittent obstruction.

ASYMMETRY

Asymmetry of vocal fold structure may cause the two vibrating folds to move out of phase with each other, with complex consequences for the acoustic waveform. This discrepancy will disrupt the fine coordination between airflow and vocal fold configuration, causing perturbation of the laryngeal waveform. Structural asymmetry is a feature of many laryngeal pathologies, including carcinoma, vocal polyps and papillomata.

TISSUE LAYER INTEGRITY

In addition to the above comments, there are considerations about the integrity of tissue layers to be taken into account. A degree of independent behaviour of the body and covering tissues is important in determining the fine detail of phonatory vibration (Smith, 1961; Perelló, 1962). Any loss of integrity between the tissue layers can therefore be expected to affect vibratory patterns by changing this relative independence.

Proposed Typology of Vocal Fold Disorders

It has already been mentioned that our immediate concern is with disorders of the true vocal fold, since these are the most likely to have direct consequences for vibration. Sub-glottic and supraglottic disorders are not considered here. The scope of this typology is further limited by excluding all disorders which are specific to childhood. The reasons for this are twofold. The first relates simply to the needs of the present project, which will use speech samples drawn largely, if not exclusively, from the adult population. The second reason is that, as mentioned earlier, the mature layered structure of the larynx is not fully developed until after puberty.

The proposed system of classification is outlined in Figures 16.8a and 16.8b. This is not intended to be a definitive solution to the problem of devising a phonatory classification of organic vocal fold pathology. It should be seen rather as a preliminary attempt to highlight some of the mechanical factors which must be considered in order to predict the vibratory characteristics of any disorder. The structural vocal fold pathologies which are most commonly described in the literature are listed in Figure 16.9, and each is given a classificatory code which corresponds with

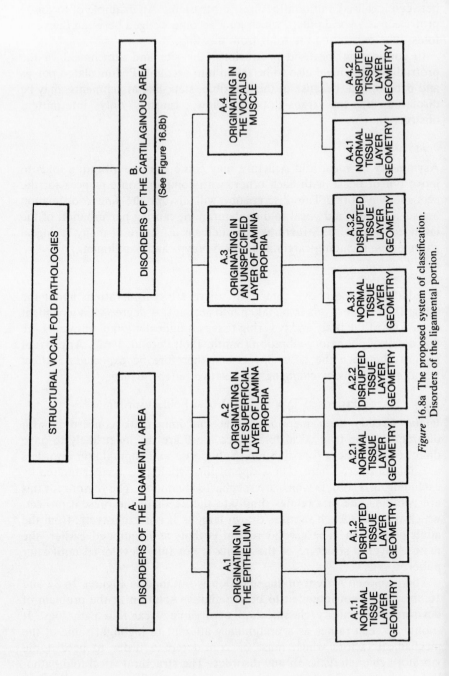

Figure 16.8a The proposed system of classification.
Disorders of the ligamental portion.

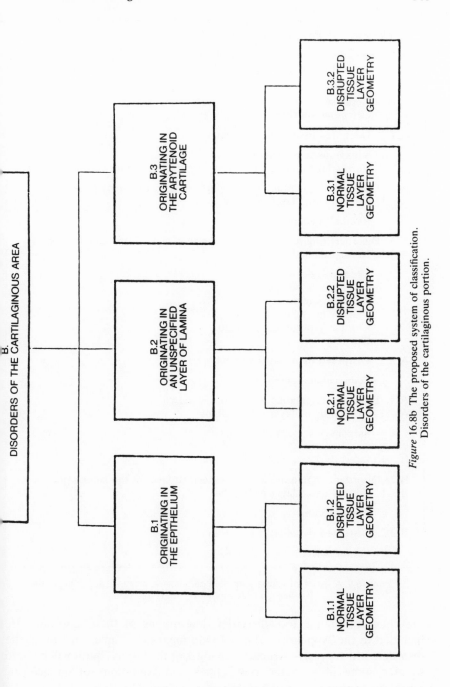

Figure 16.8b The proposed system of classification. Disorders of the cartilaginous portion.

A. *Disorders of the ligamental portion*

A.1. Disorders originating in the epithelium
A.1.1. Normal tissue layer geometry

    Hyperplasia
    Keratosis
    Carcinoma-in-situ

A.1.2. Disrupted tissue layer geometry

    Squamous cell carcinoma
    Verrucous carcinoma (a specific form of squamous cell carcinoma)

A.2. Disorders originating in the superficial layer of lamina propria
A.2.1. Normal tissue layer geometry

    Reinke's oedema

A.3. Disorders originating in any unspecified layer of the lamina propria
A.3.1. Normal tissue layer geometry

    Vocal nodules
    Sessile vocal polyps
    Acute laryngitis
    Chronic laryngitis
    Chronic hyperplastic laryngitis
    Fibroma

A.3.2. Disrupted tissue layer geometry

    Pedunculated polyp

A.4. Disorders originating in the vocalis muscle
A.4.1. Normal tissue layer relationships

    Sarcoma

B. *Disorders of the cartilaginous portion*

B.2. Disorders originating in any unspecified layer of the lamina propria
B.2.1. Normal tissue layer geometry

    Acute oedema

B.2.2. Disrupted tissue layer geometry

    Contact ulcer

Figure 16.9 A list of structural vocal fold pathologies, arranged according to the classification system outlined in Figure 16.10.

the codes in Figure 16.8a/b. Brief descriptions of these disorders are included in the Appendix. This is by no means a complete list of all the disorders which involve structural changes of the larynx, but it will be used to give some idea of the possibilities and limitations of an acoustic screening procedure for detecting vocal fold pathologies.

Allocations of disorders to categories within this framework are often tentative, because it has not yet been possible to gather sufficient information about histological details for many of the disorders mentioned. It should also be stressed that such a framework does not always necessarily relate directly to medical and pathological considerations. For example, the differing structures and mechanical properties of vocal polyps and polypoid degeneration demand that they be given different classifications in this system. They may, however, both be seen as forms of chronic inflammatory reaction to chemical or mechanical irritations, thus sharing a common underlying pathology (Luchsinger and Arnold, 1965; Boone, 1977; Aronson, 1980).

The divisions laid out in Figure 16.8 are also to some extent over-specific, in that they imply a rather more orderly situation than exists in reality. Many disorders show so much variation in form, in different individuals and at different states of their development, that they could have been allocated to more than one category. The proposed framework imposes somewhat artificial boundaries in these cases, but the allocation to categories attempts to reflect the most characteristic form of each disorder.

The combination of disorders originating in any of the three separate layers of the lamina propria into one overall category, as in categories A3 and B2, is suggested because medical writers are often not specific about which layers are involved in a structural change. It may be that such distinctions, because of a lack of a biological barrier between the layers, are of no direct medical relevance, even though there may be possible consequences for details of vibratory pattern. Further examination of individual cases may allow a more detailed categorisation.

Figure 16.10 summarises pathologies in terms of the presence or absence of mass and stiffness changes, protrusion into the glottal space, symmetry and tissue layer geometry. An important point emerges from this, concerning the potential power of acoustic screening to differentiate between disorders. Some clinically separable disorders may be expected to impose rather similar mechanical constraints on vibration, and hence on acoustic output, so that they are unlikely to be separable by a solely acoustic assessment procedure. An example of this is the grouping of papilloma, squamous carcinoma and verrucous carcinoma, all of which may show an asymmetric increase in mass and stiffness originating in the epithelium, with protrusion into the glottis and altered tissue layer geometry.

Conclusion

The three broad objectives of the project were described at the beginning of this article as being the development of an automatic screening system, the acoustic differentiation of various laryngeal pathologies, and the acoustic assessment of longitudinal change in a subject's voice. The second of these goals is perhaps the most challenging of the three. If progress is to

PATHOLOGY	Disrupted tissue layer geometry	Mass change	Stiffness change	Protrusion	Asymmetry
A. LIGAMENTAL PORTION A.1. EPITHELIAL					
A.1.1. Hyperplasia		+			+
A.1.1. Keratosis		(+)	+	(+)	+
A.1.1. Carcinoma-in-situ		+	+	(+)	+
A.1.2. Squamous carcinoma	+	+	+	+	+
A.1.2. Verrucous carcinoma	+	+	+	+	+
A.1.2. Adult papilloma	+	+	+	+	+
A.2. SUPERFICIAL L.P.*					
A.2.1. Reinke's oedema		+		N.L.	
A.3. UNSPECIFIED L.P.*					
A.3.1. Vocal nodules		+		+	(+)
A.3.1. Vocal polyps (sessile)	(+)	+	+	+	(+)
A.3.1. Acute laryngitis		+		N.L.	
A.3.1. Chronic laryngitis		+		N.L.	
A.3.1. Chronic hyperplastic laryngitis		+	+	N.L.	
A.3.1. Fibroma		+	+	+	+
A.3.2. Vocal polyps (pedunculated)	+	+	+	+	(+)
A.4. VOCALIS MUSCLE					
A.4.1. Sarcoma		+	?		+
B. CARTILAGINOUS PORTION B.1. EPITHELIAL (as under A.1.) B.2. UNSPECIFIED L.P.*					
B.2.1. Acute oedema		+		+	
B.2.2. Contact ulcer	+	+	+	+	(+)

L.P.* = lamina propria   (+) = possible or variable presence
+ = presence of a factor   N.L. = non-localised protrusion, not expected
                                       to prevent vocal fold examination

Figure 16.10 A summary of mechanical characteristics of vocal fold
pathologies.

be made towards the ability to discriminate acoustically between different vocal pathologies, then we need to have a better understanding of the relationships between the diagnosis of pathology, the structural status of the vocal folds, the mechanics of their vibration and the resulting acoustic output.

The relationships between each of these four areas are complex. There will seldom be one-to-one links to be traced between them, and this is particularly true of the link between diagnosis of pathology and the structural status of the vocal folds. A given pathology may to some extent show different structural attributes in different individuals, or at different stages of development. For example, carcinoma-in-situ may present either as a single localised area of increased epithelial thickness, or as a multifocal growth. In development in a given individual, it may progress from an area of simple thickening, with no significant alteration of stiffness, to a substantial protrusion of thickened tissue with a marked increase in stiffness due to keratinisation. In addition, two growths with quite different medical diagnoses may share a similar pattern of structural attributes. For instance, a fibroma (see Appendix) and vocal polyps may both involve very similar changes in mass, stiffness and geometry.

Our next step will be to collect patient data, in order to explore in detail the nature of the relationships mentioned above. We are fortunate in benefiting from collaboration with hospitals in Oxford and Lothian. We plan to carry out computer-based acoustic analysis, as described in Hiller, Laver and Mackenzie (1983), on tape-recordings of patients of known diagnostic status. Information about structural state and vibratory pattern will be provided by our collaborators, using fibre-optic examination of the larynx, strobolaryngoscopy and still photography, backed up by histological examination where appropriate. The hospitals involved are the Radcliffe Infirmary, Oxford, where our collaborators are Mr T. Harris (Department of Otolaryngology) and Mrs S. Collins, Department of Speech Therapy); and the Royal Infirmary, Edinburgh (Mr A. Maran, Department of Otolaryngology and Mrs M. Mackintosh, Department of Speech Therapy).

We hope that analysis of this data will allow us to approach the objectives described above, by evaluating the acoustic consequences of structural abnormalities of the vocal folds.

Appendix: Structural Vocal Fold Pathologies

This appendix includes brief notes on the individual vocal fold pathologies mentioned in the text.

Inflammation

Many of the disorders described below involve some degree of inflammation. This may play a major role in the development of a disorder, as in the various forms of chronic laryngitis, or it may occur as a secondary peripheral response, like that seen in the tissues adjacent to an advancing verrucous carcinoma (Ferlito, 1974). The descriptions of specific pathologies may therefore be simplified if they are prefaced by a brief account of the basic characteristics of inflammatory reactions. More detailed accounts of inflammation can be found in for example, Sandritter and Wartman (1969: 20–7).

Inflammation is a complex, coordinated response to tissue damage, which acts to limit infection and to repair tissue. It is convenient to view the response as a two-stage process.

THE ACUTE STAGE

The acute stage of inflammation can be thought of as an emergency reaction, which marshalls together the elements necessary for defence and repair. This stage exhibits certain common features, regardless of the size, site or type of injury. The three predominant signs are listed below:

   i) Hyperaemia
     – this simply describes an increase in blood flow to the area, which is usually achieved by capillary dilation.
  ii) Leucocyte infiltration
     – the capillaries become more permeable and allow white blood cells (leucocytes) to pass into the affected tissue. Some of these cells are active in limiting infection, by engulfing foreign bodies, or by antibody production.
 iii) Swelling due to fluid exudation (oedema)
     – fluid also passes out of the dilated capillaries and collects in the intercellular spaces of the tissue.

THE CHRONIC STAGE

The chronic stage of inflammation follows a more variable course, depending on the extent, duration and type of damage. Necrotic (dead) tissue and blood clots are resorbed by specialised cells, and the damaged area may be localised and walled off by the deposition of collagen fibres (fibrosis). Active repair of damaged tissue is brought about by the proliferation of new connective tissue and blood vessels. This proliferative repair tissue is often known as granulation tissue, but its exact morphology may vary considerably. In some cases fibrosis may predominate, with a progressive increase in collagen density, and eventually hyaline may also be deposited in the fibrosed tissue. Hyaline is the firm, glassy substance which forms the matrix of some cartilages, so that this type of granulation tissue will form areas of greatly increased stiffness. Other cases may show no sign of fibrosis, but have a marked growth of capillaries. Wherever possible in the following notes the precise nature of the inflammatory response will be specified, but most often the literature simply mentions 'inflammation', with no comment on the relative contributions of fibrosis, capillary proliferation, etc.

Disorders of the Ligamental Area of the Vocal Fold

DISORDERS ORIGINATING IN THE EPITHELIUM

A survey of epithelial disorders is complicated by the lack of a standardised terminology to describe some common types of structural disorder within the epithelium. The terms 'hyperplasia', 'keratosis', 'hyperkeratosis' and 'leucoplakia' seem all to be applied to a rather similar group of epithelial conditions which are thought to be aggravated by prolonged mechanical or chemical irritation. The common link between these conditions is the presence, in varying balance, of two types of structural change. The first, which we shall call hyperplasia, is a simple increase in cell number resulting from excessive cell division. The second, keratosis, is the formation of keratin. These two processes are described as separate disorders below, but they do commonly occur in combination. It is assumed that, alone or in varying combination, hyperplasia and keratosis cover all the labels at the beginning of this section.

There is considerable controversy over the question of whether or not these conditions should be considered as precursors of malignant change. As long as individual cells appear to have normal structure there is no evidence of malignancy, but there does seem to be a continuum from simple hyperplasia and keratosis, where cell structure is normal, to carcinoma-in-situ, where a large proportion of the epithelial cells are abnormal in structure and malignancy must be suspected. Differential diagnosis is therefore often highly problematic (Saunders, 1964; Hall and Colman, 1975; Birrell, 1977; Friedmann and Osborn, 1978).

Hyperplasia

Tissue of origin:	Epithelium.
Mechanical factors:	An asymmetric increase in mass, with normal tissue layer geometry.
Site of occurrence:	Anywhere within the laryngeal epithelium. Common at the centre of the ligamental area of the vocal fold.

Hyperplasia is an increase in cell number resulting from rapid division of the basal cell layer. The increase in basal cell number may cause buckling and distortion of the basement membrane, but the stratified arrangement of cells is maintained, and the cells appear normal.

Keratosis

Tissue of origin:	Epithelium.
Mechanical factors:	An asymmetric increase in stiffness, with normal tissue layer geometry. Eventually there may be a

significant increase in mass and protrusion into
the glottal space.

Site of occurrence: As for hyperplasia.

Keratosis is a condition in which the squamous cells of the epithelium begin
to produce keratin, which is laid down as a horny layer at the surface of the
epithelium. It may form a large, whitish mass, which protrudes into the
glottal space and may interfere with vocal fold approximation. Smoking
seems to be a major aetiological factor in the development of keratosis
(Auerbach, Hammond and Garfinkel, 1970).

Carcinoma-in-situ (intra-epithelial carcinoma)

Tissue of origin: Epithelium.
Mechanical factors: An asymmetrical increase in mass, with normal
                           tissue layer geometry. Variable increase in stiff-
                           ness and protrusion into the glottal space.
Site of occurrence: Anywhere within the laryngeal epithelium.

Carcinoma-in-situ is usually regarded as the earliest recognisable stage of
cancer of the larynx, although it is not an inevitable precursor of invasive
cancer, and not all cases of carcinoma-in-situ necessarily progress to
become fully invasive. The difficulty of making a differential diagnosis
between simple hyperplasia, keratosis and carcinoma-in-situ always
involves hyperplasia and it may co-occur with some degree of keratosis.
The feature which sets carcinoma-in-situ apart, and which indicates the
onset of malignancy, is the presence of a high proportion of abnormal cells
and the loss of the normal orderly arrangement of cells within the
epithelium. This disorder thus displays a histological pattern of haphazardly dividing cells which may have quite bizarre structure. The
abnormality spreads laterally within the epithelium, but the basement
membrane seems to act as a barrier, preventing spread into the lamina
propria. The lamina propria may, however, be inflamed (Auerbach,
Hammond and Garfinkel, 1970; Bauer and McGavran, 1972; Ferlito, 1974;
Friedmann and Osborn, 1978).

Squamous Cell Carcinoma

Tissue of origin: Epithelium.
Mechanical factors: An asymmetrical change in mass and stiffness,
                           with disrupted tissue layer geometry and protru-
                           sion into the glottal space.
Site of occurrence: Anywhere within the larynx. Most common in
                           the ligamental portion of the vocal fold.

The commonest type of laryngeal tumour is carcinoma arising in the
squamous epithelium. Carcinomatous change is characterised by a loss of

the normal control of epithelial cell division. The epithelial cells divide at an abnormal rate, and form a disorderly mass. The cells are recognised as being malignant by their abnormal structure, and by their tendency to infiltrate not just the surrounding epithelial tissue, but also the underlying tissues. Squamous cell carcinomas vary greatly in their structure, and in their pattern of invasion, so that it is difficult to generalise about their expected mechanical correlates. An increase in mass is almost always found, except in those cases with ulceration. Ulceration may occasionally expose and destroy even the laryngeal cartilages, so that a considerable amount of tissue is lost. Stiffness depends on cell density and on the degree of keratinisation, both of which are very variable. The size of the lesion may also fall within a wide range. Some specific forms of squamous carcinoma are recognised, one of which (verrucous carcinoma) is described below (Ferlito, 1974; Michaels, 1976; Friedmann and Osborn, 1978; Shaw, 1979).

Verrucous Carcinoma (a specific type of squamous carcinoma)

Tissue of origin:	Epithelium.
Mechanical factors:	An asymmetrical increase in stiffness and mass, with localised protrusion into the glottal space and disrupted tissue geometry.
Site of occurrence:	Anywhere within the larynx. Commonest in the ligamental portion of the vocal fold.

This tumour is a specific type of squamous cell carcinoma, which presents as a slowly growing warty mass, and may be multicentric. The epithelium becomes hyperplastic and highly keratinised, with fold and finger-like protrusions extending deep into the lamina propria. Epithelial pearls (dense deposits of keratin) may develop, forming localised areas of extreme stiffness. Verrucous carcinoma is of relatively low malignancy, and advances by displacement of cells rather than by infiltration. Adjacent tissue usually shows a marked inflammatory response. The tumour may grow large enough to cause dysphagia (swallowing difficulty) and respiratory obstruction (Ferlito, 1974; Biller and Bergman, 1975; Michaels, 1976; Friedmann and Osborn, 1978; Maw et al., 1982).

Adult Papilloma

Tissue of origin:	Epithelium.
Mechanical factors:	An asymmetrical increase in mass and stiffness, with disrupted tissue layer geometry and localised protrusion into the glottal space.
Site of occurrence:	Commonest at the edge of the ligamental portion of the vocal fold or at the anterior commissure.

Papilloma is a benign warty tumour, which, in adults, forms multiple branch-like projections of highly keratinised epithelium. There may be extrusion of these columns of lamina propria into the tumour, so that tissue geometry is substantially disrupted. Papillomata are usually unilateral and solitary, and most are pedunculated. These growths are not common in adults, and their medical significance derives from reports that a small proportion of papillomata undergo malignant transformation (Hall and Colman, 1975; Birrell, 1977; Friedmann and Osborn, 1978; Shaw, 1979).

DISORDERS ORIGINATING IN THE SUPERFICIAL LAYER OF THE LAMINA PROPRIA

Reinke's Oedema (Polypoid degeneration, chronic oedematous laryngitis)

Tissue of origin: Superficial layer of the lamina propria.
Mechanical factors: A symmetrical mass increase with non-localised protrusion into the glottal space. Tissue layer geometry is normal but with weakened adherence between layers.
Site of occurrence: Both vocal folds are affected along their full length.

Reinke's oedema is a specific form of chronic laryngitis which is characterised by a loosening of the attachment between tissue layers in the ligamental portion of the vocal fold. This allows oedematous collection of fluid along the full length of the vocal fold. The overlying epithelium is normal, or only slightly hyperplastic, and if fluid is allowed to drain away the lamina propria appears to be relatively normal. Only in long-standing cases does mild hyperaemia occur. Reinke's oedema is a disorder of middle age, and seems to be exacerbated by alcohol and smoking. It is interesting that clinical descriptions of Reinke's oedema suggest similarities with the age-related changes described by Hirano et al. (1982) (see section on vocal ligament). One of the main vocal symptoms is a decrease in fundamental frequency (Saunders, 1964; Fuchsinger and Arnold, 1965; Kleinsasser, 1968; Saunders, 1964; Birrell, 1977; Friedmann and Osborn, 1978; Salmon, 1979; Aronson, 1980; Fritzell, Sundberg and Strange-Ebbeson, 1982).

DISORDERS ORIGINATING IN ANY UNSPECIFIED LAYER OF THE LAMINA PROPRIA

Vocal Nodules (early stage)

Tissue of origin: Lamina propria (probably the superficial layer).
Mechanical factors: A symmetrical or asymmetrical increase in mass, with localised protrusion into the glottal space and normal tissue layer geometry. Stiffness is increased only slightly.
Site of occurrence: Usually on the edge of the vocal fold in the centre of the ligamental portion.

Vocal nodule formation is thought usually to be precipitated by local mechanical trauma. The first stage is probably a haemorrhage of the small blood vessels within the lamina propria, which is followed by a localised inflammatory response. The nodules appear as small, soft, red swellings, and they may be bilateral, at the centre of the ligamental section of each fold. Nodules may recover spontaneously if further mechanical abuse of the larynx is avoided. If they become established fibrosis, epithelial hyperplasia or capillary proliferation may occur, creating a much firmer growth. There is some disagreement about the pathological relationship between vocal nodules and vocal polyps. Some writers consider polyps to be chronically established nodules which have undergone late-stage inflammatory change, so the following section on polyps can be taken to represent a later stage in nodule development (Arnold, 1962; Luchsinger and Arnold, 1965; Michaels, 1976; Perkins, 1977; Boone, 1978; Friedmann and Osborn, 1978; Salmon, 1979; Aronson, 1980).

Sessile Vocal Polyps

Vocal polyps may be sessile or pedunculated. Pedunculated polyps have disrupted tissue layer geometry, and must therefore be placed in the category A.3.2 (see Figure 16.9). Histological characteristics of both forms are, however, similar, so they will be discussed together below.

Tissue of origin:	Lamina propria (probably the superficial layer).
Mechanical factors:	An asymmetrical (or rarely symmetrical) increase in mass and stiffness, with localised protrusion into the glottal space. Tissue layer geometry is significantly disrupted only if the growth is pedunculated.
Site of occurrence:	Usually at the edge of the ligamental portion of the vocal fold.

Long-term mechanical abuse of the vocal folds may result in the establishment of localised chronic inflammatory changes. These appear to be small, stiff swellings on the edge of the vocal fold, which may be unilateral or bilateral. In bilateral cases the polyps are seldom the same size, so that true symmetry will be rare. The extent and constancy of protrusion into the glottal space will vary, because polyps may be sessile or pedunculated. Stiffness depends on the histological make-up of each polyp. Some are predominantly fibrotic, with a dense, disorganised network of collagen fibres, and this type may eventually develop patches of hyalinisation. Others are built up largely from vascular tissue, and may be much less stiff than the fibrotic type. The epithelium overlying a polyp may also become hyperplastic (Arnold, 1962; Luchsinger and Arnold, 1965; Kleinsasser, 1968; Greene, 1972; Hall and Colman, 1975; Michaels, 1976; Birrell, 1977; Boone, 1977; Perkins, 1977; Friedmann and Osborn, 1978; Salmon, 1979; Aronson, 1980).

Acute Laryngitis

Tissue of origin:	Lamina propria.
Mechanical factors:	A symmetrical increase in mass, with normal tissue layer geometry. Approximation may be limited by associated acute oedema affecting the cartilaginous area of the fold.
Site of occurrence:	The whole of the larynx may be involved.

Acute laryngitis, which may have many causes, including infection, sudden irritation or mechanical abuse, shows all the features of a generalised acute inflammation. There is hyperaemia throughout the larynx, and infiltration of leucocytes, so that the vocal folds appear to be rounded and thickened in cross-section. The swelling due to oedema is usually most marked in the mucous covering of the arytenoids (see section on acute oedema, B.2.1.), so that approximation of the ligamental area of the vocal folds may be prevented. In severe cases the epithelium may become necrotic, and ulceration results as the dead tissue is sloughed off. The underlying muscle may also become inflamed (Luchsinger and Arnold, 1965; Hall and Colman, 1975; Boone, 1977; Birrell, 1977; Friedmann and Osborn, 1978; Salmon, 1979; Aronson, 1980).

Chronic Laryngitis

Tissue of origin:	Lamina propria.
Mechanical factors:	A symmetrical increase in mass, with non-localised protrusion into the glottal space, and normal tissue layer geometry.
Site of occurrence:	The whole larynx may be involved.

Chronic inflammation of the larynx may be rather variable in form. The simplest presentation includes hyperaemia and swelling, with an increase in mucous secretions covering the folds, and in severe cases the inflammatory response may involve the vocalis muscle. Chronis laryngitis may be a response to long-standing exposure to irritants such as dust or smoke, or to habitual Reinke's oedema and chronic hyperplastic laryngitis (Saunders, 1964; Hall and Colman, 1975; Turner, 1977; Friedmann and Osborn, 1978; Aronson, 1980).

Chronic Hyperplastic Laryngitis (chronic hypertrophic laryngitis)

Tissue of origin:	Lamina propria.
Mechanical factors:	A symmetrical increase in mass and stiffness, with non-localised protrusion into the glottal space, and normal tissue layer geometry.
Site of occurrence:	The whole larynx may be involved.

Fibroma

Tissue of origin:	Lamina propria.

| Mechanical factors: | An asymmetrical increase in mass and stiffness, with localised protrusion into the glottis, but no significant disruption of tissue layer geometry. |
| Site of occurrence: | Anywhere within the larynx. Commonest on the edge of the ligamental portion of the vocal fold. |

This rare, benign tumour usually presents as a smooth, sessile body on the edge of the vocal fold. It contains a network of collagen fibres, and may be difficult to distinguish from a fibrous polyp (Birrell, 1977; Perkins, 1977; Shaw, 1979).

Pedunculated Vocal Polyp

See earlier section on vocal polyps

DISORDERS ORIGINATING IN THE BODY OF THE VOCAL FOLD

Sarcoma

Tissue of origin:	Vocalis muscle or lamina propria.
Mechanical factors:	An asymmetrical increase in mass.
Site of occurrence:	Not specified.

Sarcoma is a very rare type of malignant tumour, which may affect connective tissue and muscle. Sarcoma arising from the vocalis muscle is one of the few disorders (excluding atrophy due to muscle paralysis) which originates in the body of the vocal fold. The rather brief comments in the references below allow only tentative suggestions about mechanical correlates (Friedmann and Osborn, 1976; Shaw, 1979).

Disorders of the Cartilaginous Area of the Vocal Fold

DISORDERS ORIGINATING IN THE EPITHELIUM

All of the epithelial disorders already described in the preceding section on disorders of the ligamental area of the vocal fold may also affect the epithelium overlying the arytenoid cartilages. Most of these are, however, more common in the ligamental area.

DISORDERS ORIGINATING IN THE LAMINA PROPRIA

Acute Oedema of the Larynx

Tissue of origin:	Lamina propria.
Mechanical factors:	Symmetrical mass increase, with non-localised protrusion into the glottal space, and normal tissue layer geometry.
Site of occurrence:	The mucosal covering of the arytenoid cartilage.

Oedema is a symptom with many possible underlying causes. These include chemical or thermal irritation, infection, allergy and cardiac or renal failure. It merits some special comment, however, because of its characteristic distribution. Fluid tends to collect first in the mucosa overlying the arytenoid cartilage, and whilst it may spread upwards to the ventricular folds and the epiglottis, the firm adherence of the tissue layers in the ligamental area limits its anterior spread. The ligamental area, therefore, tends not to be affected except when chronic inflammation leads to Reinke's oedema. The swelling will usually be symmetrical, and is likely to prevent full approximation of the unaffected ligamental portion of the vocal folds (Birrell, 1977; Friedmann and Osborn, 1978; Salmon, 1979).

Contact Ulcer (contact pachydermia, contact granuloma)

Tissue of origin: Superficial layer of the lamina propria.
Mechanical factors: An increase in stiffness with a redistribution of
                    mass, localised protrusion into the glottal space,
                    and disrupted tissue layer geometry. The degree
                    of symmetry is variable.
Site of occurrence: The mucosa overlying the vocal processes of the
                    arytenoid cartilages.

Contact ulcer is generally thought to develop from a localised area of the inflammation over the vocal process of the arytenoid cartilage, which is the point of maximum impact during adduction of the cartilages for phonation. A pile of granulation tissue develops, and the centre of this becomes worn away to expose the cartilage. The result is a central crater, surrounded by an outgrowth of connective tissue and epithelium. The epithelium may be markedly hyperplastic and keratinised. Contact ulcers are usually bilateral, but there is often some discrepancy in size of the ulcers on the two folds. Vocal abuse and psychogenic factors have both been implicated in the aetiology (Luchsinger and Arnold, 1965; Boone, 1977; Birrell, 1977; Perkins, 1977; Salmon, 1979; Aronson, 1980).

References to Chapter and Appendix

Arnold, G.E. (1962) 'Vocal nodules and polyps: laryngeal tissue reaction to habitual hyperkinetic dysfunction', *Journal of Speech and Hearing Research* 27, 205–16.

Aronson, A.E. (1980) *Clinical Voice Disorders. An Inter-disciplinary Approach*, Thieme Stratton, New York.

Auerbach, O., Hammond, E.C. and Garfinkel, L. (1970) 'Histological changes in the larynx in relation to smoking habits', *Cancer* 25, 92–104.

Baer, T. (1973) 'Measurement of vibration patterns of excised larynxes', *Journal of the Acoustical Society of America* 54, 318 (A).

Bauer, W.C. and McGavran, M.H. (1972) 'Carcinoma-in-situ and evaluation of epithelial change in laryngopharyngeal biopsies', *Journal of the American Medical Association* 221, 72–5.

Berg, J. van den (1962) 'Modern research in experimental phoniatrics', *Folia Phoniatrica* 14, 81–149.

Berg, J. van den, Vennard, W., Berger, D. and Shervanian, C.C. (1960) *Voice Production: The Vibrating Larynx (Film)*, SFW-UNFI, Utrecht.

Birrell, J.F. (1977) *Logan Turner's Diseases of the Nose, Throat and Ear* (8th ed.), John Wright and Sons, Bristol.

Boone, D.R. (1977) *The Voice and Voice Therapy*, Prentice-Hall, New Jersey.

Broad, D.J. (1977) *Short Course in Speech Science*, Speech Communications Research Laboratory, Santa Barbara.

Davies, D.V. and Davies, F. (1962) *Gray's Anatomy* (33rd ed.), Longmans, Green, London.

Farnsworth, D.W. (1940) 'High-speed motion pictures of the human vocal cords' (and film) *Bell Laboratories Record* 18, 203–8.

Ferlito, A. (1974) 'Histological classification of larynx and hypopharynx cancer', *Acta Otolaryngologica Supplement* 342, 17.

Fields, S. and Dunn, F. (1973) 'Correlation of echographic visuability of tissue with biological composition and physiological state', *Journal of the Acoustical Society of America* 54, 809–12.

Freeman, W.H. and Bracegirdle, B. (1966) *An Atlas of Histology*, Heinemann Educational Books, London.

Friedmann, I. and Osborn, D.A. (1978) 'The larynx' in Symmers W.St.C. (ed.), *Systemic Pathology* Vol. 1, 248–67.

Fritzell, B., Sundberg, J. and Strange-Ebbesen, A. (1982) 'Pitch-change after stripping oedematous vocal folds', *Folia Phoniatrica* 34, 29–32.

Greene, M.C.L. (1972) *The Voice and its Disorders* (3rd ed.), Lippincott, Philadelphia.

Goerttler, K. (1950) 'Die Anordnung, Histologie und Histogenese der quergestreiften Muskulatur in menschlichen Stimmband', *Zeitschrift für Anatomie und Entwickelungsgeschichte* 115, 352–401.

Hall, S.I. and Colman, B.H. (1975) *Diseases of the Nose, Throat and Ear: A Handbook for Students and Practitioners*, Churchill Livingstone, Edinburgh.

Hardcastle, W.J. (1976) *The Physiology of Speech Production*, Academic Press, New York.

Hiller, S.M., Laver, J. and Mackenzie, J. (1983) 'Acoustic analysis of waveform perturbations in connected speech', *Edinburgh University Department of Linguistics Work in Progress* 16, 40–68.

Hirano, M. (1974) 'Morphological structure of the vocal cord as a vibrator and its variations', *Folia Phoniatrica* 26, 89–94.

Hirano, M. (1981) *Clinical Examination of Voice*, Springer-Verlag, New York.

Hirano, M., Gould, W.J., Lambiase, A. and Kakita, Y. (1981) 'Vibratory behaviour of the vocal folds in a case with a unilateral polyp', *Folia Phoniatrica* 33, 275–84.

Hirano, M., Kurita, S. and Nakashima, T. (1981) 'The structure of the vocal folds', in Stevens, K.N. and Hirano, M. (eds), *Vocal Fold Physiology*, University of Tokyo Press, Tokyo.

Hirano, M., Kakita, Y., Ohmaru, K. and Kurita, S. (1982) 'Structure and mechanical properties of the vocal fold', pp. 211–97 in Lass, N. (ed.), *Speech and Language: Advances in Basic Research and Practice*, Academic Press, New York.

Hiroto, I. (1966) 'Patho-physiology of the larynx from the standpoint of vocal mechanism', *Practica Otologica Kyoto* 59, 229–92.

Ishizaka, K. and Flanagan, J.L. (1972) 'Synthesis of voiced sounds from a two-mass model of the vocal cords', *Bell System Technical Journal* 51, 1233–68.

Kaplan, H.M. (1960) *Anatomy and Physiology of Speech*, McGraw-Hill, New York.

Kleinsasser, O. (1968) *Microlaryngoscopy and Endolaryngeal Microscopy*, Saunders, London.

Laver, J. (1980) *The phonetic Description of Voice Quality*, Cambridge University Press, Cambridge.

Luchsinger, R. and Arnold, G.E. (1965) *Voice-Speech-Language. Clinical communicology: its Physiology and Pathology*, Constable, London.

Maw, A.R., Cullen, R.J. and Bradfield, J.W.B. (1982) 'Verrucous carcinoma of the larynx', *Clinical Otolaryngology* 7, 305–11.

Matsushita, H. (1969) 'Vocal cord vibration of excised larynges – study with ultra-high-speed cinematography', *Otologia Fukuoka* 15, 127–42 (in Japanese).

Michaels, L. (1976) 'Histopathology of nose and throat', pp. 667–700 in Hinchcliffe, R. and Hamson, D. (eds), *Scientific Foundations of Otolaryngology*, William Heinemann Medical Books, London.

New, G.B. and Erich, J.B. (1938) 'Benign tumours of the larynx; a study of 722 cases', *Archives of Otolaryngology* 28, 841.

Perelló, J. (1962) 'The muco-undulatory theory of phonation', *Annals of Otolaryngology* 79, 722–5.

Perkins, H. (1977) *Speech Pathology, An Applied Behavioural Science*, C.V. Mosby, St. Louis.

Romanes, G.J. (ed.) (1978) *Cunningham's Manual of Practical Anatomy* Vol. 3, Head and Neck and Brain (14th ed.), Oxford University Press, Oxford.

Salmon, L.F.W. (1979) 'Acute laryngitis', in Ballantyne J. and Groves J. (eds) *Scott-Brown's Diseases of the Ear, Nose and Throat* (4th ed.) Vol. 4, 345–80.

Salmon, L.F.W. (1979) 'Chronic laryngitis', in Ballantyne J. and Groves J. (eds) *Scott-Brown's Diseases of the Ear, Nose and Throat* (4th ed.) Vol. 4, 381–420.

Sandritter, W. and Wartman, W.B. (1969) *Colour Atlas and Textbook of Tissue and Cellular Pathology* (4th ed.), Year Book Medical Publishers, Chicago.

Saunders, W.H. (1964) *The Larynx*, CIBA, New Jersey.

Shaw, H. (1979) 'Tumours of the larynx', in Ballantyne J. and Groves J. (eds), *Scott-Brown's Diseases of the Ear, Nose and Throat* (4th ed.), Vol. 4, 421–508.

Smith, S. (1961) 'On artificial voice production', *Proceedings of the 4th international Congress of Phonetic Sciences*, Helsinki, pp. 96–110.

Titze, I.R. (1973) 'The human vocal cords: a mathematical model, Part I', *Phonetica* 28, 129–70.

Titze, I.R. (1974) 'The human vocal cords: a mathematical model, Part II', *Phonetica*, 29, 1–21.

Titze, I.R. and Strong, W.J. (1975) 'Normal modes in vocal cord tissues', *Journal of the Acoustical Society of America* 57, 736–44.

17 An Acoustic System for the Detection of Laryngeal Pathology

Originally published as Laver, J., Hiller, S.M., Mackenzie, J. and Rooney, E.J. (1986) 'An acoustic system for the detection of laryngeal pathology', *Journal of Phonetics*, 14: 517–24

1. Introduction

This project has two main aims: the development of a computer-based system of acoustic analysis which can screen voices for the presence of laryngeal pathologies; and the differentiation of such pathologies using acoustic measures alone. A system based on measurement of fundamental frequency and waveform perturbations has been developed (Hiller, Laver and Mackenzie, 1983; 1984; Laver, Hiller and Mackenzie, 1984). This paper is a discussion of possible procedures for distinguishing a group of speakers with known pathologies from a large control group, as a prelude to the development of screening techniques.

An automatic system which can detect possible laryngeal pathology has several potential applications.

(1) *Screening* of an unselected population, alongside existing screening programmes in hospitals, 'well man/well woman' clinics, etc. An acoustic system has the advantage of being completely non-invasive, and the recording procedure is simple, causes minimal distress to subjects and is highly portable (so that screening could be extended to schools, factories, etc.).

(2) *Assessment of priorities* among a pre-selected population, consisting of patients already complaining of hoarseness, or those visiting their GPs with voice problems. The use of an acoustic system could speed the process of referral for laryngeal examination where the possibility of serious pathology was indicated.

(3) *Diagnostic support* where a particular laryngeal pathology is already suspected. This depends on the discriminability of the various pathologies using acoustic measures.

(4) *Longitudinal monitoring* to assess change in phonatory efficiency in patients undergoing treatment (surgery, speech therapy, radiotherapy or chemotherapy), or to track deterioration in progressive disease.

2. Acoustic System

The analysis system, implemented on a VAX 11/750 computer, produces measurements of fundamental frequency (F_0) and waveform perturbations in approximately forty seconds of recorded text read from the 'Rainbow Passage' (Fairbanks, 1960). The measurement system uses an elaborated version of the Gold and Rabiner (1969) parallel processing pitch-detection algorithm, with phase compensation for low-frequency distortion introduced by tape-recording techniques; low-pass filtering to remove higher-frequency resonance effects from the waveform (600 Hz for males, 800 Hz for females); non-linear smoothing to derive an intonational 'trend-line' from the raw pitch period estimates; and parabolic interpolation at waveform peaks to provide greater resolution of pitch period values (Hiller et al., 1983; 1984).

Intonational data are derived from the smoothed F_0 trend-line, giving its mean value (F_0-AV) and its range, represented as the standard deviation of the trend-line values (F_0-DEV). Statistical analyses are then made of pitch period perturbation (jitter) and amplitude perturbation at waveform peaks (shimmer). The following measures are taken for both jitter (j) and shimmer (s).

(1) Average magnitude of excursions of the raw F_0 contour from the local trend-line (AVEX)

(2) Standard deviation of (signed) excursions from trend-line (DEVEX).

(3) Rate of excursions (RATEX): this is the percentage of points in the sample where the magnitude of excursions is greater than or equal to 3% of the local trend-line value. A value of 3% was chosen because even the healthiest of voices, performing monotone, steady-state vowels, typically shows a level of (jitter) perturbation of about 2% (Hanson, 1978).

(4) Directional perturbation factor (DPF). This measure, adapted from Hecker and Kreul (1971), is the percentage of changes in algebraic sign between adjacent pitch or amplitude estimates in the raw contours. A 3% threshold is also applied to this measure.

3. Subjects and Data Collection

The collection of data on pathological subjects has been made possible by collaboration with the ENT departments of the Radcliffe Infirmary, Oxford and the Royal Infirmary, Edinburgh. One hundred and nine speakers whose laryngeal state had been established by medical examination in these departments were recorded on high-quality analogue recorders (Revox A77 and Uher 4000). The first forty seconds of each speech sample were then digitised at 20 KHz, and analysed using the above acoustic system. A control group of 121 speakers was recorded and analysed in the same way. It has not been possible to subject the control speakers to a laryngeal examination, but none reported any history of laryngeal disorder or other relevant complaint.

Figure 17.1 gives details of each group used, including the percentage of self-reported smokers at the time of recording. Speakers from the control group are in general younger than those of the pathological group, but this

Group	Sex	Number	Age range (mean)	% Smokers
Control	M	63	18–63 (31.7)	17.5
Control	F	58	18–73 (28.7)	17.2
Pathological	M	55	25–52 (53.9)	27.3
Pathological	F	54	24–75 (53.2)	44.4

Figure 17.1 Subject data by group (n = 230)

Type of Pathology	Males	Females
Disorders of the ligamental area		
Epithelial disorders	17	2
(e.g. carcinoma, papilloma, keratosis)		
Reinke's oedema	0	4
Polyps, nodules	8	22
Cysts	2	2
Miscellaneous mild oedema, redness, laryngitis	11	15
Disorders of the cartilaginous area	8	5
Palsies	8	4
Supra-glottic lesions	1	0
Total	55	54

Figure 17.2 Classification of laryngeal disorders diagnolsed in pathological group and number of cases (n = 109).

bias will be rectified as the control group nears its target of 200 speakers (100 of each sex).

The speakers from the pathological group show a wide variety of laryngeal disorders. Figure 17.2 presents a summary of the types of disorder present in the pathological group.

4. Group Separation and Screening Procedures

The two groups of subjects may be expected to show a certain amount of internal diversity. The pathological speakers evidence a variety of disorders (as shown in Figure 17.2), each of which may have different effects on the structural – and hence vibratory properties of the vocal folds (Mackenzie, Laver and Hiller, 1983). The control group is, it is hoped, more homogeneous, but could contain speakers with undetected laryngeal pathologies or functional disorders. Some overlap between the groups' phonatory behaviour is possible, then, but in general they should be separable if a screening procedure is to be feasible.

The project has considered a number of approaches to demonstrating

Parameters	Males		Females	
	Pathological	Control	Pathological	Control
F_0-AV	12 (21.8)	3 (4.7)	12 (22.2)	2 (3.4)
F_0-DEV	7 (12.7)	2 (3.2)	8 (14.8)	5 (8.6)
J-DEVEX	14 (25.4)	2 (3.2)	15 (27.7)	2 (3.4)
J-AVEX	21 (38.2)	3 (4.7)	16 (29.6)	3 (5.2)
J-RATEX	3 (5.4)	2 (3.2)	3 (5.5)	3 (5.2)
J-DPF	34 (61.8)	2 (3.2)	31 (57.4)	2 (3.4)
S-DEVEX	25 (45.4)	4 (6.3)	20 (37.0)	2 (3.4)
S-AVEX	28 (50.1)	6 (9.5)	22 (40.7)	3 (5.2)
S-RATEX	16 (29.1)	3 (4.7)	11 (20.4)	1 (1.7)
S-DPF	42 (76.4)	2 (3.2)	35 (64.8)	1 (1.7)

Figure 17.3 Subjects deviating from control group mean for each parameter by more than two SDs (figures in parentheses are percentages).

the separation of the groups, with a view to developing screening tools. These include:

(1) a simple graphic approach, showing the relation between the groups on bivariate plots, with a plausible screening boundary to separate them,

(2) a multivariate statistical technique (linear discriminant analysis) as a means of using data from all ten parameters simultaneously.

4.1 Bivariate Plots

Our bivariate plots have a screening boundary derived from principal components analysis. This approach has the advantage of allowing the relationship between the two groups – that of individual patients to the control group – to be easily visualised. In order to facilitate the comparison of pathological subjects and controls, all subjects' scores were transformed to z-scores and expressed as multiples of the *control standard deviation* from the *control group mean* for their sex. Given that two standard deviations on any one parameter should include approximately 90–95% of control subjects (assuming normal distributions), any subject whose score on a given parameter deviates from the control group mean by more than two SDs may be considered to be at risk of pathology. Figure 17.3 presents the numbers of subjects in each group (pathological and control) who deviate from the control group mean by more than two SDs on each parameter in turn.

On this basis, no single parameter of the ten distinguishes between the two groups sufficiently for the purposes of screening; but a combination of two parameters – one F_0 parameter and one perturbation parameter, for example – is more successful (Laver et al., 1984).

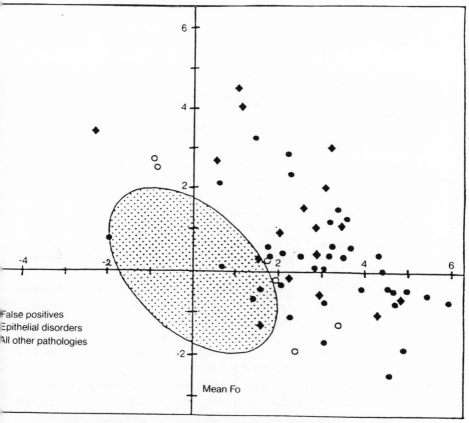

Figure 17.4 A scattergram of Directional Perturbation Factor shimmer against mean fundamental frequency for male speakers. The shaded area represents a two-Standard Deviation ellipse derived from principal components analysis of male controls.

Figure 17.4 shows fifty-five male patients with known structural pathologies of the larynx plotted on a scattergram of mean F_0 versus shimmer DPF. The axes are marked in multiples of standard deviation, and the origin of both axes corresponds to the control group mean for each parameter. S-DPF was the best single discriminator between the groups for both sexes. F_0-AV was included because of the possibility that some pathological subjects may be able to maintain normal levels of perturbation (as represented by S-DPF) by boosting laryngeal tension, at the expense of slightly higher than normal mean F_0 (Mackenzie et al., 1984). Principal components analysis was applied to the control group data to give an ellipse (at the 2 SDs level) indicating the covariance between the parameters. The boundary of this ellipse forms the screening threshold for the detection of pathology.

Fifty (90.1%) of the pathological males fall outside the ellipse, and would be recognised as pathological by this approach. Six (9.5%) control males fall outside, and register as false positives. It is worth noting that two of the pathological males who fail to be detected have epithelial disorders. Both, however, are cases of keratosis with oedema.

For the females, forty-three (79.6%) pathological subjects fall outside the ellipse, with six false positives (10.3%). Both female patients with epithelial disorders are successfully detected.

4.2 Linear Discriminant Analysis

Linear discriminant analysis (Klecka, 1980) is a statistical technique for discriminating between two (or more) nominal groups on the basis of several parameters simultaneously. A *discriminant function* is derived by weighting and combining the parameters in such a way that the groups will be maximally separated by their members' scores on this function.

The data are first assessed to see whether there is enough difference between the groups on these parameters to justify the analysis proposed. This is done by computing Wilks' λ (an inverse measure of group separation), with an associated χ^2 test of statistical significance. A significant Wilks' λ at this stage implies that the first discriminant function to be derived will itself be statistically significant. The *substantive* utility of the function can be measured by its canonical correlation: that is, the association between the function and the nominal categories representing the groups present in the data. A high canonical correlation (0.7 or upwards) indicates that the function is discriminating quite successfully between the named groups. The discriminant scores calculated for each subject can then be used to classify the subjects, allowing an additional measure of the usefulness of the function: its rate of success in allocating subjects to their correct groups.

One discriminant function, separating pathological subjects from controls, was derived for each sex separately, from subjects' raw (unstandardised) scores on all ten parameters, using the DISCRIMINANT sub-program available in the *Statistical Package for the Social Sciences* (1983). Figure 17.5 gives the resulting classifications for the males and females separately, along with the canonical correlation coefficient for each function and the Wilks' λ calculated before the derivation of that function, with a χ^2 test of statistical significance. Both functions were highly significant. Two of the incorrectly classified pathological males have epithelial disorders: one was a case of keratosis with oedema (one of the cases referred to above), the other a very early case of squamous carcinoma (undetected at the time of recording).

It is not expected that all ten parameters will be equally useful for discriminating between pathological and control subjects: some do not separate the groups very well, while others are redundant by virtue of their high correlation with those that do. The relative contribution of each

	Correct classifications	Incorrect classifications
A. Males*		
Pathological (55)	47 (85.5)	8 (14.5)
Control (63)	58 (92.1)	5 (7.9)
B. Females†		
Pathological (54)	47 (87.0)	7 (13.0)
Control (58)	55 (94.8)	3 (5.2)

* Wilks' λ before function = 0.299; χ^2 = 133.9;
 $p = < 0.0001$; canonical correlation = 0.837.
† Wilks' λ before function = 0.366; χ^2 = 105.67;
 $p = < 0.0001$; canonical correlation = 0.797.

Figure 17.5 Classification of male and female subjects into pathological and control groups by discriminant functions derived from all ten acoustic parameters (figures in parantheses are percentages).

Males		Females	
S-DPF	1.66889	S-DPF	2.05087
F_0-AV	0.96325	J-DEVEX	−1.19266
S-RATEX	−0.68534	F_0-DEV	0.78410
J-AVEX	0.54630	S-RATEX	−0.70417
J-DEVEX	−0.52852	J-DPF	−0.58023
F_0-DEV	−0.38440	J-RATEX	0.52369
J-RATEX	0.11701	F_0-AV	−0.39136
S-AVEX	0.08795	S-DEVEX	0.29108
J-DPF	−0.04024	S-AVEX	−0.19908
S-DEVEX	−0.01797	J-AVEX	0.14846

Figure 17.6 Standardised discriminant function coefficients for each of the functions described in Figure 17.5.

individual parameter to the function can be learned from the absolute values of the (standardised) weighting coefficients produced by the program. These are given in Figure 17.6, in order of importance, for both functions.

It is clear that s-DPF is by far the most important contributor to both functions. It also seems, from measurements of the correlation between individual parameters and the discriminant functions (given in Figure 17.7), that these functions are essentially functions of *perturbation*. The failure of some of the perturbation measures to achieve high weightings in the functions can perhaps be attributed to high degrees of intercorrelation among them.

Males		Females	
S-DPF	0.67050	S-DPF	0.66738
S-RATEX	0.45745	S-RATEX	0.47688
J-DPF	0.37772	J-DPF	0.26889
J-RATEX	0.27290	S-AVEX	0.24010
S-AVEX	0.26127	F_0-AV	−0.21667
J-AVEX	0.21225	J-RATEX	0.16737
F_0-AV	0.16901	J-AVEX	0.13843
F_0-DEV	0.15553	J-DEVEX	0.06467
J-DEVEX	0.12085	F_0-DEV	0.05434
S-DEVEX	0.01593	S-DEVEX	0.04271

Figure 17.7 Pooled within-groups correlation coefficients between parameters and each discriminant function.

4.3 Reservations

The results of this discriminant analysis need to be treated with caution. Linear discriminant analysis assumes that the data show a multivariate normal distribution, but given the heterogeneous composition of the pathological group it is likely that this assumption is seriously violated in this case. However, the technique is quite robust in the face of such violations. A more serious problem is the fact that the groups are still rather small, given the number of parameters being used to derive the functions, and it is therefore not possible to put great reliance on the functions obtained, despite their statistical significance. It must be remembered that a function derived for a set of data is an *optimal* one, designed to force the groups as far apart as possible. Success in achieving a high degree of separation is then a descriptive measure of structure in the actual data set. The classification rates obtained, however, cannot safely be asserted to be necessarily predictive of future success in classifying another set of subjects with the same function. The recommended procedure for testing a function's true discriminating power is to split the sample, deriving the function from, say, half of the subjects (randomly selected) and measuring its success in classifying the remainder. However, this will not be possible until the groups are larger.

It was also felt inappropriate at this stage to attempt to derive an optimal set of parameters for discrimination, despite clear indications that certain parameters (especially s-DPF) were more useful than others.

5. Conclusions

The two principal objectives of the project are (1) the development of a screening system, and (2) the differentiation of disorders. The separation of the two groups of subjects – and the feasibility of screening – have been clearly demonstrated using two techniques, both of which form potential screening tools. Work is continuing into assessing the acoustic consequences of different pathologies, but the use of a technique such as discriminant analysis for the task of differentiation, though promising, cannot be attempted without considerably larger numbers of subjects in each pathology group. The potential applications of the system to assessing priorities among patients, and monitoring progress or deterioration, remain to be examined.

Note

This project is funded by the Medical Research Council (Grant No. 8207136N: 1982–1985).

We are very grateful for the collaboration and co-operation of Mr T. Harris (Department of Otolaryngology) and Mrs S. Collins (Department of Speech Therapy), of the Radcliffe Infirmary, Oxford; and Mr A. Maran (Department of Otolaryngology), and Mrs M. Mackintosh and Mrs R. Nieuwenhuis (Department of Speech Therapy), of the Royal Infirmary, Edinburgh.

References

Fairbanks, G. (1960) *Voice and Articulation Drill Book*, Harper Row, New York.

Gold, B. and Rabiner, L. (1969) 'Parallel processing techniques for estimating pitch periods of speech in the time domain', *Journal of the Acoustical Society of America* 46, 442–8.

Hanson, R. (1978) 'A two-state model of F_0 control', *Journal of the Acoustical Society of America* 64, 543–4.

Hecker, M. and Kreul, E. (1971) 'Descriptions of the speech of patients with cancer of the vocal folds. Part 1: measures of fundamental frequency', *Journal of the Acoustical Society of America* 49, 1275–82.

Hiller, S., Laver, J. and Mackenzie, J. (1983) 'Automatic analysis of waveform perturbations in connected speech', *Edinburgh University Department of Linguistics. Work in Progress* 16, 440–68.

Hiller, S., Laver, J. and Mackenzie, J. (1984) 'Durational aspects of long-term measurements of fundamental frequency perturbations in connected speech', *Edinburgh University Department of Linguistics, Work in Progress* 17, 59–76.

Klecka, W. (1980) *Discriminant analysis* (Sage University Paper Series on Quantitative Applications in the Social Sciences 07–001), Sage, Beverly Hills, London.

Laver, J., Hiller, S. and Hanson, R. (1982) 'Comparative performance of pitch detection algorithms on dysphonic voices', pp. 192–5 in *Proceedings of the IEEE International Conference ASSP 1982.*.

Laver, J., Hiller, S. and Mackenzie, J. (1984) 'Acoustic analysis of vocal fold pathology', *Proceedings of the Institute of Acoustics* 6(4), 425–30.

Mackenzie, J., Laver, J. and Hiller, S. (1983) 'Structural pathologies of the vocal folds and phonation', *Edinburgh University Department of Linguistics, Work in Progress* 16, 80–116.

Mackenzie, J., Laver, J. and Hiller, S. (1984) 'Acoustic screening for vocal pathology: preliminary results', *Edinburgh University Department of Linguistics, Work in Progress* 17, 98–110.

SPSSSx User's Guide (1983) McGraw Hill, New York.

18 Acoustic Waveform Perturbations and Voice Disorders

Originally published as Laver, J., Hiller, S. and Mackenzie Beck, J. (1988) 'Acoustic waveform perturbations and voice disorders', *Report to the Voice Committee of the International Association of Logopedics and Phoniatrics* (pp. 1–26); to be published by *Journal of Voice* (Volume 5, in press).

Introduction

Phonation is the aerodynamic and acoustic product of an extremely complex vibratory system. Part of the evidence for this complexity is the fact that the cycle-to-cycle consistency of laryngeal vibration in phonation is never completely regular (Boves, 1984: 113). As Baken comments, 'The phonatory system is not a perfect machine, and every speaker's vibratory cycles are erratic to some extent' (1987: 166). Every act of phonation is characterised by a certain degree of apparently random variability of the cycle-to-cycle duration and/or amplitude of the pitch periods of the laryngeal waveform. The term 'perturbation' will be used throughout this article to refer to such random deviations from complete regularity of the laryngeal waveform. Perturbation is thus to be considered distinct from those more consistent low-rate oscillations of frequency and amplitude of the laryngeal pulses that form the basis of vibrato and tremolo – for example, as characterised in Michel and Grashel (1981), Shipp (1981) and Shipp, Leanderson and Haglund (1983).

Acoustic, Auditory and Physiological Definitions

Acoustically, perturbation can characterise the laryngeal waveform in both the time domain and the frequency domain. In the time domain, dysperiodic perturbation of the cycle-to-cycle duration is called 'jitter'. Perturbation of the cycle-to-cycle amplitude of successive laryngeal pulses is called 'shimmer'. In the frequency domain, a fricational element can add spectral noise to the laryngeal waveform.

From an auditory perspective, jitter and shimmer contribute to the rough perceptual effect usually called 'harshness'. Physiologically, a voice which is audibly and habitually harsh can arise either functionally from hyperkinetic adjustments of the phonatory musculature, or pathologically from disruptive mechanical effects of neoplastic growths in the laminar tissue layers of one or both vocal folds. As a very broad generalisation, the larger the neoplastic growth, the greater the perturbatory effect (Lieberman, 1963; Koike, 1967).

Spectral noise alone is associated with the auditory effect called 'whisperiness', and voices showing this effect can be called 'whispery voices'. When spectral noise is added to jitter and/or shimmer, this has the auditory effect of adding whisperiness to harshness, and the composite quality is usually called 'hoarseness', or 'hoarse voice'. Physiologically, the fricational element in whispery and hoarse voices is caused by incomplete glottal closure. The incomplete closure can be the result either of idiosyncratic, habitual adjustments of the phonatory musculature, or of mechanical intrusion into the glottis of obstructions such as vocal nodules, polyps and other types of growths, or of paralysis of one or both vocal folds.

Perturbation in the laryngeal waveform of a given speaker can occur across a wide range of incidence, from occasional to habitual, and in degree from slight to severe. Severe perturbations are almost always signs of either pathological or functional disorder, but slight perturbations occurring occasionally are evident in all speaking voices, especially at the margins of voicing episodes. The moments of onset and offset of voicing are extremely complex situations, with many aerodynamic and muscular parameters in a state of abrupt transition. Mathematically catastrophic changes of parametric relations in the myoelastic and aerodynamic adjustments of the vocal folds are then reflected in momentary irregularities of phonation before the system settles to a more consistent pattern.

The articulatory transition from one segment type to another often involves physiological and aerodynamic changes whose laryngeal consequence is a very local modulation of fundamental frequency. Baken and Orlikoff (1988) summarise a number of studies showing this effect, and their own experiments on transitions between voiced fricatives and following vowels were able to confirm that 'the laryngeal system is not compensated to maintain (fundamental frequency) in the face of transitory changes in vocal-tract dynamics that accompany voiced fricative production' (1988: 207).

Ephemeral variations in the mucal conditions of the fluid bathing the surface of the vocal folds can also cause momentary perturbations, often eliminated by the speakers clearing their throats. Other slight perturbations in healthy voices during the course of phonation probably have a neuromuscular origin (Baer, 1978; 1980; 1981). Increased perturbation is also one symptom of the ageing voice (Benjamin, 1981; Ramig and Ringel, 1983; Wilcox and Horii, 1980).

Perturbatory differences of the cycle-to-cycle period in the normal voice are very small. Lieberman (1963) found that, in normal adult male speakers, only some 15% of such differences typically exceed 0.5 ms in duration. Perturbations of the time domain below about 1% of the local fundamental frequency or intensity seem not to be audible as such, though they can be registered by acoustic or physiological analysis. An important consideration in the ability of acoustic techniques to register perturbation data is therefore the sensitivity of the acoustic technique itself. The major factor controlling such sensitivity is the sampling frequency used. If too low a frequency is employed, the minimum difference of period that can be registered when comparing successive cycles is unsuitably large (Heiberger and Horii, 1982; Hiller, 1985). Sampling frequencies giving suitable resolution to detect low levels of perturbation in waveforms from adult male speakers' and most adult female speakers' ranges should be not lower than about 20 KHz.

There is one type of dysperiodicity of laryngeal vibration that is of functional origin, but which is apparently not brought about by hyper-kinetic muscular adjustments. This is the type of phonation usually called 'creak' (in the British literature on phonation) or 'vocal fry' (which is an American usage – see for example Hollien and Michel (1968), Hollien and Wendahl (1968) and Horii (1985)). It is also increasingly being referred to as 'pulse register', following suggestions by Hollien (1974). Creaky voices show a tendency to irregular, low-frequency groupings of laryngeal pulses, such that alternations of pairs of shorter or longer cycles occur (Laver, 1980). Moore and von Leden (1958: 235) also gave this low-frequency pulse-grouping tendency the name 'dicrotic dysphonia'. Creaky phonation can be used as a habitual personal style, but it is also linguistically exploited by native speakers of English as a signal, in association with a low terminal fall in intonation-contour, of finality in an utterance. A tendency to inject audible creakiness into an utterance is also phonetically associated with the production of a glottal stop, and is often referred to as 'glottalisation' or 'laryngealisation' in the linguistic phonetic literature. Dysperiodicity of this low-frequency pulse-grouping type will not be given further specific consideration in this article.

The attempt to discover objective acoustic and physiological ways of characterising laryngeal waveforms in terms of perturbation parameters now has a history of over thirty years, starting from the pioneering work of researchers such as Moore and von Leden (1958), Moore (1962), Lieber-man (1961; 1963) and Michel (1964). From this base, the topic of perturbation has attracted many contributions from speech science, signal processing, laryngology and speech pathology. The literature of per-turbation studies is already substantial, and a thorough survey is beyond the scope of this summary review. The interested reader is directed to Hiller (1985), who reviews the studies in detail, and to Baken (1987: 113–9, 166–88), who gives a compact review of different approaches to the measurement of perturbation.

Some particularly relevant articles and books other than the ones already mentioned are: Anders, Hollien, Hurme, Sonninen and Wendler (1988); Askenfelt and Hammarberg (1980; 1981); Askenfelt and Sjölin (1980); Coleman (1969); Coleman and Wendahl (1967); Davis (1976); Deal and Emanuel (1978); Emanuel and Sansone (1969); Hammarberg, Fritzell, Gauffin, Sundberg and Wedin (1980); Hollien, Michel and Doherty (1973); Horii (1975; 1979; 1980; 1982); Isshiki, Okamura, Tanabe and Morimoto (1969); Kane and Wellen (1985); Kasprzyk and Gilbert (1975); Kasuya, Kobayashi and Kasuya (1983); Kempster and Kistler (1983); Kitajima and Gould (1976); Koike (1973); Koike, Takahashi and Calcaterra (1977); von Leden and Koike (1970); Ludlow, Coulter and Gentges (1983a; 1983b); Ludlow, Naunton and Bassich (1984); Murry and Doherty (1983); Sansone and Emanuel (1970); Sherman and Linke (1952); Shipp and Huntington (1965); Smith and Lieberman (1969); Smith, Weinberg, Lawrence and Horii (1978); Sorensen and Horii (1983; 1984); Sorensen, Horii and Leonard (1980); and Wendahl (1966).

It is important to emphasise that there are very many different ways of defining the basic data of perturbation, and that no wide consensus yet exists on definitions of the identity of the most information-rich parameters. It may be helpful, nevertheless, to give some illustrative examples of some of the types of measures used in the area. An initial distinction is possible between two broad classes of parameters in this area: that between the gross behaviour of fundamental frequency and intensity over some period of time (involving trend-line analysis), and the more local variations, within these grosser trends, of individual phonatory cycles (involving cycle-to-cycle analysis).

The fundamental frequency parameter which is based on the trend-line in the successive values of pitch periods is usually referred to as 'intonation', and the distance between the value of a given cycle and the trend-line can be regarded as an 'excursion' from the intonational trend. The trend-line can be established by various types of linear and non-linear smoothing. In Laver, Hiller, Mackenzie and Rooney (1986), the trend-line underlying the raw fundamental frequency data is created by the combined application of a five-point median smoother, together with a three-point Hanning window smoother, following the suggestions of Rabiner, Sambur and Schmidt (1975). A non-linear smoother has advantages over more conventional linear smoothers such as running averages, which tend to smear realistic discontinuities in the speech signal, as well as being grossly affected by egregious errors in the signal analysis. A median filter with a duration of five sample points smooths only those discontinuities in the signal which are one or two sample points in duration. Single very large errors of analysis thus do not contribute to the trend-line.

Descriptive parameters based on such excursions tend to be based on the magnitude, frequency and range of the excursions, and such studies normally also report the means and ranges of the intonational data.

Kitajima and Gould (1976) use a similar method, employing excursions from a least-squares trend-line as a base for their measures of shimmer. Other examples of the use of excursion measures based on a smoothed trend-line can be found in the work of Koike (1973), Kitajima, Tanabe and Isshiki (1975), Davis (1976) and Koike, Takahashi and Calcaterra (1977).

A somewhat comparable approach is taken by Ludlow, Coulter and Gentges (1983a), where perturbation is represented as a deviation from a locally-calculated trend in terms of the difference between a given period and the average of the periods two cycles to the left and right. Alternative characterisations of perturbation have tended to focus on the relationship between adjacent phonatory cycles, for instance in terms of how often the difference in value of adjacent cycles tends to change its algebraic sign (e.g. Hecker and Kreul's (1971) 'Directional Perturbation Factor'). Another approach is Horii's (1979) 'jitter ratio', which calculates the average magnitude of the differences between adjacent periods. A more computationally intensive approach is to examine the serial correlation between periods (Baken, 1987: 186). Iwata and von Leden (1970) and Iwata (1972) explore the interesting possibility that different types of serial correlation may discriminate between different types of pathology.

The studies of perturbation and laryngeal pathology so far conducted tend to fall into two rather different categories – those that use data from the production of sustained, isolated monotone vowels, versus those that take continuous speech as their material. The use of isolated vowels has the advantage that the irregularities due to segmental effects, as well as the adjustments of cyclic values that are directly due to voluntary intonational changes, can be largely eliminated from consideration (Hollien, Michel and Doherty, 1973). Processing this type of voice sample also requires less sophisticated signal analysis techniques to derive period and amplitude values, since the 'voiced' nature of the signal is not normally in doubt.

A disadvantage of taking isolated vowels is that the production of speech in such circumstances is a less demanding task for the subject, who may have learned to mask the effects of pathology by limiting his or her production to a more restricted but manageable zone of vocal performance. The representativeness of the data for the subject's everyday performance is therefore sometimes open to question.

The advantage of taking continuous speech as input to perturbation analysis is that it is more likely to yield representative data. In the case of pathological phonation, the production of continuous speech may tax the laryngeal mechanism in a manner which makes the pathology more evident (as reflected in increased magnitude of perturbatory parameter values). The analysis of period and amplitude values from continuous speech is more difficult than from sustained monotone vowels since the detecting algorithm has to examine a variety of signal structures produced by interactive segmental effects of the dynamic movements of the articulators, together with multiple voicing onsets and offsets. It is probably also thereby more subject to the risk of artefactual distortion.

If continuous speech data is used for perturbation analysis, then a minimum duration of speech material is required to stabilise long-term measurements of perturbation (e.g. the mean and standard deviation of each perturbatory parameter). In an experiment reported by Hiller (1985), it was found that a 40-second sample of read speech provided relatively stable long-term speaker-characterising parameters of perturbation for healthy male and female speakers. This finding is in general agreement with the results of previous studies of the long-term features of the voice (in particular for long-term characteristics of fundamental frequency).

Clinical Relevance of Automatic Systems for Perturbation Analysis

The articles listed above and the studies described by Hiller (1985) and Baken (1987) provide the technical basis for the discussion that follows immediately below on the applications of automatic systems for quantifying the perturbatory characteristics of phonation. Emphasis in the discussion will be placed on non-invasive acoustic methods, but some comment will also be made on physiological methods.

When patients complain of harsh or hoarse voices, an important clinical decision has to be reached about the pathological versus functional basis of their presenting symptoms. This decision, which is often initially problematic, has direct consequences for any ensuing treatment. Any objective methods for supporting such a decision, if they can be made automatic, reliable and cost-effective, are of evident otolaryngological value (not least because a disabling and potentially life-threatening disorder such as laryngeal cancer, if diagnosed sufficiently early, is amongst the most treatable types of cancer).

There are four major applications of automatic methods of perturbation-analysis which could give evidence of potential laryngeal pathology (Laver, Hiller, Mackenzie and Rooney, 1986):

1. *Screening* of a given population, to complement existing screening programmes in hospitals such as 'well man/well woman' clinics. The consequence, however, of applying a screening system for laryngeal pathology to the general population would be to overwhelm the clinical otolaryngological services, and the rehabilitative speech therapy services, in hospitals. This is because the incidence of pathological conditions needing truly urgent treatment is substantially lower than the incidence of solely functional disorders of the voice. General screening of unselected populations is therefore very unlikely to be cost-effective (Ludlow, personal communication). Limited screening of populations known to be at risk would be more feasible, nevertheless. Such populations include factory workers in potentially laryngeally-damaging environments such as

flour-mills, cement-factories and the asbestos industry, for example. A funding basis for screening systems in such applications may grow from company schemes for group medical insurance.

2. *Priority assessment* of patients visiting their general practitioner with complaints of harshness or hoarseness. The use of an automatic acoustic system could usefully accelerate referral for laryngeal examination by specialists with hospital-based fibre-optic laryngoscopic facilities in those cases where evidence of serious pathology was indicated.

3. *Diagnostic support*, where the acoustic system had shown itself to be able to provide reliable evidence discriminating one type of pathology from another, or general evidence of pathological versus functional aetiology.

4. *Monitoring*, to assess changes with time of the phonatory efficiency of patients receiving surgery, radiotherapy, chemotherapy or speech therapy, or to track deterioration or remission in progressive·disease.

It is probably reasonable to suggest that current automatic acoustic techniques of quantifying perturbatory evidence in laryngeal waveforms could reliably and cost-effectively support the functions of screening, priority assessment and monitoring described above. Figure 18.1, from Laver et al. (1986: 521), shows the results of a simple bivariate plot for a Directional Perturbation Factor in a shimmer parameter against mean fundamental frequency, for a control group of sixty-three male speakers versus a group of fifty-five male speakers known to suffer from a variety of laryngeal pathologies. The results for the control group are expressed partly in terms of an ellipse surrounding two standard deviations of the data on the two parameters. The boundary of the ellipse can be used as a practical screening threshold for the detection of vocal pathology. This can be seen from the fact that only some 9.5% of the control speakers fall outside the ellipse, and therefore register as false positives, while 90.1% of the known pathological speakers fall outside and are therefore successfully detected as probably pathological. For a similar treatment of a group of fifty-four pathological female speakers versus a control group of fifty-eight female speakers presumed healthy, 79.6% of the pathological speakers were successfully detected by this method, at a cost of 10.3% false positives.

However, it is premature to suggest that such systems can yet support a discriminative diagnostic function with any satisfactory degree of reliability. There are promising signs that such techniques are in principle capable of providing diagnostic support, but a major obstacle is the unavailability to date of adequate databases of acoustic and laryngoscopic recordings of speakers with relevant laryngeal disorders, and of comparable databases of control groups of speakers. Recommendations about establishing such databases, under standardised recording conditions and on standard equipment, are made below.

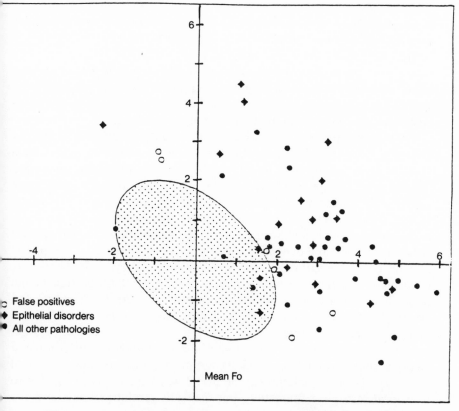

Figure 18.1 A scattergram of Directional Perturbation Factor shimmer against mean fundamental frequency for male speakers. The shaded area represents a two-Standard Deviation ellipse derived from principal components analysis of male controls.

Instrumental Techniques for Registering Perturbation Data

A wide range of different instrumental techniques has been used for registering the primary phonatory data for perturbation analysis. They fall into two main categories – acoustic techniques and physiological techniques.

Acoustic techniques, reviewed in detail in Hiller (1985), can be divided into those that address the examination of the time domain and those that explore the frequency domain. Time-domain techniques include many different types of pitch-tracking algorithms. In all cases, emphasis is placed on accurate assessment of the location in time of the individual larynx pulses. Pitch-tracking devices that smooth the acoustic waveform are thus disqualified from use in this application to the extent that they impose a time-smear on the time domain of the analysis, losing the fine detail of cycle-to-cycle information that is the basis of perturbatory analysis.

Frequency-domain techniques themselves fall into two sub-categories: those that seek to register the presence and properties of spectral noise from laryngeal friction, and those that try to recover the laryngeal waveform from the combined signal (the speech waveform) that is the result of the convolution of the laryngeal waveform with resonance effects introduced by the supraglottal vocal tract, the nasal cavity and the sub-glottal cavity. Spectrography is an example of the former type of technique, and inverse filtering an example of the latter.

The major physiological technique for gathering information about laryngeal behaviour that is indirectly relevant to perturbatory analysis is visual observation through laryngoscopy. Varieties of this technique are indirect laryngoscopy and fibre-optic laryngoscopy. Indirect laryngoscopy is useful for an initial examination of the surface geometry of the static larynx, but fibre-optic laryngoscopy is more usually used with stroboscopic illumination to allow a view of the vocal folds in motion. It is particularly important to obtain a dynamic view of phonatory action, since neoplastic growths below the surface of the vocal folds may display their effects only in terms of interference with symmetrical and regular vibration of the folds. The visibility of the normal mucal wave pattern travelling up and across the surface of the vocal fold into the laryngeal ventricle is of immediate relevance here.

Ultrasonic techniques of inspection of the vocal folds are comparable to laryngoscopic techniques in that they afford a view of the vocal fold geometry. These techniques can be useful when the patient is unable to bear laryngoscopic examination, but their low resolution tends to make them of limited value.

Neither laryngoscopy nor ultrasonic scanning techniques give directly quantifiable information about perturbation as such. But they can give crucial background information about the probable mechanical state of the vocal folds that can contribute to an interpretation of acoustic or physiological records of the dynamic behaviour of the vocal folds in vibration acquired by other means.

Electroglottography (also often called laryngography) is a valuable adjunct to laryngoscopic techniques, in that it gives plausible information about vocal fold contact area during phonation with a good degree of time-resolution (Baken, 1987; Fourcin, 1974). The technique has some limitations, notably in the cases of patients with short, fat necks where placement of the electrodes can make for difficulties in achieving adequate signal-registration.

Finally, electromyography is a technique that can lead to an understanding of the patterns of muscular action underlying to the production of different types of laryngeal adjustment, and hence to the understanding of an overall model of muscular contributions to phonation.

Equipment for Acquiring Acoustic Recordings
for Perturbation Analysis

The two chief advantages of acoustic techniques for perturbation analysis are firstly that the recording methods involved are non-invasive, non-frightening to patients, and use fairly low-cost technology within the reach of most hospitals and clinics. Secondly, techniques of analysis of acoustic perturbation data are relatively straightforward to automate, and hard-copy records which are easy to interpret can easily be made available for incorporation into the patient's file.

The two major disadvantages of the use of acoustic techniques for perturbation analysis are firstly that acoustic recordings are subject to contamination by both environmental factors and equipment-derived artefacts. Secondly, the process of automating the perturbatory analysis currently involves relatively high-cost computing equipment (though it will eventually be simple and cheap to provide low-cost solutions to this problem). The following paragraphs discuss in more detail suitable equipment and procedures for making the necessary acoustic recordings.

The cycle-to-cycle detail of perturbation data requires that pitch-detection be based on direct examination of the time-domain signal or some equivalent time-domain derivative. Any system used to capture speech signals for these purposes must therefore accurately preserve the time-amplitude structures which carry the perturbatory information about jitter and shimmer characteristics.

The ideal acoustic recording equipment for acquiring speech data for perturbation analysis should have the following features:

1. *Flat, low-frequency response* – the fundamental frequency produced by adult male speakers can be as low as 40–50 Hz. Any recording system should be able to record signals at these and lower frequencies.

2. *No signal distortion* – accurate quantification of pitch periodicity in the speech waveform can only be achieved when the signal has not been disturbed by phase distortions. Phase distortion is an inherent characteristic of most types of tape-recorders, and compensatory techniques therefore have to be applied.

3. *High signal-to-noise ratio* – most time-domain pitch-detection algorithms are not very resistant to the effects of contamination by transient noises (such as doors closing, telephones ringing, footsteps and typing), and by continuous ambient noise (such as traffic, 50/60 Hz hum from fluorescent lighting, and room ventilation/fan heating).

4. *Affordability* – the recording equipment must be within the budget of the clinics using it. Most speech pathology clinics, which are often the sources of recordings requiring perturbation analysis, have low budgets for equipment, and expensive recorders such as FM recorders are usually out of reach.

The following comments can be made about equipment and procedures which meet these requirements, in the light of a distinction between transducers for picking up the acoustic signal; recorders; and the recording environment.

Transducers – in most perturbation studies, a microphone for picking up the acoustic signal has been used as the transducer. In our own research, we have found that the electret type of microphone (e.g. as made by Sennheiser) is the most useful, since it produces a flat frequency response in the low frequencies, and is unidirectional. Noise-cancelling microphones are also available, but they are very expensive.

A number of perturbation studies have used transducers which record signals directly from the external wall of the throat. They include throat microphones, miniature accelerometers and electroglottograph electrodes. These provide signals which are relatively free of contamination by resonance effects of non-laryngeal structures. They have the drawback that they are more invasive than free-field microphones and are dependent on the fit of the transducer to the speaker's throat.

Recorders – both analogue and digital recorders are often used for perturbation analysis purposes. Pulse Code Modulation (PCM) digital audio recorders provide a flat frequency response over a wide frequency-range with minimal phase distortion. Under advice from the Speech Technology Assessment Group of the United Kingdom's Institute of Acoustics Speech Group on recommended recording standards, SONY PCM Digital Audio Systems have been adopted as standard equipment by all the major speech science laboratories in Britain.

Many clinical laboratories make recordings with analogue tape recorders. Relatively inexpensive analogue recorders of high quality are available from companies such as REVOX, AMPEX and SONY. These systems offer high recording speeds and flat frequency response down to frequencies as low as 20 Hz. However, analogue magnetic tape recorders produce phase distortion caused by the recording and playback amplifiers and pre-amplifiers. A study by Hiller (1985) revealed that phase distortions of the speech signal due to analogue recording equipment had a detrimental effect on the accurate measurement of waveform perturbations. Techniques for compensating for phase distortion caused by analogue recording have been proposed by Holmes (1975) and Berouti, Childers and Paige (1977).

Recently, the issue of recorder type has been circumvented by direct analogue-to-digital conversion of speech signals onto digital computer systems. For example, Zyski, Bull, MacDonald and Johns (1984) digitised signals directly onto a microcomputer for perturbation analysis.

Recording environment – recordings must be made in a quiet environment to ensure an adequate signal-to-noise ratio. They should preferably be made in a sound-treated booth which also provides shielding against mains current electrical signals and heavy-duty hospital equipment such as radiographic machinery.

Contribution to the Theory of Speech Production

The research on perturbation has made a contribution, indirectly, to our understanding of the detailed anatomy of the vocal folds, and of the importance of the mucal wave for normal, healthy phonation. The leading figure in advancing a model of the vocal fold as a mechanically complex, layered structure is Hirano (1981; Hirano et al. 1981; 1982). Disruption of the laminar coherence of these layers by neoplastic growth changes the mass, stiffness and geometry of the affected fold in relation to that of its otherwise symmetrical partner, and perturbed phonatory behaviour is the consequence. If the change in vibratory pattern can be acoustically detected, an analysis of the acoustic details may lead to a clinically relevant hypothesis about the pathological cause of the vibratory disturbance. It may therefore be helpful, following Hirano and his colleagues, to offer here a brief discussion about the anatomy of the laminar structure of the vocal fold. This discussion was originally presented in an unpublished paper given to a Voice Foundation meeting in Denver by Laver, Mackenzie, Hiller and Rooney (1985).

The geographical limits of the area of laryngeal interest here lie within the true vocal fold, and in particular round the ligamental part of the fold. The ligamental area is the part most freely involved during phonation, and is also the area most prone to pathological change. If we look in more detail at the tissue make-up of the ligamental border of the fold, then it can be seen that there are five different types of tissue layers involved (Mackenzie, Laver and Hiller, 1983).

Figure 18.2 shows the vocal fold in vertical cross-section through the thickest part of the fold. The layered nature of this section is very evident. The body of the fold, made up of the vocalis muscle, lies under a cover of mucous membrane. This flexible cover is itself made up of four thin layers, each with different mechanical properties. The outer layer is the epithelium, and the next three layers make up the lamina propria.

We can consider the layered cover and the body in a little more detail, in terms of the different types of tissue shown in Figure 18.3. The epithelium is thin, relatively stiff and inelastic and isotropic – that is, it has the same degree of stretchability lengthwise and crosswise. It rests on a very thin basement membrane which acts as a biological barrier to infection. Many disorders arise in the epithelium, but do not necessarily spread into the lamina propria or the vocalis muscle.

The lamina propria is made up of three layers of connective tissue. The superficial layer has been likened by Hirano (1981: 5) to soft gelatin. Cells are embedded in a semi-fluid matrix, with a loose, haphazard network of elastic and collagen fibre. With the epithelium, this layer acts like a liquid

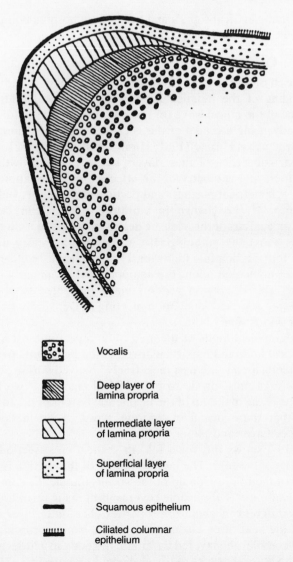

Vocalis

Deep layer of
lamina propria

Intermediate layer
of lamina propria

Superficial layer
of lamina propria

Squamous epithelium

Ciliated columnar
epithelium

Figure 18.2 Laminar tissue-structure of the vocal fold, shown in vertical cross-section (adapted from Hirano, 1981; Hirano, Kurita and Nakashima, 1981; and Hirano, Kakita, Ohmaru and Kurita, 1982).

with a very high surface tension, and forms the medium through which the surface wave of the mucal ripple travels in phonatory vibration.

The intermediate layer is much more tightly packed with fibres. These are elastic fibres in an orderly arrangement parallel to the free border of the vocal fold. They are like elastic bands, stretchable and flexible. They are anisotropic, in that they are elastic along the length of the fibres, but

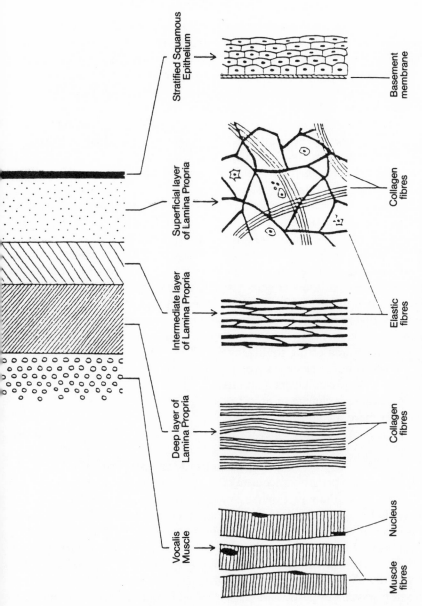

Figure 18.3 A diagrammatic representation of tissue-structure in the vocal fold.

stiffer across the grain. The tissue is assumed to be incompressible (Titze, 1973).

The deep layer is similar to the intermediate layer, but the fibres are mostly formed of collagen. They are flexible, but difficult to stretch. Hirano's analogy here is with cotton thread, emphasising the relative non-elasticity of collagen compared with elastin (Freeman and Bracegirdle, 1966; Fields and Dunn, 1973). Like the intermediate layer, the deep layer is assumed to be anisotropic and incompressible.

The final layer is made up of the vocalis muscle, part of the thyro-arytenoid muscle. The fibres run parallel to the free border of the fold, but their elasticity will depend very much on their state of contraction. Hirano et al. (1982) cite research establishing as much as a tenfold difference in elasticity between resting and contracted muscle. The vocalis muscle is anisotropic, being much more elastic longitudinally than crosswise, and is relatively incompressible.

These five different layers behave basically like three relatively independent masses, with the epithelium and the superficial layer of the lamina propria forming one semi-fluid layer, the intermediate and the deep layers of the lamina propria forming a stiffer layer within the cover, and the vocalis muscle forming the third mass as the body. If any of these layers change in mass, stiffness or geometry, then the vibratory pattern of the fold changes. A number of questions can then be asked about such changes of mass, stiffness and geometry to help to formulate a hypothesis about acoustic consequences. Typical questions would be:

– which area of the fold is involved?
– which tissue layer is involved?
– are the tissue layers disrupted?
– is there a change in mass?
– is there a change in stiffness?
– does any surface mass protrude into the glottis and prevent full glottal approximation?
– is any structural change symmetrical, or asymmetrical?

Each change brings an acoustic consequence, more directly understood in some cases than in others. For example, an increase in mass will normally bring about a drop in fundamental frequency, and an increase in stiffness will normally generate a rise in fundamental frequency and a drop in intensity. Prevention of full glottal approximation by the intrusion of a surface mass will inject interharmonic noise into the glottal spectrum (giving audible whisperiness), and asymmetrical structural changes will increase waveform perturbation, increasing frequency jitter and intensity shimmer factors. From an analysis of the acoustic detail, one can therefore to some extent work backwards, and use the acoustic information as evidence of the possible existence of a given class of laryngeal disorder, which can in turn be checked by laryngological and histological examination.

The process of arguing from acoustic evidence to physiological and anatomical causes is, nevertheless, still broadly speculative. This is not least because of the complexity of the potential interaction between different mechanical effects. For example, a counteracting relationship between a rise in mass and a rise in stiffness of laryngeal tissues may well leave mean fundamental frequency as such only marginally displaced, though the range of fundamental frequency and the mean intensity would be affected.

Needs for Technological Development

Our understanding of the different acoustic parameters which can be used to characterise perturbation is already in a reasonably serviceable state. Unfortunately, the same cannot be said for the corresponding physiological parameters, nor for the correlation between the acoustic and the physiological information, as indicated above.

One technological advance which would be of great assistance in this area would be the development of a graticule-based quantification of images of the vocal folds seen through fibre-optic viewing systems. This would allow the analyst to estimate discrepancies of vibration in mucal wave movement and in glottal excursions.

Electroglottography probably has something to add here as well, apart from its possible use as a trigger for stroboscopic illumination (which can probably be supplied by a pitch-detection system simultaneously at work on the acoustic wave).

A clear need also exists for an archive of high-quality fibre-optic colour photographs, and of colour cinefilms, of pathological larynges, annotated for their diagnostic status. A corresponding need exists for a similar archive of records of healthy larynges.

One major exception to the adequate nature of our understanding of acoustic correlates of perturbation is the absence to date of a system for quantifying the fricational element of spectral noise in the whispery component associated with so much of pathological perturbatory phonation.

Finally, a scheme for quantifying the acoustic and phonatory consequences of increased and decreased muscular tension at the laryngeal level is needed.

Needs for Databases

There is a need for at least three types of databases, which should be recorded under standard acoustic conditions, on standard linguistic material within a language and comparable linguistic material across languages, on standard equipment, under standard procedures, with standard bio-graphical documentation of the speakers involved.

The first is a database of voice samples of patients known to be suffering from specific voice disorders, both pathological and functional. This database should include graded samples of a wide range of disorders at different degrees of severity, from males, females and children.

The second is a database of speakers suspected to be suffering from laryngeal pathology or dysfunction, recorded prior to diagnosis, with information available about the later diagnoses.

The third is a database of a control group of speakers, matched in sex, age, socio-economic status, general physique and general state of health to the speakers of the first two databases. This control database should be divided into two halves – smokers and non-smokers. Neither group of control speakers should have a reported history of voice disorders.

A major part of the study of perturbation has examined the speech waveforms of young, healthy adults (usually university students), together with the phonation of speakers with abnormal laryngeal conditions. In the latter group, the speakers are often older than the healthy speakers and are predominantly male. For a control group, data should be collected from a wider age- and sex-range of speakers to provide more representative normative information. For the pathological group, data should be collected from as wide a range of disorders as possible. The voice samples in the databases should include not only the production of sustained vowels, but also a sample of continuous speech.

Major Issues

The major issue in perturbation remains the correlation between the acoustic characteristics of perturbed phonation and the anatomical, physio-logical and aerodynamic situation to which they correspond. Once a better understanding is achieved of the mechanical consequences for phonation of different types of disruption of laminar tissue relationships, the search for an automatic system that is capable of providing diagnostic support to clinicians will be able to proceed on a sounder footing. An important part of this development will be the optimisation of the choice of perturbation parameters for the different types of disorder.

An important practical objective is the development of a microprocessor-based version of perturbation analysis for low-cost use in ENT clinics and speech pathology clinics, to provide quantified support for remedial aid monitoring functions.

In the meantime, progress in this area is likely to be focused on correlational studies of the connection between types and degrees of perturbation and the typology of laryngeal disorder that a combination of acoustic analysis, fibre-optic laryngoscopic inspection and histological examination can reveal. The potential usefulness of perturbation measures for assessing laryngeal pathology seems beyond doubt. The nature of the approaches to perturbation that will be the most profitable for patients suffering from laryngeal pathology remains to be established.

References

Anders, L.C., Hollien, H., Hurme, P., Sonninen, A. and Wendler, J. (1988) 'Perception of hoarseness by several classes of listeners', *Folia Phoniatrica* 40, 91–100.

Askenfelt, A. and Hammarberg, B. (1980) 'Speech waveform perturbation analysis', *Speech Transmission Laboratory – Quarterly Progress and Status Report* 4, 40–9, Royal Institute of Technology, Stockholm.

Askenfelt, A. and Hammarberg, B. (1981) 'Speech waveform perturbation analysis revisited', *Speech Transmission Laboratory – Quarterly Progress and Status Report* 4, 49–68, Royal Institute of Technology, Stockholm.

Askenfelt, A. and Sjölin, A. (1980) 'Voice analysis in depressed patients, rate of change of fundamental frequency related to mental state', *Speech Transmission Laboratory – Quarterly Progress and Status Report* 2–3, 71–84, Royal Institute of Technology, Stockholm.

Baer, T. (1978) 'Effect of single-motor-unit firings on fundamental frequency of phonation', *Journal of the Acoustical Society of America* 64, S90(A).

Baer, T. (1980) 'Vocal jitter, a neuromuscular explanation', pp. 19–24 in Lawrence, V. and Weinberg, B. (eds) *Transcripts of the Eighth Symposium on 'Care of the Professional Voice' Part 1, Physical Factors in Voice, Vibrato, Registers*, The Voice Foundation, New York.

Baer, T. (1981) 'Investigation of the phonatory mechanism', pp. 38–46 in Ludlow, C. and Hart, M.O. (eds) *Proceedings of the Conference on the Assessment of Vocal Pathology, ASHA Reports* 11, American Speech-Language-Hearing Association, Rockville, MD.

Baken, R.J. (1987) *Clinical Measurement of Speech and Voice*, College-Hill Press, Little, Brown and Company, Boston, MA.

Baken, R.J. and Orlikoff, R.F. (1988) 'Changes in vocal fundamental frequency at the segmental level, control during voiced fricatives', *Journal of Speech and Hearing Research* 31, 207–11.

Benjamin, B.J. (1981) 'Frequency variability in the aged voice', *Journal of Gerontology* 36, 722–6.

Berouti, M., Childers, D.G. and Paige, A. (1977) 'Correction of tape recorder distortion', *ICASSP–77*, 397–400.

Boves, L. (1984) *The Phonetic Basis of Perceptual Ratings of Running Speech*, Foris Publications, Dordrecht, Holland, and Cinnaminson, NJ.

Coleman, R.F. (1969) 'Effect of median frequency levels upon the roughness of jittered stimuli', *Journal of Speech and Hearing Research* 12, 330–6.

Coleman, R.F. and Wendahl, R.W. (1967) 'Vocal roughness and stimulus duration', *Speech Monographs* 34, 85–92.

Davis, S.B. (1976) 'Computer evaluation of laryngeal pathology based on inverse filtering of speech', *Speech Communication Research Laboratory*, SCRL Monograph 13, Santa Barbara, CA.

Deal, R. and Emanuel, F. (1978) 'Some waveform and spectral features of vowel roughness', *Journal of Speech and Hearing Research* 21, 250–64.

Emanuel, F.W. and Sansone, F.E. Jr. (1969) 'Some spectral features of normal and simulated rough vowels', *Folia Phoniatrica* 21, 401–15.

Fields, S. and Dunn, F. (1973) 'Correlation of echographic visuability of tissue

346 *The Description of Voice Quality*

with biological composition and physiological state', *Journal of the Acoustical Society of America* 54, 809–12.

Fourcin, A.J. (1974) 'Laryngographic examination of vocal fold vibration', pp. 315–33 in Wyke, B. (ed.), *Ventilatory and phonatory Control Systems*, Oxford University Press, Oxford.

Freeman, W.H. and Bracegirdle, B. (1966) *An Atlas of Histology*, Heinemann Educational Books, London.

Hammarberg, B., Fritzell, G., Gauffin, J., Sundberg, J. and Wedin, L. (1980) 'Perceptual and acoustic correlates of abnormal voice qualities', *Acta Otolaryngologica* 90, 441–51.

Hecker, M. and Kreul, E. (1971) 'Descriptions of the speech of patients with cancer of the vocal folds. Part 1, Measures of fundamental frequency', *Journal of the Acoustical Society of America* 49, 1275–82.

Heiberger, V.L. and Horii, Y. (1982) 'Jitter and shimmer in sustained phonation', pp. 299–332 in Lass, N. (ed.) *Speech and Language, Advances in Basic Research and Practice*, Vol. 7, Academic Press, New York.

Hiller, S.M. (1985) 'Automatic acoustic estimation of waveform perturbations'. PhD dissertation, University of Edinburgh.

Hirano, M. (1981) *Clinical Examination of Voice*, Springer-Verlag, New York, NY.

Hirano, M., Kurita, S. and Nakashima, T. (1981) 'The structure of the vocal folds', in Stevens, K.N. and Hirano, M. (eds) *Vocal Fold Physiology*, University of Tokyo Press, Tokyo, Japan.

Hirano, M., Kakita, Y., Ohmaru, K. and Kurita, S. (1982) 'Structure and mechanical properties of the vocal fold', in Lass N. (ed.)*Speech and Language, Advances in Basic Research and Practice*, Academic Press, New York, NY.

Hollien, H. (1974) 'On vocal registers', *Journal of Phonetics* 2, 125–43.

Hollien, H. and Michel, J.F. (1968) 'Vocal fry as a phonational register', *Journal of Speech and Hearing Research* 11, 600–4.

Hollien, H., Michel, J. and Doherty, E.T. (1973) 'A method for analysing vowel jitter in sustained phonation', *Journal of Phonetics* 1, 85–91.

Hollien, H. and Wendahl, R.W. (1968) 'Perceptual study of vocal fry', *Journal of the Acoustical Society of America* 43, 506–9.

Holmes, J.N. (1975) 'Low-frequency phase-distortion of speech recordings', *Journal of the Acoustical Society of America* 58, 747–9.

Horii, Y. (1975) 'Some statistical characteristics of voice fundamental frequency', *Journal of Speech and Hearing Research* 18, 192–201.

Horii, Y. (1979) 'Fundamental frequency perturbation observed in sustained phonation', *Journal of Speech and Hearing Research* 22, 5–19.

Horii, Y. (1980) 'Vocal shimmer in sustained phonation', *Journal of Speech and Hearing Research* 23, 202–9.

Horii, Y. (1982) 'Jitter and shimmer differences among sustained vowel phonations', *Journal of Speech and Hearing Research* 25, 12–14.

Horii, Y. (1985) 'Jitter and shimmer in sustained vocal fry phonation', *Folia Phoniatrica* 37, 81–6.

Isshiki, N., Okamura, H., Tanabe, M. and Morimoto, M. (1969) 'Differential diagnosis of hoarseness', *Folia Phoniatrica* 21, 9–19.

Iwata, S. (1972) 'Periodicities of pitch perturbations in normal and pathological voices', *Laryngoscope* 82, 87–95.

Iwata, S. and Leden, H. von (1970) 'Pitch perturbations in normal and pathological voices', *Folia Phoniatrica* 22, 413–24.

Kane, M. and Wellen, C.J. (1985) 'Acoustical measurements and clinical judgments of vocal quality in children with vocal nodules', *Folia Phoniatrica* 37, 53–7.

Kasprzyk, P.L. and Gilbert, H.R. (1975) 'Vowel perturbation as a function of vowel height', *Journal of the Acoustical Society of America* 57, 1545–6.

Kasuya, H., Kobayashi, Y. and Kasuya, T. (1983) 'Characteristics of pitch period and amplitude perturbations in pathologic voice', *ICASSP-83* 1372–5.

Kempster, G.B. and Kistler, D.J. (1983) 'Selected acoustic characteristics of pathological and normal speakers, a re-analysis', *Journal of Speech and Hearing Research* 26, 159–60.

Kitajima, K. and Gould, W.J. (1976) 'Vocal shimmer in sustained phonations of normal and pathological voices', *Annals of Otolaryngology* 85, 377–81.

Kitajima, K., Tanabe, M. and Isshiki, N. (1975) 'Pitch perturbations in normal and pathological voice', *Studia Phonetica* 9, 25–32.

Koike, Y. (1967) 'Application of some acoustic measures for the evaluation of laryngeal dysfunction', *Journal of the Acoustical Society of America* 42, 1209.

Koike, Y. (1973) 'Application of some acoustic measures for the evaluation of laryngeal dysfunction', *Studia Phonetica* 7, 17–23.

Koike, Y., Takahashi, H. and Calcaterra, T.C. (1977) 'Acoustic measures for detecting laryngeal pathology', *Acta Laryngologica* 84, 105–17.

Laver, J. (1980) *The Phonetic Description of Voice Quality*, Cambridge University Press, Cambridge, England.

Laver, J., Hiller, S. and Hanson, R. (1982) 'Comparative performance of pitch detection algorithms on dysphonic voices', *ICASSP-82* 192–5.

Laver, J., Mackenzie, J., Hiller, S.M. and Rooney, E. (1985) 'Acoustic screening for vocal pathology', unpublished paper presented to the *Voice Foundation Conference on the Care of the Professional Voice*, Denver, June 1985.

Laver, J., Mackenzie, J., Hiller, S.M. and Rooney, E. (1986) 'An acoustic screening system for the detection of laryngeal pathology', *Journal of Phonetics* 14, 517–24.

Leden, H. von and Koike, Y. (1970) 'Detection of laryngeal disease by computer techniques', *Archives of Otolaryngology* 91, 33–40.

Lieberman, P. (1961) 'Perturbations in vocal pitch', *Journal of the Acoustical Society of America* 33, 597–603.

Lieberman' P. (1963) 'Some acoustic measures of the fundamental periodicity of normal and pathological larynges', *Journal of the Acoustical Society of America* 35, 344–53.

Ludlow, C.L., Coulter, D.C. and Gentges, F.H. (1983a) 'The differential sensitivity of frequency perturbation to laryngeal neoplasms and neuropathologies', pp. 381–92 in Bless, D.M. and Abbs, J.H. (eds) *Vocal Fold Physiology, Contemporary Research and Clinical Issues*, College Hill, San Diego, CA.

Ludlow, C.L., Coulter, D.C. and Gentges, F.H. (1983b) 'The effects of change in vocal fold morphology on phonation', pp. 77–89 in Lawrence, V.L. (ed.) *Transcripts of the Eleventh Symposium 'Care of the Professional Voice' Part 1*, The Voice Foundation, New York, NY.

Ludlow, C.L., Naunton, R.F. and Bassich, C.J. (1984) 'Procedures for the selection of spastic dysphonia patients for recurrent laryngeal nerve section', *Otolaryngology Head and Neck Surgery*, 92, 24–31.

Mackenzie, J., Laver, J. and Hiller, S.M. (1983) 'Structural pathologies of the vocal folds and phonation', *Edinburgh University Department of Linguistics Work in Progress* 16, 80–116.

McDonald, W.E., Zyski, B.J., Johns, M.E. and Bull, G.L. (1981) 'Adjunctive use of perturbation analysis for projective assessment of laryngeal surgery', *IEEE Proceedings of the 5th Annual Symposium of Computer Applications in Medical Care.*

Michel, J. (1964) 'Vocal fry and harshness'. PhD dissertation, University of Florida.

Michel, J. and Grashel, J. (1981) 'Vocal vibrato as a function of frequency and intensity', pp. 45–8 in Lawrence, V. and Weinberg, B. (eds) *Transcripts of the Ninth Symposium on 'Care of the Professional Voice'*, The Voice Foundation, New York,

Moore, P. (1962) 'Observations on the physiology of hoarseness', *Proceedings of the 4th International Congress of Phonetic Sciences*, Helsinki, pp. 92–5.

Moore, P. and Leden, H. von (1958) 'Dynamic variations of the vibratory pattern in the normal larynx', *Folia Phoniatrica* 10, 205–38.

Murry, T. and Doherty, E.T. (1980) 'Selected acoustic characteristics of pathological and normal speakers', *Journal of Speech and Hearing Research* 23, 361–9.

Murry, T. and Doherty, E.T. (1983) 'Selected acoustic characteristics of pathological and normal speakers, a re–analysis, a reply to Kempster and Kistler', *Journal of Speech and Hearing Research* 26, 16O.

Rabiner, L.R., Sambur, M.R. and Schmidt, C.E. (1975) 'Applications of a non-linear smoothing algorithm to speech processing', *IEEE Transactions on Acoustics, Speech and Signal Processing*, ASSP–22, 552–7.

Ramig, L.A. and Ringel, R.L. (1983) 'Effects of physiological ageing on selected acoustic characteristics of voice', *Journal of Speech and Hearing Research* 26, 22–30.

Sansone, F.E. and Emanuel, F.W. (1970) 'Spectral noise levels and roughness ratings for normal and simulated rough vowels produced by adult males', *Journal of Speech and Hearing Research* 13, 489–502.

Sherman, D. and Linke, E. (1952) 'The influence of certain vowel types on degree of harsh vowel quality', *Journal of Speech Disorders* 17, 401–8.

Shipp, T. (1981) 'Variability in vibrato rate, extent and regularity', in Lawrence, V. and Weinberg, B. (eds) *Transcripts of the Ninth Symposium on 'Care of the Professional Voice'*, The Voice Foundation, New York.

Shipp, T., Leanderson, R. and Haglund, S. (1981) 'Contribution of the cricothyroid muscle to vocal vibrato', pp. 131–3 in Lawrence, V. and Weinberg, B. (eds) *Transcripts of the Ninth Symposium on 'Care of the Professional Voice'*, The Voice Foundation, New York.

Smith, B.E., Weinberg, B., Lawrence, L.F. and Horii, Y. (1978) 'Vocal roughness and jitter characteristics of vowels produced by esophageal speakers', *Journal of Speech and Hearing Research* 21, 240–9.

Smith, W.R. and Lieberman, P. (1969) 'Computer diagnosis of laryngeal lesion', *Computers and Biomedical Research* 2, 291–303.

Sorensen, D. and Horii' Y. (1983) 'Frequency and amplitude perturbation in the voices of female speakers', *Journal of Communication Disorders* 16, 57–61.

Sorensen, D. and Horii, Y. (1984) 'Directional perturbation factors for jitter and shimmer', *Journal of Communication Disorders* 17, 143–51.

Sorensen, D., Horii, Y. and Leonard, R. (1980) 'Effects of laryngeal topical anesthesia on voice fundamental frequency perturbation', *Journal of Speech and Hearing Research* 23, 274–83.

Titze, I. (1973) 'The human vocal folds, a mathematical model, Part 1', *Phonetica* 28, 129–70.
Wendahl, R.W. (1966) 'Some parameters of auditory roughness', *Folia Phoniatrica* 18, 26–32.
Wilcox, K.A. and Horii, Y. (1980) 'Age and changes in vocal jitter', *Journal of Gerontology* 35, 194–8.
Zyski, B.J., Bull, G.L., McDonald, W.E. and Johns, M.E. (1984) 'Perturbation analysis of normal and pathological larynges', *Folia Phoniatrica* 36, 190–8.

19 The Analysis of Vocal Quality: from the Classical Period to the Twentieth Century

Originally published as Laver, J. (1981) 'The Analysis of Vocal Quality: from the Classical Period to the Twentieth Century', in Asher, R.E. and Henderson, E.J.A (eds) *Towards a History of Phonetics*, Edinburgh University Press (pp. 79–99)

In the early literature of phonetics, discussion of speaker-characterising voice quality is often merged with that of paralinguistic tone of voice. This paper is an attempt to trace the history of this interest in these two areas of vocal quality, from the classical period until the beginning of the twentieth century. Indian and Arabic sources have not been included, and comment is confined mostly to Roman, British and American writers.

Classical Writings on the Voice

The explicit classification on a phonetic basis of different voice qualities and tones of voice really began only in the nineteenth century. An interest in the voice goes back, however, to a very much earlier point in time. Hunt (1858) stated that, in ancient Greece:

> The discipline for the formation and improvement of the voice among the Athenians was so comprehensive that, as we are informed by the Roman writers, not less than three different classes of teachers were employed for this purpose, viz. the *vociferarii*, *phonasci* and *vocales*. The object of the first class seems to have been to strengthen the voice and extend its compass, the office of the second to improve its quality, so as to render it full, sonorous and agreeable; while the efforts of the third, who, perhaps, were considered as the finishing masters, were directed to the proper intonation and inflection. (quoted by Browne and Behnke, 1984: 8)

Stanford (1967: 148–9) says that:

> Besides teachers and performers, two other professional groups in ancient Greece took a special interest in vocal qualities. The physicians . . . listened to them in making their diagnoses. Also the writers on 'physiognomics', the art or science of deducing character from physical qualities, had a good deal to say about the supposed relationship between certain kinds of voices and certain kinds of people. Some believed, for example, that people with deep and tense

voices were brave, those with high and slack voices cowardly; if disgruntled, one that rises from low to high. If spiteful and morally lax, you are likely to speak with a nasal quality. Greedy and vain people have high, clangy voices like birds; stupid ones bleat like sheep or goats. If you hear a dry quality in someone's voice, look out – he is probably a wily fellow. And a man's cracked or broken tone should warn you against his gluttony and violence. If he talks with pararhotacism like Alcibiades, he must be haughty, proud and hard-hearted. So, at least, the physiognomists thought.

Part of this earliest interest in voice quality sprang from the classical concern with oratory, and a useful commentary on Greek and Latin writings on oratory, including voice quality and tone of voice, is Austin's *Chironomia* (1806). Like Hunt, he refers to the different sorts of teachers concerned with the voice:

> Phonasci, Vociferarii (and) Vocales, were the common appellations of those who taught the exercise and management of the voice. Tertullian called them Edomatores Vocis. Galen says they recommended to their disciples the frequent use of the warm bath. Cresollius mentions other practices of the Phonasci, some of which are curious, and some he considers useful. (Austin, 1806: 557)

Commenting specifically on the role of the Phonascus, Austin (1806: 22–3) writes that:

> It was the custom for the Roman youth to recite weekly, chosen passages from the poets . . . They frequently employed . . . Phonasci, whose sole business it was to regulate the modulations of the voice, to manage it by peculiar regimen, and to administer remedies when it happened to be deranged.

In a footnote to this, he quotes a passage from Cresollius' *Vacationes Autumnales*, which can be translated as follows:

> Octavius Augustus . . . paid constant attention to the Phonascus, and by these efforts he achieved the object of pronouncing everything with a pleasant and characteristic sort of tone of voice. Galen, who was a very learned and intelligent man, writes of himself 'and I adopted what the Phonasci call voice exercises'. The Emperor Nero, who took great care of his voice, and gave remarkable attention to it, neither said nor attempted virtually anything without the help of a Phonascus.

(Ludovicus) Cresollius was a French Jesuit priest of the seventeenth century called Louis de Cressolles. *Vacationes Autumnales* (1620) was one of the many Jesuit books on rhetoric about that time (Sandford, 1938: 72). Austin supports this last comment by Cresollius on Nero with a quotation (Austin, 1806: 24) from chapter 26 of Suetonius' *Nero*, which is translated in the Loeb edition as:

> So far from neglecting or relaxing his practice of the art after this, he never addressed the soldiers except by letter or in a speech delivered

by another, to save his voice, and he never did anything for amusement or in earnest, without a phonascus by his side to warn him to spare his vocal organs and hold a handkerchief to his mouth.

A theme running through much of classical writing on voice delivery in oratory was the avoidance of unpleasant quality. Stanford comments that:

> Another aspect of the speaking voice which the Greeks often mentioned was its quality in terms of timbre and resonance. Modern writers variously describe unpleasant voices as 'throaty' or 'nasal' or 'guttural' or 'hoarse' or 'thin' or 'harsh' or 'chesty' or 'breathy' and so on . . . . Pleasant voices are 'rich', 'vibrant', 'warm', ... The Greeks deployed a rich vocabulary for qualities of this kind. They especially disliked hollowness, coarseness, thickness, roughness, breathiness, throatiness, brokenness. (Stanford, 1967: 148)

A final point in Austin's *Chironomia* that is of interest illustrates this 'cosmetic' approach, as it were, to pleasant and unpleasant aspects of vocal quality. As an Appendix to his book (1806: 553ff.) he gives a long list of labels for vocal quality from the Greek writer Julius Pollux. Pollux was a 'professor of literature at Athens under the reign of Commodus' (Sweet, 1899: 212), in the second century AD, the author of a work called *Onomasticon*. Austin quotes from the fourth chapter of Book 2, in the 1706 Amsterdam edition. Austin's English translations of the Greek and Latin labels listed by Pollux are as follows (only the Latin version of the original is given here). Firstly, for the 'good' qualities:

> Altam, high; excelsam, powerful; splendidam, brilliant; mundatam, pure; suavem, sweet; illecebrosam, attractive; exquisitam, melodious, cultivated; persuasibilem, persuasive; pellacem, tractabilem, engaging, tractable; flexilem, flexible; volubilem, executive; dulcem, sweet; stridulam, sonorous, harmonious; manifestam, distinct; perspicuam, perspicuous, articulate.

Secondly, for the 'bad' qualities:

> nigram, obscure; fuscam, dull; injucundam, unpleasing; exilem, pusillam, small, feeble; angustam, thin; difficilem auditu, molestam, faint; subsurdam, obscuram, hollow, indistinct; confusam, confused; absonam, discordant; inconcinnam, neglectam, unharmonious, uncultivated; intractabilem, unattractive, unmanageable; impersuasibilem, uninteresting; rigidam, rigid; asperam, harsh; distractam, cracked; tristem, doleful; infirmam, raucam, unsound, hoarse; aeneam, brassy; acutam, shrill, sharp.

Pollux' list is very unsatisfactory, and in the light of the typological labelling principles suggested in Laver (1974) can be seen to be based on no single criterion of description.

Two writers were outstanding in the classical period for analytic comment on voice quality and tone of voice. The first was Cicero, in the first century BC, in his two treatises *De oratore* and *Brutus*. The second was

Quintilian, in the first century AD, in his *Institutiones oratoriae*. Of the two, Quintilian made the more extensive and systematic comment, but it is as true of both Quintilian and Cicero as it is of almost all writers on the subject until the nineteenth century that they mixed, in their descriptive labelling, features of vocal quality with features of voice dynamics such as pitch, loudness, tempo and continuity (Abercrombie, 1967: 95–110), and with features of segmental pronunciation. Even when writers in this span of two thousand years successfully managed to isolate a feature that could reasonably be allocated to vocal quality, the labels they chose to use were most often impressionistic imitation labels (such as Cicero's use of a label like 'rough'), or were indexical labels for some physical, psychological or social attribute of the speaker to which the writer imagined the vocal quality was acting as an index (as in Quintilian's use of a label like 'effeminate').

The conflation of impressionistic description and indexical comment can be seen in the following extracts from Cicero's treatises *De oratore* and *Brutus*, (in Watson's translations, 1889):

> Any illiterate Athenian will easily surpass the most learned Asiatics, not in his language, but in sweetness of tone, not so much in speaking well as speaking agreeably. Our citizens pay less attention than the people of Latium, yet among all the people that you know in the city, who have the least tincture of literature, there is not one who would not have a manifest advantage over Quintus Valerius of Sora, the most learned of all Latins, in softness of voice, in conformation of the mouth, and in the general tone of pronunciation. (*De oratore*, Book III, c.XI)

(on Antonius) 'his voice was strong and firm, though naturally hoarse' (*Brutus*, c.XXXVIII); (on Cnaeus Pompeius) 'his voice was sonorous and manly' (*Brutus*, c.LXVIII); (on Catullus) 'his reputed purity of diction was owing chiefly to the sweetness of his voice and the delicacy of his accent' (*Brutus*, c.LXXIV). Cicero also discusses the communication of attitude and emotion in speech, in his commentary on 'tones':

> For every emotion of the mind has from nature its own peculiar look, tone, and gesture; and the whole frame of a man, and his whole countenance, and the variations of his voice, sound like strings in a musical instrument, just as they are moved by the affections of the mind. For the tones of the voice, like musical chords, are so wound up as to be responsive to every touch, sharp, flat, quick, slow, loud, gentle; and yet, among all these, each in its kind has its own middle tone. From these tones, too, are derived many other sorts, as the rough, the smooth, the contracted, the broad, the protracted, and interrupted; the broken and divided, with varieties of modulation; for there is none of these, or those that resemble them, which may not be influenced by art and management; and they are presented to the

orator, as colours to the painter, to produce variety. (*De oratore*, Book III, C.LCIII)

Cicero's notion that there are certain features of communication of emotional states that are universal to all human beings, on which are superimposed modulations which are (presumably) culturally relative, recurs repeatedly in writings on the voice up to the present day.

Quintilian, in his very modern-sounding *Institutiones oratoriae*, was the first writer to try to separate features of vocal quality from those of voice dynamics. He had only partial success, but his ideas can be seen to have anticipated major distinctions drawn in the description of vocal quality in current phonetic writing. He also distinguished between a speaker's natural voice (the features arising from the speaker's individual anatomy) and the aspects of voice capable of voluntary control by the speaker (Abercrombie, 1967: 92; Laver, 1968).

Quintilian's often quite phonetically specific ideas can be seen in the following extracts from c.III of Book XI of his *Institutiones* (again translated by Watson, 1899):

> The first thing to be considered is *what sort of voice we have*, and the next, *how we use it*. The natural power of the voice is estimated by its *quantity* and its *quality*. Of these, the quantity is the more simple consideration, for it may be said in general that it is either *much* or *little*; but between the extremes of these quantities there are many diversities, and many gradations from the lowest tone to the highest, and from the highest to the lowest. *Quality* is more varied; for the voice is either *clear* or *husky*, *full* or *weak*, *smooth* or *rough*, of *smaller* or *larger compass*, *hard* or *flexible*, *sharp* or *flat* . . . .
>
> The general tone of the voice, however, ought to be sweet, not grating.
>
> In the *management of the voice* there are many particulars to be observed: for besides the three main distinctions of *acute*, *grave*, and *intermediate*, there is need of many other kinds of intonation, as the *forcible* and the *gentle*, the *higher* and the *lower*; and of *slower* or *quicker* time. But between these varieties there are other intermediate varieties: and as the face, though it consists of very few features, is infinitely diversified, so the voice, though it has very few variations that can be named, has yet a peculiar tone in each individual; and the voice of a person is as easily distinguished by the ear as the face by the eye.

It would be tempting to see in this last passage an adumbration of a componential approach to the description of vocal quality, where the 'infinite diversification' Quintilian writes of should come about by the combinations of a small number of basic components, with each component divisible into very many gradations. But it seems more likely that this diversification should properly be thought to mean the variability of the qualities of individual voices due at least in part to the involvement of the variety of anatomically derived features.

Like Pollux, mentioned earlier, Quintilian was interested in the 'cosmetic' aspects of voice production, in oratory at least:

As to *rules for delivery*, they are precisely the same as those for language.

For as language ought to be *correct*, *clear*, *elegant*, and *to the purpose*, so delivery will be correct, that is, free from fault, if our pronunciation be *easy*, *clear*, *agreeable* and *polished*, that is, of such a kind that nothing of the rustic or the foreign be heard in it; for the saying *Barbarum Graecumve*, that a man is 'Barbarian or Greek' is not without good foundation, since we judge of men by their tones as of money by its clink. (*Institutiones*, Book XI, c.III)

This last evocative phrase could hardly put the function of the phonetic, controllable element of vocal quality, as an index of social and psychological characteristics, more concisely. Quintilian continues his comment on 'cosmetic' qualities of the voice, saying that:

If the voice, too, be naturally, so to speak, sound, it will . . . not be *dull sounding*, *gross*, *bawling*, *hard*, *stiff*, *inefficient*, *thick*, or on the contrary, *thin*, *weak*, *squeaking*, *small*, *soft*, *effeminate* . . . .

That delivery is *elegant*, which is supported by a voice that is *easy*, *powerful*, *fine*, *flexible*, *firm*, *sweet*, *well-sustained*, *clear*, *pure*, *that cuts the air and penetrates the ear*. (ibid.)

His discussion of cosmetic aspects leads Quintilian on to comment on indexical factors to do with the effect on the voice of various sorts of vocal abuse, and of fatigue:

The voice must not be strained beyond its natural power, for, by that means, it is often choked, and becomes less clear the greater the effort that is used; and sometimes, if urged too far, it breaks out into the sound to which the Greeks have given a name from the crowing of young cocks . . . .

But the good qualities of the voice, like those of all our other faculties, are improved by attention and deteriorated by neglect. The attention to be paid to the voice by orators, however, is not the same as that which is required from singing-masters; though there are many things equally necessary to both; as strength of body, for instance, that the voice may not dwindle down to the weak tone of eunuchs, women, and sick persons . . . . It is necessary that the throat be in good condition, that is, soft and flexible, for by any defect in it the voice may be rendered broken, husky, rough or squeaking; . . . the throat, when swollen, strangles the voice, when not clear, stifles it, when dry, roughens it, and when affected by spasms, gives forth a sound like that of broken pipes . . . . Too much moisture also impedes the voice, and too little weakens it. As to fatigue, it affects the voice as it affects the

whole body, not for the present merely, but for sometime afterward.
(*Institutiones*, Book xi, c.iii)

Like Cicero, Quintilian has something to say about the function of the
voice in the communication of emotional states.

> The voice is the index of the mind, and has as many variations as the
> mind itself. Hence, in speaking on cheerful subjects, it flows in a *full*
> and *clear* tone, and is itself, as it were, *cheerful*; in argument, it
> arouses itself with its full force, and strains, so to speak, every nerve;
> in anger, it is fierce, rough, thick . . . . (ibid.)

Voice Quality and Paralinguistic Description of Tone of Voice

We see thus that phonetic, controllable aspects of speech were of interest
to Cicero and Quintilian in their paralinguistic function of acting as
'affective indices' (Abercrombie, 1967: 9) to a speaker's ostensible
emotional state as expressed in his tone of voice. This clearly derives
directly from their concern with spoken delivery as an art that can be
cultivated, and we shall find that comments on voice quality are often
found embedded in a discussion of paralinguistic uses of the voice. There
are two facets here that are of immediate interest.

The first is that the description of paralinguistic features making up tone
of voice is almost always relevant to the description of phonetic voice
quality features, because the main difference between vocal paralinguistic
features and voice quality's phonetic component is the time-scale involved
and not so much the identity of the features used (Laver, 1980).
Paralinguistic features are used on a relatively ephemeral medium-term
basis, while the same features, when used as phonetic components in voice
quality, are quasi-permanent. The way that different writers in the history
of phonetics go about the business of constructing a descriptive vocabulary
for handling paralinguistic features is thus interesting to a study of voice
quality precisely because many of the same phenomena are involved in the
two areas.

The second facet is that analytic decisions about which phonic events of
vocal quality should be deemed linguistically relevant in a particular
accent, which paralinguistically relevant to tone of voice, and which
relevant to person-characterising voice quality, cannot be taken in isolation. All three strands have to be considered together, and a decision about
any one of them has immediate reciprocal implications for the other two.
While analytic schemes for describing the phonetic substance of linguistic
units are thoroughly well established, the same cannot be said for the
substance of paralinguistic units; we have an opportunity here to see the
description of voice quality against the background of emerging systems for
the description of spoken paralanguage.

There is one further qualification that needs to be made before coming
to the work of the early British phoneticians: that is, many writers from the

time of Wallis (1653) to the present day comment specifically on the hypothesised long-term articulatory settings (Honikman, 1964) of the vocal apparatus that they held to characterise the phonetic aspects of different languages. The concept of an articulatory setting is so central to a phonetic approach to describing voice quality that the account of the historical development of the concept deserves a separate presentation. This can be found in Laver (1978) (reprinted as Chapter 20 in the present volume).

Leaving detailed discussion of language-characterising settings aside, this paper will be concerned with two other broad aspects of the history of the analysis of vocal quality. We shall trace the development of the various comprehensive schemes for classifying voice quality on a general, componential basis, which begin to appear in the nineteenth century; and we shall try to follow a number of threads of development in the earlier, less systematic observations on voice quality and paralinguistic features that are scattered through the phonetic literature.

Early British Writings on the Voice

The first systematic commentary on vocal quality in early British works appeared early in the eighteenth century, when Maittaire (1712) wrote about the phonetic, controllable aspects of voice quality and voice dynamics, in a passage which, without acknowledgment, is mostly an extension of some of Quintilian's comments quoted above:

THE VOICE Two things in it are carefully to be observed; what voice you have, and how to use it.

It may be, as to its Quantity, Great or Small.

As to its Quality, Clear or Thick, Full or Slender, Soft or Harsh, Contracted or Spread, Hard or Easy to be managed, Sharp or Blunt.

The Breath is either Long or Short.

The Good Qualities, as of all other things, so of the Voice are bettered with Care, and impaired through Negligence. Frequent Exercise, Temperance and Frugality conduce much to their improvement.

. . . Tis a fault of the voice to be too much stretched or rowling: the mouth is best, when it is Ready, no Precipitate; Moderate, not Slow. . . . Nothing can be worse than a Tone or Cant. A true Pronunciation is ever suited to what we speak. The Affections are either Real and Natural, which need no Art: or else Feigned and Put on; and in these the great Art is to be first moved with them, as if they were Real; then the Voice, as a faithful Interpreter of the Mind, will convey what impressions it has received from our Soul, into those of the Judges or Auditors. It is capable of as many Changes as our Minds; Easy in Chearful Matters; Erect and Firm, when we strive as for the Mastery; Fierce, Harsh and Thick in Anger; Soft, in Begging; Grave, in Persuading; Short, in Fear; Strong, in Exhortation or Narration,

Even, between Acute and Grave; in short, it Riseth or Falleth, as the
Affections are Raised or Composed. (Maittaire, 1712: 239–40)

Maittaire also includes an interesting comment one facial expression in
speech: 'Small is the motion of the Nostrils and Lips, unless in Scorn and
Contempt. We ought always to speak more with the Mouth than the Lips'
(ibid., p. 241).

An important work in the eighteenth century was Mason's (1784) *Essay
on Elocution*. According to R.C. Alston, the *Essay*

has a particular historical significance because it represents a renewed
interest in a neglected art. The interest in pronunciation which is so
characteristic of writers on English in the second half of the eighteenth
century, and finds expression in numerous treatises on pronunciation
and elocution as well as in dictionaries of English, can be traced back
to sixteenth-century manuals of pulpit oratory, but the movement
which was to reach fruition in the works of writers such as Sheridan
and Walker has its origins in a complex coincidence of
interests: among which are the improvement of dramatic speech (to
which Garrick contributed so effectively) and parliamentary debate;
the public recitation of poetry; and a concern to 'fix' pronunciation
and formulate a universal standard. Mason's *Essay* thus appears at the
beginning of an important movement. (Alston, in editorial note to
facsimile reprint (1968) of Mason (1748)

Although Mason shared 'a concern to fix pronunciation and formulate a
universal standard', and contributed some impetus to the movement
Alston describes, he can also be seen as continuing a long-established
tradition of an interest in prescriptive cosmetic aspects of voice, started in
the classical period and notable in the works of Cicero and Quintilian.
Alston acknowledges this, and says that the *Essay's*

immediate significance can be seen as related to the re-appraisal of the
great classical treatises on oratory by Longinus, Cicero and Quintilian.
William Smith's translation of Longinus (1739) was to be reprinted
numerous times between 1740 and 1800; William Guthrie's translation
of Cicero's *De oratore* appeared in 1742 . . . and his translation of
Quintilian followed in 1756 . . . .

Mason's *Essay* was reprinted in the same year as the first edition,
and again in 1751, 1757, 1761 and 1787. (Alston, ibid.)

Mason himself was quite explicit about the value of classical writings:

Those who desire to be more particularly acquainted with this Subject,
and with the several other Branches of Oratory, I would advise not to
trust altogether to the Rules of Modern Writers, but to repair to the
Fountain Head; and converse with the great Masters and Teachers of
this Art among the Antients; particularly, Dionysius of Halicarnassus,
Cicero, Quintilian, and Longinus. (Mason, 1748: 39)

It may be necessary to mention here that while Cicero and Quintilian wrote at some length on aspects of spoken delivery relevant to vocal quality, neither Dionysius of Halicarnassus nor Longinus gave it any particular attention. Mason begins with some sensible comments on using a conversational tone of voice in public speaking and reading aloud:

> To avoid all kinds of unnatural and disagreeable Tones, the only Rule is to endeavour to speak with the same Ease and Freedom as you would do on the same Subject in private Conversation. You hear no body converse in a Tone; unless they have the Brogue of some other Country, or have got into a Habit (as some have) of altering the natural Key of their Voice when they are talking of some serious Subject in Religion. But I can see no Reason in the World, that when in common Conversation we speak in a natural Voice with proper Accent and Emphasis, yet as soon as we begin to read, or talk of Religion, or speak in Publick, we should immediately assume a stiff, awkward, unnatural Tone. If we are indeed deeply affected with the Subject we read or talk of, the Voice will naturally vary according to the Passion excited; but if we vary it unnaturally, only to seem affected, or with a Design to affect others, it then becomes a Tone and is offensive. (Mason, 1748: 17–18)

The notion of a 'Tone', although rather vague, was widespread in writings on elocution in the eighteenth century. Very often, it seems to be used in the same way that we use the term today in phrases like 'tone of voice'; that is, as a cover term for a wide variety of phonetic phenomena used as paralinguistic cues for conveying emotional information. But there is also a tendency to use 'Tone' to refer to paralinguistic behaviour that the writer condemns as insincere or inappropriate for the particular situation, as in the last sentence of the passage quoted from Mason immediately above. Appropriateness of vocal cues to the speaker's emotional state seems often to be judged on the basis of an imagined iconic resemblance between the vocal behaviour and the mental state to which it is taken to be acting as an index. This may be seen in the following passage from Mason (1748):

> The Voice must express, as near as may be, the very Sense or Idea designed to be conveyed by the emphatical word; by a strong, rough and violent, or a soft, smooth, and tender Sound.
>
> Thus the different Passions of the Mind are to be expressed by a different Sound or Tone of Voice. *Love*, by a soft, smooth, languishing Voice; *Anger*, by a strong, vehement, and elevated Voice; *Joy*, by a quick, sweet, and clear Voice; *Fear*, by a dejected, tremulous, hesitating Voice; *Courage*, hath a full, bold, and loud Voice; and *Perplexity*, a grave, steady, and earnest one. Briefly, in *Exordiums* the Voice should be low; in *Narrations*, distinct; in *Reasoning*, slow; in *Perswasions*, strong: it should thunder in *Anger*, soften in *Sorrow*, tremble in *Fear*, and melt in *Love*. (Mason, 1748: 25–6)

This attribution of indexical characteristics of the speaker to the speaker's voice is easily understandable if we remember the very strong influence on writers such as Mason of Quintilian.

Mason also mentions one specific type of inappropriate use of a 'Tone':

> It is false Oratory . . to seek to perswade or affect by mere Vehemence of Voice. A Thing that hath been often attempted by Men of mean Furniture, low Genius, or bad Taste, among the Antients as well as the Moderns. A Practice which formerly gave the judicious *Quintilian* great Offence: Who calls it not only clamouring, but *furious Bellowing*; not Vehemence, but downright *Violence*.
>
> Besides, an overstrained Voice is very inconvenient to the *Speaker*, as well as disgusting to judicious Hearers. It exhausts his Spirits to no Purpose. And takes from him the proper Management and Modulation of his Voice according to the Sense of his Subject. And, what is worst of all, it naturally leads him into a Tone. (Mason, 1748: 7–8)

Bayly (1758), in a phonetically sophisticated book, discusses 'tones', and distinguishes clearly between anatomically derived and phonetic, controllable features of the voice:

> The voice itself is indeed a gift of nature; but with respect to the tone it is extremely in the power of affectation, or ill habit to hurt it, and of art to improve it. The most remarkable ill tones are perhaps such as arise from what is called speaking through the nose and in the throat. Of guttural tones there is great variety. Some are like the bleating of a sheep, or noise of a raven; some resemble the croaking of a frog, and quacking of a duck: All which seem to be owing to some trick of compressing the wind pipe in such a manner as to confine the tone in the throat instead of letting it pass freely out. The voice is also often hurt by another trick; that of shutting the teeth, and confining the tone within the mouth instead of opening the teeth and lips properly so as to bring it out with fulness and rotundity. (Bayly, 1758: pt. 3, pp. 180–1)

Thomas Sheridan (1762) follows Cicero in asserting the universality of vocal means for communicating strong emotions, and he distinguishes very clearly between language and 'tones':

> Every one will at once acknowledge that the terms anger, fear, love, hatred, pity, grief, will not excite in him the sensations of those passions, and make him angry or afraid, compassionate or grieved; nor, should a man declare himself to be under the influence of any of these passions, in the most explicit and strong words that the language can afford, would he in the least affect us, or gain any credit, if he used no other signs but words. If any one should say in the same tone of voice that he uses in delivering indifferent propositions from a cool understanding, 'Sure never any mortal was so overwhelmed with grief as I am at this present' . . . . Sure, no one would feel any pity for the distress of the [speaker] . . . . We should either believe that he jested,

or if he would be thought serious, we should be moved to laughter at his absurdity. And why is this? But because he makes use of words only, as the signs of emotion, which it is impossible they can represent; and omits the use of the true signs of the passions, which are the tones, looks and gestures.

This will serve to shew us that the language or sensible marks by which the emotions of the mind are discovered, and communicated from man to man, are entirely different from words, and independent of them . . . the language of the animal passions of man . . . should be fixed, self-evident, and universally intelligible. (Sheridan, 1762: 100–2)

In 1781, Sheridan gets closer to a modern conception of the coded, arbitrary nature of paralinguistic features, while still maintaining the universality of affective indices to the most basic emotional states:

Tones may be divided into two kinds; natural, and instituted. The natural, are such as belong to the passions of man in his animal state; which are implanted in his frame, by the hand of nature; and which spontaneously break forth, whenever he is under the influence of any of these passions. These form a universal language, equally used by all the different nations of the world, and equally understood and felt by all. Thus, the tones expressive of sorrow, lamentation, mirth, joy, hatred, anger, love, pity, etc. are the same in all countries, and excite emotions in us analogous to those passions, when accompanying words which we do not understand.

The instituted tones, are those which are settled by compact, to mark the different operations, exertions, and emotions of the intellect and fancy, in producing their ideas; and these in a great measure differ, in different countries, as the languages do.

The former of these, it is evident, neither require study nor pains, when we are ourselves under the influence of any of those passions, as they are necessarily produced by them; . . . .

With respect to the latter, it will require great pains, and much observation, to become master of them. (Sheridan, 1781: 120–1)

Nowadays, we would prefer to believe that many of his 'natural tones' are more culturally relative, more 'instituted' than Sheridan suggests, but he puts the distinction between 'natural' and 'instituted' elements in the communication of attitude and emotion very succinctly.

Fenning (1771: 180–1), without acknowledgement, copies Mason (1748: 25–6) in the passage quoted above ('Love [is expressed] by a soft, smooth, languishing Voice', etc.), for which Fenning has 'Love is expressed by a soft, smooth, languishing tone', and so on.

Herries, in his book *The Elements of Speech* (1773), makes some of the most perceptive and phonetically interesting comments on vocal quality to be found before the nineteenth century. He writes, for example, that

Others, who are not accustomed to expel their breath with the same freedom through the nostrils as through the mouth, pronounce the three nasals m, n, and ng, very imperfectly, which produces that dull disagreeable sound, which we call sneveling or SPEAKING THROUGH THE NOSE. The latter term is entirely wrong, because it is the defect of NOT speaking thro' the nose which occasions that impropriety in articulation. Sometimes this habit arises from an excess in taking snuff, which ought always to be avoided by a publick speaker or singer. (Herries, 1773: 55–6)

Herries also has a nice comment on a particular type of voice used in public speaking:

Many of our public speakers have had their powers of utterance enervated and restrained in their younger years. At home and at school they have been put under a false *regimen*. They perhaps have been told 'that it was not *pretty*, it was not genteel to breathe too strongly, to roar out the words, and bellow like a clown; it was quite vulgar, it grated their ears, it was enough to fright a person'. The young gentleman takes the hint. He begins to speak *fine*. He minces out his words, and warbles his modulations like an Italian singer. What is the consequence? His voice as he grows up retains the same unmanly quality. He dare not, he cannot exert it. He speaks upon the most important, the most alarming subjects, with the delicate tone of a waiting-gentlewoman.

Let this effeminate mode of education be banished from our land. (Herries, 1773: 99–100)

This theme is continued, in a discussion about the function of the voice as an indexical clue to physical features such as a speaker's physique, and the possibility of drawing wrong indexical conclusions:

Do we not often behold men of the most robust habit of body, speaking in public, with such a weak, puerile voice, that if we were to trust to the testimony of our ears alone, we should conclude that their constitution was quite enfeebled and decayed. From hence we may infer, that a strong *body* is not always accompanied with a strong *voice*. (Herries, 1773: 106)

Finally, Herries discusses some details of the inter-relationship of factors of pitch with those of vocal quality:

The true criterion of just speaking is, when each of the articulate sounds is uttered forcibly and distinctly. But we find that whenever we go beyond our natural pitch, we lose the command of articulation. Our tones are weak, shrill, and broken. Every excess of passion has a tendency to straiten the glottis, and render the voice more acute. This we may observe in the sharp, hurrying voice of anger, the plaintive wailings of grief, the clear-gliding warblings of joy. If, therefore, a public speaker is deeply animated with his subject, his voice insensibly ascends, and sometimes is carried to such a pitch that he loses all command of it. Cicero informs us, that when Gracchus, an eminent pleader at Rome, was in the vehement parts of his discourse, his voice became too high and squeaking. To remedy this inconvenience, he placed a servant behind him, with a pitch-pipe in his hand, who, at such a time, sounded a note in unison with the medium of his voice, on which he immediately descended to his usual sweetness. (Herries, 1773: 152)

It may be of interest here to note that James Rush, who was a major figure in the later history of analysis of vocal quality, was very scathing about this anecdote, and about classical writings generally. In his characteristically jaundiced and irascible tone he wrote that:

If one should be disposed to believe in the vocal perfection of the Greeks, through any other than their own testimony, he might well question the authority of their Roman eulogists: since they themselves, the pupils of the Greeks, display no better analysis and system in their institute of elocution. We may fairly estimate their discrimination, when with the same pen that deals out the extravagancies of praise upon the oratorical action of their masters, they gravely give us, as proof of their own nicety in vocal matters, the story of one of their famous orators having occasion for a Pitch-pipe, to enable him to recognise his own voice, and affectedly to govern his melody, through the more acute perceptions of a slave, who now and then blew this little regulating trumpet at his elbow!! (Rush, 1859: 675n (5th edition of *Philosophy of the Human Voice* (1827))

Writings on Vocal Quality in the Nineteenth Century

In the nineteenth century, attempts at explicit, general componential schemes for describing voice quality begin to appear. Interest in the subject of delivery, and of tone of voice was also still maintained (particularly in America). We have noted Austin's *Chironomia* (1806). Although this had only one British edition, and no American edition, Haberman (1954: 117–18) says:

it exerted an enormous influence upon elocutionists. In England, A.M. Hartley called it 'incomparably the ablest treatise on delivery in general that has yet appeared in our language'. In America, a lot of writers, among them Caldwell, Bronson, Bacon, Fulton and Trueblood, and, as late as 1916, Joseph A. Mosher, were indebted to this extraordinary book.

This is to overestimate its value, but it gives us an idea of the general interest during the nineteenth century in the voice.

In Britain during this time, Willis (1829) wrote that 'Thus we say that a man has a clear voice, a nasal voice, a thick voice . . .', and by Sweet's time, attempts to set up a voice quality classification on a phonetic basis were becoming frequent (in America, at least), although none of them began to approach any degree of comprehensiveness. Sweet (1877: 97–9) distinguished between 'clear', 'dull', 'harsh' and 'nasal' qualities, and expanded this list in his *Primer of Phonetics* (1890b: 69), to the following set of qualities: 'clear quality', 'dull quality', 'nasality', 'wheeziness' and 'gutturality'. Sweet was probably the first writer to assert quite explicitly that vocal quality is susceptible of systematic componential description, when he wrote that 'besides the various modifications of stress, tones, etc., the quality of the voice may be modified through whole sentences by various glottal, pharyngeal and oral influences' (1877: 97). This position was re-asserted in *The History of Language* (1900: 136), when he wrote 'the general quality of the voice is likely to be modified by changes in the shape of the throat and mouth passages, which give rise to the various qualities of voice known as clear, dull, muffled, nasal, wheezing, strangled voice'. He also drew a clear distinction between anatomically derived features of the voice and controllable, phonetic modifications, when he wrote that modifications of voice quality

> must be carefully distinguished from those which are due to peculiarities in the organs of speech themselves. Thus defects in the palate may cause permanent nasality (together with a peculiar hollowness of sound), an abnormally large tongue, gutturality, etc. All of these peculiarities are inseparable from the individual. (1877: 99)

It is perhaps a little surprising that Sweet stopped short, in considering anatomically derived aspects of the voice, at those that arise from some abnormal anatomical factor, and did not go on to the logical conclusion that nearly *all* speakers can be distinguished on the basis of differences of organic anatomy even within the range of whatever might be considered normal variations of anatomy.

The interests of vocal quality classification in the nineteenth century were probably most advanced by the efforts of the American elocutionists. The first and most influential of these was James Rush. Son of one of the signers of the Declaration of Independence, Dr Benjamin Rush, James Rush was a physician who was educated at Princeton and at the University of Pennsylvania, where he was awarded his MD degree. He then spent a year at the University of Edinburgh in 1810, as a student of Moral Philosophy under the Scottish philosopher Dugald Stewart. It was during the year he spent in Edinburgh that he became interested in the writings of Bacon (Gray, 1943), and from then on put great emphasis, following Bacon, on the value of objective scientific observations, which had its influence on his approach to the description of speech.

In 1827, he published the first of six editions of *The Philosophy of the Human Voice*. Hale (1954–226) comments that 'In publishing a vocal philosophy which gave a physiological foundation and explanation of vocal theory, Rush gave an entirely new and different emphasis to the study and teaching of speech'. (By 'the study and teaching of speech' Hale is referring to the American tradition of interest in rhetoric and elocution.)

Rush gives an extensive commentary on the description of vocal quality. He deserves to be considered in some detail; the quotations given below are taken from the enlarged fifth edition published in 1859. Early in his book he gives a very clear enunciation of one of the most basic characteristics of phonetic analysis:

A description of the different modes and forms of sound in the human voice, without exemplification by actual utterance, is always insufficient and often unintelligible. With a view to facilitate instruction, it is desirable to discover the mechanical movements of the organs, together with action of the air upon them; that a reference to conformations and changes of the organs, and to the impulses of the air, may enable an observer to exemplify to himself, the description of vocal sounds, by using the known physical means which produce them. (Rush, 1859: 131)

Rush begins with his divisions of 'vocal sound':

All the constituents of the human voice may be referred to the five following Modes: Quality, Force, Time, Abruptness, Pitch. The details of these five modes, and of the multiplied combination of their several forms, degrees, and varieties, includes the enumeration of all the Articulation and the Expressive powers of speech. (Rush, 1859: 67)

The first mention of vocal qualities states that

The thirty-five elements of speech may be heard under four different kinds of voice; the Natural, the Falsette [sic], the Whispering, and that improved quality, to be presently described under the name of the Orotund (Rush, 1859: 138).

He discusses the 'natural' voice in these terms:

The natural voice is said to be produced by the vibration of the glottis. This has been inferred, from a supposed analogy between the action of the human organ, and that of the dog, in which the vibration has been observed, and on exposing the glottis during the cries of the animal; and from the vibration of the chords, by blowing through the human larynx, when removed from the body. The conclusion is therefore probable, but until it is seen in the living function of the part, or until there is sufficient approximation to this proof by other means, it cannot be admitted as a portion of exact physiological science. (Rush, 1859: 139

It is a little surprising that Rush, by 1859, had not heard of Manuel Garcia's success with a dental mirror as a laryngoscope in seeing the vocal folds in action, reported in 1854.

'Falsette' is described as follows:

> The Falsette is a peculiar voice, in the higher degrees of pitch, beginning where the natural voice breaks, or outruns its compass. The piercing cry, the scream and the yell are various forms of the falsette . . . . The striking difference in quality, between the natural and the falsette voices, has created the idea of a difference in the respective mechanisms, not only of their kind of sound, but likewise of their pitch. It has been supposed that the falsette is produced at the 'upper orifice of the larynx, formed by the summits of the arytenoid cartilages and the epiglottis' (Dodart): and the difficulty of joining it to the natural voice, which is thought to be made by the inferior ligaments of the glottis, is ascribed to the change of mechanism in the transition. On this point I have only to add that the falsette . . . may be brought downward in pitch, nearly to the lowest degree of the natural voice; . . . and since the natural voice may by cultivation be carried above the point it instinctively reaches, it suggests the inquiry, whether these voices may have a different agency of mechanism [rather than by] an extension of the powers of the same organisation. (Rush, 1859: 142)

Rush starts his discussion of 'Whispering' by saying that 'The Whispering voice is well known', but goes on to declare that

> We are not acquainted with the mechanical cause of *whisper*, as distinguished from *vocality*. It has been ascribed to the operation of a current of air on the sides of the glottis, while its cords are at rest; whereas vocality is said to proceed from the agitation of the air by the vibration of those cords. This however is merely an inference from analogy, and has a claim to possibility, but no more. (Rush, 1859: 146)

A longer section is devoted to the description of 'Orotund' voice:

> The voice now to be described, is not perhaps in its mechanism, different from the natural; but it is rather to be regarded as an eminent degree of fulness, clearness and smoothness in quality; and this may be either native or acquired.
>
> The limited analysis, the vague history of speech by the ancients, and the further confusion of the subject by commentators upon them, leave us in doubt whether the Latin phrase, 'os rotundum'; used more to our purpose in its ablative, 'ore rotundo', by Horace, in complimenting Grecian eloquence; referred to the construction of periods, the predominance or position of vowels, or to quality of voice. Whatever may have been the original signification of the phrase, the English term 'roundness of tone', specifying as we may suppose the kind of quality, seems to have been derived from it. (Rush, 1859: 151)

Rush goes on to give a specification of what he meant by 'orotund' voice, although he concedes that he knows 'how difficult it is to make such descriptions definite, without audible illustration' (p. 152). He writes:

On the basis of the Latin phrase, I have constructed the term Orotund; to designate that assemblage of attributes which constitutes the highest character of the speaking voice.

By the Orotund, or adjectively, the Orotund voice, I mean a natural, or improved manner of uttering the elements with a fulness, clearness, strength, smoothness, and if I may make the word a subsonorous quality; rarely heard in ordinary speech, and never found in its highest excellence, except through long and careful cultivation.

By Fulness of voice, I mean a grave and hollow volume, resembling the hoarseness of a common *cold*.

By Clearness, a freedom from aspiration, nasality, and vocal murmur.

By Strength, a satisfactory loudness or audibility.

By Smoothness, a freedom from all reedy or guttural harshness.

By a Sub-sonorous quality, its muffled resemblance to the resonance of certain musical instruments. (Rush 1859: 151)

By 'vocal murmur', Rush meant 'an obscuring accompaniment of sound, as if the whole of the voice had not been *made-up* into articulation. It is not an unfrequent cause of indistinctness in speakers' (Rush, ibid.). He also had this to say about his use of the phrase 'guttural harshness':

There is a harsh quality of voice called Guttural; produced by a vibratory current of the air, between the sides of the pharynx and the base of the tongue, when apparently brought into contact above the glottis. If then the term 'voice from the throat' which has been one of the unmeaning or indefinite designations of vocal science, were applied to this guttural quality, it would precisely assign a locality to the mechanism. (Rush, 1859: 153)

It *is* very difficult to know what he meant, in the absence of an audible demonstration, particularly when many of the aspects of orotund voice that he specifies are only the absence of another quality of the voice (aspiration, nasality, vocal murmur, reedy or guttural harshness). There is also the difficulty that two of the factors he prescribes seem to be mutually contradictory – 'a satisfactory loudness' and a 'muffled resemblance to the resonance of certain musical instruments'.

There is, however, one possibility of establishing what it was that Rush meant by labels such as 'Orotund voice'. I have quoted Rush at some length because of the remarkable influence he exercised on the field of elocution. Nearly all the terminologies for the description of voice quality published by American elocutionists for a hundred years after the first appearance of his *Philosophy of the Human Voice* in 1827, up to and including Woolbert (1927), were based on that of Rush. It would be possible, in principle, to elucidate the meaning of some of Rush's terms, if a reasonably detailed continuity of influence could be established from Rush to writers in the twentieth century. It would be too sanguine to hope for more than the most approximate hint of Rush's conceptualisation, but a continuity of teaching and influence *can* be shown. The following discussion is based in part on two interesting review articles about the history of American elocution in the nineteenth century by Gray (1943) and Robb (1954).

William Russell was the first editor of the *American Journal of Education*, from 1826. He was a prolific writer, and of his thirty books sixteen were concerned with elocution. He was a contemporary of Rush, and strongly influenced by him as well as by Austin's *Chironomia* of 1806 (Robb, 1954: 187–8). With Goldsbury, Russell wrote an American School Reader (1844), in which the following labels were applied to voice qualities: 'harsh', 'smooth', 'aspirated' (whispery or breathy voice), 'pectoral', 'guttural', 'oral' 'orotund' and 'pure tone'. They have no specific label for Rush's 'natural' quality, and do not mention his 'falsette' quality.

Russell founded the School of Practical Rhetoric and Oratory in 1844 with James Murdoch, a well-known actor who had been taught the principles underlying the *Philosophy of the Human Voice* by Rush himself. Robb (1954: 189) describes Murdoch as 'a leader in the elocutionary movement for fifty years'.

Murdoch and Russell collaborated to produce *Orthophony*, or *Vocal Culture in Elocution* (1845), which was phenomenally successful, having eighty-four impressions by 1882. They give four basic qualities: 'Whispering', 'Pure Tone', 'Orotund' and 'Aspirated'. In a 'cosmetic' approach, they list various potential faults in quality, such as 'the hollow and false pectoral murmur', 'the aspirate', 'the nasal' and 'the oral' (presumably meaning denasal voice). Again, they do not include 'falsette'.

Hamill was a student of Murdoch, and in 1882 published his *Science of Elocution*. In this he lists 'Pure Tone', 'Orotund', 'Aspirate', 'Pectoral', 'Guttural', 'Oral' and 'Nasal'. In the 1886 edition, he added 'Falsetto' [sic].

Fulton and Trueblood (mentioned earlier as having been influenced by Austin's *Chironomia* of 1806), studied under both Murdoch and Hamill, and in 1893 published *Practical Elocution*. They listed 'Normal', 'Orotund', 'Oral', 'Aspirate', 'Guttural', 'Pectoral', 'Nasal' and 'Falsetto' qualities. One of the most interesting aspects of their work is that they chose to call one of their qualities 'Normal', and said that 'the Normal is the natural basis upon which all the other qualities rest, each of which is some modification of or variation from the Normal' (Fulton and Trueblood, 1893: 41).

Finally, Woolbert (1927) is the last writer to be considered here in the continuous succession from Rush, studying under Trueblood. Woolbert is the link with American 'speech science' of the twentieth century, and begins to move towards an acoustic specification, very speculatively and imprecisely, of the qualities he suggests. 'Orotund' is the 'All-round

Resonance', 'Pectoral' the 'Chest Resonance', and 'Guttural' the 'Throat Resonance'. He mentions the term 'Falsetto', but without any acoustic description.

It would be pleasant to be able to demonstrate that the evolution of the descriptive system that had its genetic origin in the work of Rush in 1827 had produced a competent and comprehensive structure by the time Woolbert made his contribution in 1927, a century later. Unfortunately, it has to be said that Woolbert's attribution of particular qualities to principal locations where 'resonance' takes place is not a major improvement on the 'metaphorical' system that Rush himself castigates in his discussion of 'that improved quality of the singing voice, called by vocalists "Pure Tone" '. Rush wrote that

> there are several terms used to describe the mechanical causes of its different characters and qualities. Among these, the causations implied by the phrases 'voce di testa', and 'voce di petto', or the voice from the head, and from the chest, must be considered as not yet manifest in physiology; and the notions conveyed by them must be hung up beside those metaphorical pictures, which with their characteristic dimness or misrepresentation have been in all ages, substituted for the unattainable delineations of the real processes of nature. (Rush, 1859: 153)

This is perhaps a little harsh as a judgment on Woolbert. The main point to be made here is that enough of Rush's system is visible in Woolbert's work – and more particularly in that of Fulton and Trueblood (1893) – to demonstrate a continuity of teaching and influence spanning the century between Rush and Woolbert. Some hint also emerges from the later writers of what Rush was referring to by his descriptive terms. The chief significance of Rush's work of course extends well beyond the analysis of vocal quality as such: its importance lies, as Hale suggested (1954: 226) in the insistence he placed on a physiological foundation for the study of speech.

Conclusion

In his article (1949) on 'Forgotten Phoneticians', complementing Firth's (1947) paper on 'The English School of Phonetics', David Abercrombie wrote that 'our antecedents are older and better than we think'. In even this cursory exploration of aspects of vocal quality in the literature on speech, it becomes very clear that modern phonetics has much to gain from the insights offered by our predecessors.

References

Abercrombie, D. (1949) 'Forgotten phoneticians', *TPhS 1948*, 1–34.
Abercrombie, D. (1967) *Elements of General Phonetics*, Edinburgh University Press, Edinburgh.
Alston, R.C. (1968) Editorial 'Note' to facsimile reprint of Mason (1748).

Austin, G. (1806) *Chironomia: or a Treatise on Rhetorical Delivery*, T. Cadell, and W. Davies, London.

Bayly, A. (1758) *An Introduction to Languages, Literary and Philosophical, especially to the English, Latin, Greek and Hebrew*, J. and J. Rivington, J. Fletcher, P. Vaillant, R. and J. Dodsley, London.

Browne, L. and E. Behnke (1884) *Voice, Song and Speech*, London (Sampson Low, Marston), G.P. Putnam's Sons, New York.

Cicero *Brutus*, trans. J.S. Watson (1889) George Bell and Sons, London.

Cicero, *De oratore*, trans. J.S. Watson (1889) George Bell and Sons, London.

Fenning, D. (1771) *A New Grammar of the English Language*, London.

Firth, J.R. (1947) 'The English School of Phonetics', *TPhS 1946*, 92–132.

Fulton, R. and Trueblood, T. (1893) *Practical Elements of Elocution*, Ginn, Boston.

Goldsbury, J., and Russell, W. (1844) *The American Common-School Reader and Speaker*, Tappan and Whitmore, Boston.

Gray, G.W. (1943) 'The "voice qualities" in the history of elocution', *Q.J. Speech* 29.

Haberman, F.W. (1954) 'English sources of American elocution', in K.R. Wallace (ed.) *History of Speech Education in America*, Appleton-Century-Crofts, New York, 105–26.

Hale, L.L. (1954) 'Dr. James Rush', in K.R. Wallace (ed.) *History of Speech Education in America*, Appleton-Century-Crofts, New York, 219–37.

Hamill, S. (1882) *The Science of Elocution*, Phillips and Hunt, New York.

Herries, J. (1773) *The Elements of Speech*, E. and C. Dilly, London.

Honikman, B. (1964) 'Articulatory settings', in Abercrombie et al. (eds.) *In Honour of Daniel Jones*, Longmans, London, 73–84.

Hunt, J. (1858) *Philosophy of Voice and Speech*, Longman, Browne, London.

Laver, J. (1968) 'Voice quality and indexical information', *Br. J. Disorders Comm.* 3, 43–54.

Laver, J. (1974) 'Labels for voices', *J. Int. Phonetic Ass.* 4, 62–75.

Laver, J. (1976) 'Language and nonverbal communication', in E.C. Carterette and M.P. Friedman (eds.), *Handbook of Perception* vol. VII, Academic Press, New York, pp. 345–62.

Laver, J. (1978) 'The concept of articulatory settings: an historical survey', *Historiographia Linguistica* 5, 1–14.

Laver, J. (1980) *The Phonetic Description of Voice Quality*, Cambridge Studies in Linguistics 31, Cambridge University Press, London.

Maittaire, M. (1712) *The English Grammar*, H. Clements, London.

Mason, J. (1748) *An Essay on Elocution, or Pronunciation*, M. Cooper, London; facsimile reprint, Scolar Press, London 1968.

Pollux, J. *Onomasticon*, Amsterdam edition 1706.

Quintilian *Institutiones oratoriae*, J.S. Watson (1899) *Quintilian's Institutes of Oratory, or, Education of an Orator*, George Bell and Sons, London.

Robb, M.M. (1954) 'The elocutionary movement and its chief figures', in K.R. Wallace (ed.) *History of Speech Education in America*, Appleton-Century-Crofts, New York, 178–201.

Rush, J. (1827) *The Philosophy of the Human Voice*, Griggs and Elliot, Philadelphia; 5th ed. B. Lippincott, Philadelphia 1859.

Russell, W. and Murdoch, J.E. (1845) *Orthophony or Vocal Culture in Elocution*, Ticknor, Boston.

Sandford, W.P. (1938) *English Theories of Public Address, 1530–1828*, H.L. Hedrick, Columbus, Ohio.

Sheridan, T. (1762) *A Course of Lectures on Elocution*, London.
Sheridan, T. (1781) *A Rhetorical Grammar of the English Language*, Dublin.
Stanford, W.B. (1967) *The Sound of Greek*, University of California Press, Berkeley and Los Angeles.
Sweet, H. (1877) *Handbook of Phonetics*, Clarendon Press, Oxford.
Sweet, H. (1890) *A Primer of Phonetics*, Clarendon Press, Oxford; 3rd ed., rev., 1906.
Sweet, H. (1899) *The Practical Study of Languages*, Dent, London.
Sweet, H. (1900) *The History Language*, Dent, London.
Wallis, J. (1653) *Grammatica linguae Anglicanae*, Leon Lichfield, Oxford.
Willis, R. (1829) 'Vowel sounds', *Transactions of the Cambridge Philosophical Society*.
Woolbert, C.H. (1927) *The Fundamentals of Speech – a Textbook of Delivery*, Harper, New York.

20 The Concept of Articulatory Settings: an Historical Survey

Originally published as Laver, J. (1978) 'The concept of articulatory settings: an historical survey', *Historiographia Linguistica* 5: 1–14

The characterising quality of every speaker's voice is the product of two sorts of vocal features, namely intrinsic and extrinsic features (Laver, 1975). Intrinsic features are those whose auditory quality is directly due to the invariant anatomy of the speaker's vocal apparatus. Extrinsic features derive their auditory quality from long-term muscular adjustments of the intrinsic vocal apparatus, which were once acquired by social imitation or individual idiosyncrasy, and have become habitual (Abercrombie, 1967; Laver, 1967; 1968). Extrinsic features normally lie outside the speaker's conscious awareness. One example of an extrinsic adjustment would be the tendency to maintain the lips in a rounded posture throughout speech. Another would be the habitual use of a 'whispery' voice.

It was Beatrice Honikman (1964) who first gave the name 'articulatory settings' to these long-term, extrinsic adjustments. But while the term itself is new, the general concept is not. In fact, one finds phonetic comment on settings in voice quality (as quasi-permanent tendencies underlying and colouring the moment-to-moment segmental articulations), and on settings in voice dynamics (as constraining tendencies in long-term aspects of factors such as pitch-range, loudness-range and tempo), in early writings from the mid-seventeenth century onwards. The purpose of this article[1] is to explore some aspects of the historical development of the concept of articulatory settings, particularly with regard to voice quality.

Writers on phonetics have made appeal to the concept of settings most often in the discussion of the ways in which general tendencies in pronunciation characterise different languages. A very early forerunner was Isidore of Seville (seventh century AD), mentioned by Fromkin and Rodman (1974: 230) as having observed that

> All the Oriental nations jam tongue and words together in the throat, like the Hebrews and Syrians. All the Mediterranean peoples push their enunciation forward to the palate, like the Greek and the Asians. All the Occidentals break their words on their teeth, like the Italians and Spaniards. . .

John Wallis (1616-1703), in his *Tractatus de Loquela* prefaced to his *Grammatica Linae Anglicanae* (1653), appears to have been the first in the phonetic tradition in Britain to discuss the topic, when he wrote:

> It is worth noting . . . that differences in pronunciation occur in various languages which are not attributable so much to the individual letters, as to the whole style of speech of the community. For instance, the English as it were push forward the whole of their pronunciation into the front part of the mouth, speaking with a wide mouth cavity, so that their sounds are more distinct. The Germans, on the other hand, retract their pronunciation to the back of the mouth and the bottom of the throat, so that they have a stronger and more forceful pronunciation. The French articulate all their sounds nearer the palate, and the mouth cavity is not so wide; so their pronunciation is less distinct, muffled as it were by an accompanying murmur. The Italians, and the Spaniards even more, speak with a slow tempo, the French speak faster, and the English are in between. The French, and the Scots equally, raise or sharpen the pitch of the last syllables of sentences or clauses, while the English lower or deepen it; this is a characteristic not of individual words but of the sentence taken as a continuous whole. I leave it to others to observe differences of this kind among other peoples, as the opportunity presents itself. (Quoted from the translation of the 6th ed. (1765) by Kemp, 1972: 209–11).

Kemp (p. 62) points out that 'in describing the English pronunciation as at the front of the mouth Wallis is not referring to the place of articulation, but rather to the comparative lack of interference with the airstream at this point'.

Kemp also notes that 'Wallis's account of the speech habits of different communities is imitated by Wilkins (1668: 380–1), who also mentions variations in style of speech between individual members of one speech community' (ibid.). This is certainly the case, but Wilkins does more in his comments about settings than merely suggest that both languages and individuals can be characterised by them, as can be seen in the following quotation:

> Though each of the Letters have their distinct powers naturally fixed, yet that difference which there is in the various manner of *Pronunciation*, doth somewhat alter the sound of them. And there are no two Nations in the world that do exactly agree in the same way of pronouncing any one Language (suppose the *Latin*). Amongst persons of the same Nation, some pronounce more *fully* and *strongly*, others more *slightly*, some more *flatly*, others more *broadly*, others more *mincingly* . . . 'Tis obvious to anyone to observe, what great difference there will be in the same words, when spoken *slowly* and *treatably*, and when tumbled out in a *rapid precipitate* manner. And this is one kind of difference in the pronunciation of several Nations;

the *Spaniards* and *Italians* pronouncing more *slowly* and *Majestically*, the *French* more *volubly* and *hastily*, the English in a middle way betwixt both. Another different mode of Pronunciation betwixt several Nations may be in regard of strength and *distinctness* of pronouncing, which will specially appear in those kind of Letters which do most abound in a Language. Some pronounce more deeply *Guttural*, as the *Welsh*, and the *Eastern* people, the *Hebrews*, and *Arabians*, etc. Others seem to thrust their words more *forwards*, towards the *outwards* parts of the mouth, as the *English*; others more *inward* towards the palate, as the *French*; some speak with stronger collisions, and more vehement aspirations, as the *Northern* people generally . . . others more *lightly* and *softly*, as the Southern Nations . . . (Wilkins 1668: 380–1)

What is important to note here, for the study of the contribution of articulatory settings to voice quality, is Wilkins' originality in approaching the idea that the setting which characterises a speech-community can be seen as the product of the nature and distributional frequency of the segmental stock of their phonology. In other words, the characterising setting represents the long-term, highest common factor of all the articulations of the phonology, weighted for frequency of occurrence. The relevant part of the quotation from Wilkins is where he suggests that 'Another . . . mode of pronunciation betwixt several Nations may be in regard to *strength* and *distinctness* of pronouncing, which will specially appear in those kind of Letters which do most abound in a Language . . .'. That Wilkins was thinking chiefly in articulatory terms here is supported by the fact that it is only at this point in his discussion that he deals in unequivocally articulatory descriptions of the shape of the vocal tract ('thrust their words more *forwards*, towards the *outward* parts of the mouth . . . more *inward* towards the palate . . .'), where elsewhere his descriptions rather concern voice-dynamic aspects such as tempo, or are couched in terms of auditorily-based imitation labels (Laver, 1974).

William Holder (1616–98), in his *Elements of Speech* (1669), also discusses, briefly, the various ways in which languages, and individual speakers of the same language can be differentiated. He deals first with lexical, phonological and phonetic differentiation:

There are other differences of Sound in Speaking, by which the Tone of several Nations, and oft of several persons in the same Nation, is rendred distinct, which are partly to be referred to their Alphabets, and partly to their Words and manner of Pronunciation, and Accent. (Holder, 1669: 74–5)

He later discusses differentiation by means of some extrinsic settings and by intrinsic features:

Many more observations of these kinds might easily be made, and are to be found in different Languages, all over the habitable world. And in general, the Freedom or Apartness and vigour of pronouncing (as is particularly observed in the *Bocca Romana*) and giving some what more of Aspiration; and on the other side, the *closeness* and Mufling, and (as I may say) Laziness of Speaking (which varieties are found in several Nations comparatively, and by the different natural shapes of the Mouth, and several conformations of the organs of speech in those of the same Language) render the sound of their speech considerably different, though they all should use the same Alphabet. (Holder, 1669: 78–9)

In this passage, Holder distinguishes between potentially controllable extrinsic aspects of pronunciation to do with the characteristic amount (and presumably speed) of mouth opening, and aspects of speaker-specific anatomy. He contrasts a wide dynamic range of mouth opening ('Apartness and vigour of pronouncing') and a narrow, inhibited range ('*closeness* and Mufling, and . . . Laziness of Speaking'). Uncontrollable anatomical features are referred to in his phrase 'the different natural shapes of the Mouth, and several conformations of the Organs of speech'.

Christopher Cooper (1646?–98), in his own English translation (1687: 10–11) of a passage from his *Grammatica Linguae Anglicanae* (1685: 18), gives clearer expression to an idea already sketched in by Wallis, Wilkins and Holder, when he states:

Each of the vowels may be pronounced in a slender, middle, or gross sound; as the Organs are greater or less; the Appulse of the Active Instruments, Tongue, Lips, to the passive, Teeth, Palate, stronger or weaker. Or as the passage of the Breath from the Lungs thorow the wind-pipe, Larynx or Mouth is longer or shorter, broader or narrower, emitted with greater or less force. Whereby the same motion of the breath, made by the same specifical Organs, causing the same specifical sound, may be spoken in divers Tones: as appears from the speech of persons of both Sexes, young and old, healthful and sickly, and men of several countries, some speak very *broad* and openly, others *fine* and *inwardly*, and some others in a *mean*. The German and Welsh speak *roughly* and *difficulty* [sic] in the Throat; so the *Hebrew* Tongue abounds in Gutturals. The *French* quick and hasty, full of Vowels, as the *Greek*, the *English* speak their syllables and words distinctly and outwardly from the Lips.

The crucial section is 'Whereby the same motion of the breath, made by the same specifical Organs, causing the same specifical sound, may be spoken in divers Tones'. The implication is that the auditory quality of a sound can be considered at a number of different levels. If the perceptual correlate of the acoustic totality is called 'phonic quality', then at least two different components of phonic quality can be distinguished – 'phonic quality' and 'voice quality'. We have seen that voice quality itself derives from two sources, the anatomical foundation and the extrinsic settings.

Phonetic quality might then be thought of as the continually changing auditory product of the momentary articulatory gestures superimposed on the underlying voice quality.[2] In these terms, Cooper is able to distinguish phonetic quality ('the same specifical sound') from phonic quality ('the same specifical sound may be spoken in divers Tones'), where the 'phonic' diversity arises either from anatomical voice quality differences ('the speech of persons of both Sexes, young and old'), or from voice quality setting differences ('the Germans and the Welsh speak *roughly* . . . in the Throat').

The same triple distinction between phonic, phonetic and voice quality seems to be implicit in a number of comments by the scholars quoted above, e.g. by Wallis ('differences in pronunciation occur in various languages which are not attributable so much to the individual letters, as to the whole style of speech of the community'); by Wilkins ('Though each of the Letters have their distinct powers naturally fixed, yet that difference which there is in the various manner of *Pronunciation*, doth somewhat alter the sound of them'); and by Holder, in his comment that voice quality differences in speakers 'render the sound of their Speech considerably different, though they all should use the same Alphabet'.

Joseph Aickin (1693: 6), without acknowledgment, gives a re-ordered, free translation of Wallis's comments on language-characterising setting. James Greenwood (d. 737) makes acknowledgment to 'the Learned Dr Wallis', and translates the whole *Tractatus*, appending it to his *Essay towards a Practical Grammar* (1711: 283–310).

Anselm Bayly (d. 1794) mentions a number of phonetic observations that clearly relate to voice quality settings:

> The voice itself is indeed a gift of nature; but with respect to the tone it is extremely in the power of affectation, or ill habit to hurt it, and of art to improve it. The most remarkable ill tones are perhaps such as arise from what is called speaking through the nose and in the throat. Of guttural tones there is great variety. Some are like the bleating of a sheep, or noise of a raven; some resemble the croaking of a frog, and quacking of a duck; all which seem to be owing to some trick of compressing the wind pipe in such a manner as to confine the tone in the throat instead of letting it pass freely out. The voice is also often hurt by another trick; that of shutting the teeth, and confining the tone within the mouth instead of opening the teeth and lips properly so as to bring it out with fulness and rotundity. (Bayly, 1758, Pt.3: 180–1)

In this passage, by 'The voice itself', Bayly must mean the intrinsic component of vocal performance. Extrinsic settings are indicated by 'tones . . . such as arise from what is called speaking through the nose and in the throat'. The reference to nasality is straightforward, but 'speaking . . . in the throat' is less obviously interpretable. The auditory impressions he offers as examples of these 'guttural tones' might be equatable with an articulatory tendency to constrict the pharynx, but his articulatory explanation about 'compressing the wind pipe' is much more likely to be a comment about muscular adjustments in the larynx. It may be that both pharyngeal and laryngeal settings are involved in the effects he was considering. At the end of the passage, he is concerned with settings of the jaw and lips.

Bayly's approval of articulatory settings that give a voice 'rotundity' is echoed by John Herries, in his *The Elements of Speech* (1773), who observes:

> Endeavour to acquire a ROUNDNESS and openness in your speech. Let there be nothing shrill or squeaking in it. Some speakers pronounce with great distinctness, and yet there is a smallness and a puerility in their tone, which is very unsuitable to the grandeur and dignity of publick Eloquence. The Greeks who carried the fine arts to greater perfection than any nation whatsoever, were remarkable for this OSROTUNDUM, this full and flowing articulation. Roundness of voice may be acquired by depressing tongue and jaw, and enlarging the cavity of the mouth in the pronunciation of vowels. (Herries, 1773: 117)

Noah Webster (1758–1843), like Bayly and Herries, mentions the effect of jaw settings on speech, in discussing the 'drawling nasal manner of speaking in New England' (Webster, 1789: 60). He is commenting on the speech of country people in New England, which he thinks attracts the ridicule of other listeners. He attributes the quality of their speech to the habit of not opening the mouth sufficiently, and writes that:

> Nothing can be so disagreeable as that drawling, whining cant that distinguishes a certain class of people; and too much pains cannot be taken to reform the practice. Great efforts should be made by teachers of schools, to make the pupils open the teeth, and give a full clear sound to every syllable. The beauty of speaking consist in giving each letter and syllable its due proportion of sound, with a prompt articulation (Webster, 1789: 108–9)

One might look askance at the prescriptive aspect of Webster's concern to impose an aesthetic conformity on the speech habits of different communities: his commentary is mentioned here as an example of the interest which writers in the eighteenth century took in voice quality settings.

We have seen that the general concept of an overall articulatory setting was quite clearly established over three hundred years ago by Wallis (1653); the concept had to wait for a specific name until the second half of the nineteenth century, however, when phoneticians such as Sweet, Sievers, Storm, Jespersen and Viëtor became interested in the topic. Kelz (1971) gives an excellent account of the widespread adoption of Felix Franke's (1860–86) term 'Artikulationsbasis', coined earlier but published posthumously in an article in 1889 edited by Jespersen. Franke's term replaced slightly earlier terms such as Siever's 'Operationsbasis', Storm's 'Mundlage' and Sweet's 'Organic basis'. Discussion here will be confined mainly to Sweet's contributions, because of his importance in the more general field of voice quality analysis.

Henry Sweet (1845–1912) first wrote about this topic in 1877, in a discussion of 'varieties of voice quality', which he said were 'mostly individual or national peculiarities' (Sweet, 1877: 98). He gave (ibid.) the following examples:

> Narrowing of the upper glottis . . . gives an effect of strangulation. It is common among Scotchmen, and combined with high key gives the pronunciation of the Saxon Germans its peculiarly harsh character.
>
> Partial closure of the mouth is a common English peculiarity. It has a tendency to labialise back vowels, and even when there is not actual labialisation, it gives the vowels generally a muffled sound, so that *a* for instance, is not easily distinguished from *ɔ*. It also tends to make the general speech nasal, for the breath being impeded in its passage through the mouth, naturally seeks another through the nose. Germans sometimes say of the English, with humorous exaggeration, that they speak, not with their mouth like other people, but with their nose and throat!

It is interesting to note that Sweet isolated exactly the same aspects of voice quality for comment, namely the setting of the jaw and its auditory consequences, as Bayly, Herries and Webster before him.

In 1884, Wilhelm Viëtor (1850–1918) published his *Elemente der Phonetik* (translated into English by Walter Ripman (1869–1947) in 1899), in which the term 'Artikulationsbasis' first appeared. Sweet used this term in 1885, in his *Elementarbuch des gesprochenen Englisch*, the German version of his *A Primer of Spoken English*, which was not published in English until 1890. In the English version, Sweet rendered 'Artikulationsbasis' as 'organic basis', in the following discussion:

> The general character of English speech depends on the following peculiarities of its organic basis: The tongue is broadened and flattened, and drawn back from the teeth (which it scarcely ever touches), and the forepart of it is hollowed out, which gives a dull sound, especially noticeable in *l* (Sweet, 1890a: 4)

In his *A Primer of Phonetics* (1890b), Sweet expands the comments he made on voice quality in his *Handbook of Phonetics* (1877) to suggest that while intrinsic peculiarities of anatomy 'are inseparable from the individual', voice quality modifications 'which are the result of controllable organic positions . . . may – and often do – characterise the speech of whole communities' (1890b: 73). He then goes on to give a more extended description of his idea of an 'organic basis' than in his *Primer of Spoken English*, explicitly equating 'organic basis' with 'basis of articulation':

> Every language has certain general tendencies which control its

organic movements and positions, constituting its organic basis or basis of articulation. A knowledge of the organic basis is a great help in acquiring the pronunciation of a language. (Sweet, 1890b: 74)

Sweet then proceeds to compare the organic basis of English with that of French and German. His description of 'organic basis' is repeated in its essentials in his *The Sounds of English* (1908: 57), and in his article 'Phonetics' (*Encyclopaedia Britannica*, 11th edition, 1911: 466).

The term that is mostly used nowadays to refer to the concept of an organic basis is 'basis of articulation'. Heffner (b. 1892), for example, uses this term in discussing the 'Indifferenzlage' (a term also used by Franke) or 'habitual attitude' of the vocal organs, Heffner's (1950) discussion advances the descriptive power of the concept, in introducing a more detailed consideration of the relationship between the basis of articulation and the individual segmental articulations. It is therefore worth looking at Heffner's treatment at greater length:

It is clear that there are certain general peculiarities of utterance which characterise the speech movements of whole groups of speakers. One of the most important of these is sometimes spoken of as the general basis of articulation. The matter deserves much more careful treatment than it has yet received. It has, however, been observed that in some dialects or languages the position of the tongue from which its articulatory movements start and to which it tends to return is relatively low and retracted, with the tongue surface quite broad. All the movements of the tongue are made to harmonise with this habitual attitude, or 'Indifferenzlage' of the organ, and the vowels particularly are then marked by dullness rather than by brightness of timbre. Some groups of speakers join with this generally low tongue position a tendency to allow the lips to remain largely passive. In other regions the whole level of the tongue in its speech movements is higher and more in the front of the mouth. The tongue is more tense and the movements are quicker. Often in such cases the lips are notably active. French is a language which is usually spoken from a high and tense forward basis of articulation. German is intermediate between French and English in this respect, for English is spoken from a comparatively low and relaxed basis of articulation. On the whole, American English is even less energetically articulated than British English. These are broad generalisations to which there are many individual exceptions. They are, moreover, supported only by the observations of men like Storm, Sievers and Jespersen. No method of measurement has been devised which would permit the mathematical description of a basis of articulation. (Heffner, 1950: 98–9)

The last two sentences of the passage reveal Heffner's adherence to an instrumentally-supported approach to phonetic theorising. No-one would with to deny the valuable role of analytic instruments in phonetic observation, but Heffner's implicit devaluation of the contribution of auditory skills is to be regretted, not least in its unfairness to 'men like Storm, Sievers and Jespersen'. The contribution of auditory judgment to the analysis of settings in voice quality is particularly important, since the clues that are available are slight and subtle, and have to be gathered from an impression of 'colourings', as it were, of the stream of individual segments. Methods of measurement are indeed now available, such as the calculation of long-term averages of formant-frequency ranges, but they are not simple, and are usefully complemented by the auditory skills of trained phoneticians.

Heffner's comments about the different language-characterising settings are perceptive, particularly in contrasting the tense, palatalised setting for French with the laxer, more centralised settings of German and British and American English. Heffner's major contribution to the concept of articulatory settings, as reflected in the 'basis of articulation', is his notion of the harmonisation of individual segmental articulations with the underlying articulatory setting ('All the movements of the tongue are made to harmonise with this habitual attitude, or "Indifferenzlage" of the organ').

The best extended discussion of the concept of a setting is by Beatrice Honikman (b. 1905), the originator of the term, when she writes:

> Articulatory setting does not imply simply the particular articulations of the individual speech sounds of a language, but is rather the nexus of these isolated facts and their assemblage, based on their common, rather than their distinguishing, components. The isolated articulations are mutually related parts of the whole utterance; they are clues, as it were, to the articulatory plan of the whole; the conception of articulatory setting seeks to incorporate the clues or to see them as incorporated in the whole. Thus an articulatory setting is the gross oral posture and mechanics, both external and internal, requisite as a framework for the comfortable, economic and fluent merging and integrating of the isolated sounds into that harmonious cognisable whole which constitutes the established pronunciation of a language. (Honikman, 1964: 73)

Honikman's approach to a concept of a setting characterising the pronunciation of a language emphasises two particular aspects. These are to do firstly with the highest common factor in the various segmental articulations of a language, and secondly with the need to give a statistical weighting to the contribution of individual segments to a setting on the basis of their frequency of occurrence in the spoken language. The first aspect is seen in her comment that 'Articulatory setting does not imply simply the particular articulations of the individual speech sounds of a language, but is rather the nexus of these isolated facts and their assemblage, *based on their common, rather than their distinguishing components*' (Honikman, 1964: 73; my emphasis). The second aspect is expressed in a sentence which, though independently conceived, remarkably resembles an idea put forward by Wilkins in 1668, and mentioned above: Wilkins' comment was to the effect that 'Another different mode of Pronunciation betwixt several Nations may be in regard of *strength and distinctness* of pronouncing, which will most specially appear in those kind of Letters which do most abound in a Language' (Wilkins, 1668: 381). Honikman's suggestion is that 'The . . . articulatory setting of language is determined, to a great extent, by the *most frequently occurring sounds and sound combinations in that language*' (Honikman, 1964: 76; my emphasis).

Honikman gives a very detailed account of the articulatory settings that characterise Received Pronunciation of British English, and more briefly discusses many other languages in the same terms, being particularly concerned to show the relationship between a long-term setting and the momentary articulations of segments.

The last writer to be considered in this discussion of the development of the concept of articulatory settings in voice quality is Abercrombie (1967). Abercrombie (b. 1909) uses the idea of certain muscular tensions, or adjustments, held throughout speech, to explain the phonetic basis of voice quality (Abercrombie, 1967: 93). The notion of a long-held muscular adjustment is essentially the same as Honikman's 'setting', and Abercrombie cites Honikman's article for a 'very full and clear account of adjustments of this sort' (Abercrombie, 1967: 171 note).[3]

We have seen that the concept of a setting is fairly abstract. In particular, its 'statistical' aspect has been emphasised in the discussion, concerned as it is with characteristic common denominators underlying the rapidly fluctuating and spasmodic muscular activities which constitute the speech of a given individual or group of individuals. In taking into account these long-term aspects of muscular activity in speech, the analytic process may here parallel the perceptual process applied to voice quality by the human listener. When meeting a speaker for the first time, a listener seems likely to perceive his voice quality by some process of abstraction of relevant features gathered over a period of time from spasmodic and ephemeral clues in the moment-to-moment fluctuations of segmental and suprasegmental articulations. The most obvious example of this is that perceptual clues to voice quality lie chiefly, though not exclusively, in the intermittently occurring voiced segments, where such features as the acoustic resonatory characteristics of the vocal tract are most easily audible.

This comment about the intermittent, spasmodic nature of clues in segmental performance to a speaker's voice quality leads on to an important reservation about the relationship between segments and settings. That is, no articulatory setting normally applies to every single segment a speaker utters. The performance of a given segment may override the parametric values of a setting, as in the case of a velar stop in the speech of someone generally characterised by velarisation, or a nasal stop in the speech of a speaker with a nasal voice quality. In these examples, the contribution of a setting to segmental articulation is redundant. Alternatively, the performance of a given segment may momentarily reverse the value of a parameter normally exploited by a setting, as in oral stops performed by a speaker with a nasal voice quality.

In future discussion about the relationship between segments and settings, it may be useful to propose a distinction between segments which are *susceptible* to the influence of a given setting, and those which are *non-susceptible*, because of their pre-emptive articulatory requirements. Any given setting will apply to all segments susceptible to its influence in the speech of the speakers concerned. It is partly the intermittency of occurrence in the stream of speech of these susceptible segments that constrains definitions of voice quality such as Abercrombie's (1967: 91) to qualify the permanence of voice quality by mitigators such as '*quasi-permanent quality*', and 'characteristics which are present *more* or *less* all the time that a person is talking' (my emphasis).

Notes

1. A preliminary version of this article was published in the *University of Edinburgh Department of Linguistics Work in Progress* 10: 64–75, 1976, entitled 'Early phoneticians and the concept of articulatory settings'. I gratefully acknowledge the benefit I have had of critical comments from David Abercrombie, Alan Kemp and Konrad Koerner.
2. The analytic separation of phonetic quality from the extrinsic component of voice quality is convenient for the present discussion. But in a more rigorous treatment, it would be preferable to propose a different grouping of components of auditory quality: phonetic quality and voice quality would overlap, sharing the extrinsic setting component of voice quality. Phonetic quality would then be the qualitative aspect of all learned, controllable vocal activity on the part of the speaker, i.e. the product of extrinsic activity, whether short-term or long-term. This approach is preferable because it is semiotically unbiased. The former proposal encourages the identification of phonetic quality with the manifestations of linguistic units, and voice quality with a speaker-characterising function. There is, however, no *a priori* means, in considerations of auditory quality as such, of reserving certain sorts of vocal quality for phonological purposes and other sorts for characterising speakers. All types of vocal quality can be used for either purpose. A distinction of this kind can be made on the basis of duration: phonological (and paraphonological) uses of vocal quality tend to involve a much shorter time-span than the quasi-permanent vocal effects in voice quality. But to make appeal to factors of duration in an internal classification of quality is not the most rigorous of procedures.

    One consequence of adopting the second proposal is that the task of describing the extrinsic component of voice quality is seen as a legitimate task for general phonetic theory, extending its range and power. The power of phonetic theory is extended in the sense of being able to move beyond the description of vocal manifestations of language, to the description of all controllable, learnable activity in vocal communication.

3. Abercrombie published this account of muscular adjustments in voice quality in 1967. The general topic of voice quality, including this particular aspect, had been discussed by him in lectures from a much earlier point in time, however: and it was as an undergraduate and postgraduate student of Professor Abercrombie from 1958 onwards that my own interest in voice quality, and in the history of phonetics, was first stimulated. I am happy to acknowledge my special debt to him.

References

Abercrombie, D. (1967) *Elements of General Phonetics*. Edinburgh University Press, Edinburgh.

Aickin, J. (1693) *The English Grammar*, printed for the author, London (Repr., Scolar Press, Menston, 1967).

Bayly, A. (1758) *An Introduction to Languages, Literary and Philosophical, especially to the English, Latin, Greek and Hebrew*, Rivington, J. and J., Fletcher, P., Vaillant, R. and Dodsley, J., London (Repr., Scolar Press, Menston, 1967).

Cooper, C. (1685) *Grammatica Linguae Anglicanae*, Tooke, B., London; (Re-ed. by Jones, J.D., Halle/S., Niemeyer, M., 1911).

Cooper, C. (1687) *The English Teacher*, printed for the author, London (Repr., Scolar Press, Menston,1967).

Franke, F. (1889) 'Die Umgangssprache der Niederlausitz in ihren Lauten', *Phonetische Studien* 2, 21–60. (Edited posthumously by Otto Jespersen).

Fromkin, V.A. and Rodman R. (1974) *An Introduction to Language*, Holt, Rinehart and Winston, New York.

Greenwood, J. (1711) *Essay towards a Practical English Grammar*, Tookey, R., London (Repr., Scolar Press, Menston, 1967).

Heffner, R.-M.S. (1950) *General Phonetics*, University Wisconsin Press, Madison.

Herries, J. (1773) *The Elements of Speech*, Dilly, E. and C., London (Repr., Scolar Press, Menston, 1967).

Holder, W. (1669) *Elements of Speech*, Martyn, F., London (Repr., Scolar Press, Menston, 1967).

Honikman, B. (1964) 'Articulatory Settings', *In Honour of Daniel Jones*, ed. by Abercrombie, D. et al., 73–84, Longmans, London.

Kelz, H.P. (1971) 'Articulatory Basis and Second Language Teaching', *Phonetica* 24, 193–211.

Kemp, J.A. ed. (and transl. 1972) *John Wallis: Grammar of English Language with an Introductory Treatise on Speech*, Longman, London.

Laver, J. (1967) 'Synthesis of Components in Voice Quality', *Proc. VIth Int. Congr. Phonetic Sciences*, 523–25, Academia, Czechoslovak Academy of Sciences, Prague.

Laver, J. (1968) 'Voice Quality and Indexical Information', *British Journal of Disorders of Communication* 3, 43–54.

Laver, J. (1974) 'Labels for Voices', *Journal of the International Phonetic Association* 4, 62–75.

Laver, J. (1975) *Individual Features in Voice Quality*, PhD diss University of Edinburgh.

Sweet, H. (1877) *Handbook of Phonetics*, Clarendon Press, Oxford.

Sweet, H. (1885) *Elementarbuch des Gesprochenen Englisch*, ibid.

Sweet, H. (1890a) *A Primer of Spoken English*, ibid.

Sweet, H. (1890b) *A Primer of Phonetics*, ibid. (3rd rev. ed., 1906).

Sweet, H. (1908) *The Sounds of English*, ibid.

Sweet, H. (1911) 'Phonetics', *Encyclopaedia Britannica*, 11th ed., 458–67. Cambridge University, Press, Cambridge.

Viëtor, W. (1884) *Elemente der Phonetik des Deutschen, Englischen und Französischen*, Reisland, Leipzig (Transl. into English by Ripman, W. as *Elements of Phonetics*, Dent, London, 1889).

Wallis, J. (1653) *Grammatica Linguae Anglicanae. Cui praefigitur, De Loquela; sive sonorum formatione, tractatus grammatico-physicus*, London (Repr., Scolar Press, Menston, 1969).

Webster, N. (1789) *Dissertations on the English Language*, Thomas, J., London (Repr., Scolar Press, Menston, 1967).

Wilkins, J. (1668) *An Essay towards a Real Character, and a Philosophical Language*, Martyn, J., London (Repr., Scolar Press, Menston, 1967).

Name Index

Topic Index

Note: Numbers in italics refer to figures where these are separate from their textual reference. Numbers in brackets refer to notes.